# Computer Communications and Networks

**Series editor**
A.J. Sammes
Centre for Forensic Computing
Cranfield University, Shrivenham Campus
Swindon, UK

The **Computer Communications and Networks** series is a range of textbooks, monographs and handbooks. It sets out to provide students, researchers, and non-specialists alike with a sure grounding in current knowledge, together with comprehensible access to the latest developments in computer communications and networking.

Emphasis is placed on clear and explanatory styles that support a tutorial approach, so that even the most complex of topics is presented in a lucid and intelligible manner.

More information about this series at http://www.springer.com/series/4198

Zaigham Mahmood
Editor

# Connectivity Frameworks for Smart Devices

## The Internet of Things from a Distributed Computing Perspective

Springer

*Editor*
Zaigham Mahmood
Department of Computing and Mathematics
University of Derby
Derby, UK

Business Management and Informatics Unit
North-West University
Potchefstroom, South Africa

ISSN 1617-7975 ISSN 2197-8433 (electronic)
Computer Communications and Networks
ISBN 978-3-319-33122-5 ISBN 978-3-319-33124-9 (eBook)
DOI 10.1007/978-3-319-33124-9

Library of Congress Control Number: 2016943429



Printed on acid-free paper

This Springer imprint is published by Springer Nature
The registered company is Springer International Publishing AG Switzerland

*To*
*Arif Zafar and Hanya Zaigham:*
*Happy first wedding anniversary*
*and best wishes.*

# Preface

## Overview

The Internet of Things (IoT) is a dynamic global network infrastructure of self-configuring physical objects, embedded with connectivity protocols to enable collection and exchange of data and communication with other smart objects. The objects, or *things* in the network, react autonomously to events, without requiring man-machine intervention in real time. The IoT vision revolves around increased machine-to-machine communication, built on the cloud computing paradigm and networks of data-gathering sensors. This is now the vision of the *Internet of the future* that has the potential to revolutionize pervasive computing and its applications.

The IoT is transforming our lives, e.g., through the use of intelligent wearables, living in self-governing smart cities and driving autonomous cars in the *Internet of Vehicles* on smart roads. It is also transforming the business sector where the growth potential is explosive, as billions of smart interconnected units are already generating more than $1 trillion in revenue. According to analysts, the market for intelligent systems will reach nearly four billion connected devices by 2016, representing more than $2 trillion in revenue. Experts predict that there will be anywhere from 20 to 50 billion connected objects by 2020.

As perhaps the biggest of the latest technology trends, IoT is going to give us the most disruption, driving profound changes in many dimensions of our lives, as well as the most opportunity over the next few years. However, success of the IoT vision is highly dependent on the system architectures, network capabilities, communication protocols, and ubiquitous computing technologies to support effective and reliable physical and cyber interconnections. The IoT environment is heterogeneous where devices are supplied by a variety of vendors that follow different communication protocols and utilize diverse technologies. In this case, achieving interoperability can be highly complex, as data formats and encryptions also vary. Since seamless connectivity and interoperability are prerequisites in a multi-network heterogeneous distributed environment such as the IoT, achieving reliable and resilient connectivity has already become a challenge. Besides, as *objects* are becoming more and more intelligent, device connectivity is also beginning to impact on regulatory compliance.

With this background, there is an urgent need for properly integrated solutions taking into account data and device security, signaling and device detection, device and data management, communication protocols and platforms, network bandwidth and topology, seamless connectivity and interoperability, and worldwide regulations and legal compliance. A major challenge that the IoT ecosystem must also overcome is the risks resulting from legal issues and performance problems caused by the mass deployment of inefficient, insecure, and/or defective IoT devices which may lead to further serious problems.

In this context, this book, *Connectivity Frameworks for Smart Devices: The Internet of Things from a Distributed Computing Perspective*, aims to capture the state of the art on the current advances in the connectivity of diverse devices. Majority of the contributions focus on the communication, security, privacy, access control, and authentication aspects of the device connectivity in distributed environments. Twenty-seven researchers and practitioners of international repute have presented latest research developments, frameworks and methodologies, current trends, state-of-the-art reports, case studies, and suggestions for further understanding, development, and enhancement of the IoT vision.

## Objectives

The aim of this volume is to present and discuss the state of the art in terms of frameworks and methodologies for connecting diverse *things* in relation to the IoT vision. The objectives include:

- Capturing the state-of-the-art research and practice relating to the IoT and distributed environments
- Discussing developments with respect to connectivity of heterogeneous smart and sensory devices
- Analyzing the relevant theoretical frameworks, practical approaches, and methodologies for machine-to-machine communication
- Discussing the latest advances, current trends, and future directions in the subject areas relating to the IoT
- In general, advancing the understanding of the emerging new methodologies relevant to the Internet of Things vision

## Organization

There are 14 chapters in *Connectivity Frameworks for Smart Devices: The Internet of Things from a Distributed Computing Perspective*. These are organized in three parts, as follows:

- Part I: *Device Connectivity in the Internet of Things*. This section has a focus on device connectivity within the IoT. There are four chapters. In the first two chapters, the emphasis is on security aspects of interconnections. The third contribution discusses machine-to-machine connectivity presenting an agent-based framework relevant to the IoT environment. The fourth contribution discusses vehicle-to-vehicle connectivity, presenting evolution of VANET in relation to the Internet of Vehicles.
- Part II: *Architecture and Frameworks for the Internet of Things*. This part of the book comprises six chapters that focus on frameworks and methodologies. The first chapter presents a resource-based architecture for IoT, whereas the second contribution presents integration approaches for the IoT environment. The next chapter proposes a resource management framework for corporate device clouds. The fourth contribution suggests a novel solution for interoperable data management in multi-clouds. The next contribution has a focus on the performance optimization of intelligent home networks, and the final contribution in this section presents a fuzzy cognitive map extend technology roadmap with respect to network neutrality in the IoT environment.
- Part III: *Security Mechanisms for the Internet of Things*. There are four chapters in this section that focus on security of connectivity mechanisms. The first two chapters present data security, privacy, access control, and authentication mechanisms with respect to the interconnection of varied devices in the distributed IoT environment. The third contribution presents a security perspective in relation to developing smart sustainable cities. The final chapter addresses generic security challenges within the IoT environment.

## Target Audiences

This volume is a reference text aimed at supporting a number of potential audiences, including the following:

- *Communication engineers* and *network security specialists* who wish to adopt the newer approaches to ensure the security of data and devices for seamless connectivity
- *Students and lecturers* who have an interest in further enhancing the knowledge of technologies, mechanisms, and frameworks relevant to the IoT environment from a distributed computing perspective

- *Researchers* in this field who require up-to-date knowledge of the current practices, mechanisms, and frameworks relevant to the IoT vision, to further enhance the connectivity between heterogeneous devices

Derby, UK Zaigham Mahmood
Potchefstroom, South Africa

# Acknowledgments

The editor acknowledges the help and support of the following colleagues during the review, development, and editing phases of this text:

- Dr Alfredo Cuzzocrea, CAR-CNR and Univ. of Calabria, Rende (CS), Italy
- Dr Emre Erturk, Eastern Institute of Technology, New Zealand
- Prof Jing He, Kennesaw State University, Kennesaw, GA, USA
- Josip Lorincz, FESB-Split, University of Split, Croatia
- Dr N Maheswari, School of CS and Eng, Chennai, Tamil Nadu, India
- Aleksandar Milić, University of Belgrade, Serbia
- Prof Sulata Mitra, Indian Institute of Eng Science and Tech, Shibpur, India
- Prof Saswati Mukherjee, Anna University, Chennai, India
- Dr S Parthasarathy, Thiagarajar College of Eng, Tamil Nadu, India
- Daniel Pop, Institute e-Austria Timisoara, West Univ. of Timisoara, Romania
- Dr Pethuru Raj, IBM Cloud Center of Excellence, Bangalore, India
- Dr Muthu Ramachandran, Leeds Becket University, Leeds, UK
- Dr Lucio Agostinho Rocha, State University of Campinas, Brazil
- Dr Saqib Saeed, University of Dammam, Saudi Arabia
- Prof Claudio Sartori, University of Bologna, Bologna, Italy
- Dr Mahmood Shah, University of Central Lancashire, Preston, UK
- Dr Fareeha Zafar, GC University, Lahore, Pakistan

I would also like to thank the contributors of this book: 27 authors and coauthors, from academia as well as industry from around the world, who collectively submitted 14 chapters. Without their efforts in developing quality contributions, conforming to the guidelines, and meeting often the strict deadlines, this text would not have been possible.

Grateful thanks are also due to the members of my family—Rehana, Zoya, Imran, Hanya, Arif, and Ozair—for their continued support and encouragement. Every good wish, also, for the youngest in our family: Eyaad Imran Rashid Khan.

Zaigham Mahmood

Department of Computing and Mathematics
University of Derby
Derby, UK

Business Management and Informatics Unit
North-West University
Potchefstroom, South Africa
29 Feb 2016

# Other Springer Books by Zaigham Mahmood

## Cloud Computing: Challenges, Limitations and R&D Solutions

This reference text reviews the challenging issues that present barriers to greater implementation of the cloud computing paradigm, together with the latest research into developing potential solutions. This book presents case studies, and analysis of the implications of the cloud paradigm, from a diverse selection of researchers and practitioners of international repute. ISBN: 978-3-319-10529-1.

## Continued Rise of the Cloud: Advances and Trends in Cloud Computing

This reference volume presents latest research and trends in cloud-related technologies, infrastructure, and architecture. Contributed by expert researchers and practitioners in the field, this book presents discussions on current advances and practical approaches including guidance and case studies on the provision of cloud-based services and frameworks. ISBN: 978-1-4471-6451-7.

## Cloud Computing: Methods and Practical Approaches

The benefits associated with cloud computing are enormous; yet the dynamic, virtualized, and multi-tenant nature of the cloud environment presents many challenges. To help tackle these, this volume provides illuminating viewpoints and case studies to present current research and best practices on approaches and technologies for the emerging cloud paradigm. ISBN: 978-1-4471-5106-7.

## Software Engineering Frameworks for the Cloud Computing Paradigm

This is an authoritative reference that presents the latest research on software development approaches suitable for distributed computing environments. Contributed by researchers and practitioners of international repute, the book offers practical guidance on enterprise-wide software deployment in the cloud environment. Case studies are also presented. ISBN: 978-1-4471-5030-5.

## Cloud Computing for Enterprise Architectures

This reference text, aimed at system architects and business managers, examines the cloud paradigm from the perspective of enterprise architectures. It introduces fundamental concepts, discusses principles, and explores frameworks for the adoption of cloud computing. The book explores the inherent challenges and presents future directions for further research. ISBN: 978-1-4471-2235-7.

## Data Science and Big Data Computing: Frameworks and Methodologies

This reference text has a focus on data science and provides practical guidance on big data analytics. Expert perspectives are provided by an authoritative collection of 36 researchers and practitioners, discussing latest developments and emerging trends, presenting frameworks and innovative methodologies, and suggesting best practices for efficient and effective data analytics. ISBN: 978-3-319-31859-2.

# Contents

# Contributors

**Stephen Kwamena Aikins** School of Public Affairs, University of South Florida, Tampa, FL, USA

**Shruti Bansal** Infosys Limited, Pune, India

**Eleri Cardozo** Department of Computer Engineering and Industrial Automation, School of Electrical and Computer Engineering, University of Campinas, Campinas, SP, Brazil

**Hema Date** IT Applications Group, National Institute of Industrial Engineering (NITIE), Mumbai, India

**Odej Kao** Complex and Distributed IT Systems, Faculty of Engineering and Computer Science, Technische Universität Berlin, Berlin, Germany

**Attila Kertesz** Software Engineering Department, University of Szeged, Szeged, Hungary

**Andreas Kliem** Complex and Distributed IT Systems, Faculty of Engineering and Computer Science, Technische Universität Berlin, Berlin, Germany

**K'Obwanga M. Kevin** Department of Computer Science, Faculty of ICT, Tshwane University of Technology, Pretoria, South Africa

**Okuthe P. Kogeda** Department of Computer Science, Faculty of ICT, Tshwane University of Technology, Pretoria, South Africa

**Manoj Lall** Department of Computer Science, Faculty of ICT, Tshwane University of Technology, Pretoria, South Africa

**Somayya Madakam** IT Applications Group, National Institute of Industrial Engineering (NITIE), Mumbai, India

**Amir Manzoor** Bahria University, Karachi, Pakistan

**Sulata Mitra** Department of Computer Science and Technology, Indian Institute of Engineering Science and Technology, Shibpur, India

**Atanu Mondal** Department of Computer Science and Technology, Indian Institute of Engineering Science and Technology, Shibpur, India

**Tamas Pflanzner** Software Engineering Department, University of Szeged, Szeged, Hungary

**K. Prathapchandran** Department of Computer Science and Applications, Gandhigram Rural Institute – Deemed University, Gandhigram, Tamil Nadu, India

**Pethuru Raj** Infrastructure Architect, IBM Global Cloud Center of Excellence, IBM India, Bangalore, India

**S. Rajaraajeswari** Department of Computer Applications, Raja Rajeswari College of Engineering, Bangalore, India

**Aditya Kaushal Ranjan** Department of Computer Science and Engineering, Central University of Rajasthan, Ajmer, India

**A. Sebastian** Department of Computer Science and Applications, Gandhigram Rural Institute, Deemed University, Gandhigram, Tamil Nadu, India

**R. Selvarani** Computer Science and Engineering Department, Alliance University, Bangalore, India

**S. Sivagurunathan** Department of Computer Science and Applications, Gandhigram Rural Institute – Deemed University, Gandhigram, Tamil Nadu, India

**Gaurav Somani** Department of Computer Science and Engineering, Central University of Rajasthan, Ajmer, India

**Ricardo Souza** Department of Computer Engineering and Industrial Automation, School of Electrical and Computer Engineering, University of Campinas, Campinas, SP, Brazil

**Roland Tornyai** Software Engineering Department, University of Szeged, Szeged, Hungary

**Vijayaraghavan Varadharajan** Infosys Limited, Bangalore, India

**Bo Xing** Computational Intelligence, Robotics, and Cybernetics for Leveraging E-future (CIRCLE), School of Mathematical and Computer Sciences, Faculty of Science and Agriculture, University of Limpopo, Limpopo, South Africa

# About the Editor

**Professor Dr Zaigham Mahmood** is a published author of 16 books, 5 of which are dedicated to electronic government and the other 11 focus on the subjects of cloud computing, data science, and the Internet of Things, including *Cloud Computing: Concepts, Technology & Architecture* which is also published in Korean and Chinese languages; *Cloud Computing: Methods and Practical Approaches*; *Software Engineering Frameworks for the Cloud Computing Paradigm*; *Cloud Computing for Enterprise Architectures*; *Cloud Computing Technologies for Connected Government*; *Continued Rise of the Cloud: Advances and Trends in Cloud Computing*; *Cloud Computing: Challenges, Limitations and R&D Solutions*; and *Data Science and Big Data Computing: Frameworks and Methodologies*. Additionally, he is developing two new books to appear later in 2017. He has also published more than 100 articles and book chapters and organized numerous conference tracks and workshops.

Professor Mahmood is the editor in chief of *Journal of E-Government Studies and Best Practices* as well as the series editor in chief of the IGI book series on *E-Government and Digital Divide*. He is a senior technology consultant at Debesis Education, UK, and associate lecturer (research) at the University of Derby, UK. He further holds positions as foreign professor at NUST and IIU in Islamabad, Pakistan, and professor extraordinaire at the North-West University, Potchefstroom, South Africa. Professor Mahmood is also a certified cloud computing instructor and a regular speaker at international conferences devoted to cloud computing and e-government. His specialized areas of research include distributed computing, project management, and e-government.

Professor Mahmood can be reached at *z.mahmood@debesis.co.uk*

# Part I
# Device Connectivity in the Internet of Things

# Chapter 1
# Securing Device Connectivity in the Industrial Internet of Things (IoT)

**Amir Manzoor**

## 1.1 Introduction

Internet linked computers, originally, but now billions of devices (smartphones, sensors, actuators, energy meters, etc.) connect to each other through the Web. In the coming decade, the quantity and types of devices linked to the Web and the software apps that will run on this expanding IoT will explode, driving a new Internet revolution. According to [1], 99 % of physical objects, which may one day join the network, still remain unconnected.

The current form of the Internet has evolved through many phases. In the first phase (1960–1980), we see mainframe computers dominating the Internet sphere and this use of the Internet was restricted to academics and researchers. In the second phase (1981–2012), the Internet became available for use by individuals and businesses. In the third phase, in the last decade, IoT emerged with the aim to connect everything. Figure 1.1 shows the projected increase in the number of connected devices in the years to come. Figure 1.2 suggests the projected number of connected device per person [2].

In an IoT environment, objects (such as people and devices) are assigned unique identifiers and are able to exchange data over a network without any human-to-human or human-to-computer interaction. Furthermore, the huge increase in the address space due to IPV6 has fueled the growth of IoT. According to an estimate, address space provided by IPV6 is so huge that every atom on earth can have an IP address assigned and enough IP addresses will still remain available to cater for another 100+ earths [3]. There exist big opportunities for businesses to help governments and other businesses in navigating the convergence of the digital

A. Manzoor (✉)
Bahria University, Karachi, Pakistan
e-mail: amirmanzoor@yahoo.com



Z. Mahmood (ed.), *Connectivity Frameworks for Smart Devices*,
Computer Communications and Networks, DOI 10.1007/978-3-319-33124-9_1

**Fig. 1.1** Projected number of connected devices

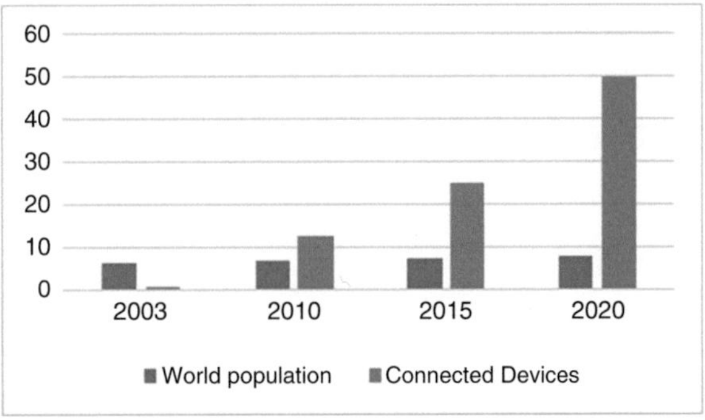


**Fig. 1.2** Projected number of connected devices per person

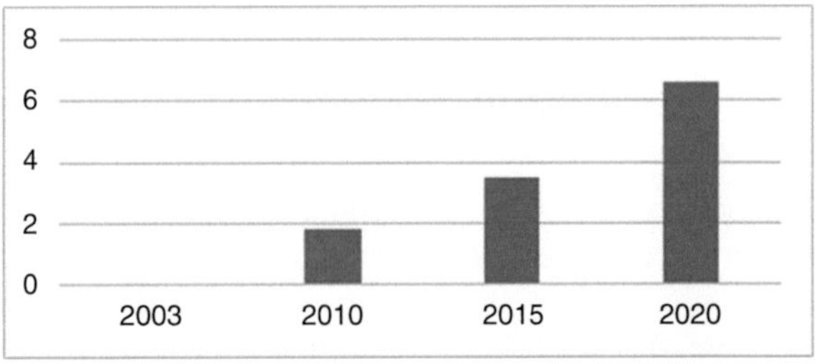


**Table 1.1** IoT initiatives

| Initiative | Company |
|---|---|
| Central nervous system for earth | HP |
| Industrial Internet | General electric |
| Planetary skin | Cisco |
| Powerful answers | Verizon |
| Smart community | Toshiba |

and broader physical worlds. Table 1.1 shows many initiatives in progress, in this context.

## 1.2 Securing Device Connectivity in the IoT

In the context of Internet of Things, it is important to understand why securing the device connectivity is important. In the IoT domain, everything is connected whether it is a smartphone, washing machine, or energy meter. However, such connectivity can expose large amounts of sensitive data such as location of a person. While sharing information among devices can provide many benefits, unauthorized access to this information can pose serious risks to data security and privacy. For sensitive data, we also need to protect it to maintain the confidentiality, integrity, and availability of the data. By compromising machines or things, a hacker can harm real people. Imagine someone disabling a car breaks while driving the car on a highway. Even if no real persons are involved, exposure of sensitive data can seriously damage reputation of companies. With increasing number of device being connected with each other and increasing amount of data being collected, it is very important that connectivity among these devices is secured [4].

However, securing device connectivity in IoT exposes many challenges. The first challenge is that IoT devices are generally constrained by way of computing power and memory capacity, and therefore using resource-intensive cryptographic algorithms with these devices can be challenging. Another challenge refers to the IoT devices that are often connected with each other using an unreliable connection. For security of these devices, it is important that any updates are rolled out to all the relevant connected devices. However, with unreliable connection between devices, this task becomes difficult to accomplish. An additional challenge is to make security intuitive for the users. This is because device installation and maintenance have to be easy in order to gain user acceptance of the device [5, 6].

After providing the introduction and a discussion on the importance and challenges of securing device connectivity in the industrial IoT, the following section provides a discussion of various connectivity protocols in relation to industrial IoT. Section 1.4 discusses various important security issues related to industrial IoT such as authentication, authorization, encryption, digital signing, and infrastructure security. This section also provides some strategies to strengthen security of device connectivity in industrial IoT. Concluding remarks are provided in Sect. 1.5.

## 1.3 Connectivity Protocols for Industrial IoT

Devices in the IoT connect with each other using a variety of protocols. This section aims to discuss some of the most commonly used protocols in industrial IoT. In industrial settings, there still exist a large number of legacy equipment that use older protocols but have diverse real-time needs. In this context, it is difficult to imagine a single data-connectivity standard despite several documented benefits that industrial IoT can provide. These benefits include increased revenue, reduced costs, and energy efficiency. A serious problem with constrained devices is the realization of secure communication. The devices only have limited system resources such as memory, stable storage (such as disk space), and transmission capacity and often lack input/output devices such as keyboards or displays. Therefore, they are not readily capable of using common protocols. In the near future, we can say that industrial IoT will be an environment in which many protocols will coexist, and to gain the benefits of industrial IoT, we need to ensure that data must be secure. This security is needed both to secure data transfer and data storage in order to ensure data accessibility.

In an industrial IoT environment, a range of different protocols are used for data transfer/sharing among devices [7, 8]. Some important protocols are listed in Table 1.2; some of these are discussed in the following subsections.

**Table 1.2** Important connectivity protocols for industrial IoT

| Protocol | Provider | Connectivity | Purpose |
|---|---|---|---|
| Data distribution service for real-time systems (DDS) | The Object Management Group (OMG) | Device to device | Provides sharing of device data |
| Advanced message queuing protocol (AMQP) | OASIS | Server to server | Provides messaging between servers |
| MQ telemetry transport (MQTT) | OASIS | Device to server | Collects device data for server use |
| Constrained application protocol (CoAP) | Internet Engineering Task Force (IETF) | Device to server | Collects device data for server use |
| Extensible messaging and presence protocol (XMPP) | Internet Engineering Task Force (IETF) | Device to people | Provides access to device data |

### *1.3.1 Message Queue Telemetry Transport (MQTT)*

MQTT is a many-to-many communication protocol for passing messages between multiple clients through a central broker. It is suited to messaging for live data and MQTT clients make a long-lived outgoing TCP connection to the broker. MQTT provides no support for labeling messages with types or other metadata to help clients understand it. MQTT messages are used for many purposes. However, all clients need to know message format beforehand in order communicate. IBM and Eurotech created MQTT. It is a TCP-based lightweight publish/subscribe protocol with smallest packet size of 2 bytes and reduced client footprint. It is reliable and provides bidirectional message delivery with protection against packet loss on client disconnection. With MQTT, it is easy to add new message producers or consumers. MQTT is a small protocol with small clients (kilobytes) and implementable on low-power devices. MQTT uses small headers and avoids polling to provide network efficiency. MQTT provides near real-time notification of events and provides exactly once delivered (where required). Because of its compact wire format, MQTT involves lower network costs than an HTTP equivalent. MQTT is event driven and a single MQTT server can support a million connected devices or users. It is possible to add additional functionality to MQTT application without changing existing application code. MQTT supports easy set of verbs that developers can easily learn [9].

MQTT protocol itself specifies few security mechanisms. This is because MQTT protocol, by design, is a lightweight and easy-to-use communication protocol for IoT. To provide security, this protocol uses other generally accepted state-of-the art security standards such as SSL/TLS for transport security. MQTT protocol provides security at multiple layers and each layer handles different kinds of security risks. To secure communication between clients and broker, network layer can provide protection in terms of a physically secure network or VPN. To ensure data confidentiality, TLS/SSL encryption is a generally used protection provided by the transport layer. On the application layer, MQTT protocol uses a client identifier and username/password credentials for authentication of devices. However, the device authorization is dependent on broker implementation. MQTT protocol can also provide payload encryption at the application layer for secure device communication without implementing a full-fledged encryption at the transport layer [10, 11].

### 1.3.2 Advanced Messaging Queuing Protocol (AMQP)

AMQP is an advanced messaging queuing protocol that allows messages exchange between applications. A new standard designed to meet the needs of the institutions enables the interoperation communication and showing resources between new and legacy applications. It allows businesses to work together to provide infrastructure. Middleware acts like a conduit between applications, businesses, and shared resources. It ties together organizations and technologies across time and space. AMQP is the communication glue that binds together message vehicle and the transport mechanism [12, 13].

AMQP supports various broker architectures that are able to receive, queue, route, and deliver messages. AMQP is interoperable, reliable, open, standardized, complete, and safe. It provides an efficient wire protocol, which separates the wire from broker architectures and management. Additionally, it supports multiple broker architectures including peer to peer, message security, global addressing, and support for multiple messaging standards including JMS, WCF, and many others [14].

AMQP protocol does not include security layers as part of the protocol specification. It uses generally accepted standards for security, for example, TLS for data encryption. There is one exception though. AMQP standard specifies Simple Authentication and Security Layer (SASL) that enables AMQP to negotiate an agreed authentication mechanism [15].

### 1.3.3 Constrained Application Protocol (CoAP)

CoAP is a one-to-one protocol for transferring information between clients and servers. CoAP is state based and not purely event based. CoAP clients and servers both send and receive UDP packets. This protocol provides built-in support for content negotiation and discovery allowing devices to probe each other to find ways of exchanging data. It is an efficient RESTful protocol, ideal for constrained devices and networks. It is especially suited for M2M applications and provides easy mapping to/from HTTP. CoAP is not a replacement of HTTP and does not provide HTTP compression. CoAP is also restricted to isolated automation networks. CoAP is based on an open IETF standard. It uses compact 4-byte header. It uses UDP, SMS, and TCP support and provides asynchronous subscription and built-in discovery. CoAP is designed for IoT and compatible with proxy infrastructures. Legacy protocols can be easily mapped to CoAP [16].

**Table 1.3** Comparison of IPSec and DTLS

| Security feature | IPSec | DTLS |
|---|---|---|
| Access control | No | No |
| Authentication | Yes | Partial (server only) |
| Non-repudiation | Depends on authentication method. Constrained devices do not support PKI | Depends on authentication method |
| Confidentiality | Yes | Yes |
| Communication security | Yes | Yes |
| Integrity | Yes | Yes |
| Availability | No | Yes |
| Privacy | No | No |

CoAP is built on top of UDP. CoAP uses two security protocols to secure CoAP network and its traffic: DTLS and IPsec. According to a CoAP's draft, CoAP defines four security modes in order to achieve security services required. These modes are NoSec, PreSharedKey, RawPublicKey, and Certificate. In the NoSec model, DTLS is disabled, and this model can be combined with alternative security (e.g., IPsec). In PreSharedKey mode, DTLS is enabled and preshared keys authenticate peers or group of peers. In RawPublicKey model, DTLS is enabled and asymmetric keys without certificates are used. In the Certificate model, DTLS is enabled, and asymmetric keys with X.509 certificates are used. However, DTLS only works with unicast not multicast. Second, our current DTLS transport only supports UDPV4 and not UDPV6. Finally, transport-level security just does not provide fine-grained configuration on a per topic basis [17].

There are some disadvantages of using DTLS. Firstly, DTLS protocol does not support multicast communications, which is an essential part of CoAP protocol and key feature in IoT [18]. Also, DTLS security features do not fit well for CoAP. For instance, the loss of a message in flight requires the retransmission of all messages in flight. In addition to DTLS security protocol (as a security means for CoAP), other implementations and applications could use IPsec. Table 1.3 provides a comparison between DTLS and IPsec.

### *1.3.4 Data Distribution Service for Real-Time Systems (DDS)*

DDS is a standard developed by Object Management Group (OMG). This standard is designed as a high-performance completely decentralized architecture that provides secure publish/subscribe. DDS provides dynamic discovery so that matching peers can communicate automatically. A rich set of QoS service provided by DDS ensures that all aspects of data distribution (such as availability, resource usage, traffic prioritization, etc.) can be controlled [19]. If a server wants to communicate with a client over DDS securely, there are few options available. One option is to stay within the domain boundary like a secure network. The problem is that anyone inside the domain boundary can easily infiltrate the network. Another option is to use a secure transport such as TLS or DTLS, which authenticates and encrypts everything that goes on the network. DDS security standard defines five plug-in interfaces to take care of security specific operations that middleware should not worry about. These are authentication, access control, cryptographic (which focuses on key exchange and steady-state communication), logging (i.e., recording important security-related events for auditing purposes), and data tagging (i.e., labeling user data for access control purposes). The DDS security specification also defines a set of standard interface and implementations so that every secured DDS implementation will interoperate out of the box. The middleware becomes aware of security and reacts to security operations while remaining decoupled from the details of those operations. Plug-in architecture provides the flexibility to de-secure in the desired manner. It integrates easily with existing security infrastructure and operations. Servers and clients who communicate different data with different security needs can use DDS to work securely as one [20].

### *1.3.5 Extensible Messaging and Presence Protocol (XMPP)*

Extensible messaging and presence protocol (XMPP) is a communication protocol for message-oriented middleware based on XML (extensible markup language). The protocol was originally named as *jabber* and developed by the jabber open-source community in 1999 for near real-time instant messaging (IM), presence information, and contact list maintenance. Designed to be extensible, the protocol has also been used for publish/subscribe systems, signaling for video file transfer, gaming, Internet of Things (IoT) applications such as the smart grid, and social networking services. Unlike most instant messaging protocols, XMPP is defined as an open standard and uses an open system approach of development and application by which anyone may implement an XMPP service and interoperate with other organizations implementations. Because XMPP is an open protocol, implementations can be developed using any software license although many server, client, and library implementations are distributed as free and open-source software. Numerous freeware and commercial software implementations also exist. The Internet Engineering Task Force (IETF) formed the next MPP working group in 2002 to formalize the core protocols as an IETF instant messaging and presence technology. The XMPP working group produced four specifications: RFC 3920, RFC 3921, RFC 3922, and RFC 3923 which were approved as proposed standards in 2004. In 2011, RFC 3920 and RFC 3921 were superseded by RFC 6120 and RFC 6121, respectively, with RFC 6122 specifying the XMPP address format. In addition to these core protocols standardized at the IETF, the XMPP Standards Foundation (formally the jabber software foundation) is active in developing open XMPP extensions. XMPP-based software is deployed widely across the Internet and, by 2003, was used by over 10 million people worldwide according to the

XMPP Standards Foundation. To provide security, an XMPP server uses server certificate, allows no clear-text communications, and uses XEP-198 [21].

## 1.4 Security of Connectivity Protocols

The protocols used for device connectivity in industrial IoT face many security issues. This section reviews and discusses some of the important issues.

Some of the most important concerns are related to authentication, authorization, encryption, digital signing, and infrastructure security. Most protocols that offer security use standard IT (information technology) security solutions and these are the core security mechanisms for these protocols. These approaches are often based on standards such as TLS, IPSec/VPN, SSH, SFTP, secure boot loader and automatic fallback, filtering, HTTPS, SNMP v3, encryption and decryption, DTLS (for UDP-only security), etc.

### *1.4.1 Authentication*

Authentication is the process of identifying an individual, usually based on some user credentials such as a username and password. It is a process in which individuals gain access to system objects, based on their identity [22]. Authentication and authorization are key aspects for every Internet of Things application. The following paragraphs discuss some commonly used authentication protocols.

MQTT protocol identifies a client by its unique client identifier, user ID, or a client digital certificate. The MQTT server authenticates the client. The MQTT server authenticates the client either by using SSL protocol to authenticate the client certificate or by using a password sent by the client. Based on client identity, the MQTT server grants the client access to the resources. The client authenticates MQTT server by authenticating the certificate sent by the server. This authentication is done by using SSL protocol [23]. MQTT provides encryption as a security mechanism at transport and application layers. Authentication at the transport layer is the job of TLS to authenticate the digital certificates of client and server. On the application layer, a combination of client username and password provides the means for authentication. Different broker implementations can add different mechanisms on top of that authentication mechanisms provided by MQTT [24]. According to MQTT specification 3.1, a client can send the server a username without a password. However, vice versa is not possible. When using MQTT's built-in authentication mechanism, the username and password sent to the broker in plain text. Therefore, an eavesdropper can easily compromise client credentials. Only transport layer encryption can provide completely secure transmission of user credentials to the broker. Every client in MQTT has a unique client identifier based on username and password. Besides using a 36-character long UUID, any other unique information (such as MAC address of the device) may serve as client identifier. MQTT also allows authentication just against the client identifier while completely ignoring the username and the password. Another possible authentication source from the client is a X.509 client certificate. A client presents its X.509 certificate to the broker during the MQTT TLS handshake. Once the TLS handshake is successful, it is also possible to use the information in the certificate for application layer authentication. This way, a broker can read all information in the certificate and can use this information for authentication [25].

AMQP uses Simple Authentication and Security Layer (SASL) to authenticate client connections to the broker. Typically, the PLAIN mechanism is used, and so the authentication parameters consist of a username and password. This method is vulnerable to man-in-the-middle attacks unless SSL (Secure Sockets Layer) is also used. Without SSL, it is a recommendation to disable PLAIN authentication in the broker [26].

XMPP uses the standardized Simple Authentication and Security Layer (SASL) to publish an extensible set of authentication methods that the client can use. One advantage of this approach is that it provides new authentication methods. One drawback of this approach is that clients may choose an unsecure authentication mechanism and become vulnerable to credential theft. As a recommended practice, organizations should make sure that clients only use secure authentication mechanisms such as SCRAM-SHA-1 or SCRAM-SHA-1-PLUS. If clients' certificates are used, it is a recommendation to use EXTERNAL method only. If use of an unsecure method is necessity, then organizations should make sure of logging all authentication activities. This allows organizations to detect attackers [27].

CoAP does not have a standardized way of performing authentication. In CoAP, such authentication is built on top of the protocol as security options. The lack of such options in the standard affects interoperability negatively [28].

### *1.4.2 Authorization*

Authorization specifies who has access to what resources. Authorization in MQTT is not part of the protocol provided by the MQTT servers. Since MQTT servers are publish/subscribe brokers, authorization means controlling access to the server by clients and controlling which topics a client can publish or subscribe to. MQTT servers generally group clients by profile to facilitate large number of clients. Without proper authorization, a client can publish and subscribe to all types of messages. In most cases, it is preferred to use fine-tuned restrictions to restrict what types of messages a client can publish and subscribe. Implementing such restrictions requires implementation of configurable/adjustable topic permissions on the broker side. There are many possible topic permissions. MQTT brokers can use these topic permissions to specify authorization policies for clients and to limit their ability to subscribe and publish messages. The current MQTT version 3.1.1 specification does not inform the client about any unauthorized publishing. Rather, the broker disconnects the client in case of any unauthorized publishing. It is a good practice to restrict client publishing only to allowed topics by including the client id in the permissions. One can also use the similar strategy for topic subscription [29].

MQTT uses TCP and therefore, by default, the communication is in encrypted form. It is a good practice, implemented by many MQTT implementations, to use TLS to encrypt the whole MQTT communication. However, there is a drawback of using MQTT over TLS. Using MQTT over TLS requires additional CPU usage. This CPU usage can be negligible for the MQTT broker but it can be significant for tiny devices not designed for resource-intensive tasks. Here the use of session resumption technique can greatly enhance TLS performance. Session resumption allows reuse of an already negotiated TLS session after reconnecting to the server. This way, a full TLS handshake between client and server is not required. However, organizations should remember that not all TLS libraries implement all session resumption techniques. Some TLS libraries do not implement any session resumption. There are two techniques of session resumption: session IDs and session tickets. Not all MQTT implementation supports both techniques. For short-lived client connections, the communication overhead of the TLS handshake can be significant [30].

A new TLS connection may take up to a few kilobytes of bandwidth since each packet over TLS is in encrypted form and can have additional overhead compared to the unencrypted packets. Depending on the ciphers used, TLS can be very compute intensive and can take tens of kilobytes of memory. It is a good practice to use long-lived client connections so that the TLS overhead can be negligible. The TLS overhead can be significant if there are many reconnects, it is not possible to use session resumption technique, there are constrained devices with insufficient resources, and broker needs to publish many small MQTT messages. In each MQTT implementation, organizations should measure the TLS overhead to determine whether MQTT over TLS is the best solution or not. If TLS is not possible with the devices, organizations should think about using payload encryption for their publish messages. Another option is to use TLS-PSK ciphers that do not use resource-intensive public key operations. One drawback of TLS-PSK ciphers is that they are not widely adopted. As a best practice, all IoT protocol implementations should always use protocol over TLS if the CPU and bandwidth overhead are affordable. A properly implemented protocol over TLS ensures no eavesdropping can take place. Organizations should also use the highest possible version of TLS that is feasible for their implementation. Choosing the highest possible version of TLS also ensures that this updated version can mitigate the security risks of using previous TLS versions. Organizations also get additional security for application-level authentication and authorization. It is a recommendation always to use encrypted communication channels for other protocols such as HTTP. One should avoid the use of SSL V3 or prior versions as the latest POODLE attack showed that SSL V3 and previous versions of SSL are broken. Validation of client X.509 certificate from broker is a useful technique to prevent man-in-the-middle attacks. In all cases, one must avoid using an allow-all client implementation used in combination with self-signed server certificate. Self-signed certificates do not work well with TLS implementation and many times result in non-validation of certificate that can open possibilities of man-in-the-middle attacks. Organizations should always use official certificates from official certificate authorities (CAs). That could mean extra cost but it is worth it specially in case organization is using protocol over Web sockets since most modern Web browsers have Web-socket connections to resources with untrusted certificates. The use of client certificates provides many advantages. It is also possible to verify the identity of MQTT clients and authenticate clients at transport level. It is possible to lock invalid clients before connecting to the broker [31].

The use of X.509 client certificates can also save resources on broker side if there are many clients trying to use broker service since the clients are disconnected before any broker communication ever takes place. This resource saving can be significant when broker is using costly authentication mechanisms (such as database lookups or Web service calls). However, using client certificates is costly because of the complex process of client provisioning and certificate revocation. Client provisioning means securely deploying X.509 certificates to clients. If the organization owns the devices, then it is possible to provide client certificates as part of the update of device firmware and client provisioning will be easier. However, if organization does not own the devices (such as mobile devices), client provisioning can be very difficult. In case of many clients, organizations also need to come up with a way to manage client certificate life cycle. In a public key infrastructure (PKI) implementation, managing client certificate life cycle becomes easy. In the absence of PKI, managing life cycle of a large number of clients can be very challenging. It is important to have a client-certification revocation process. This is because server needs a way to identify the invalid certificate and prohibit clients connecting with that certificate. One option to provide this mechanism is to use Certificate Revocation List (CRL) that includes all invalid certificates. This list is a good option if organizations have few MQTT clients to manage. To deal with the client certificates deployed on a large number of MQTT clients, using Online Certificate Status Protocol (OCSP) is a better option. OCSP responder, an HTTP server, responds to certificate revocation check requests. Though OCSP responder setup is tricky, their use allows revocation of a large number of client certificates easier because organization does not have to distribute the CRL to the brokers. Organizations should keep this in mind that typically the use of X509 client certificates makes sense if organization controls the whole system, from broker to clients. If organization cannot control the provisioning of clients, it is better to rely on other authentication mechanisms [23–25].

In addition to TLS, it is a good idea to use additional security measures such as payload encryption, payload signature verifications, and authorization mechanisms. When selecting a cipher suite for protocol implementation, organization should make sure to select the secure cipher suite for communication. This is important because many cipher suites are known to be broken, and if organization is not cautious in the selection of cipher suite, it may create a false sense of security [32].

In AMQP, authorization can be rule based and uses an access control list (ACL) that is part of AMQP broker. The use of encryption ensures that no plain-text data transfer takes place as such hackers can intercept and read such data transfer. Digital signatures provide proof of sending a given message by a known sender. SSL is used for encryption and signing. SASL can be used for encryption and signing, but SSL provides stronger encryption. CoAP provides for a simple authorization mechanism but has no means to distinguish access rights for different clients [33].

#### 1.4.2.1 OAuth

This is an open standard for authorization. OAuth provides client applications *a secure delegated access* to server resources on behalf of a resource owner. In OAuth implementations, an authorization server, with the approval of the resource owner, issues access tokens to the third-party clients. The client then uses the access token to access the protected resources hosted by the resource server. The official OAuth website describes OAuth "as an open protocol to allow secure authorization in a simple and standard method from the Web, mobile and desktop applications." The OAuth 2.0 authorization framework enables a third-party application to obtain limited access to an HTTP service [34]. OAuth, by design, is suitable to work with HTTP. According to OAuth specification, this specification is designed for use with HTTP. The use of OAuth over any protocol other than HTTP is out of scope [34]. As such, OAuth is not a good choice for a constrained IoT device that works in the field with no human interaction.

In OAuth, there are different flows or message exchange patterns such as code flow, client credential flow, resource-owner credential flow, and implicit flow. The most common flow is code flow, which is used, e.g., when a website wants to access an API on a user's behalf. In client credential flow, the client holds the credentials. Only the client credential flow makes sense without human interaction which is common in constrained environment, e.g., IoT. However, it also means that everything is dependent on the use case and environment – how organizations are provisioning clients, into which devices user has access, how we can store the keys, etc. [35]. Another problem with using this flow is that organizations may come across a situation where human intervention is required, e.g., when using a mobile app with an IoT protocol such as MQTT. In case of XMPP, OAuth access tokens are acquired outside the XMPP (i.e., via HTTP as defined in the core OAuth specification) and merely presented over XMPP when sending a protocol-specific access request. In case of CoAP, after initial DTLS-based client authentication, authorization servers decide whether a client may access specific resources. Resource servers do enforce the presence of authorization information [36].

## *1.4.3 Encryption*

### 1.4.3.1 Encryption Scenarios

We present two scenarios: end-to-end (E2E) encryption and client-to-broker encryption.

In the E2E approach, the application data stays encrypted all the time and the broker cannot look into the encrypted data. To decrypt the data, trusted clients need the decryption key. If organizations do not use TLS or the authentication/authorization mechanism is not set up properly, an attacker can get access to the protocol packets. If organizations have applied end-to-end encryption, the attacker cannot decrypt the data if he does not have access to decryption key. This type of encryption is broker implementation independent. It is a recommendation to use end-to-end encryption to protect application data from attackers and other clients if organizations do not have proper mechanisms of authentication/authorization [37].

In the client-to-broker approach, the message payload is in encrypted form during communication between a client and broker. In contrast to E2E encryption, the broker can decrypt the message. This way broker is able to distribute the original, unencrypted message to all subscribers. If organizations are not using TLS and want to protect data from attackers on the publishing side, client-to-broker implementation is a good option. The trusted subscribers use a communication channel secured by using TLS. As such, they can receive the data in plain text. To use client-to-broker encryption, organizations need a broker plug-in that broker uses to perform on-the-fly decryption of the messages [38].

### 1.4.3.2 Encryption Mechanisms

There are generally two popular mechanisms of data encryption: asymmetric encryption and symmetric encryption.

Asymmetric encryption (also known as public/private key encryption) is an encryption mechanism in which two keys are used: public key and private key. Public key is used for encrypting the data and private key is used for decrypting the data. Once data is encrypted with a public key, it can only be decrypted with a private key. Asymmetric encryption for payload encryption is a good option if few trusted subscribers are involved that have access to private key. When this approach is used, it is a recommendation that each topic used by subscribers has its own public/private key [39, 40].

In the symmetric approach, data can be encrypted/decrypted using the same key (e.g., a password) [39]. It is a recommendation to use symmetric encryption in secure IoT environments. This encryption approach is easy to implement as compared to asymmetric encryption. It is a good practice that each topic has its own key. This way, if attacker gets access to key of a certain topic, they won't be able to decrypt the messages on other topics.

#### 1.4.3.3 Payload Encryption

Payload encryption is the encryption of application-specific data on the application level. Payload encryption provides end-to-end encryption for application data. Message metadata remains intact while the payload of the message is encrypted. This type of encryption is not defined in the IoT protocol specification and is completely application specific. If a protocol's payloads are binary (such as MQTT protocol payloads), there is no need to encode the encrypted message to a textual encoding. This could save bandwidth because text encodings are typically more bloated than the raw byte representation. Payload encryption ensures that broker side needs no custom mechanism for decrypting the data to route the messages to the subscribers. In any implementation, one should check it and broker must not decrypt the data if the payload encryption is used. Custom broker plug-ins can also be developed that can decrypt the data on the broker side [26]. In AMQP, SSL is used for encryption. To provide encryption, broker must have SSL support and have a certificate signed by a certification authority (CA). Clients must also trust this certificate. If client authentication is required in addition to server authentication, it is a requirement that a CA signs the client's certificate and the broker trusts this signed certificate. The certificate database is generally be password protected [33].

Payload encryption provides a completely secure end-to-end encryption of application data and is well suited for constrained devices that cannot use TLS due to limited resources. Payload encryption provides another layer of security for messages that contain confidential information. Still the process of encryption/ decryption can be resource intensive for constrained IoT devices and require secure provisioning of the keys to the clients. Payload encryption cannot protect against man-in-the-middle attacks and replay attacks [38].

#### 1.4.3.4 TLS vs. Payload Encryption

One should note that TLS works on network layer, while payload encryption works on application layer. Therefore, it is possible to use TLS and payload encryption in conjunction. Payload encryption provides protection of application messages against eavesdroppers or untrusted clients. It is still possible that an attacker can replay the entire message or parts of message if the messages are not communicated on a secure communication channel such as one secured by using TLS. Payload encryption alone without TLS (e.g., when organizations have constrained devices) is a good option if organizations do not want to send application data in plain text. Since process of encryption/decryption consumes large amounts of processing power, it is a recommendation to choose an encryption algorithm that provides the best mix of performance and security [41].

### 1.4.4 *Digital Signatures, Message Authentication Code Algorithms (MACs), and Checksums*

In an IoT system with many untrusted clients or clients over which we have no control, accessing the broker and checking data integrity of sent messages are very important. This integrity check becomes more important if the broker implementation does not use TLS. With data integrity checks in place, organizations ensure that no one can modify the contents of the messages sent.

The packets of communication can include a digital signature/MAC/checksum of the contents of the packet. These are typically part of the payload as a calculated stamp. The receiver of the packet can verify the integrity of the packet by recalculating the stamp. Here the term stamp refers to an umbrella term that includes digital signatures, MACs, and checksums. It is a good practice to include only the payload and the topic of the message as part of the stamp. The three important and generally used mechanisms of creating stamps include checksum/hash algorithms (e.g., MD5, CRC, etc.), MAC (e.g., HMAC), and digital signatures [24, 25]. Table 1.4 gives an overview of the guarantees the individual mechanisms can provide.

Non-repudiation means that only the message creator can create the stamp with the private key he has. Other parties may verify the stamp with the public key but cannot create the stamp themselves. In MQTT, the MQTT PUBLISH Payload and the topic of the MQTT PUBLISH packet are parts of the stamp.

#### 1.4.4.1 Checksums

Checksum algorithms are typically very fast, but an attacker can alter them. This is because attackers having knowledge of checksum algorithm can apply this algorithm after modifying the communication packet. If organizations do not use TLs, it is a good practice that they use a MAC algorithm or digital signatures. In case of MQTT, it is a recommendation to avoid the use of checksum [24, 25].

#### 1.4.4.2 Message Authentication Code Algorithms (MACs)

In general, MACs are much faster than digital signatures. MACs can provide good security if, prior to the communication, a shared key is exchanged. HMAC is a

**Table 1.4** Guarantees provided by different mechanisms

| | Checksum | MAC | Digital signature |
|---|---|---|---|
| Data integrity | Yes | Yes | Yes |
| Authentication | No | Yes | Yes |
| Non-repudiation | No | No | Yes |
| Key | None | Symmetric | Asymmetric |

MAC that includes a hash function and cryptographic key. Senders having the secret key can create the stamp. Another advantage of HMAC is that it can work securely if TLS is used. HMAC is typically very fast and works great on constrained devices. One significant disadvantage of HMAC is that it uses the same key for encryption and decryption. As such, all clients that have access to the secret key can sign and verify the communication [25, 26].

#### 1.4.4.3 Digital Signatures

When using digital signatures, the sender signs the message with a private key that receiver validates by using a public key of the sender. In MQTT Publish/Subscribe environment, the receiver typically is unaware of the identity of the message sender. If a good authorization mechanism is in place that could guarantee that a specific client can publish to a specific topic, digital signatures can provide an additional layer of security. Digital signatures can provide a number of security services, including message authentication, message integrity, and non-repudiation. There are many use cases for digital signatures in the XMPP.

#### 1.4.4.4 Data Integrity and Encryption

To provide confidentiality of the payload, it must be in encrypted form, but to provide only integrity of the payload, organizations needs a hashing algorithm to process a signature. In that case, an attacker can see the data but cannot temper it. Data integrity checks with stamps are a good addition to encrypting messages. If the attacker tries to temper the data (i.e., decrypt the message and encrypt it after modification), the data integrity check at server fails and server rejects the message. One good example is a factory automation system. Here, it may not be important whether the temperature readings sent by the automation system to the cloud are in encrypted form or not. However, it is very important that the temperature readings arrive at the destination without any modifications. This is because automation system should not act erroneously on incorrect temperature readings. In such cases, organizations can use simple hashing algorithms on constrained devices. There are other examples where confidentiality of the data can be of prime importance. One such case is a doctor accessing status of a patient at home. In this case, confidentiality of health information as it travels from home to hospital is very important. If organizations are not using TLS, the use of hashing algorithm can provide an additional layer of security. In case TLS is deployed and proper authentication and authorization mechanisms are in place, data integrity checks are not useful. Using non-repudiation checks, along with digital signature with public/private key, can provide additional security. This is especially important when organizations are dealing with highly confidential data [40].

## 1.4.5 *Infrastructure Security*

Many brokers are deployed in a network environment, and understanding the network topology of the target system helps lock out attackers as soon as possible in order to prevent damage and downtime on downstream systems. Some security mechanisms are detailed below.

### 1.4.5.1 Firewall

As a recommended practice, one should place at least one firewall in between broker and the clients. There are many commercial and open-source firewall solutions available. This firewall should implement sophisticated rules aimed at blocking attackers at the firewall level. The most appropriate firewall rules vary from case to case and there is no one-size-fits-all approach. In general, a firewall should allow only expected traffic to the downstream objects. In MQTT environments, it is a recommendation to block all UDP datagram packets. This is because MQTT uses TCP. If a particular implementation of protocol does not require any particular ports, a firewall should also block all traffic to these ports. In MQTT environment, port 1883 is the default MQTT port and port 8883 is default MQTT over TLS port. A firewall in MQTT environment should only allow traffic on these two ports. If organizations know the IPs of all clients in their system, the firewall should only allow traffic from the given IP range to lock any clients not included in the defined IP range [25, 26].

### 1.4.5.2 Load Balancer

The function of a load balancer is to distribute protocol traffic to different brokers, e.g., if brokers are operated in a cluster environment. A load balancer typically does not provide much security but can prevent overloading of brokers and can also throttle unusually high traffic. This throttling is important because few malicious clients with enough bandwidth available can overload the system very quickly and consume all the bandwidth, which may lead to service degradation and can be very expensive. For example, MQTT allows throttling on a global and per-client basis. Organizations can limit the total incoming bytes per second and the total outgoing bytes per second independently. In many protocol deployment scenarios, messages are much smaller, often small than a kilobyte. It is a recommendation that organizations determine their usage scenario and know the maximum message size that can occur. With this information, organizations can decrease the maximum allowed message size to that limit. Malicious clients could send huge messages otherwise, which may result in excessive memory consumption and unneeded bandwidth usage [33].

#### 1.4.5.3 Demilitarized Zone (DMZ)

A DMZ is a subnetwork that protects access to all downstream objects by providing an additional firewall. The purpose of the DMZ is to stop the attacker at the DMZ level by using a dual firewall system. A DMZ should utilize two firewalls from different vendors. This is because the same exploitation techniques known for one firewall cannot be used against the second firewall. Some broker implementation, such as MQTT, provides plug-ins that are used to access internal services (e.g., authentication services). In this case, one should not deploy a DMZ [33].

#### 1.4.5.4 Operating System

Brokers are, typically, installed on servers. These servers can be physical or virtual. It is important to note that, in many cases, attackers utilize security holes in operating systems to compromise the broker itself. It is therefore important that operating system software be updated all the time.

## 1.5 Conclusion

Each IoT protocol has certain strengths and weaknesses with respect to securing device connectivity. A careful analysis of these strengths and weaknesses is required in order to choose the best mix of protocols for a given scenario. Different protocols provide different levels of interoperability for information exchanges between applications and subsystems. Each protocol varies in its QoS capabilities and the architecture and the message/data sharing requirements for each target system varies. These capabilities and characteristics can affect the protocol's ability to provide basic message reliability. For example, DDS can provide tailored data management that enables applications to specify the reliability of data exchanges. TLS and payload encryption can work in conjunction. Checksums are vulnerable to attacks. Digital signatures can provide multiple security services such as message authentication, message integrity, and non-repudiation. MACs are much faster than digital signatures. The use of encryption can help ensure confidentiality of the payload. The use of a firewall can be helpful in restricting traffic to certain ports. The use of load balancer can help in reducing excessive memory consumption and unneeded bandwidth usage. If plug-ins are available in a particular broker implementation for accessing internal services, deployment of a DMZ can be helpful. All IoT protocols provide transport-level data encryption based on TLS or DTLS. AMQP and XMPP also use SASL for authentication. DDS provides a comprehensive security framework that provides a complete end-to-end security for DSS-based IoT environment. It is clear that selecting an option that provides secure device connectivity in IoT is challenging. This challenge becomes much bigger in case when one considers multiple key system requirements (such as QoS and interoperability) along with security. This is because the complex IoT environments seldom use a single data connectivity standard. In order to reap the benefits of industrial IoT, we need a solution that would enable multiple protocols that would then work together efficiently and securely.

## References


1. Cisco (2014) The Internet of everything: bringing the future to life. Retrieved from www.cisco.com/web/offer/grs/176780/The_Internet_of_Everything_Bringing_the_future_to_life_FINAL.PDF
2. Govtech (2014) FutureStructure: the new framework for communities (Infographic). Retrieved 24 September 2015, from http://www.govtech.com/dc/articles/FutureStructure-The-New-Framework-for-Communities.html
3. Evocca A (2015) Internet of Things (IoT). Retrieved from http://itnews.evocca.com.au/author/angela-lovett/. Accessed Jul 2015
4. Babar S, Mahalle P, Stango A, Prasad N, Prasad R. (2010). Proposed security model and threat taxonomy for the internet of things (IoT). In Recent trends in network security and applications. Springer, Berlin/Heidelberg, pp 420–429
5. Heer T, Garcia-Morchon O, Hummen R, Keoh SL, Kumar SS, Wehrle K (2011) Security challenges in the IP-based Internet of things. Wirel Personal Commun 61(3):527–542
6. Garcia-Morchon O, Kumar S, Struik R, Keoh S, Hummen R (2013) Security considerations in the IP-based internet of things. IETF, The Netherlands
7. Gazis V, Gortz M, Huber M, Leonardi A, Mathioudakis K, Wiesmaier A, Vasilomanolakis E (2015, August). A survey of technologies for the internet of things. In Wireless Communications and Mobile Computing Conference (IWCMC), International. IEEE, Croatia, pp 1090–1095
8. Al-Fuqaha A, Guizani M, Mohammadi M, Aledhari M, Ayyash M (2015) Internet of things: a survey on enabling technologies, protocols, and applications. IEEE Commun Surv Tut 17 (4):2347–2376
9. Antonic A, Marjanovic M, Skocir P, Zarko IP (2015) Comparison of the CUPUS middleware and MQTT protocol for smart city services. In Telecommunications (ConTEL), 2015 13th international conference on (pp 1–8). IEEE
10. De Caro N, Colitti W, Steenhaut K, Mangino G, Reali G (2013) Comparison of two lightweight protocols for smartphone-based sensing. In Communications and vehicular technology in the Benelux (SCVT), 2013 I.E. 20th symposium on (pp 1–6). IEEE
11. Hunkeler U, Truong HL, Stanford-Clark A (2008) MQTT-S—a publish/subscribe protocol for wireless sensor networks. In Communication systems software and middleware and workshops, 2008. comsware 2008. 3rd international conference on (pp 791–798). IEEE
12. Vinoski S (2006) Advanced message queuing protocol. IEEE Internet Comput 6:87–89
13. Pesch D, Timm-Giel A, Agüero R, Wenning B-L, Pentikousis K (2013) Mobile networks and management: 5th international conference, MONAMI 2013, Cork, Ireland, September 23–25, 2013, Revised Selected Papers. Springer
14. AMQP (2015) AMQP is the Internet protocol for business messaging. Retrieved 24 September 2015, from https://www.amqp.org/about/what
15. Oasis (2012) OASIS Advanced Message Queuing Protocol (AMQP) version 1.0, Part 0: overview. Retrieved 24 September 2015, from http://docs.oasis-open.org/amqp/core/v1.0/os/amqp-core-overview-v1.0-os.html
16. Shelby Z, Hartke K, Bormann C (2014) The constrained application protocol (CoAP). IETF, USA

17. Alghamdi TA, Lasebae A, Aiash M (2013) Security analysis of the constrained application protocol in the Internet of Things. In Future Generation Communication Technology (FGCT), 2013 second international conference on (pp 163–168). IEEE
18. Khan S, Pathan A-SK (2013) Wireless networks and security: issues, challenges and research trends. Springer-Verlag, Berlin/Heidelberg
19. Schmidt DC, Corsaro A, Hag H (2008) Addressing the challenges of tactical information management in net-centric systems with DDS. Prism Tech Corp, USA
20. OMG (2014) DDS-Security Beta1. Retrieved 24 September 2015, from http://www.omg.org/spec/DDS-SECURITY/1.0/Beta1/
21. Saint-Andre P (2011) Extensible messaging and presence protocol (XMPP): core. IETF, USA
22. Jøsang A, Pope S (2005) User centric identity management. In AusCERT Asia Pacific information technology security conference, p 77
23. Lampkin V, Leong WT, Olivera L, Rawat S, Subrahmanyam N, Xiang R, Keen M (2012) Building smarter planet solutions with mqtt and ibm websphere mq telemetry. IBM Redbooks, IBM, USA
24. Hivemq (2015a) MQTT security fundamentals – MQTT message data integrity. Retrieved from http://www.hivemq.com/blog/mqtt-security-fundamentals-mqtt-message-data-integrity
25. Hivemq (2015b) MQTT security fundamentals: TLS/SSL. Retrieved from http://www.hivemq.com/blog/mqtt-security-fundamentals-tls-ssl
26. Apache (2011) Apache ActiveMQ security guide. Retrieved 24 September 2015, from https://access.redhat.com/documentation/en-US/Fuse_ESB/4.3.1/html-single/Apache_ActiveMQ_Security_Guide/index.html
27. XMPP (2015) Extensible Messaging and Presence Protocol (XMPP): core. Retrieved 24 September 2015, from http://xmpp.org/rfcs/rfc3920.html
28. Waher P (2015) Learning internet of things. Packt Publishing Ltd, Birmingham
29. Schofield A (2014) Security and MQTT – middleware conversations [ZZ999]. Retrieved 24 September 2015, from www-304.ibm.com/connections/blogs/aim/entry/security_and_mqtt?lang=en_us
30. Infoq (2013) Practical MQTT with Paho. Retrieved 24 September 2015, from http://www.infoq.com/articles/practical-mqtt-with-paho
31. Hivemq (2015c) MQTT security fundamentals: authentication with username and password. Retrieved 24 September 2015, from http://www.hivemq.com/blog/mqtt-security-fundamentals-authentication-username-password
32. OWASP (2015) Transport layer protection cheat sheet – OWASP. Retrieved 24 September 2015, from https://www.owasp.org/index.php/Transport_Layer_Protection_Cheat_Sheet
33. Apache (2015) 1.5. security. Retrieved 24 September 2015, from https://qpid.apache.org/releases/qpid-0.14/books/AMQP-Messaging-Broker-CPP-Book/html/ch01s05.html
34. OAuth (2015) OAuth community site. Retrieved 24 September 2015, from http://oauth.net/
35. Oracle (2015) Oracle fusion middleware user guide. Retrieved from http://docs.oracle.com/cd/E65459_01/user.1112/E65456_01.pdf
36. Saint-Andre P (2008) OAuth over XMPP [XMPP extension protocol]. Retrieved 24 September 2015, from http://www.geopapier.pl/katalogbiurowy/xmpp.org/extensions/attic/xep-0235-0.4.html
37. Saint-Andre P (2004) End-to-end signing and object encryption for the extensible messaging and presence protocol (XMPP). IETF, USA
38. says P (2015) MQTT security fundamentals: MQTT payload encryption. Retrieved from http://www.hivemq.com/blog/mqtt-security-fundamentals-payload-encryption
39. Microsoft (2015) Description of symmetric and asymmetric encryption. Retrieved 24 September 2015, from https://support.microsoft.com/en-us/kb/246071
40. Microsoft (2003) How TLS/SSL works: logon and authentication. Retrieved 24 September 2015, from https://technet.microsoft.com/en-us/library/cc783349(v=ws.10).aspx
41. Singh G, Supriya A (2013) A study of encryption algorithms (RSA, DES, 3DES and AES) for information security. Int J Comput Appl 67(19):33–38

# Chapter 2
# Security Mechanisms for Connectivity of Smart Devices in the Internet of Things

**Somayya Madakam and Hema Date**

## 2.1 Introduction

We have already connected cars, homes, refrigerators, thermostats, spoons, and many other appliances and devices to the Internet. In fact, in the near future, even more physical things will get connected to the Future Internet (FI). A complete IoT corporate's vision is that a world of low-cost sensors will be designed, developed, and embedded into our daily eating utensils, mattresses, and home lighting systems, to name but a few, for better services to the human being through smart device connectivity. The term smart device (SD) designates any physical object associated with computing resources and capable of communicating with other similar objects via physical transmission medium and logical protocols or with humans via a standard user interface. The scale spans from big smart devices such as personal digital assistants (PDAs) to small ones such as radio-frequency identification (RFID) tags [1]. Smart devices can be programmed, sometimes hardwired, to tell us to reduce the amount of caffeine we consume after 8 pm or train one's bedroom lights to gradually increase their brightness precisely at the moment one comes out of deep sleep. Sensors can work around the clock ($24 \times 7$) to measure and monitor everything from one's diet to one's sleeping behavior and then use this information to modify future actions for a better future. A recent observation at Seven Hills Hospital at Marol in Mumbai (India) was that the patient's entire blood pressure, electro cardio graphy (ECG), sugar content level, oxygen, water amount, and other allied medical parameters were completely measured by sensors, computers, and allied medical smart devices for monitoring, automation, and controlling. This was finally intimated to the concerned nurses and doctors for further treatment. This is an ideal example how smart devices can be used for better medical treatment. This

S. Madakam (✉) • H. Date
IT Applications Group, National Institute of Industrial Engineering (NITIE), Mumbai, India
e-mail: somu4smart@gmail.com



Z. Mahmood (ed.), *Connectivity Frameworks for Smart Devices*,
Computer Communications and Networks, DOI 10.1007/978-3-319-33124-9_2

kind of device connection is called the Internet of Things. The Internet of Things is a new paradigm shift in IT world, where things have digital identities, monitoring functionalities with artificial intelligence (AI), and can be located, tracked, automated, monitored, and controlled automatically.

In the rest of this chapter, we explore the concept of smart devices and their connectivity from the viewpoint of scholars, academicians, practitioners, and developers. Furthermore, we also discuss in detail the security mechanisms of smart devices within the Internet of Things (IoT) scenario, with emphasis on both physical and logical remedy mechanisms.

## 2.2 Internet of Things

As discussed before, a smart device is an electronic device, generally connected to other electronic devices through high-speed bandwidth networks with the help of wireless technologies such as Bluetooth, near-field communication (NFC), Wi-Fi, and 4G, capable of communication with other devices. These smart devices can be smartphones, androids, tablets, iPads, computers, laptops, television, consoles, and IP cameras. Next-generation smart cards, also called smart devices, are regarded as personal devices providing a secured execution and storage environment for application tasks and sensitive secrecy/privacy of the data or information, respectively [2].

In the beginning, the Internet was designed and used only for communication and to access websites/web portal through mobiles or computers to download information. However, with the help of advanced technological tools and techniques and more powerful smart devices with high speed, extra capabilities, and more intelligence abilities, its connotation changed. Advances in technologies like very large-scale integration (VLSI) chips and microcontrollers are also creating smarter devices with low power consumption; this means that large networks of sensors can be created, with the ability to obtain information, process it, and act accordingly. 3D computer-aided design system uses the common multi-touch gestures associated with smart devices to keep the modeling operations simple and easy for users. However, it is difficult to input the precise geometric information to generate 3D CAD models by such gestures [3]. Here it shows how the idea of the Internet of Things arises [4]. Though the term IoT was coined by Kevin Ashton in 1999 at the Auto-ID Center in MIT, the IoT was the seventh technology in the series defined by the International Telecommunication Union (ITU) in their reports originally launched in 1997 under the title *Challenges to the Network*.

The Internet of Things describes the evolution from systems linking digital information to systems relating digital information to real-world physical items. In this sphere, the Internet connects with our routines through this network of connected objects [5]. The rise of the Internet of Things provides an environment where everyday objects are allied to the Internet and contribute together on a system, which gives way to the convergence of smart appliances and conventionally connected to devices. There were approximately 6.3 billion people living on the planet in 2003, and 500 million devices connected to the Internet as per Cisco's statistics. This indicates that there was less than one (0.08) device for every person. Based on Cisco's Internet Business Solutions Group (IBSG)'s definition, the IoT did not exist in the year 2003. The number of connected devices was relatively very small given that ubiquitous smart devices such as smartphones were introduced only in the year 2007. Hence, Cisco's IBSG reported that the IoT was born way back between 2008 and 2009. Today, the Internet of Things is quite prosperous, as initiatives such as Cisco's planetary skin, smart grid, and intelligent vehicles continue to progress. Cisco's IBSG predicts that there will be 25 billion smart devices connected to the Internet by 2015 and 50 billion by 2020. Some other projections indicate that up to 100 billion smart devices or objects will be connected to the Internet by the end of the year 2020. According to the seventh EMC digital universe study report, India's digital universe shall grow ninefold by 2020. Out of which data generated by the IoT shall be 10 %. The IoT is considered as the world's third wave of the information industry after the inventions of computer and the Internet [6]. The base for any smart device to function efficiently is the help of embedded Internet of Things technologies. Speaking about smart devices, it includes even the existing electronic devices that have computational capabilities as well as physical things, acquiring the power of intelligence through various artificial intelligence capabilities to perform tasks efficiently and effectively.

The Internet of Things is the next evolution of the Internet, which is positively affecting human life. The Internet of Things is a technological revolution that represents the future of computing and communications, and its development depends on the dynamic technical innovation in a number of important fields, from wireless sensors to nanotechnologies. Primarily, the Internet of Things is aimed at making our daily life more sophisticated and flexible. The IoT is a network of smarter objects, which includes people too. These devices will have communication and computation capabilities [7]. The IoT, also called Cyber-Physical Systems, is now going to reign over all earthly things, living as well as nonliving. It will be present everywhere (omnipresent) through various connected technologies and will have the potential to automate, monitor, and control things even in situations of disasters. According to one estimate, there could be around 86,000 trillion devices that connect to the future Internet, soon.

In the Internet of Things, everything real becomes virtual, which means that each person and thing has a locatable, addressable, and readable counterpart on the Internet [8]. In the Internet of Things, every existing object can be connected to the Internet and can exchange data with other objects. By allowing everything to be interconnected, objects will have recognition, localization, sensing, control, and management. The basic objective of any device or thing or object connection to the Internet varies from device to device. This connection can be done through various technologies including RFID, IPv6, EPC, bar code, ZigBee, Wi-Fi, Bluetooth, NFC, sensor, actuator, data analytic, ambient intelligence (AI), and Web 2.0.

The IoT is a paradigm shift that takes advantage of sensor networks. It is rapidly gaining ground in modern wireless communications, with its position and status known, where services and intelligence are added to this expanded Internet, fusing the digital and physical world. The basic concept is the pervasive presence of objects, such as radio-frequency identification (RFID) tags, actuators, mobile phones, and sensors [9]. The benefits of the IoT to developing and emerging economies are significant, and strategies to realize these need to be found. As a result, applying the IoT for modeling logistic system is a promising solution for researchers [10]. The prospects of a world of smart things that virtually talk to each other are fascinating, leading to many new applications and opportunities [11]. The pervasive and ambient intelligence (AI) will involve interaction coordination and cooperation among more and more smart devices [12].

## 2.3 Security in the IoT

Security is not a new concept. Right from birth to death, one has to take care of several security mechanisms in terms of food, shelter, children, articles, finance, and many more aspects, in which we are experiencing very well. Similarly, when the billions of smart devices are connecting to the Internet under the umbrella of IoT phenomena, there needs to be robust security mechanisms to get the right information to the right things, at the right place at the right time through the right channel. At the same time, when the communication is happening among all people, objects, and machines, security is absolutely required. Sometimes one may be unable to receive data due to device failure, due to in turn, to noise or channel failure. Besides, there may be more hackers who often try to hack strategic information for their own business without following any cyber laws or ethics. Organizations need to protect their own information from attackers or competitors as these could lead to loss of professional data. Information security refers to measures adopted to prevent the unauthorized use, misuse, modification, or denial of knowledge, facts, data, or capabilities [13]. The basic security issues in the IoT are the same as the security issues in general IT; however, in the case of the IoT, much more sensitivity and confidentiality are a must. The sensitivity of IoT technologies is based on different security requirements such as confidentiality, integrity, authenticity, privacy, availability, and regulation. As every player with a stake in the IoT is well aware, security is paramount for the safe and reliable operation of connected devices. The security of smart device issues generally includes physical and logical issues. The logical issues are many in the form of malware counting into virus, worms, Trojan horse, and spyware. Smart devices have limited capabilities, in terms of computational power and memory, and might be battery-powered devices, thus raising the need to adopt particularly energy-efficient technologies. These devices generate a large amount of data per second, even in peta-bytes per second. The deployment of the IoT raises many security issues coming from (1) the very nature of smart objects, e.g., the adoption of lightweight cryptographic algorithms, in terms of processing and memory requirements, and (2) the use of standard protocols, e.g., the need to minimize the amount of data exchanged between nodes [14]. The integration of the physical world into the fabric of Web imposes advanced security requirements that need to be satisfied in order to ensure a stringent control over IoT service interaction. Security and privacy trials of the Internet of Things (IoT) that appear are due to the connection of diverse technologies [15].

The Internet of Things is a topic that has been studied by many researchers, either trying to create a trustworthy infrastructure to enhance the privacy of the Internet of Things or creating developments secure enough to provide applications on fields as healthcare [16]. Design principles and methods for securing the IoT are yet to be explored. Security in the IoT device is a crucial aspect that applies at different levels, ranging from technological issues to more philosophical ones, such as privacy and trust, especially in scenarios like smart toys. The security challenges derive from the very nature of smart objects and the use of standard protocols. In [17], the security challenges and requirements for an IP-based IoT have been presented by analyzing existing Internet Protocols to be applied to the IoT and the limitations and problems that such a solution might introduce. The technique of the Internet of Things is a new application technique, and people are often more focused on novel applications, neglecting the security problem, which is more important in the case of wireless sensor network in the IoT [18]. Towards particular IoT security, there are several open issues such as cryptographic algorithms, authentication protocols, access control, trust or privacy, and governance frameworks [19]. Hence, the research status of key technologies including encryption mechanism, communication security, protecting sensor data, and cryptographic algorithms must be taken care of [20]. However, it is the need of the hour that we need to work for more advanced security mechanisms in the forthcoming years in securing smart device communications under the umbrella of the Internet of Things.

## 2.4 Security in Smart Devices

Security has been defined as the ability to deal with a specific threat by somehow neutralizing it. A broader definition refers to relative freedoms from various kingdoms of dangers and risks. This definition includes cognitive and psychological aspects innate in a security system. Security is, thus, an attitude which depends heavily upon the perceived nature of an environment [21]. The market for devices like mobile phones, multi-functional watches, and personal digital assistants is growing rapidly. Most of these mobile user devices need security for their prospective electronic commerce applications. While new technology has simplified many business and personal transactions, it has also opened the door to high-tech crime [22]. Many corporate people for their business activities, and common people for their daily work, use smart devices around the clock and throughout the globe. Tablets, Apple iPads, and Android-based phones are now being used by millions of employees worldwide to send and receive official information for business operations. These smart devices are embedded with many applications like software utilities in office applications, phone call, email, WhatsApp, LinkedIn, Facebook, and Instagram are sending the data including audio, video, and entertainment apps. These devices need to be secured from the vulnerabilities from both physical mode and logical point of view. Not astonishingly, security has emerged as the primary challenge posed by the smart devices at par with BYOD (bring your own device). Therefore, both physical and logical security of devices is the need of the hour. Security services, like authentication and access control, have to be non-intrusive, intelligent, and able to adapt to the rapidly changing contexts of the spaces [23].

### 2.4.1 Physical Security

Physical security is one of the essential parts of smart and Internet of Things devices. Physical security includes not only the area containing system hardware but also locations of wiring used to connect the systems, supporting services, backup provisions, and any other part of the systems counting as smart devices. Physical things in a house include beds, fans, curtains, windows, bedsheets, chairs, and other home appliances like kitchen utensils among others. When installing a network or connecting our home to the home area network (HAN) and wide area network (WAN) or the Internet, we are building an infrastructure that people depend on. Security measures exist to ensure that the network and devices are reliable for home owners and their family members. For many installations, outages often occur due to human tampering, whether accidental or non-accidental. Networks have physical components, such as wires, modems, firewalls, boxes, and Wi-Fi devices, which can be easily disturbed. In many installations, people will not understand the purpose of the installed electronic equipment, and curiosity may lead them to experiment. They may not realize the importance of a cable connected to an I/O ports. Someone may unplug an Ethernet cable or turn our camera direction so that they can connect their laptop or smart mobile for 5–10 min or consecutively carry out the theft or move a switch because it is in their way. A plug might be removed from a power bar because someone needs that receptacle. Assuring the physical security of an installation is supreme, signs and labels will only be useful to those who can read our language. Putting things out of the way and limiting the access are the best means to assure that accidents and tinkering do not occur. Sometimes, people are so fond of smart devices, the latest gadgets, and electronic devices and do the theft by taking the opportunity. Smart washing machines, tumble dryers, air conditioners, refrigerators, electric water heaters, and electric space heating may come under this section. Hence, physical security is one of the vital aspects in smart devices communication security.

## 2.4.2 *Logical Security*

Logical security uses technology to allow individuals to access the data, information, things, devices, and systems based on who they are and what is their role within an organization or residential place or could be a network. Access to information resources should be restricted to those individuals with a need to access. Determining data and information ownership and access rights to the process for a monitor that individuals have appropriate access are all a part of an effective security strategy. The elements of logical security include authentication, privacy, policies' standardization, and monitoring. Security services, like authentication and access control, have to be nonintrusive, intelligent, and able to adapt to the rapidly changing contexts of the spaces. Logical security is in different methods as explained in the next following sections.

### 2.4.2.1 Authentication

Before being granted access to network resources and devices in the Internet of Things, users should first be authenticated. In an ideal world, every wired and wireless user would have an identifier that is unique, unchangeable, and addressable, which cannot be impersonated by other users. Otherwise, this will turn out to be a very difficult problem to solve in the realistic world. Consider a medical application in which patient's information is stored in medical information system (MIS) and health information system (HIS) records. The medical data access for authentication by several users including the hospital, medical practitioners, staff nurses, medical researchers, and insurers should be authentic. Devices should be secured with the help of CCTV/IP cameras/physical security guards. This authentication of smart people and smart devices is by different means including MAC address, QR codes, RFID, and IPv4/IPv6.

### 2.4.2.2 Medium Access Control (MAC)

One of the closest features in authentication is to have a unique identifier like the medium access control (MAC) address. This is the 48 bit number assigned by the manufacturer to every wireless and Ethernet device. By employing MAC filtering on our access points, we can authenticate users based on their MAC address. With this feature, the access point keeps an internal table of approved MAC addresses. When a wireless user tries to associate to the access point, the MAC address of the client must be on the approved list; otherwise, association will be denied. Alternately, the access point (AP) may keep a table of known and bad MAC addresses and not permit other devices that are not in the list. IEEE 802.15.4 MAC layer offers some facilities, which can be used by upper layers to achieve a good level of security. It is said that companies like alarm.com are taking advantage of wireless networks to let one arm or disarm their system remotely, watch live videos, detect water in the basement, trigger real-time email notifications, and control critical systems like lights, thermostats, and small appliances remotely.

#### 2.4.2.3 The Radio-Frequency Identification (RFID)

The radio-frequency identification (RFID) technology has advanced significance over several other technologies. RFID is a powerful technology, not only for automated inspection or identification of products but also for augmenting conventional positioning systems [24, 25]. Radio-frequency identification applications are in military, airline, library, security, healthcare, sports, animal farms, and others below. RFID is the wireless, noncontact use of radio-frequency electromagnetic fields to transfer data, for the purposes of automatically identifying and tracking tags attached to objects. Without proper security controls, tags embedded in consumer products could leak potentially embarrassing information. Even if the tag contents are secured, predictable tag responses could be tracked, violating one's location privacy [26]. In a bottom-up approach, cryptography is the cornerstone for network infrastructure protection. Although it is possible to implement existing standards, such as Advanced Encryption Standard (AES), some IoT devices, such as passive RFID tags, might be extremely constrained. Cryptographic mechanisms must be smaller and faster but with little or no reduction in security level.

#### 2.4.2.4 Quick Response (QR) Code

QR code is one of the latest authentication techniques in which objects, things, or events can be identified or distinguished from the world. Once scanned through mobile, this code will take one to the main home page of that particular product description, which is given in detail. QR codes are two-dimensional barcodes that visually encode bits of information characterized as black square dots placed on a white square grid. QR code security protocols allow the code creator to protect data stored in QR codes by encryption. This allows the end users to verify that message did not tamper with the previous one. The initial usage of these codes is spread more in Japan, China, and the rest of world.

#### 2.4.2.5 IPv4/IPv6

In comparison with IPv4, IPv6 has an increased set of capabilities to simplify end-system auto-configuration, which includes the automated discovery of routers, neighbor's resolution, duplicate address detection, and neighbor unreachability detection. Refer to Table 2.1. These enhancements bring along with them a different set of security vulnerabilities that must be addressed. According to Scott Hogg, IPv6 security author and CTO of GTRI, "All security practitioners should

**Table 2.1** Comparison between IPv4 and IPv6

| IPv4 | IPv6 |
|---|---|
| The address space is 32 bits | The space is 128 bits |
| The length of the header is 20 bytes | The length of the header is 40 bytes |
| Four bytes for each address in the header | Fifteen bytes for each address in the header |
| The number of header field is 12 | The number of header field is 8 |
| Checksum field, used to measure error in the header, required | Checksum field eliminated from the header as error in the IP header is very crucial |
| Internet Protocol Security (IPSec) with respect to network security is optional | Internet Protocol Security (IPSec) with respect to network security is mandatory |
| No identification to the packet flow (lack of QoS handling) | The flow-level field on the header portion identifies the packet flow and directs to the router (efficient QoS handling) |
| The fragmentation is done both by sending host and routers | The fragmentation is done both by sending host; there is no role of the routers |
| No identification to the packet flow (lack of QoS handling) | The flow-level field on the header portion identifies the packet flow and directs to the router (efficient QoS handling) |
| Clients have to approach the dynamic host configuration server (DHCS) whenever they connect to a network | Clients do not have to approach any such server as they are given permanent addresses |
| www.certiology.com, website accessed dated on | 12/12/2015 |

learn about IPv6 now because all organizations have IPv6 capable and enabled operating systems in their environments. Failure to secure the IPv6 system is like allowing a back-door to exist." There are 16 different tunnels and transition methods, not to mention upper layer tunnels. A general myth and misunderstanding about IPv6 is that it is more secure than IPv4. This assertion stems from the original mandated use of IPSec in host-to-host communication, as specified in RFC 2401. Certainly, if IPSec is implemented, it would provide confidentiality and integrity between two hosts, but it still would not address any link operation vulnerabilities, attacks, and most of the denial-of-service (DoS) attacks. DoS is one of the most aggressive and menacing intrusive behaviors. It severely degrades availability of a victim, such as a smart device or even the network by imposing computationally intensive tasks, using exploitation of system vulnerability. The victim is then forced to stop providing services for some time to other devices of the network. Hence, effective approaches for detecting DoS attack are significantly important to protect on-line services, and many efforts have been made to enable this process.

### *2.4.3 Security Tools and Software*

Software is a set of logical instructions executed for problem solving. Securing software is a computer program designed to enhance information security. The explosion of Internet traffic has created enormous demand for information system security professionals. In this mode, all files that the operating system (OS) opens or uses are scanned first before they are fully opened. Security must be addressed throughout the smart device software life cycle, right from the initial design, coding, and development to operational and maintenance environment. To deal with the distributed denial-of-service attacks, the information security personnel should ensure that critical network connections have enough bandwidth and redundancy to prevent easy attacks [27]. Authors of [28] have reported that lower connection speeds can easily be overwhelmed by the attacker. The distributed denial-of-service attacks cannot just be eliminated by having sufficient bandwidth; additional techniques for dealing with these attacks should also be employed [29]. This includes the installation of intrusion detection systems to foresee a possible attack [30], the intrusion detection systems as network burglar alarms, and listening to the network for traffic that matches common attack signatures stored in the database [31]. Security codes, motion detectors, and cameras provide information to a smart home security system, allowing it to determine whether an individual is a resident, a cleared visitor, or an intruder. Motion detectors trigger an alert, letting the artificial intelligence program know that there is someone or something to be evaluated. Facial recognition software and security codes allow the security system to allow residents into the home, while based on preprogrammed information restrict access to other individuals [32, 33]. The malfunctioning software in smart environments is of two/many forms including:

- Mobile Viruses: These can be the main threat, particularly with devices that have significant computational capabilities. Mobile devices, in general, are susceptible to viruses in several ways. Viruses can take advantages of security holes in applications or in underlying OS and cause damage. Applications downloaded to mobile devices like android can be as virus prone as desktop applications. In some of the mobiles, malfunctioning SMS can also crash the OS.
- Bluejacking: This refers to sending nameless, unwanted messages to other users with Bluetooth-enabled mobile phones or laptops. Bluejacking depends on the capability of Bluetooth phones to detect and contact another Bluetooth-enabled device. Bluejacking can be a problem if it is used to send obscene or threatening messages or images or to send advertising. If we want to avoid such malicious messages, we can turn off Bluetooth or set it to "undiscoverable."

Apart from this, secure boot, when electrical power is first supplied to a smart device, and the authenticity and integrity of the system software on the smart device should be verified using cryptographically generated digital signatures. In the same way, the person who signed on a legal certificate through a digital signature attached to the software copy should be verified by the device to ensure only the duly authorized software to run on that device at the time of booting. The foundation of reliance has been established, but the device still needs protection from various runtime threats and malicious intents. Infineon Pvt. Ltd. and many other companies have developed a broad range of semiconductor technologies for counter-growing security threats. These technological solutions permit system and device manufacturers as well as service providers to capitalize on growth opportunities by integrating the right level of security without compromising on user experience. Complemented by software and supporting services, their hardware-based products also create an anchor of trust for security, supporting device integrity checks, authentication, and secure key management.

#### 2.4.3.1 System-Level Security

System-level security is essential for smart devices, computers, tablets, and servers. The firewall of smart devices should be always enabled in the operating system (OS) level. The device protocols in which the object or electronic device in a home area network (HAN), local area network (LAN), or world area network (WAN) should be defined very specifically. All the connected home devices are protected with login names and passwords. If it is required, one should keep double-level entry password security mechanisms like banking security systems. This ensures that third-party or rouge devices cannot steal personal home information. One should clearly caution one's children against even sharing the smart home security passwords with their friends. The same also applies to one's laptop and computer passwords, smart door key, smart gas connection, smart meter distribution, and any other locking smart fridge. Along with these, one should always update the latest versions of software. The patches will help for better smart device security operation level, leading to better and safe communication.

#### 2.4.3.2 Antiviruses

Any smart device can be affected by malware. Malware software is an all-inclusive term for malicious programs like viruses, Trojan horse, worms, and spyware, which are designed to poison and take control of smart devices. One's smart device has been infected, rogues can capture all the keystrokes, steal one's vital information, and use the devices. Hence, antivirus software is required. Antivirus consists of computer programs that attempt to identify, prevent, and eliminate computer viruses and other malware software. Antivirus typically uses two different techniques to accomplish its mission: (1) examining files to look for known viruses matching definitions in a virus dictionary and (2) identifying suspicious behavior from any computer program that might indicate infection. Such analysis may include data captures, port monitoring, and other methods. These programs have two basic modes: (1) static file scanning, useful for when you have to scan a file to check to see if any of the files are currently infected with malware, and (2) real-time "dynamic" scanning, which is really what is needed to prevent the computer from getting infected in the first place. For better security, one should use fully licensed software with the latest/updated patches.

#### 2.4.3.3 Firewalls

The firewall is an integrated collection of security measures designed to prevent unauthorized electronic access to a networked computer system as well as IoT devices. The same principle will work for all smart devices. A network firewall is similar to firewalls in building construction, because in both cases they are intended to isolate one "network" or "compartment" from one another. The successful use of a firewall is dependent on the selection of an appropriate product. Packet filtering in firewalls accepts or denies based on numerous rules that depend on the source and destination ports of packets and other diffusion criteria. The level of security for smart devices in the Internet of Things (IoT) depends on the customization/settings of the firewall software.

#### 2.4.3.4 Monitoring

Monitoring the people or things or events using smart devices is one of the vital tasks in home/building/company. This can be done by CCTV (closed-circuit television) or IP (Internet Protocol) camera or human physical security. It is extremely difficult to monitor the objects/procedures in continuous in all the places without CCTV/IP cameras. For example, the number of participants and their safety in NITIE, Mumbai, in its convocations for 6 h without any hazardous can be possible using IP cameras. Another example is the monitoring of growth patterns of rose/lotus/jasmine plant using Koubachi sensor for its life. The Sensor will give notifications to its user's smart mobile about basic requirements of light, hydrogen, humidity, oxygen, and carbon dioxide measurements.

CCTV/IP Camera

We know that an IP camera [34] is a video camera that can be directly connected to the Internet without the need of a separate computer. Camera devices are in use in public places as well as in homes which have the capacity to gather large amounts of image material. Fortunately, for the time being, there are effective ways to analyze the mass of video data automatically and recognize potential risk situations in advance by analytical software. In industrial plants, CCTV equipment may be used to observe parts of the process from a central control room, when the environment is not suitable for humans. CCTV [35] systems may operate continuously or only as required to monitor a particular event. [36] have worked upon calibration techniques of CCTV camera. CCTV is one part of the solution and not a panacea for public safety and security. CCTVs improve public perception of safety and deter and displace antisocial behavior and crime. For applications network security is an important concern; the deployment of IP cameras in the network address translation (NAT) environments with dynamic locations is usually desired. However, without static IP address information, accessing the Web server associated with IP Cameras will be difficult [37]. In the mining applications, IP cameras and RFID devices are being used very effectively in order to provide security for workers and detection of landslides or unexpected explosion of water sprouts in $24 \times 7$ round the years.

Wireless Sensor Network (WSN)

WSN is one of the most popular forms of connected smart devices deployed in smart home or smart office security systems. They often integrate various wireless devices into our home to enable remote intruder detection and image streaming to our cell phone over a combined security platform, which can be remotely controlled from our mobile device. Security plays an important role in WSN since the nodes are exposed to attacks even in a ruthless environment. The original motivation behind the research into WSNs was military applications. Examples of military sensor networks include large-scale acoustic ocean surveillance systems for the detection of submarines, self-organized and randomly deployed WSNs for battlefield surveillance, and attaching microsensors to weapons for stockpile surveillance [38]. According to the author Suraiya Tarannum in his book *Wireless Sensor Networks*, the application space for WSNs is quite large and continues to expand vigorously, encompassing habitat, ecosystem, seismic and industrial process monitoring, security, and surveillance as well as rapid emergency response and wellness maintenance. The lifetime of the network can be enhanced by providing security and privacy against network layer attacks when the nodes are scattered in an unsupervised environment. In order to protect a network, few of the routing protocols such as sensor protocols for information via negotiations [39] and path redundancy-based security algorithm for homogeneous-based wireless sensor networks [40] address the security mechanism and authentication against the various attacks. Some of the secured routing protocols of heterogeneous sensor networks [41] can detect the malicious nodes and deliver the packets to sink successfully. wireless sensors networks are vulnerable to many types of attacks.

As WSNs are based on communication standards and data sent over a broadcast channel, it is possible to make packet sniffing and data spoofing attacks. In recent years, there have been many proposals using cryptography to ensure secure communication [42]. Nevertheless, cryptography alone is not sufficient for node compromise attacks and novel misbehavior in sensor networks [43]. However, in the future, the security software developers or coders should keep in mind 100 % security mechanisms while writing the codes of applications.

## 2.5 Privacy of Smart Devices

The term privacy is derived from the Latin word "privatus" [44] and "privo", meaning to deprive [45]. In English language dictionaries, privacy is defined as "withdrawal from public view or company and one's private life" [46]. The term privacy is used frequently in ordinary language as well as in philosophical, political, legal discussions and the Internet of Things (IoT), yet there is no standard single definition or analysis or meaning of the term. Perceived privacy has long been accepted as the right of individuals, groups, or institutes, and they decide for themselves when, how, and what kind of information they need to deal with during communication with others [47].

With the advancement of the digital age and IoT technology, personal information vulnerabilities have increased. Information privacy may be applied in numerous ways, including encryption, authentication, and data masking—each attempting to ensure that it is available only to those with authorized access. Information privacy is considered an important aspect of information sharing during smart devices' communication. The need to maintain information privacy is applicable to collected personal information, such as medical records, financial data, criminal records, and political information. According to [48], perceived privacy includes both reliability and credibility dimensions, which are related to sharing of information among users of IT. During communication on the website, many users handle a lot of information on certain procedures. Credibility and reliability, thus, are important issues in these transactions [49]. Jingjun [50] says that mobile nodes in the IoT often move from one cluster to another, in which cryptography-based protocols are required to provide rapid identification authentication and privacy protection. In an advanced technological communication of the Internet of Things, where each and every object is connecting to object-human-machine to communicate, credibility and reliability are essential. All the private data generated by things should strictly follow security standards.

A single-step protocol was presented for the occasion that the mobile node joins a new cluster. The literature describes teenagers as active users of social media, who seem to care about privacy, but who also reveal a considerable amount of personal information. There is an evidence that concerns about who would get access to their health information or learn about their medical consultation affect actual or intended healthcare-seeking behaviors by adolescents [51, 52]. Burgoon defined social privacy as having control over the actual interaction with others and the frequency, length, and content of that interaction. Psychological privacy protects the individual from intrusions upon one's thoughts, feelings, and values and the freedom to decide to whom to disclose certain personal thoughts and feelings. Informational privacy refers to the ability to control whoever gathers and disseminates information about oneself and under what circumstances. Hence it is an eleventh hour that we need to work for the development of devices with privacy.

## 2.6 IT Act 2000

Much has been talked about the Internet of Things and smart devices. Embedded networked devices including sensors and actuators are everywhere nowadays. They are in our fridges and on our washing machines. They are in our smartphones, our houses, hospitals, offices, ships, planes, buses, trains, and automobiles. Some of the smart devices are helping us do exercise enough for good health and measuring our sleep. In this light, Internet of Things security mechanisms are essential in the mushrooming Cyber-Physical Systems arena. Indian (Information Technology) IT Act 2000 started in 2000 to look after IT communication issues. Later, the Indian Ministry of IT department released a new version in 2008, in the form of IT Act 2008. Besides, the Energy Independence and Security Act (EISA) of 2007 gave the National Institute of Standards and Technology (NIST) primary responsibility to coordinate development of a framework that includes protocols and model standards to achieve interoperability of smart grid devices and systems. In the same way, there needs to be an IoT act, device standards to cooperate, monitor, and control miscommunication of text, pictures, audio, and videos. In October 2012, the government of India unveiled its plan of training around 500,000 cybersecurity professionals in its 5 year plan. However, India's cybersecurity industry was practically nonexistent. Most of the Indian IT companies depend on international service providers to overcome their security threats. The consequent lack of a job market has also resulted in the education system completely ignoring the cyber security field. Most of Indian technical educational institutes do not even offer the cyber security subject as a specialization. They concentrate more on lucrative subjects like software design, development, and languages like C, C++, testing, DBMS, Oracle, and Web portal. The best part is that recently Gujarat University started a course on data, forensic, and Cyber laws. In today's technological arena, data and information are perchance the key to fighting any kind of crime. That is why safe city projects got initiated in 1992. In India with an investment of circa 1200 crore rupees, the security project is aiming to install approximately 1700 CCTVs. These are being mounted at more than 50 public markets and 15 national borders. In addition to these places, they are present at almost every critical traffic intersection. This array of IP Cameras and CCTVs would create a web of surveillance setup that would form a foundation of the integrated intelligence surveillance systems. In this light, Surat City in Gujarat (India) is also one of the best examples in IP camera installations in the city public places for prevention of crimes. This project was mainly supported by public funds. These security systems generally seamlessly pass the data to police departments through their PDAs for crime analysis. Even in Delhi, the capital city of India, the public places are fixed with IP cameras for social security. Mobile apps can also be downloaded in smart mobiles at no charge. During emergencies, anybody can easily call number (911), which will give complete details of a victim with the location using GIS technologies. At the global level, the New Zealand Police, a national law enforcement agency, is using Intergraph Mobile Responder apps (software), which allow police officers to access real-time data about events for enhanced public safety.

Software can be protected by hardware. Secured hardware protects the processing and storage of code using encryption, fault and manipulation detection, and secure code and data storage. Software programs thus become trustworthy by combining it with secured hardware. This has been proven by extensive experience in trusted computing, the use of secured elements in mobile phones, and protection of smart grids. In all of these cases, secured hardware provides the extra protection needed for security-sensitive code and data. To protect both privacy and smart device data security, M/s Emory Company has created a new smart device security policy that lays out security requirements for both Emory-owned and personally owned devices that access Emory exchange email or store-sensitive information. This policy does not grant Emory access to information stored on our devices; it only requires a handful of security settings to be enabled, including a four-digit password and data encryption technique.

Security of the IoT raises numerous open legal and ethical issues that are currently being addressed at academic, research, corporate, government, and personal levels. Many of these issues are raised for some clear conflicts between the global versus national interests and government versus public interests. These IoT security policies and associated Codes of Practice set out the responsibilities for ensuring the security of IoT devices within personal or within the organization or within the home network or global level. The contents of respective legislation must encompass right to information, provisions prohibiting or restricting the use of mechanisms of the Internet of Things, and rules on IT security legislation [53]. The procedures to be followed to safeguard resources provide confidentiality and integrity of the information held thereon.

## 2.7 Methodology

This chapter is basically conceptual and grounded on the secondary data in various research articles, general articles, and corporate white papers which are grounded on on-line database. Besides the experience of the authors in the same domain on both information technology (IT) and computer science (CS) and working on the research topic "Internet of Things Technologies" since 2012 made the concepts very clear to authoring this manuscript. The beauty of this artifact is that it is composed of various thought processes gathered from authors' and experts' discussions in conferences, workshops, and symposiums on this topic. The data was in different formats including text, picture, and videos. The research method used here is exploratory, qualitative research type, and with a thematic narration.

## 2.8 Discussion and Conclusion

When all things are connected to the Internet and are ready to be accessed from the smartphones and other PDAs from anywhere at anything for any services, the security issues should not be nullified. Security of smart devices, basically into the assessment of the risk of threats which causes some loss of value to devices, is heightened through device vulnerabilities. For better security, the safeguards can be detection, prevention, and correction. Today's development of smart labels, memory amplifiers, and smart dust seems to mirror the sudden technology shifts by Warren and Brandeis, opening up new forms of social interactions that change one's expectation of privacy or secrecy.

Devices may be left unsecured because their owners expect that they will remain in their physical control; however, if they leave the physical control of their owners, they are open to be used by anyone. Hence, physical security through surveillance systems is essential. There should be ethical design, development of smart hardware, and software from the software coders or developers along with proper deployment in appropriate applications. The international standardization bodies have to monitor the development of devices, software, and networks. Ultimately, there should be trustworthy interoperability among the Internet of Things devices to get connected. The end user/netizen also plays an important role in accessing the data and information. People have to practice international cybersecurity laws for smooth and better communication. There should be punishment for cybercrimes in order to prevent data miscommunication. The International Telecommunication Union (ITU), Institute of Electrical and Electronics Engineers (IEEE), Internet of Things-Architectures (IoT-A), and National Institute of Standards and Technology (NIST) are some of the global standardizing institutes in device standards and communication without any security breaches. The smart device security is becoming a basic need nowadays in this technical world. Hence, it is a need of hour for smart device security under the umbrella of the IoT.

## References

1. Carabelea C, Boissier O (2003) Multi-agent platforms on smart devices: dream or reality. In: Proceedings of the Smart Objects Conference (SOC03), Grenoble, France, pp 126–129
2. Noda C, Walter T (2005) Smart devices for next generation mobile services. In: Construction and analysis of safe, secure, and interoperable smart devices. Springer, Berlin Heidelberg, pp 192–209
3. Kang Y, Kim H, Suzuki H, Han S (2015) Editing 3D models on smart devices. Comput Aid Des 59:229–238
4. Doukas C (2012) Building internet of things with the arduino. CreateSpace, North Charleston
5. Doody P, Shields A (2012) Mining network relationships in the Internet of things. In: Proceedings of the 2012 international workshop on Self-aware Internet of Things. ACM, pp 7–12
6. Yuan Y, Ma L, Zhang J (2014) Patented network analysis on cloud computing technology in internet of things. In Identification, information and knowledge in the internet of things, 2014 International Conference, Beijing, IEEE, pp 248–251
7. Agrawal S, Das ML (2011) Internet of things: a paradigm shift of future internet applications, Engineering (NUiCONE), Nirma University International Conference, Ahmedabad (India) IEEE, pp 1–7
8. Yong W et al (2006) A Survey of security issues in wireless sensor networks. Commun Surv Tutorials IEEE 8:2–23
9. Atzori L, Iera A, Morabito G (2010) The internet of things: a survey. Comput Netw 54:2787–2805

10. Coetzee L, Eksteen J (2011) The internet of things—promise for the future? An introduction. In: Proceedings of the IST Africa 2011, Gaborone, Botswana, 11–13 May
11. Mattern F (2003) From smart devices to smart everyday objects. In: Proceedings of smart objects conference, April 2003
12. Ramparany F, Boissier O, Brouchoud H (2003) Cooperating autonomous Smart Devices. In Proceedings of the Smart Objects Conference (sOc'2003), Grenoble, France (pp.182–185)
13. Maiwald E (2004) Fundamentals of network security. McGraw-Hill Technology Education, New York
14. Cirani S, Ferrari G, Veltri L (2013) Enforcing security mechanisms. In: IP-based internet of things: an algorithmic overview algorithms, ISSN 1999-4893
15. Mayer CP (2009) Security and privacy challenges in the internet of things.In: Proceedings of the KiVS workshop on Global Sensor Networks (GSN09)
16. Gessner D, Olivereau A, Segura AS, Serbanati A (2012) Trustworthy infrastructure services for a secure and privacy-respecting internet of things, pp 998–1003
17. Zhang XM, Zhang N (2011) An open, secure and flexible platform based on internet of things and cloud computing for ambient aiding living & telemedicine, pp 1–4
18. Heer T, Garcia-Morchon O, Hummen R, Keoh SL, Kumar SS, Wehrle K (2011) Security challenges in the IP-based internet of things. Wirel Pers Commun 61:527–5421
19. Srivastava L (2006) Pervasive, ambient, ubiquitous: the magic of radio. In: European Commission conference, From RFID to internet of things, Bruxelles, Belgium
20. Suo H, Wan J, Zou C, Liu J (2012) Security in the internet of things: a review. In: Computer Science and Electronics Engineering (ICCSEE), 2012 international conference on, vol 3, pp 648–651, IEEE
21. Gariup M (2013) European security culture: language, theory, policy. Ashgate Publications
22. Pfitzmann A, Pfitzmann B, Schunter M, Waidner M (1997) Trusting mobile user devices and security modules. Computer 2:61–68
23. Al-Muhtadi J, Ranganathan A, Campbell R, Mickunas MD (2003) Cerberus: a context-aware security scheme for smart spaces. In: Pervasive computing and communications, (PerCom 2003), Proceedings of the first IEEE international conference on. IEEE, pp 489–496
24. Roman R, Najera P, Lopez J (2011) Securing the internet of things. Computer 44(9):51–58. doi:10.1109/MC.2011.291
25. Takizawa O, Hosokawa M, Takanashi K, Hada Y, Shibayama A, Jeong B (2008) Pinpointing the place of origin of a cellular phone emergency call using active RFID tags. In: Proceedings of 22nd international conference on advanced information networking and applications–workshops, Gino Wan, Okinawa, Japan, pp 1123–1128
26. Weis SA (2003) Security and privacy in radio-frequency identification devices. Doctoral dissertation, Massachusetts Institute of Technology
27. Li B, Li W (2008) Logistics information fusion application research based on RFID and GPS. In: Proceedings of 27th Chinese control conference, China, pp 389–393
28. Manion M, Goodrun A (2000) Terrorism or civil disobedience: towards a hacktivist Ethic. ACM SIGCAS Comput Soc 30(2):14–19
29. Katz FH (2006) Campus-wide spyware and virus removal as a method of teaching information security. In: Proceedings of the 3rd annual conference on information security curriculum development, 1–4
30. Nolan J, Levesque M (2005) Hacking human: data-archaeology and surveillance in social Networks. SIGGROUP Bull 25(2):33–79
31. Sukhai NB (2004) Hacking and cybercrime. In: Proceedings of 1st annual conference on information security curriculum development, pp 128–132
32. Nicks V (2009) AI enhances the smart home security system
33. Robles RJ, Kim TH, Cook D, Das S (2010) A review on security in smart home Development. Int J Adv Sci Technol 15: 13–22
34. Yung, Nelson HC, Pang Grantham KH, Fung George SK (2000) A novel camera calibration technique for visual traffic surveillance. In Proc

35. Ganeriwal S, Srivastava MB (2004) Reputation-based framework for high integrity sensor networks. In Proceedings of ACM SASN
36. CCTV Digital Video Recorders (DVRs), sourcesecurity.com. Retrieved 29 June 2013
37. Hintermaier W, Steinbach E (2010) A system architecture for IP camera based driver assistance applications, IEEE Intelligent Vehicles Symposium (IV), San Diego, 21–24 June, pp 540–547
38. Dagada R, Eloff MM (2013) Integration of policy aspects into information security issues in South African organizations. 7(31):3069–3077, 21 doi:10.5897/AJBM12.979
39. Pister KSJ (2000) Military applications of sensor networks, of Institute for Defence Analyses, Paper P-3531, Defense Science Study Group
40. Perrig A, Szewczyk R, Wen V, Culler D. Tygar JD (2001) SPINS: security protocols for sensor networks. In: Proceedings of ACM annual international conference on mobile computing and networking, pp 189–199, ISBN:1-58113-422-3, Rome, Italy
41. Sami, Al-Wakeel S, Al-Swailem A (2007) PRSA: a path redundancy based security algorithm for wireless sensor networks. Proceedings of IEEE wireless communication and networking conference, pp 4156–4160, ISBN: 1-4244-0658-7, Kowloon, China
42. Xiaojiang Du, Sghaier Giyani, Yang Xiao, Hsiao-Hwa Chen (2006) A secure routing Protocol for heterogeneous sensor networks. In: Proceedings of IEEE Global Telecommunication Conference (GLOBECOM'06), pp 1–5, ISBN: 1-4244-0356-1, San Francisco, California, December, IEEE
43. Perrig A (2001) SPINS: security protocols for sensor networks. In Proceedings of ACM MobiCom
44. Chien-Min Ou, Wei-De Wu (2012) Automatic service discovery of IP cameras over wide area networks with NAT traversal. Adv Int Things 2:23–36
45. Curtin L (1981) Privacy: belonging to oneself. Perspect Psychiatry Care 19(3–4):112–115
46. Rawnsley M (1980) The concept of privacy. Adv Nurs Sci 2(2):25–31
47. Webster's New World Dictionary (1986) Prentice-Hall, New York
48. Westin A (1967) Privacy and freedom. Atheneum, New York
49. Yousafazi SJ, Pllister JG, Foxall GR (2003) A proposal model of e-trust for electronic banking. Technovation 23:847–860
50. Choate T (2000) 5 keys to customer conversion, Catalog Age, I Merchant, August,14–15
51. JingjunMiao, Liangmin Wang (2012) Rapid identification authentication protocol for mobile nodes in internet of things with privacy protection. J Netw 7(7):1099–1105
52. Britto MT, Tivorsak TL, Slap GB (2010) Adolescents' needs for health care privacy. Paediatrics 126:1469e76
53. Weber RH (2010) Internet of things – new security and privacy challenges. Comput Law Secur Rev 26(1):23–30

# Chapter 3
# Agent-Based Machine-to-Machine Connectivity Analysis for the Internet of Things Environment

**Bo Xing**

## 3.1 Introduction

With vast technological advancements and the growing popularity of digital assistance in everyday life and work environments that go along with it, technologies are needed to evolve these application domains to the next level. One vision for this is the Internet of Things (IoT): interconnected devices, embedded in all kinds of objects. In order to turn this vision into reality, routing protocols are needed to aid the communication between these things in a decentralized, self-organized, and changing infrastructure. The IoT vision and emerging 4G services, fueled with the flexibility of mobility, is expected to transform the structure of wireless networks from the current single-hop access networks to large dense multi-hop wireless networks. Multi-hop wireless networks have the capability of conveying information through multiple hops and include the wireless mesh networks (WMN), mobile ad hoc networks (MANET), wireless sensor networks (WSN), vehicular ad hoc networks (VANET), etc., which are envisioned to be formed among large number of nodes in the near future. One major challenge of multi-hop wireless networks is the path finding or routing, which is further deteriorated by the heterogeneous nodes imposed by multi-hop transmissions.

In the rest of this chapter, we first, in Sect. 3.2, outline some background knowledge of the field. Then, Sect. 3.3 details the motivations of this study. Next, the employed methodology is explained in Sect. 3.4, followed by an elaborated experimental environment setup in Sect. 3.5. The simulation result analysis is provided in Sect. 3.6; the limitations and future work of the present study are

B. Xing (✉)
Computational Intelligence, Robotics, and Cybernetics for Leveraging E-future (CIRCLE), School of Mathematical and Computer Sciences, Faculty of Science and Agriculture, University of Limpopo, Limpopo, South Africa
e-mail: bxing2009@gmail.com



Z. Mahmood (ed.), *Connectivity Frameworks for Smart Devices*,
Computer Communications and Networks, DOI 10.1007/978-3-319-33124-9_3

highlighted in Sect. 3.7. Finally, the conclusion drawn in Sect. 3.8 closes the chapter.

## 3.2 Background

### 3.2.1 Internet of Things (IoT)

The phrase "IoT" was originally coined by the cofounder and former head of the MIT Auto-ID Center, with special mention to Kevin Ashton in 2002. So what is the IoT? Basically, it describes the vision of pervasive and "hidden" computing in which a large range of devices will be embedded in the environment all around us. More precisely, the IoT can be defined as the network of physical objects or "things" embedded with different technologies and connectivity to enable it to support greater value and service via the Internet [1]. Nowadays, with the move towards 5G, IoT will reach a new level of maturity connecting everything anytime. Cisco, a technology company, predicts that 50 billion connected devices will be in circulation by the end of the decade, up from 11 billion in 2013. Applications include retail, logistics [2, 3], healthcare [4–7], smart home [8, 9], and education [10].

Logically, a fundamental enabler of IoT would be the identity knowledge of the "self" and of the others. According to the International Telecommunication Union (ITU) report, the key technological drivers behind the IoT are likely to be radio-frequency identification (RFID), sensors, actuators, and intelligent system [11]. In addition, the authors of [12] pointed out that those enabling technologies need to be studied together with the hybrid wireless sensor networks, since they have to be wireless, robust, and most of all, energy efficient. Furthermore, the ITU report at the same time identifies some challenges that need to be considered, such as standardization and harmonization (e.g., new mobile communication protocols and sustainable standards), privacy, and socio-ethical issues.

### 3.2.2 Wireless Sensor-Actuator Networks

As the field of microelectromechanical systems (MEMS) and wireless communications has been expanding over recent years, the new types of micro-engineered devices (e.g., sensors and actuators) are evolving all the time. A sensor is a hardware device that converts a physical phenomenon (e.g., temperature, pressure, and humidity) into an electrical signal, i.e., capture information. As such, sensors represent part of the interface between the physical world and the world of electrical devices. The other part of this interface is represented by actuators, which convert electrical signals into physical phenomena for further processing, i.e., make decisions and acting upon sensed events. Typically, a distributed system composed of wirelessly connected smart sensor and actuator nodes is referred to as wireless sensor/actuator networks (WSANs). In general, a sensor node is equipped with a power supply, transceiver, memory, analog to digital converter, and processing and sensing unit, whereas an actuator node has ample power supply, transmission, processor, storage, controller, digital to analog converter, and actuation [13]. Nowadays, there are various applications of such distributed task, such as home automation [14], traffic light control [15], and agricultural monitoring [16]. It is advantageous in several aspects: first, it communicates with both sensor and actuator node types to reach network's goals [17]; second, it facilitates fine-grained monitoring and control [18]; and third, WSAN with Internet connectivity makes IoT realistic [19].

Despite such advances, large-scale WSAN is incredibly hard to design and deploy. Paper [18] considered the problem of node failures and link failures (i.e., failure detection) which are caused by topology changes in a WSAN. Since the WSANs are mainly used for distributed control systems, several authors (e.g., [20, 21]) paid more attentions to the control domain. In addition, under the vision of IoT paradigm, service gateways (SGs) play an important role in bridging WSANs with the Internet, user requests, and the sensor/actuator information flow through. To provide efficient services, Paper [22] presented reflective SGs, which can self-adapt to WSAN changes and enable WSANs to customize their activities according to the application services involved. Moreover, the security issues in WSANs have been studied in [23]. For more information about WSANs, refer to a comprehensive survey by [13].

### *3.2.3 Wireless Multi-hop Communication Network*

In traditional single-hop network operating modes, mobile stations (MSs) directly communicate with either a base station (BS) or access point (AP) that can provide direct access to the Internet, whereas in multi-hop network operating modes, MSs usually communicate with a BS/AP through relay stations (or informally intermediate MSs) for the purpose of increasing the single-hop networks' capacity and coverage.

Loosely speaking, wireless multi-hop communication network refers to a network that uses wireless multi-hopping for data transmission. The backbone of this communication paradigm lies in the ability to act as a source, a destination, or a relay when a node (part of WSAN under the umbrella of IoT) needs to send a packet to a destination out of its transmission range. This concept plays an important role in enabling connectivity issue within the realm of IoT due to its efficient and low-cost deployment characteristics. According to the literature, wireless multi-hop network can be classified into various categories such as wireless sensor networks (WSNs), mobile ad hoc networks (MANETs), vehicular ad hoc networks (VANETs), and wireless mesh networks (WMNs). Nowadays, the applications ranging from personal electronics to industrial machines and sensors/actuators are getting continuously and wirelessly connected to one or more abovementioned wireless network paradigms. For instance, audio/video conferences communicate through MANETs, smart home devices send data via WSNs, assistive healthcare devices connected based on WMNs, and driverless cars oriented by VANETs. Therefore, future heterogeneous sensor-/actuator-integrated IoT environments are expected to comprise distinct wireless technologies that are built on respective different network architectures. It is thus reasonable to envision that various wireless network technologies would be integrated into the next-generation wireless systems for compensating for the shortcomings of standard network to have architectures with global connectivity.

To summarize, in this chapter, we envisage an IoT architecture that is constructed on the basis of a key idea of extending the coverage of heterogeneous sensors and actuators by employing multi-hop communication mechanism. The links of within a multi-hop network can be utilized for not only load balancing but also capacity increasing of single-hop networks. For example, in a simplified scenario, a BS/AP can be communicated directly by individual MSs as long as they are within the coverage. In some cases, however, it is impossible to connect in a direct manner (e.g., a poor MS coverage or outside a BS/AP's coverage area), and thus an MS can only communicate with the BS/AP with the help of intermediate relay MSs. That is, before a BS/AP is reachable, the information packets will continuously be forwarded by relay MSs to their neighboring MSs.

The merits of such futuristic view of WSAN may include the following [24]:

- The integrated multiple wireless sensor/actuator networks cannot only increase both the coverage and capacity, but also result in an efficiency way of energy and time consumption.
- An MS may communicate with the BS/AP in two ways: either directly (i.e., through single hop) or indirectly (via multi-hop).
- Enabling dynamic reconfiguration and routing, utilizing multimode devices and multi-hop communication for the purpose of avoiding data congestion and collision.
- Equipping MSs with a convenient interface for the sake of selectively connecting to a network whenever and wherever it is necessary.

## 3.3 Motivation

One of the main research challenges for realizing the abovementioned future IoT environment with the ingredient of WSAN is to come up with mobility management solutions that enable seamless connectivity across heterogeneous networks. In this chapter, we define seamless connectivity as the ability of an MS to maintain connectivity with a network of things without any significant quality of service degradation for ongoing application's sessions. As an essential part of such scheme, routing is a critical element in the design of networks and networking-based applications. In a multi-hop network, there is no predetermined topology. Therefore, for a packet to be sent from one node to another, it is the responsibility of the routing protocol to find the "next hop" of the nodes along the route. Having multiple intermediate nodes results in having multiple potential paths to be followed. So, the role of a multi-hop routing protocol is not only finding a path, but finding the optimal one that satisfies the needed performance requirements from a set of candidate paths.

As we know that within the paradigm of multi-hop communication, different types of wireless networks can be classified as wireless multi-hop networks. Being multi-hop networks, these paradigms depend on a sequence of intermediate nodes for routing packets from a source to a destination. Some protocols may have the merits of avoiding noise propagation, and thus they can provide a better connectivity reliability; whereas if the cooperative relay in each hop of the multi-hop transmission system is selected among several adjacent relays, better transmission reliability may be provided by achieving diversity gain through the cooperation among cluster nodes. Under such a scheme, each relay node participates in an ad hoc routing protocol that allows to discover the best multi-hop path through the network towards the destination node.

Although there are some differences in routing characteristics and functionalities of these discrete network paradigms, which may result in having different routing protocols specifically designed for each network paradigm, they all share some common features, e.g., these network frameworks are inherent heterogeneous in the era of IoT that they consist of diversity of sensor and actuators being grouped into multiple clusters with a variety of different distances and numbers of relays.

This commonality emerges from sharing uniform characteristics and challenges that impose requirements on the routing functions for all paradigms, which also motivates us to perform an analysis regarding the performance of heterogeneous multi-hop WSANs. The goal of this study is thus twofold: first, the macro aim is to quantify how design parameters affect the network efficiency, and second, the ad hoc objective is to reduce number of hops from the source to the destination. The reduction in the number of hops eliminates various undesired issues of WSAN (e.g., connection latency, jitter, and packet losses) that may otherwise hinder the development of a fully deployed IoT environment.

## 3.4 Employed Methodology

This section elaborates the theory and methodology, namely, multi-agent systems (MAS) and agent-based modeling and simulation (ABMS) utilized in this study.

### 3.4.1 Multi-Agent System (MAS)

A MAS is a system that applies various autonomous agents to accomplish some specified goals. Based on the inherent features (i.e., autonomy, reactivity, sociality, and proactivity), agents are able to cooperate, coordinate, and negotiate with each other. As a result, the MAS is most appropriate for domains with a high degree of geographically dispersed heterogeneous resources [25]. These domains certainly include mobile wireless computing environment.

Mobile wireless networks can be broadly classified into two categories: cellular (i.e., single hop) and ad hoc (i.e., multi-hop) wireless links. Since mobile network has rapidly developed in recent years, the latter category is more preferred. However, existing research on mobile multi-hop networks poses a hot spot problem due to those networks that have a complex wireless path from a source to a destination. As a result, how to find the optimal communicate routes to the correct destination becomes a main concern. To cope with this problem, the authors of [26] presented an efficient data-gathering system to the mobile wireless network with multi-agents. In addition, several bioinspired MAS has been proposed for optimizing the route selection in the mobile wireless networks, such as ant routing algorithm [27, 28], termite [29], and bee algorithm [30].

### 3.4.2 Agent-Based Modeling and Simulation (ABMS)

Agent-based modeling and simulation (ABMS) is a popular modeling approach that has gained increasing attention over the past decades. This growth trend is evidenced by the increasing numbers of applications in various domains, such as supply chain [31, 32], manufacturing [33], market diffusion [34], product diffusion [35], robotics [36], social science [37], and economics [38]. But why is it becoming widespread? The answer is threefold [39–41]: first, it has capabilities of capturing more realistic characteristics; second, it provides a powerful analytical method that enables the modeling of many heterogeneous real-world agents as individual software programs; and third, it is not only related to the fields of MAS and robotics from the field of artificial life, but also be commonly used in modeling human social behavior and individual decision-making.

Among others, NetLogo, developed by Uri Wilensky [42], is one of the best ABMS prototyping environments; particularly it is well suited for modeling complex systems consisting of hundreds or thousands of agents [43, 44]. It is free and written in Java, so users can easily and quickly build their models on it. In general, there can be four types of agents in NetLogo worlds, i.e., turtles, patches, links, and observer. Turtles are agents that move around in the simulation world; each path is a square piece of "ground" over which turtles can move; links are agents that connect two turtles; finally, the observer is constantly looking out over the world of turtles and patches. Moreover, equipping with a well-designed graphical interface,

NetLogo allows both the novice and expert alike to run, adjust, and develop models with ease. Examples include healthcare [45], robotics [46], social science [47, 48], manufacturing [49], and modeling diffusion [50].

## 3.5 Experimental Environment Setup

In this study, the connectivity of a network (either a social network or computer network) is measured via the means of "the degree of separation." In practice, super-node is often found in many types of networks where lots of other sub-nodes are super-connected to this hub. Hence the amount of connections that a hub has with other sub-nodes is usually much larger than the average amount of connections per node. The purpose of introducing hubs is to improve the speed of communication in the process of spreading over the network. Due to the inherent characteristics, as soon as a piece of message is received via a hub, a greater part of the network can almost immediately receive the information as well without having to wait for each intermediate nodes to be visited. In the forthcoming IoT era with a highly interwoven WSAN, for the purpose of improving the connectivity of thousands of connected devices, we can first identify a hub and then work out its associated degree of separation, i.e., the number of nodes that need to be passed from a particular node (where an information requiring device is located at) to the hub, so as to pave the way of obtaining the shortest information traveling path.

Nevertheless, the complexity of a network (e.g., configuration) often hinders the identification of a hub or goal node. Bearing this in mind, we are going to create a model that implements various algorithms in searching for a hub in a network. Since different paths (linking the starting node with the hub) may exist, the model is built on multi-agent system concepts where interaction and knowledge sharing is happening in a real-time manner between agents.

For the rest of this section, the definition of agent types is first described in Sect. 3.5.1; the core rules which govern the model are then detailed in Sect. 3.5.2; finally, the main elements of the model (e.g., buttons, switches, choosers, sliders, and plots) are elaborated in Sect. 3.5.3.

### *3.5.1 Agents*

A school of turtle walker (arrow type in NetLogo environment) is employed for the agents that need to roam around the simulation environment trying to reach the hub. The information about the present search state (e.g., the taken path) is kept by these searcher agents. Each arrow type of searcher agent expands its search via following suggested (as a result of the adopted knowledge-sharing strategy) outgoing paths that lead out of the present node. Meanwhile, another group of walker agents (human type in NetLogo environment) is designed to move through the network during the execution of Dijkstra's algorithm. This mechanism can then be used to compute the separation degree of every node in the network from the hub.

### 3.5.2 *Rules*

Since NetLogo is suitable for realizing agent-oriented approach, the search algorithms employed in this model are implemented by utilizing this advantage so that the information can be distributed among the agents. Unlike the traditional uninformed search algorithms (e.g., depth-first search and breadth-first search [51]) or the informed search approaches (e.g., A* and greedy best-first search [51]), the agents in our model perform the search via knowledge-sharing strategy with other peer agents that are also involved in the search. Such strategy (see Fig. 3.1 for illustration) is fulfilled through the following ways:

- *Word of mouth* methodology: If the hub is found by some agents (successful agents), then this information is shared with the other agents (unsuccessful agents) which the succeeded ones meet on their way to the hub. Those unsuccessful agents are either still busy with search or simply returning to their starting node.
- *Blackboard* technique: With this approach, communal blackboards are integrated into each node and the useful information are written down on the blackboards by the agents who own these knowledge. The latter coming agents can then read the information shared on the blackboards.
- *Hybrids 1* and 2: Meanwhile, two hybrid types of knowledge-sharing methods—both combining two abovementioned approaches but in slightly different manners—are also implemented in our model.

### 3.5.3 *Key Elements of the Model*

Due to the easy-to-code nature and graphic display feature of NetLogo, many functions, parameters, and the results of our model are fulfilled, adjusted, and

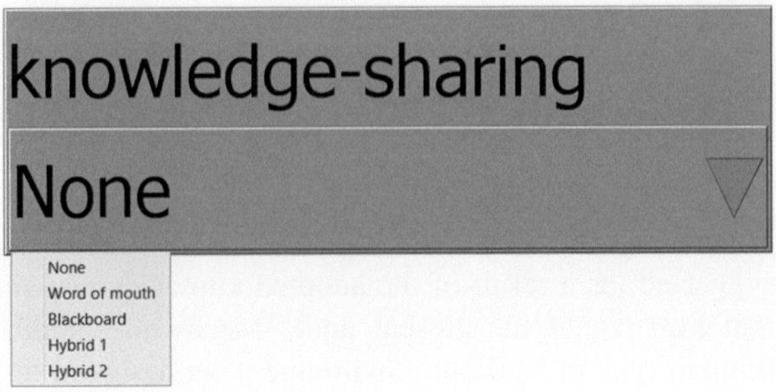


**Fig. 3.1** Various choices of knowledge-sharing strategy

illustrated, respectively, via a set of elements such as buttons, switches, sliders, choosers, and plots. In this section, we will give a brief discussion of some key elements that are very useful in understanding the working principles of our model.

#### 3.5.3.1 Key Buttons

The selected key buttons are illustrated in Fig. 3.2; their functions are presented below:

- *Setup WSAN*: When this button is pressed, the simulation environment will be cleared and all variables will be set to their default values. Meanwhile, a random WSAN network (see chooser *type-of-network* in Sect. 3.5.3.3 for details) will also be established. The layout of the chosen network is determined by chooser *type-of-layout* as described in Sect. 3.5.3.3.
- *Setup roamers*: The function of this button is to create a group of new roamers where the amount is controlled by *new-roamers-per-tick* slider (see Sect. 3.5.3.4 for details). The duty of these roamers is to walk within the network with the goal of finding the hub.
- *Reset layout*: As the name implies, this button can help one to change the network layout if desired. The available layout types are circle, spring, and radial (see chooser *type-of-layout* as described in Sect. 3.5.3.3).
- *Go Dijkstra*: This button is used to activate Dijkstra's algorithm for the purpose of computing the shortest travel distance (the results are illustrated in plot *shortest travel distance* which can be found in Sect. 3.5.3.5) and finding the average separation degree from the hub. In this model, the measure used for determining the hub is Erdős number.
- *Roamers move once*: In order to get a closer observation, this button is designed to help observer view the simulation tick by tick. In other words, when this button is pressed, the simulation will proceed only one time step and then pause.
- *Roamers move forever*: On the contrary, this button will make the simulation run continuously until it meets some of the termination criteria such as a hub is

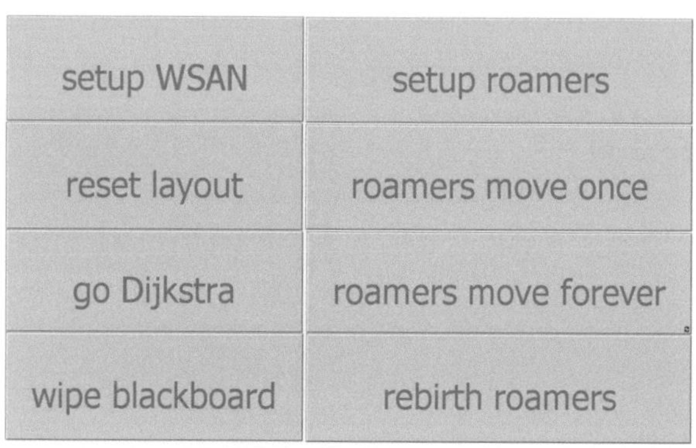


**Fig. 3.2** Key buttons of the model

found, the number of ticks is reached (see slider *stopping-criteria-#-of-ticks* in Sect. 3.5.3.4 for more details), or ultimately the model gets stuck.
- *Wipe blackboard*: As described in Sect. 3.5.2, in our model, each node has an associated blackboard if the blackboard under the *knowledge-sharing* chooser is selected. As such, this button helps to eliminate the information kept by these blackboards.
- *Rebirth roamers*: This button allows one to remove all existing roamers and create new ones. The number of newly born roamers is still regulated by *new-roamers-per-tick* slider (see Sect. 3.5.3.4 for details).

#### 3.5.3.2 Key Switches

The selected key switches are illustrated in Fig. 3.3 and their functions are presented below:

- *Dijkstra-Animation*?: The on/off state of this switch will determine whether animating the execution of Dijkstra's algorithm or not given the *go Dijkstra* (see Sect. 3.5.3.1) button is activated.
- *Revisits-permitted*?: This switch is used to control whether or not the roamer agents are allowed to visit the nodes that have already been visited before during a round of search.

#### 3.5.3.3 Key Choosers

The selected key choosers are illustrated in Fig. 3.4; their functions are introduced below:

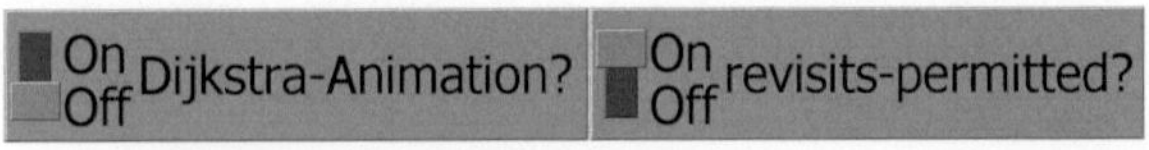


**Fig. 3.3** Key switches of the model

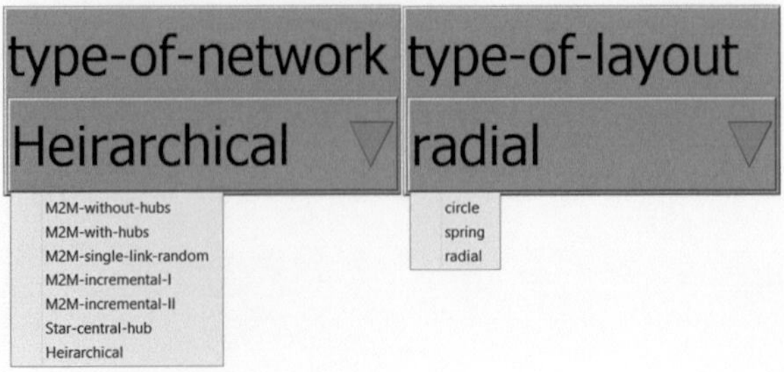


**Fig. 3.4** Key choosers of the model

- *Type-of-network*: This chooser selects a particular network type that is going to be created given the *setup WSAN* button is pressed. The available network types are outlined as follows:
  - "M2M-without-hubs" and "M2M-with-hubs": These two choices mimic a scenario of machine-to-machine network without/with hubs.
  - "M2M-single-link-random": This choice simulates a machine-to-machine network where only one link can be established between each node and another random node.
  - "M2M-incremental-I" and "M2M-incremental-II": These choices create a simulated machine-to-machine network environment by incrementally establishing the links with other random nodes in two manners: either one at a time (i.e., type I) or with no restriction (i.e., type II).
  - "Star-central-hub": This choice constructs a network with one goal node as its central hub which means all other nodes are connected only to this central hub instead of any other sub-nodes.
  - "Hierarchical": If this choice is chosen, a tree type of network will be created with the goal node at its root.
- *Type-of-layout*: This chooser has three choices, namely, circle, spring, and radial. Each selected choice helps to specify how to arrange a network when it is visualized.

#### 3.5.3.4 Key Sliders

The selected key sliders are illustrated in Fig. 3.5; their functions are discussed below:

- *#-of-nodes*: This slide can be used to adjust the number of nodes to be created in our WSAN network.
- *#-of-hubs*: The number of hubs to be established within the model. By definition, the hubs are nodes which have significantly more connections (determined by the next slider, i.e., *connections-per-node*) than any other sub-nodes have.
- *Connections-per-node*: This slider determines the maximum number of connections (or links) that a sub-node could have. In the simulation, the actual number

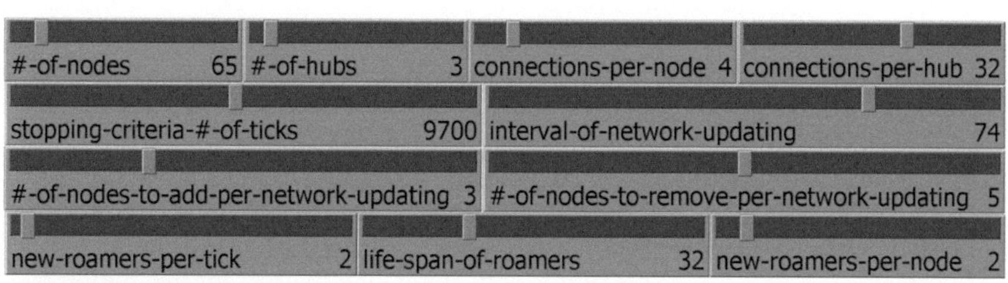


**Fig. 3.5** Key sliders of the model

of connections selected for a specific node is a random number within the range of [1, number shown on *connections-per-node* slider].

- *Connections-per-hub*: Similarly, this slider is used to specify the maximum number of connections that a hub can possess. In the simulation, the actual number of connections selected for a specific hub is a random number within the range of [1, number shown on *connections-per-hub* slider].
- *Stopping-criteria-#-of-ticks*: This slider specifies the time span of a round of simulation, that is, how long could a simulation last for. As soon as the number of ticks is reached, the simulation will be terminated, whether or not the roamer agents have finished their search.
- *Interval-of-network-updating*: The selected number slider can cause the WSAN network to be updated at intervals which is based on a random number chosen within the range of [0, number shown on the slider].
- *#-of-nodes-to-add-per-network-updating*: This slider can help us to fulfill the function of adding a specified number of nodes (determined by the chosen number shown on the slider) to the network each time when a network updating occurs.
- *#-of-nodes-to-remove-per-network-updating*: On the contrary, this slider can assist us in removing a specified number of nodes (determined by the chosen number shown on the slider) to the network each time when a network updating takes place.
- *New-roamers-per-tick*: The number of new roamer agents that needs to be added into the simulation on a per-tick base can be achieved via adjusting this slider.
- *Life-span-of-roamers*: In the simulation, although roamer agents are actively involved in search, some of them could not find the hub for various reasons. This slider helps the observer to set how long a group of roamers could remain alive before they are eliminated.
- *New-roamers-per-node*: This slider specifies the number of roamers to be born at each node for continuing the search towards the multiple directions. Please note that if the number shown on this slider is greater than 1, the simulation environment will soon be full of searching agents which will turn the simulation speed very slow.

#### 3.5.3.5 Key Plots and Monitors

The selected key plots are illustrated in Fig. 3.6; their functions are depicted below:

- *Number of roamers*: This plot illustrates the fluctuation of total number of roamers per tick.
- *Successful searches*: In our model, a successful search is defined as each time when a hub is found by roamer agents. Hence the number of successful searches per tick is showed by this plot.
- *Shortest travel distance*: This plot is activated when the *go Dijkstra* button (see Sect. 3.5.3.1) is pressed. It shows the shortest travel distance from each node to the hub.

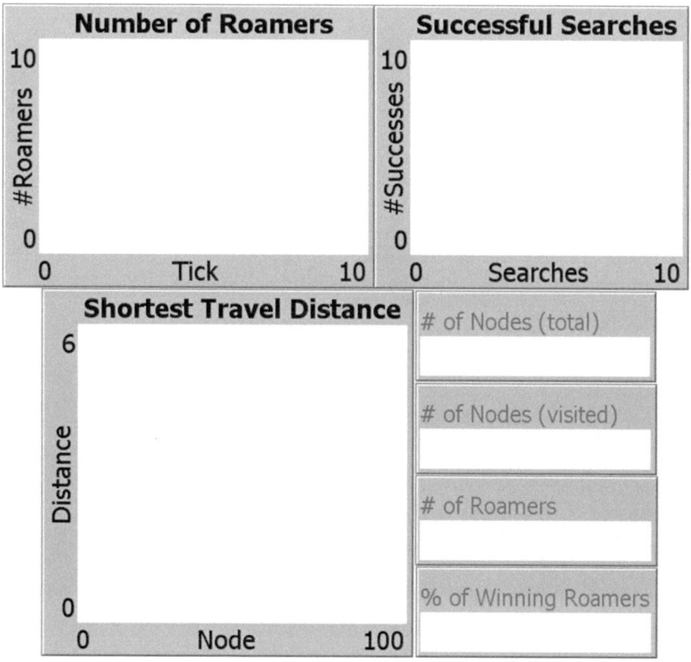


**Fig. 3.6** Key plots and monitors of the model

- *# of nodes* (*total*): The total number of nodes within the network is reported by this monitor. This number is largely influenced by the selected values of some sliders (introduced in Sect. 3.5.3.4) such as interval-of-network-updating, #-of-nodes-to-add-per-network-updating, and #-of-nodes-to-remove-per-network-updating.
- *# of nodes* (*visited*): As the name suggests, the number of visited nodes by the roamer agents is returned by this monitor.
- *# of roamers*: This monitor shows the number of roamer agents that are still actively involved in searching within the network.
- *% of winning roamers*: This monitor tells the percentage of winning roamer agents who have succeeded in reaching the hub.

## 3.6 Analysis of Simulation Results

A screenshot of the simulation window is shown in Fig. 3.7. A randomly generated network was first created and then used for simulating and comparing the efficiency of distinct communication strategies in assisting with the message spread

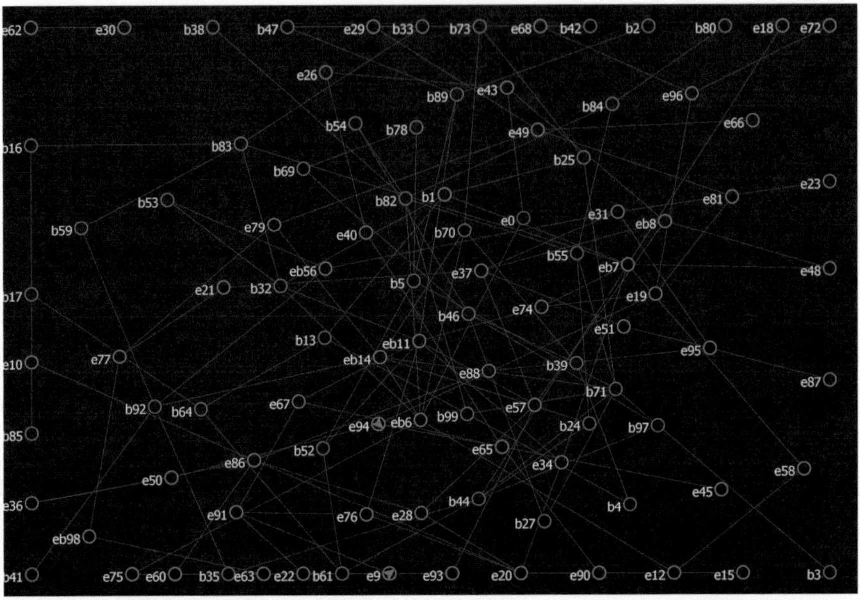


**Fig. 3.7** Screenshot of simulation environment

throughout the WSAN network. In this selected run, the network has 100 nodes, 4 of them are hubs. Sub-nodes have a random number of connection falls within the range of [1, 5], and the connections of hubs are set to a random number chosen from the range of [1, 40].

As soon as the simulating environment is ready to use, we can let the roamer agents set out to scout around the network for accomplishing different duties, e.g., search hubs and calculating the average separation degree of sub-nodes within the network from a specific hub. In this illustrative simulation, when one of the stopping criteria, i.e., 500 ticks, is met, we can get a searching result as shown in Fig. 3.8.

In order to carry out the distance computation, a simple but well-known Dijkstra's algorithm is implemented in our model. The working principle of the employed algorithm is to let the roamer agents update the shortest travel distance while they are patrolling the network. An array data structure (an extension to NetLogo) is used for keeping these results. The calculations are performed within model's procedure section by making use of the return data stored at distance array. The detailed process is out the scope of this chapter, but the results shown in Fig. 3.9 can give readers a glimpse of how distance is fluctuated as the search proceeds.

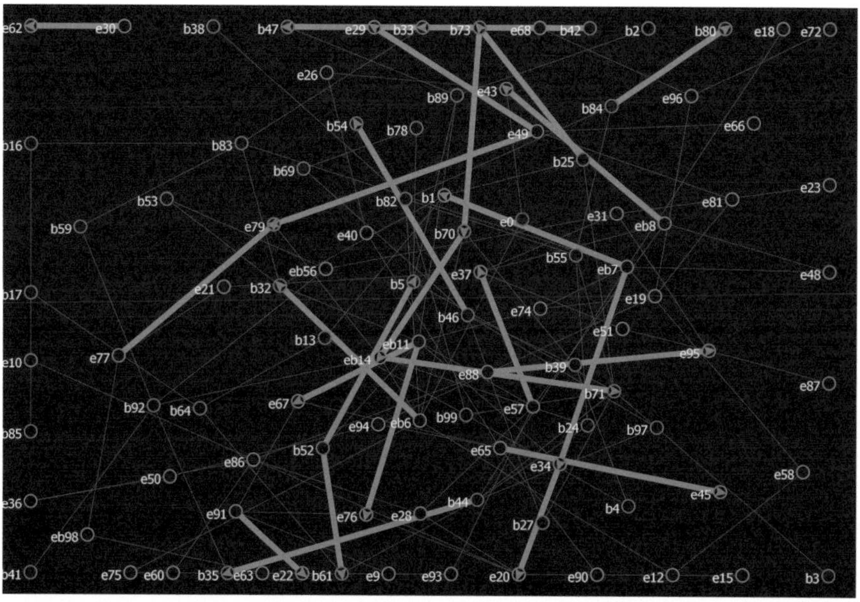


**Fig. 3.8** Screenshot of preliminary search results (stopped after 500 ticks)

**Fig. 3.9** Screenshot of shortest travel distance plot

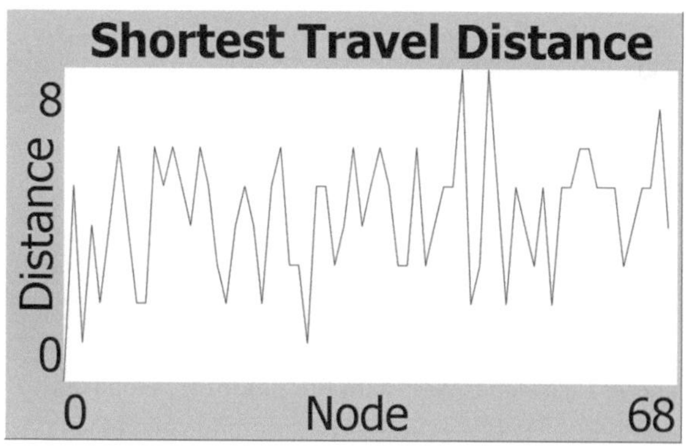


## 3.7 Limitations and Future Work

### *3.7.1 No Differentiation Among Various Multi-hop Network Paradigms*

In this study, we do not distinguish different types of paradigms from each other which means differentiating the individual routing components of each paradigm is not the main concern of this chapter. Nevertheless, the individual unique characteristics and challenges do impose specific requirements on the routing functions for each paradigm. So the future work can extend the current simulation environment to each particular network paradigm for capturing better system performance.

### 3.7.2 *Omitting the Energy Consumption Issue in Multi-hop Network*

Large and dense multi-hop WSAN is expected to form the structure of the IoT world in the near future. However, the hidden terminal problem emerges and constitutes the reason for a significant number of packet collisions and energy losses. By taking this factor into consideration, IoT vision also needs to embrace green networking, which is defined as a way to reduce energy required to carry out a given task while maintaining the same level of performance [52]. Therefore, another major challenge of multi-hop WSAN is the limited or costly energy, which is further reduced by the additional load imposed by multi-hop transmissions [53]. Energy efficiency is a cross layer issue and is affected by the following three major functions at the protocol stack differently in multi-hop wireless networks compared to single-hop networks: (1) the data rate at the physical layer, (2) medium access control protocol at the data link layer, and (3) routing protocol at the network layer. The future work of this research direction is thus concluded as first, identify the reason of packet losses, either collision or channel error, and reacting accordingly becomes important in multi-hop wireless networks, and second, layout guidelines for energy efficiency in multi-hop WSAN considering these three functions at the lower three layers.

## 3.8 Conclusion

The IoT vision, fueled with the flexibility of mobility, is expected to transform the structure of wireless networks from the current single-hop access networks to large dense multi-hop wireless networks. Multi-hop wireless networks (e.g., WMN, MANET, WSN, VANET, etc.) have the capability of conveying information from one node to other nodes in the network that may not be within direct wireless transmission range of each other and thus are envisioned to be formed among large number of nodes in the near future. In the light of this statement, the connectivity issue in the era of IoT is thus largely influenced by the efficacy of wireless multi-hop network.

The focus of this chapter is placed on a general routing performance analysis of a heterogeneous WSAN with possibly different numbers of relays in clusters of various separations. For clustered multi-hop relaying systems, hop-by-hop routing, the route to a destination is distributed in the "next hop" of the nodes along the route, is known as an efficient decentralized routing algorithm which selects the best relay node in each hop using local channel state information.

This chapter conducts a modeling and simulation scenario analysis via agent technology. For the simulations presented, we made use of the NetLogo. In the simulation, we investigate the distinctive properties in terms of network type, knowledge sharing, and mobility patterns. In addition, we consider various well-known algorithms, e.g., Dijkstra's algorithm, which have different characteristics. We evaluate those algorithms under different scenarios and the simulation results demonstrate the usefulness of the presented analyses.

## References

1. Höller J, Tsiatsis V, Mulligan C, Karnouskos S, Avesand S, Boyle D (2014) From machine-to-machine to the internet of things: introduction to a new age of intelligence. Academic, Elsevier Inc., 32 Jamestown Road, London NW1 7BY, UK. ISBN 978-0-12-407684-6
2. Macaulay J, Buckalew L, Chung G (2015) Internet of things in logistics. DHL Trend Research & Cisco Consulting Services, DHL Customer Solutions & Innovation, 53844 Troisdorf, Germany
3. Xing B, Gao W-J, Nelwamondo FV, Battle K, Marwala T (2011) e-RL: the Internet of things supported reverse logistics for remanufacture-to-order. In: Fifth international conference on Advanced Engineering Computing and Applications in Sciences (ADVCOMP), 20–25 November, Lisbon, Portugal, pp 84–87
4. Díaz M, Juan G, Lucas O, Ryuga A (2012) Big data on the Internet of things: an example for the E-health. In Sixth International Conference on Innovative Mobile and Internet Services in Ubiquitous Computing (IMIS), 4–6 July, Palermo, Italy, pp 898–900
5. Paschou M, Sakkopoulos E, Sourla E, Tsakalidis A (2013) Health Internet of things: metrics and methods for efficient data transfer. Simul Ion Model Pract Theory 34:186–199
6. Turcu CE, Turcu CO (2013) Internet of things as key enabler for sustainable healthcare delivery. Proc Soc BehavSci 73:251–256
7. Domingo MC (2012) An overview of the internet of things for people with disabilities. J Netw Comput Appl 35:584–596
8. Piyare R (2013) Internet of things: ubiquitous home control and monitoring system using android based smart phone. Int J Int Things 2:5–11
9. Kyas O (2015) How to smart home, 3rd edn, Key Concept Press e.K., Wyk, Germany, ISBN: 978-3-944980-06-5
10. Thin AG (2008) Capturing curiosity—mobile learning and the Internet of things. Centre for Bioscience Bulletin 1
11. ITU (2005) The internet of things: executive summary. International Telecommunication Union (ITU), Geneva ITU Internet Reports 2005, November
12. Santucci G, Lange S (2008) Internet of things in 2020: a roadmap for the future. Information Society and Media Directorate-general of the European Commission (DG INFSO) & European Technology Platform on Smart Systems Integration (EPoSS) Report, 05 September
13. Salarian H, Chin K-W, Naghdy F (2012) Coordination in wireless sensor–actuator networks: a survey. J Parallel Distrib Comput 72:856–867
14. Gauger M, Minder D, Marron PJ, Wacker A, Lachenmann A (2008) Prototyping sensor–actuator networks for home automation. In: Proceedings of the workshop on real-world wireless sensor networks, Glasgow, Scotland, pp 1–10

15. Zou F, Yang B, Cao Y (2009) Traffic light control for a single intersection based on wireless sensor network. In: Proceedings of international conference on electronic measurement and instruments, pp 1–10
16. Evans R, Iversen W, Kim Y (2008) Remote sensing and control of an irrigation system using a distributed wireless sensor network. IEEE Trans Instrum Meas 57:1379–1387
17. Rezgui A, Eltoweissy M (2007) Service-oriented sensor–actuator networks: promises, challenges, and the road ahead. Comput Commun 30:2627–2648
18. Zia HA, Sridhar N, Sastry S (2009) Failure detectors for wireless sensor-actuator systems. Ad Hoc Netw 7:1001–1013
19. Stankovic JA (2008) When sensor and actuator networks cover the world. ETRI J 30:627–633
20. Cao X, Chen J, Gao C, Sun Y (2009) An optimal control method for applications using wireless sensor/actuator networks. Comput Electr Eng 35:748–756
21. Ben-Tzvi P, Goldenberg AA, Zu JW (2010) Articulated hybrid mobile robot mechanism with compounded mobility and manipulation and on-board wireless sensor/actuator control interfaces. Mechatronics 20:627–639
22. Kim SH, Kim D, Kang J-S, Park HS (2012) A reflective service gateway for integrating evolvable sensor–actuator networks with pervasive infrastructure. J Parallel Distrib Comput 72:1237–1253
23. Hu F, Siddiqui W, Sankar K (2007) Scalable security in wireless sensor and actuator networks (WSANs): integration re-keying with routing. Comput Netw 51:285–308
24. George A, Kumar A, Cavalcanti D, Agrawal DP (2008) Protocols for mobility management in heterogeneous multi-hop wireless networks. Pervasive Mob Comput 4:92–116
25. Parunak HVD, Savit R, Riolo R (1998) Agent-based modeling vs. equation-based modeling: a case study and users' guide. presented at the Proceedings of the international workshop on multi-agent systems and agent-based simulation, Paris, France, July 4–6, pp 10–25
26. Dong M, Ota K, Yang LT, Chang S, Zhu H, Zhou Z (2014) Mobile agent-based energy-aware and user-centric data collection in wireless sensor networks. Comput Netw 74:58–70
27. Kumar DS, Bhuvaneswaran RS (2007) Proposal on multi agent ants based routing algorithm for mobile ad-hoc networks. Int J Comput Sci Netw Secur 7:260–268
28. Deepalakshmi P, Radhakrishnan S (2009) Ant colony based QoS routing algorithm for mobile ad hoc networks. Int J Recent Trends Eng 1:459–462
29. Roth M, Wicker S (2006) Termite: a swarm intelligent routing algorithm for mobile wireless Ad-Hoc networks. In: Studies in Computational Intelligence (SCI) 31. Springer, Berlin, pp 155–184
30. Dhurandher SK, Misra S, Pruthi P, Singhal S, Aggarwal S, Woungang I (2011) Using bee algorithm for peer-to-peer file searching in mobile ad hoc networks. J Netw Comput Appl 34:1498–1508
31. Holmgren J, Ramstedt L, Davidsson P (2010) Roles and responsibilities in supply chains An agent simulation modeling framework. In: Proceedings of IEEE ITSC2010 workshop on Artificial Transportation Systems and Simulation (ATSS'2010)
32. Santa-Eulalia LAd, D'Amours S, Frayret J-M (2010) Modeling agent-based simulations for supply chain planning: the FAMASS methodological framework. presented at the Proceedings of IEEE International Conference on Systems, Man, and Cybernetics (IEEE SMC 2010), Istanbul, Turkey, pp 1710–1717
33. Rolón M, Martínez E (2012) Agent-based modeling and simulation of an autonomic manufacturing execution system. Comput Ind 63:53–78
34. Kiesling E, Günther M, Stummer C, Wakolbinger LM (2009) An agent-based simulation model for the market diffusion of a second generation biofuel. In: Proceedings of the 2009 winter simulation conference, pp 1474–1481
35. Amini M, Wakolbinger T, Racer M, Nejad MG (2012) Alternative supply chain production-sales policies for new product diffusion: an agent-based modeling and simulation approach. Eur J Oper Res 216:301–311

36. Edelen MR (2003) Swarm intelligence and stigmergy: robotic implementation of foraging behavior. Master of science, University of Maryland
37. Kiim W-S (2009) Effects of a trust mechanism on complex adaptive supply networks: an agent-based social simulation study. J Artif Soc Soc Simul:12:1–4. http://jasss.soc.surrey.ac.uk/12/3/4.html
38. Cui B, Wang H, Ye K, Yan J (2012) Intelligent agent-assisted adaptive order simulation system in the artificial stock market. Expert Syst Appl 39:8890–8898
39. Macal CM, North MJ (2009) Agent-based modeling and simulation. In: 2009 Winter Simulation Conference (WSC 2009), pp 86–98
40. Nikolai C, Madey G (2009) Tools of the trade: a survey of various agent based modeling platforms. J Artif Soc Soc Simul:12:1–2. http://jasss.soc.surrey.ac.uk/12/2/2.html
41. Bousquet F, Page CL (2004) Multi-agent simulations and ecosystem management: a review. Ecol Model 176:313–332
42. Wilensky U (1999) "NetLogo," 4.1 ed. Center for Connected Learning and Computer-Based Modeling, Northwestern University, Evanston, IL. Available at http://ccl.northwestern.edu/netlogo/
43. Berryman MJ, Angus SD (2010) Tutorials on agent-based modelling with NetLogo and network analysis with Pajek. In: Dewar RL, Detering F (eds) Complex physical, biophysical and econophysical systems. World Scientific Publishing, Hackensack, pp 351–375
44. Sklar E (2007) Software review: NetLogo, a multi-agent simulation environment. Artif Life 13:303–311
45. Keane C (2014) Modeling behavior in complex public health systems: simulations and games for action and evaluation. Springer Publishing Company, LLC, 11 West 42nd Street, New York, NY 10036. ISBN 978-0-8261-1017-6
46. Dixon C, Winfield AFT, Fisher M, Zeng C (2012) Towards temporal verification of swarm robotic systems. Robot Auton Syst 60:1429–1441
47. Román B (2010) Complexity, culture, and tolerance: a new methodology for studying the hispanic culture. PhD thesis, University of Western Ontario, London, Ontario, Canada
48. Diaz MBA (2010) Agent based models on social interaction and demographic behaviour. Doctoral thesis, Institut für Wirtschaftsmathematik, Fakultät für Mathematik und Geoinformation, Vienna University of Technology
49. Rolón M, Martínez E (2012) Agent learning in autonomic manufacturing execution systems for enterprise networking. Comput Ind Eng 63:901–925
50. Sapkota P (2010) Modeling diffusion using an agent-based approach. Master thesis, University of Toledo
51. Russell S, Norvig P (2003) Artificial intelligence: a modern approach, 2nd edn. Prentice Hall, Upper Saddle River
52. Bianzino AP, Chaudet C, Rossi D, Rougier J-L (2015) A survey of green networking research. IEEE Commun Surv Tutor 14:3–20
53. Gupta P, Kumar P (2000) The capacity of wireless networks. IEEE Trans Inf Theory 46:388–404

# Chapter 4
# Secure Inter-Vehicle Communication: A Need for Evolution of VANET Towards the Internet of Vehicles

**Sulata Mitra and Atanu Mondal**

## 4.1 Introduction

The Internet of Things (IoT) connect nearly anything with an electronic subsystem to the existing Internet infrastructure. It suggests a vision of a connected world where smart devices, intelligent objects, and Web-based systems are autonomously linked via the Internet and communicate with each other to improve the quality of life of their owners/users.

The new era of IoT is driving the evolution of conventional Vehicle Ad hoc Networks (VANET) into the Internet of Vehicles (IoV) paradigm. According to recent predictions, 25 billion of "things" will be connected to the Internet by 2020 among which vehicles will constitute a significant portion. In VANET, a vehicle is mainly considered as a node to disseminate messages among vehicles. In IoV paradigm, vehicles are not merely considered as just like traditional vehicles in VANET. Rather vehicles are considered as an intelligent device/smart device which has encompassed strong information communication system, reliable security concern, and capability of computation, storage, and learning to anticipate customers' intention. The dynamic mobile communication systems such as vehicle to vehicle (V2V), vehicle to infrastructure (V2I), and vehicle to human (V2H) enable secure information sharing, releasing, gathering, and processing in IoV due to the inevitable convergence of these technologies. Based on this paradigm, the vehicles can effectively guide and supervise other vehicles and provide secure and reliable information services. So, to accomplish these operations, inter-vehicle communication (IVC) is a manifest of IoV.

S. Mitra • A. Mondal (✉)
Department of Computer Science and Technology, Indian Institute of Engineering Science and Technology, Shibpur, India
e-mail: bulu456@yahoo.co.in

 
Z. Mahmood (ed.), *Connectivity Frameworks for Smart Devices*,
Computer Communications and Networks, DOI 10.1007/978-3-319-33124-9_4

Security in IVC is a major challenge, having a great impact on future deployment and applications of IoV. Authentication and authorization are important counterattack measures in IoV deployment, allowing only authorize nodes to be connected for secure communication between vehicles. But the adversaries may misuse the resource by generating and communicating message with other vehicles. Moreover, the behavior of authentic vehicles may deviate from the required standard behavior. Such vehicles are known as misbehaving vehicles. The misbehaving vehicles may jeopardize the safety of other vehicles, drivers, and passengers as well as the efficiency of the transportation system. The misbehaving vehicles can adversely impact IVC by replaying and suppressing messages. They may send false message to other vehicles like to clear the road for selfish reason, may fabricate the message, and also may introduce delay in message communication. But any modification and delay of such messages may cause injuries even deaths. However message exchange between vehicles is based on VANET. Hence, the identification and revocation of unauthentic and misbehaving vehicles from VANET are essential for its future evolution towards IoV. It is also essential to track the vehicles at various checkpoints within a boundary or premises in high-mobility VANET to manage the security and safety of vehicles in case of theft or any unwanted incident. It needs to protect VANET from unauthorized message injection and message alteration to avoid road accidents and to ensure security and privacy of inter-vehicle communication. This chapter addresses the problem of revocation of unauthentic and misbehaving vehicles from VANET. The schemes are elaborated in two phases:

- In the first phase (Phase_I), the identification and authentication of vehicles are verified.
- In the second phase (Phase_II), the misbehaving vehicles are detected and revoked from the set of authentic vehicles as identified in Phase_I.

In Phase_I, two schemes are proposed to identify authentic vehicles in VANET. Both the schemes use identification algorithm to identify a vehicle uniquely and authentication algorithm to verify the authentication of a vehicle using an initial registration phase and tracking algorithm to track an authentic vehicle within the coverage area of VANET. The first scheme (Authentication_Scheme_I) [1] is implemented in a centralized VANET which is a hierarchy having certifying authority (CA) at the root level, base stations (BSs) at the intermediate level, and vehicles at the leaf level. This scheme is extended in Authentication_Scheme_II [2] for accommodating more vehicles in VANET. It is implemented in a distributed VANET which is a hierarchy having CA at the root level (R_CA) and also at the first level (F_CA), BSs at the second level and vehicles at the leaf level. The F_CAs are maintained at the first level of the hierarchy to increase the coverage area of VANET which in turn helps to accommodate more vehicles in [2] than [1]. But the authentic vehicles may misbehave by generating false message, by introducing delay in message communication, by suppressing emergency message, etc. Two schemes are proposed in Phase_II to detect and revoke such misbehaving vehicles from the set of authentic vehicles as identified in Phase_I. In both the schemes, each vehicle receives a beacon message periodically and service message (S_MSG) after the occurrence of an event from the vehicles which are within its coverage area. The steganography method is used to protect S_MSGs from the access of intruder. Each vehicle identifies misbehaving vehicles from the received S_MSGs, generates a certificate revocation list (CRL), and sends the CRL to its parent BS. Each BS receives CRLs from the vehicles under it, generates a final CRL from the received CRLs, and sends final CRL to CA. The CA receives CRLs from the BSs under it, generates CA_CRL from the received CRLs, and broadcasts CA_CRL among the vehicles under it. Hence, in both the schemes of Phase_II, detection and revocation of misbehaving vehicles are performed jointly by CA, BS, and vehicles.

In the first revocation scheme (Revocation_Scheme_I) [3], CA, BS, and the vehicle execute their operations sequentially, whereas in the second revocation scheme (Revocation_Scheme_II) [4], the independent operations of the vehicle, BS and CA, are executed in parallel for reducing the generation time of CA_CRL. The operations at each vehicle, BS and CA, are divided into blocks for parallel execution [4]. The maximum size of data packet is assumed as 64 bytes (Size_DP) [5] in [4]. Hence in [4], the CRL of vehicle, final CRL of BS, and CA_CRL of CA are fragmented into data packets if their size exceeds Size_DP by their sender, whereas the CRLs are regenerated from the received data packets by their receiver.

The remainder of this chapter is structured as follows. In Sect. 4.2, some of the published work related to the verification of vehicle authentication and revocation of misbehaving vehicles is presented briefly. Both the phases of work are elaborated in Sect. 4.3. The simulation results of Phase_I and Phase_II are reported in Sect. 4.4. Section 4.5 concludes the chapter. The name and description of parameters are shown in the appendix at the end of the chapter.

## 4.2 Previous Work

Several vehicle authentication and vehicle revocation schemes have been proposed in the literature. Here, we present some of these.

Sensors can be used for vehicle detection and tracking. But sensors may not be able to collect accurate information regarding vehicle identification due to the interference of any Bluetooth signal or microwave signal with the collected information during transmission. It needs sophisticated and expensive technologies to collect high-quality information. Moreover, a lot of sensors are required to collect the traffic status [6] from the entire coverage area of the transportation network due to the limited effective range of most of the sensors. The power consumption of sensors is also a concerning factor. The closed-circuit television (CCTV) technology [7] may be used in vehicle tracking system. But the image quality is affected by the lighting or the presence of trees. The CCTV images cannot be preserved for a long time, so police investigation is under time pressure to locate relevant material. The images can be of poor quality and may not be a reliable means of verifying identity. It also needs data protection and legislation. The automatic vehicle identification techniques are discussed in [8]. One such technique uses barcode which is affixed to each vehicle. The optical reader may be used to read it. But its quality is affected by weather and in case of dirty vehicles. Most current automatic vehicle identification technology relies on radio-frequency identification in which an antenna is used to communicate with a transponder on the vehicle using dedicated short-range communication (DSRC). It has excellent accuracy even at highway speed. But the major disadvantage is the cost of transponder. The automatic number plate recognition may also be used to identify a vehicle. The image of the number plate is captured using camera but it has a significant error rate and significant cost of transaction processing. The global positioning system (GPS) may be used to know the current position of a vehicle [9]. But it cannot distinguish one vehicle from another. Moreover satellite communication is required to process data which is obtained from GPS. But satellite communication is not adequate at urban and forest area. Any storms having ionized particle may introduce noise in the collected information.

Each vehicle has a unique identity along with a public and private key as considered in [10]. The public key is used to encrypt the unique identity before sending it to the receiver and the private key is used to decrypt any received message. But the pattern of the unique identity is not mentioned in this scheme. Moreover it needs considerable amount of time for encryption. The biometric information of the driver is used for authentication as mentioned in [11]. It hampers the privacy of the driver. Moreover it is applicable if the driver in the vehicle is a fixed person. In [12], CA assigns a public key to each vehicle for V2V and V2I communication. The vehicle uses the public key for encryption. CA generates a signature from the said public key and assigns it to the vehicle in case the vehicle wants to get any service from the network. But any intruder may get the public key of a vehicle and may start some communication. Broadcast authentication is mentioned in [13]. Here source node sends packet to the destination node. In this packet the source node specifies the error correction bits. After receiving all the packets from source node, the destination verifies the authenticity of the source node using the error correction bits. So the destination end takes considerable amount of time to verify the authenticity of the source node which is not permitted in the VANET environment due to the high velocity of vehicles.

The authors of [14] divide the network into clusters. Each cluster is under the control of a local certifying authority, each road side unit (RSU) monitors and senses the incoming adversary for generating report quickly. But the cluster formation overhead is not evaluated in [14].

In a decentralized solution [15], vehicles are evicted from the network by their peers. The CA can be notified to revoke the keys of the misbehaving vehicles. However the eviction decision is taken and performed by the vehicles in the network. But each vehicle has to report the reason of revocation to CA.

A flexible, simple, and scalable design for VANET certificates and new methods for efficient certificate management are proposed in [16]. It reduces channel overhead by eliminating the use of CRL. It issues valid certificate to valid vehicles and adversary certificate to adversary vehicles, hence protects the system from adversary vehicles by distributing information about them among the whole network and by revoking the certificates of adversary vehicles. But the performance of the scheme is not evaluated on the basis of overhead and delay.

The CA divides the entire CRL into pieces and signs in each piece to protect integrity before distributing them among RSUs as proposed in [17]. Each RSU receives the complete CRL file, verifies its authenticity, and broadcasts it among board units of vehicles within its coverage area. Though it reduces wireless medium contention and keeps the medium available for transmission of time-critical safety messages, there is a little chance of collision. Moreover the performance of the scheme depends on RSU deployment.

The scalable methods of distributing CRL and other large files over VANET using V2V and V2I communications while taking advantage of the multichannel operations in IEEE 1609.4 are proposed in [18]. The wireless channel contention is reduced in [18] by limiting the number of broadcasting nodes to a single node. It uses most pieces of broadcast method in which only the node with the maximum number of CRL file pieces is selected to broadcast within a given radio broadcast range. But the overhead of generating CRL pieces is not computed. The size of the CRL and number of CRL pieces increase with vehicle density. Hence it is difficult to distribute the CRL over the entire network with minimum delay and network congestions.

## 4.3 Present Work

In this section both the phases, as mentioned earlier in the chapter, are elaborated.

### *4.3.1 Phase_1: Vehicle Identification and Authentication*

Two schemes for identification, authentication, and tracking of vehicles using vehicle identification number (VIN) are proposed in this phase of work. Both the schemes use a modified VIN structure to identify more manufacturers than identified in [19].

Figure 4.1i, ii shows the hierarchical VANET as proposed in [1] and [2], respectively. The coverage area of CA, R_CA, F_CAs, and BSs is assumed to be as Rm. So the maximum distance from vehicle to BS (Dist_V_BS) as mentioned in [1, 2], BS to CA (Dist_BS_CA) as mentioned in [1], BS to F_CA (Dist_BS_FCA) as mentioned in [2], and F_CA to R_CA (Dist_FCA_RCA) as mentioned in [2] is also R m to ensure communication among them. Let C1 in Fig. 4.1iii be the CA of [1]. As the sum of angle BAD, angle DAE, and angle EAB in Fig. 4.1iii is 360°, the maximum possible number of BSs under the coverage area of CA in [1] (NO_OF_BS) is 3. Due to the same reason, the maximum number of BSs under

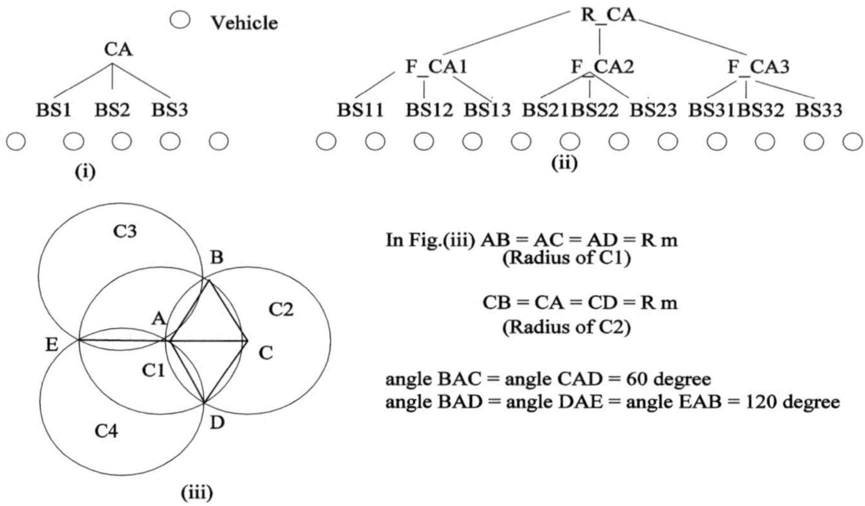


**Fig. 4.1** System architecture

the coverage area of each F_CA (NO_OF_BS) and the maximum number of F_CAs under the coverage area of R_CA (NO_OF_FCA) in [2] are also 3.

Both the schemes consider V2I communication among the vehicles, CA and BS. The DSRC is proposed for such fast short-distance V2I communication. The range of frequency provided by DSRC is 5.850–5.925 GHz. So the available bandwidth at each BS is 75 MHz, out of which 70 MHz is usable and rest 5 MHz is used as guard frequency. The 70 MHz bandwidth at each BS is divided into seven links, out of which six links are reserved for service and one link is used for control purposes. So the bandwidth of each link is 10 MHz, and it is allocated to authentic vehicle on demand at a rate 1.28 MHz for data service, 2.56 MHz for audio service, and 3.84 MHz for video service. Both the schemes consider V2I communication in the form of data. So each 10 MHz link is divided into (10 MHz/1.28 MHz) $\approx$ 8 channels and the total number of available channels to provide service at each BS is 48. Each BS allocates one channel to each authentic vehicle within its coverage area and so can provide service to 48 vehicles using 48 channels.

In both the schemes, it is assumed that each vehicle has an electronic license plate (ELP) in which its modified VIN is embedded in encrypted form (E_VIN) by the vehicle manufacturer. The ELP of a vehicle broadcasts (as per IEEE P1069 and IEEE 802.11p) E_VIN after entering into the coverage area of a new BS. The new BS verifies the authentication of the vehicle using an initial registration phase and assigns a digital signature (D_Sig) to the vehicle if it is authentic.

Both CA and R_CA maintain a VIN database (VIN_CA) to store the VINs of the vehicles that are already manufactured. It is updated when a new vehicle is manufactured. Both CA and R_CA gather knowledge about the available pattern of each character in VIN of the vehicles which are already manufactured by consulting with VIN_CA after updating it. Each BS also maintains a VIN database

(VIN_BS) to store (E_VIN, D_Sig) pair of the authentic vehicles that enters into the coverage area of CA in [1] whereas into the coverage area of its parent F_CA in [2].

The modified VIN structure is discussed in this section. The identification, authentication, and tracking algorithms are elaborated for $v^{th}$ vehicle ($V_v$, $1 \leq v \leq TOT\_V$, where TOT_V is the total number of vehicles in VANET).

#### 4.3.1.1 Modified VIN Structure

VIN has 17 characters which are divided into three fields [19]. The field_1 is World Manufacturing Identification (WMI). It is used to identify the manufacturer at different countries and so it is required to know the manufacturing details of a vehicle. The field_2 is Vehicle Description Section (VDS). It includes various description of the vehicle such as engine type, assembly point, body type, break type, etc., and so it is required to know any detail description of a vehicle. For example, the number of cylinders in the engine helps to decide the amount of load it can carry, break type is required to change wheel of a vehicle, assembly point is required to know for purchasing any parts of a vehicle, etc. The field_3 is Vehicle Identifier Section (VIS). It indicates a serial number of a vehicle and so it can be used to distinguish a vehicle from others.

There are four competing standards to represent VIN worldwide [19]. The first standard (S1) is FMVSS 115, Part 565, the second standard (S2) is ISO 3779, the third standard (S3) is SAEJ853, and the fourth standard (S4) is ADR 61/2. The field_1 contains three characters for all the four standards; field_2 contains six characters for S2, S3, and S4 whereas five characters for S1. The field_3 contains eight characters for all the four standards. In S1 the ninth character is used to detect error in VIN which may occur during its communication through unreliable channel. In S2, S3, and S4, out of six characters in field_2, five characters are used as VDS and the sixth character which is actually the ninth character of VIN remains unused [19].

The above VIN structure is modified in the proposed scheme to accommodate more manufacturers. The field_1 has four characters in the modified VIN. Each character in field_1 is valid if it is in the ranges A–H, J–N, P, R–Z, and 0–9 [20]. The field_2 has five characters in the modified VIN. The first character and second character in field_2 are valid if they are in the ranges A–H, J–N, P, and R–Z [20]. The third character and fourth character in field_2 are valid if they are in the range 0–9 [20]. The fifth character in field_2 is valid if it is in the ranges A–H, J–N, P, R–Z, and 0–9 [20]. The field_3 has eight characters in the modified VIN. The first character in field_3 is valid if it is in the ranges A–H, J–N, P, R–T, V–Y, and 1–9 [20]. The second character in field_3 is valid if it is in the ranges A–H, J–N, R–Z, and 0–9 [20]. The third character in field_3 is valid if it is in the ranges A–H, J–N, P, and R–Z [20]. The last five characters in field_3 are valid if they are in the range 0–9 [20].

Let the number of manufacturers in the world be M and the number of countries be K. Now if all the countries have M number of manufacturers, then the total number of manufacturers will be M×K. Again the number of available alphabet is 23 (except I, O, Q as they are very similar to 0 and 1) and the number of available numeric is 10 to construct VIN [20]. Now currently available number of manufacturers is 836 and the number of countries is 78 [21]. So it is required to identify 65,208 numbers of manufacturers. It is possible to identify only 35,035 numbers of manufacturers using three characters in field_1. The use of four characters in field_1 helps to identify 1,155,517 number of manufacturers. The extra 1,090,309 number of manufacturers may be utilized to satisfy any future requirement if M×K increases. The possibility of error in the proposed fast short-distance V2I communication is assumed as negligible. So an extra character for error detection like S1 is not required in the modified VIN. However the ninth character which is the error detection character in S1 and unused character in S2, S3, and S4 is incorporated in field_1 of the modified VIN structure to identify more manufacturers.

#### 4.3.1.2 Identification, Authentication, and Tracking Algorithm

Let $V_v$ enters into the coverage area of $B^{th}$ BS ($BS_B$, $1 \leq B \leq NO\_OF\_BS$). $BS_B$ is under CA in [1] and under $C^{th}$ F_CA ($F\_CA_C$, $1 \leq C \leq NO\_OF\_FCA$) in [2]. The ELP of $V_v$ broadcasts E_VIN ($E\_VIN_v$). $BS_B$ receives $E\_VIN_v$ and triggers identification algorithm.

Identification Algorithm

This algorithm adds $E\_VIN_v$ in a VIN queue ($BS_B\_VIN\_Queue$) and searches VIN_BS at $BS_B$ ($VIN\_BS_B$) for $E\_VIN_v$ using VIN_SEARCH function (refer to Listing 4.1).

If found $V_v$ is an authentic vehicle and its initial registration phase is over. The identification algorithm at $BS_B$ reads the digital signature of $V_v$ ($D\_Sig_v$) from the record of $V_v$ in $VIN\_BS_B$ and triggers tracking algorithm by sending $D\_Sig_v$ to it. Otherwise the identification algorithm at $BS_B$ starts the initial registration phase of $V_v$ by triggering authentication algorithm.

Authentication Algorithm

The authentication algorithm at $BS_B$ calls the verification function at CA as mentioned in [1] and authentication algorithm at $F\_CA_C$ as mentioned in [2] by sending $E\_VIN_v$. The authentication algorithm at $F\_CA_C$ calls the verification function at R_CA by sending $E\_VIN_v$. The CA in [1] and R_CA in [2] add $E\_VIN_v$ in CA_VIN_Queue and R_CA_VIN_Queue, respectively.

```
{ Str_R ← Received VIN from vehicle
  Size ← Number of encrypted VIN in VIN_BS
  If (Size=0)
    Go to LOOP
  Else
   { Length_R ← Length of Str_R
     D ← 1
L1:  Str_D ← Dth encrypted VIN in VIN_BS
     Length_D ← Length of Str_D
     If (Length_R ≠ Length_D)
       Go to LOOP1
     Else
       { B ← 1
L2:      Str_R(B) ← Bth character of Str_R
         Str_D(B) ← Bth character of Str_D
         If (Str_R(B) ≠ Str_D(B))
           Go to LOOP1
         Else
           {B ← B+1
            If (B ≤ Length_R)
              Go to L2
            Else
              Str_R is found in VIN_BS}}}}
LOOP: Trigger authentication algorithm
LOOP1: {D ← D+1
        If (D ≤ Size)
          Go to L1
        Else
          Go to LOOP}
```

**Listing 4.1** VIN_SEARCH function at BS

### *Verification Function*

It decrypts $E\_VIN_v$ to generate $D\_VIN_v$ using RSA algorithm [22] and verifies each character in field_1, field_2, and field_3 of $D\_VIN_v$ for its validity as discussed in Sect. 4.3.1.1. If $D\_VIN_v$ is not valid, the verification function generates a security message for the police or checking personnel to make them aware about $V_v$. Otherwise the verification function generates $D\_Sig_v$ from $D\_VIN_v$ using SHA-1 algorithm [22]. It also generates $B_v$ which is ($E\_VIN_v$, $D\_Sig_v$) pair.

In [1], the verification function at CA calls the insertion function at all the BSs under it by sending $B_v$. In [2] the verification function at R_CA calls the insertion function at $F\_CA_C$ which in turn calls the insertion function at all the BSs under it by sending $B_v$.

The insertion function at each BS under CA in [1] and under $F\_CA_C$ in [2] inserts $B_v$ in their VIN_BS. During this span of time, $V_v$ may reside within the coverage area of $BS_B$ or may move to the coverage area of another BS under CA in [1] and under $F\_CA_C$ in [2]. The insertion function at the BS within which $V_v$ is currently passing through ($Current\_BS_v$) triggers the tracking algorithm.

*Tracking Algorithm*

The tracking algorithm at Current_BS$_v$ assigns D_Sig$_v$ to $V_v$ and allocates a channel (CH$_v$) to $V_v$. It also switches on a timer and initializes it to $\tau_v$. The timer $\tau_v$ indicates the time span during which D_Sig$_v$ is assigned to $V_v$. It senses CH$_v$ when $\tau_v$ expires. If CH$_v$ is free, the tracking algorithm removes $\tau_v$ and frees CH$_v$. Otherwise it reassigns D_Sig$_v$ to $V_v$ and switches on $\tau_v$ again.

The use of VIN for identification and authentication of a vehicle is advantageous as it is impossible to transfer VIN among vehicles and to alter the information on it. Moreover VIN of a vehicle remains intact even in typical environmental condition. It contains information about the manufacturer of the vehicle and description of the vehicle as discussed in Sect. 4.3.1.1. So other than identification and authentication, VIN can also be used to know the manufacturing details and the detail description of a vehicle which may require in case of accidents, etc.

As the insertion function at each BS inserts the encrypted VIN and digital signature pair of an authentic vehicle in VIN_BS only once, i.e., at the end of initial registration phase of a vehicle, so the proposed scheme has no Denial-of-Service (DoS) and distributed Denial-of-Service (DDoS) attack.

During initial registration phase, the digital signature of the vehicle is generated from its decrypted VIN so no extra data is required to generate the digital signature for an authentic vehicle other than its VIN.

The insertion function at CA in [1] and at F_CA in [2] sends the encrypted VIN and digital signature pair of an authentic vehicle to all the BSs under it. So even if a vehicle moves to another BS during its initial registration phase, it will receive its digital signature from the new BS as all the BSs have a copy of the same digital signature. Therefore the initial registration phase of a vehicle is independent on its velocity which is an obvious requirement in VANET due to its high-mobility model.

Finally the ELP of a vehicle broadcasts its encrypted VIN after entering into the coverage area of a new BS. The new BS verifies the authentication of this vehicle. It allocates a channel and assigns a digital signature to that vehicle if it is authentic. It also reassigns the digital signature to that vehicle periodically using the same channel. So the BS is able to track an authentic vehicle within its coverage area as long as this channel is busy.

### 4.3.2 Phase_2: Misbehaving Vehicle Detection and Revocation

Two schemes for the detection and revocation of misbehaving vehicles from the set of authentic vehicles as identified in Phase_I [1] are proposed in this phase of work. In both the schemes, the misbehaving vehicles are detected and revoked jointly by CA, BS, and vehicles. The operations at each vehicle, BS and CA, are executed sequentially in [3] whereas divided into a few blocks for parallel execution in [4].

This phase of work is elaborated for $V_v$ within the coverage area of $BS_B$ under CA. $V_v$ receives S_MSGs from the vehicles within its coverage area, identifies misbehaving vehicles from the received S_MSGs, generates a CRL ($CRL_v$) by specifying the E_VINs of misbehaving vehicles, and sends $CRL_v$ to $BS_B$. $BS_B$ collects CRLs from the vehicles within its coverage area, identifies the E_VINs of misbehaving vehicles from the received CRLs, generates a final CRL ($CRL_B$) by specifying the E_VINs of misbehaving vehicles, and sends $CRL_B$ to CA. CA collects CRLs from the BSs under it, identifies the E_VINs of misbehaving vehicles from the received CRLs, generates CA_CRL by specifying E_VINs of misbehaving vehicles, and broadcasts CA_CRL among the vehicles under it. $CRL_v$, $CRL_B$, and CA_CRL are fragmented into data packets by $V_v$, $BS_B$, and CA, respectively, if their size exceeds Size_DP in [4].

Let $V_v$ receive $j^{th}$ S_MSG ($S\_MSG_j$) in the form ($D\_Sig_j$, $E\_VIN_j$, $H\_MSG_j$, $O\_MSG_j$) from $j^{th}$ vehicle ($1 \leq j \leq TOT\_V$, $j \neq v$) within its coverage area. $D\_Sig_j$, $E\_VIN_j$, $H\_MSG_j$, and $O\_MSG_j$ are the digital signature, E_VIN, hidden message, and the operational part to retrieve the message ($MESS_j$) from $H\_MSG_j$, respectively. $MESS_j$ is retrieved from $H\_MSG_j$ by performing bit-wise logical operations among $E\_VIN_j$ and $H\_MSG_j$. The $O\_MSG_j$ field contains the bit pattern corresponding to the different bit-wise operators (AND, OR, XOR). Each bit-wise operator is represented by Size_BWO number of bits, and the size of $O\_MSG_j$ ($Size\_O\_MSG_j$) is an exact multiple of Size_BWO. The number of bit-wise operations ($Number\_BWO_j$) among $H\_MSG_j$ and $E\_VIN_j$ is computed as ($Size\_O\_MSG_j$/Size_BWO).

In this section, the data packet format of $CRL_v$, $CRL_B$, and CA_CRL in [4] is considered for discussion. The function of $V_v$ is elaborated for $S\_MSG_j$. The function of $BS_B$ and CA is elaborated assuming the number of vehicles within the coverage area of $BS_B$ as $NO\_OF\_V_B$.

#### 4.3.2.1 Data Packet Format

The data packet of $CRL_v$ is in the form of (E_MARK, SL_NO, $E\_VIN_v$, E_VINs of misbehaving vehicles identified by $V_v$), $CRL_B$ is in the form of (E_MARK, SL_NO, $BS_B$, E_VINs of misbehaving vehicles identified by $BS_B$), and CA_CRL is in the form of (SL_NO, E_VINs of misbehaving vehicles identified by CA). The value in the E_MARK field is 0 in all the data packets of $CRL_v$ and $CRL_B$ except the last one to identify the last data packet associated with a particular CRL. The value in the SL_NO field represents the serial number of the data packet after fragmentation. $E\_VIN_v$ in the data packet of $CRL_v$ is the E_VIN of the vehicle that sends $CRL_v$ and $BS_B$ in the data packet of $CRL_B$ is the identification of the BS that sends $CRL_B$.

The size of data packet is Size_DP. The size of E_VIN (Size_E_VIN) is 17 characters [19], and the size of each character is assumed as 8 bits (extended ASCII format). Hence Size_E_VIN is 136 bits. The size of E_MARK field is 1 bit, whereas the size of SL_NO (Size_SLNO) field is varied during simulation depending upon the number of data packets in $CRL_v$, $CRL_B$, and CA_CRL after fragmentation. Hence the maximum possible number of E_VINs of misbehaving vehicles that can be specified in each data packet of $CRL_v$ ($M_v$) is $\lfloor(375\text{-Size\_SLNO})/136\rfloor$, of $CRL_B$ ($M_B$) is $\lfloor(511\text{-Size\_SLNO-}\log_2(\text{NO\_OF\_BS}))/136\rfloor$, and of CA_CRL ($M_{CA}$) is $\lfloor(512\text{-Size\_SLNO})/136\rfloor$. So the maximum possible value of $M_v$, $M_B$, and $M_{CA}$ is assumed as 2, 3, and 3, respectively.

#### 4.3.2.2 Function of $V_v$

$V_v$ uses ALGO_MESS algorithm to retrieve $MESS_j$ from $H\_MSG_j$ and ALGO_V algorithm to generate $CRL_v$ both in [3, 4]. In [3], $V_v$ receives CA_CRL from $BS_B$ and stores it. It switches on a timer and initializes it to $\tau_v$. It receives $S\_MSG_j$ and searches CA_CRL for $E\_VIN_j$. If $E\_VIN_j$ is in CA_CRL or if ($Size\_O\_MSG_j\%$ $Size\_BWO \neq 0$), it discards $S\_MSG_j$. Otherwise, it stores $S\_MSG_j$ in a FIFO queue ($Q_v$), increases a counter ($NS\_MSG_v$) by 1, computes $Number\_BWO_j$, and triggers ALGO_MESS algorithm. The retrieval of $MESS_j$ from $H\_MSG_j$ is shown in Listing 4.2.

The ALGO_MESS algorithm inserts a record ($R_j$) in the form ($E\_VIN_j$, $MESS_j$, $REMARK_j$) in a data table ($DT_v$) for $S\_MSG_j$. Initially the value of the $REMARK_j$ field in $R_j$ is null. The algorithm repeats the same steps of operation for the other received S_MSGs till the timer expires. The maximum number of S_MSGs in $Q_v$ and the maximum number of records in $DT_v$ is $NS\_MSG_v$.

$V_v$ triggers ALGO_V algorithm to detect the misbehaving vehicle after the expiry of the timer. The function of this algorithm is elaborated for $R_j$ in $DT_v$. It compares $MESS_j$ attribute of $R_j$ with the value of the MESS attribute field of all other records in $DT_v$. In case of match, it increases $Match_j$ counter and in case of mismatch, it increases $Mismatch_j$ counter by 1 after each comparison. If $Match_j$ = $Mismatch_j$, it ignores $R_j$. If $Match_j > Mismatch_j$, the ALGO_V algorithm inserts

```
    {  i←1
       k←1
while (k < Number_BWOj){
if (O_MSGj (i, i+Size_BWO-1) represents AND bit wise operator)
   {MESSj←H_MSGj∧E_VINj
    Go to L1}
else if (O_MSGj (i, i+Size_BWO-1)represents OR bit wise operator)
   {MESSj←H_MSGj∨E_VINj
    Go to L1}
else if (O_MSGj (i, i+Size_BWO-1)represents XOR bit wise operator)
   {MESSj←H_MSGj⊕E_VINj
   Go to L1}
else
   Go to L1
L1: { i←i + Size_BWO
      k←k + 1} } }
```

**Listing 4.2** Retrieval of $MESS_j$ from $H\_MSG_j$

TRUE in the $REMARK_j$ attribute field of $R_j$. Otherwise it inserts FALSE in the $REMARK_j$ attribute field of $R_j$, inserts $E\_VIN_j$ in $CRL_v$, and increases a counter ($NEVIN\_CRL_v$) by 1. The ALGO_V algorithm repeats the same steps of operation for all the records in $DT_v$ to generate $CRL_v$. $V_v$ sends $CRL_v$ to its parent BS. The maximum number of E_VINs in $CRL_v$ is $NEVIN\_CRL_v$.

The sequential operation of $V_v$ in [3] is divided into five blocks in [4] as given below:

Block_1

- Receives the data packets of CA_CRL from $BS_B$
- Reads the E_VINs of misbehaving vehicles from each data packet and inserts them in a set CA_CRL
- Repeats the same steps of operation till the value in the SL_NO field of the received data packet is higher than the same in previously received data packets of CA_CRL
- Stores CA_CRL

Block_2

- Switches on a timer and initializes it to $\tau_v$
- Triggers Block_3 and Block_4
- Stops Block_3 and Block_4 and triggers Block_5 after the expiry of the timer

Block_3

- Receives $S\_MSG_j$
- Either accepts or discards $S\_MSG_j$
- Stores $S\_MSG_j$ in $Q_v$ if accepted
- Increases $NS\_MSG_v$ by 1
- Repeats the same steps of operation for all the received S_MSGs till it stops by Block_2

Block_4

- Reads $S\_MSG_j$ from $Q_v$
- Executes ALGO_MESS algorithm
- Inserts $R_j$ in $DT_v$
- Repeats the same steps of operation for the other S_MSGs in $Q_v$ till it stops by Block_2

Block_5

- Executes ALGO_V algorithm for all the records in $DT_v$ to generate $CRL_v$
- Fragments $CRL_v$ into data packets if $NEVIN\_CRL_v \times Size\_E\_VIN$ is greater than Size_DP
- Sends the data packets of $CRL_v$ to $BS_B$

#### 4.3.2.3 Function of $BS_B$

This function is elaborated for the schemes as mentioned in [3, 4]. In [3], $BS_B$ receives CA_CRL from CA and broadcasts it among vehicles under it. $BS_B$ switches on a timer and initializes it to $\tau_B$. It receives CRLs from the vehicles which are within its coverage area, stores them in a FIFO queue ($Q_B$), increases a counter (NB_CRL) after receiving each CRL by 1, and assigns the first received CRL to $CRL_B$. It starts to update $CRL_B$ by performing union operation among the existing $CRL_B$ and the received CRLs in $Q_B$ as soon as NB_CRL becomes equal to 2 and repeats the same steps of operation for the other received CRL till the timer expires. $BS_B$ sends $CRL_B$ to CA after the expiry of $\tau_B$. The maximum number of CRLs in $Q_B$ is NO_OF_$V_B$ and the maximum number of E_VINs in $CRL_B$ is assumed as NEVIN_$CRL_B$.

The sequential operation of $BS_B$ in [3] is divided into four blocks in [4] as given below:

Block_1
- Receives the data packets of CA_CRL from CA
- Broadcasts them among the vehicles under it

Block_2
- Switches on a timer and initializes it to $\tau_B$
- Triggers Block_3 and Block_4
- Stops Block_3 and Block_4 after the expiry of the timer

Block_3
- Receives the data packets of $CRL_v$ from $V_v$
- Reads the E_VINs of misbehaving vehicles from each data packet and inserts them in a set $CRL_v$
- Repeats the same steps of operation for all received data packets of $CRL_v$ till the value in the SL_NO field of the received data packet is higher than the same in previously received data packets and till the value in the E_MARK field of the received data packet becomes equal to 1
- Stores $CRL_v$ in $Q_B$
- Increases NB_CRL by 1
- Repeats the same steps of operation for the CRLs of other vehicles under $BS_B$ till it stops by Block_2

Block_4
- Starts to perform union operation among the CRLs in $Q_B$ for generating $CRL_B$ as soon as NB_CRL becomes equal to 2
- Repeats it till it stops by Block_2
- Fragments $CRL_B$ into few data packets if NEVIN_$CRL_B \times$Size_E_VIN is greater than Size_DP
- Sends the data packets of $CRL_B$ to CA

#### 4.3.2.4 Function of CA

It is elaborated for the schemes as mentioned in [3, 4]. In [3] CA switches on a timer and initializes it to $\tau_C$. It receives CRLs from the BSs within its coverage area, stores them in a FIFO queue ($Q_C$), increases a counter (NC_CRL) after receiving each CRL by 1, and assigns the first received CRL to CA_CRL. It starts to update CA_CRL by performing union operation among the existing CA_CRL and the received CRLs in $Q_C$ as soon as NC_CRL becomes equal to 2 till the timer expires. CA broadcasts CA_CRL among the vehicles within its coverage area after the expiry of $\tau_C$. The maximum number of CRLs in $Q_C$ is NO_OF_BS and the maximum number of E_VINs in CA_CRL is assumed as NEVIN_CA_CRL.

The sequential operation of CA in [3] is divided into three blocks in [4] as given below:

Block_1

- Switches on a timer and initializes it to $\tau_C$
- Triggers Block_2 and Block_3
- Stops Block_2 and Block_3 after the expiry of the timer

Block_2

- Receives the data packets of $CRL_B$ from $BS_B$
- Reads the E_VINs of misbehaving vehicles from each data packet and inserts them in a set $CRL_B$
- Repeats the same steps of operation for all the received data packets of $CRL_B$ till the value in the SL_NO field of the received data packet is higher than the same in previously received data packets and till the value in the E_MARK field of the received data packet becomes equal to 1
- Stores $CRL_B$ in $Q_C$
- Increases NC_CRL by 1
- Repeats the same steps of operation for the CRLs of other BSs under CA till it stops by Block_1

Block_3

- Starts to perform union operation among the CRLs in $Q_C$ for generating CA_CRL as soon as NC_CRL becomes equal to 2
- Repeats it till it stops by Block_1
- Fragments CA_CRL into few data packets if NEVIN_CA_CRL$\times$Size_E_VIN is greater than Size_DP
- Broadcasts the data packets of CA_CRL among the vehicles under it

Unlike [16, 18], the present work uses steganography to protect S_MSGs from intruder in VANET. The use of encryption/decryption algorithm for secure message transmission consumes a considerable amount of time due to their computational hardness. Moreover the length of message may increase during encryption which increases storage overhead along with communication overhead. In the present work, CA_CRL consists of E_VIN of the misbehaving vehicles instead of their IP address like [23]. So only the E_VIN of a vehicle is sufficient to identify, detect, and revoke misbehaving vehicles from VANET. Unlike [23] the present work performs well in high density of vehicles. In [23] CA distributes pieces of CRL among vehicles via RSUs. So in the worst case, a vehicle needs to encounter all the RSUs for collecting all the pieces of CRL. Hence the performance of CRL generation degrades if congestion occurs, if vehicles move slowly, and if the distance between RSUs increases. The misbehaving vehicles are identified by their E_VINs during V2V communication in [3, 4]. So no extra task is required to assign to a vehicle for identifying misbehaving vehicle like [24]. There is no requirement of reporting the reason of revocation to CA in [3, 4] like [15] which helps to reduce the delay in revocation.

## 4.4 Simulation

In this section, the simulation results of both the phases of work are reported.

### *4.4.1 Simulation Results of Phase_I*

The simulation parameters are considered for discussion in this section. The performance of the schemes as discussed in [1, 2] is evaluated and compared qualitatively and quantitatively.

#### 4.4.1.1 Simulation Parameters

The Size_E_VIN is 17 N bits where $N=\log_2[2^{\max(P,Q)}-1]$ and P, Q are prime numbers used in RSA algorithm. The size of D_Sig (Size_D_Sig) is 160 bits [22].

The value of R is assumed as 1000 m to support DSRC. The transmission time of $E\_VIN_v$ from $V_v$ to $BS_B$ is TT_VBS_E_VIN and from $BS_B$ to CA is TT_BSCA_E_VIN in [1]. The transmission time of $E\_VIN_v$ from $BS_B$ to $F\_CA_C$ is TT_BSFCA_E_VIN and from $F\_CA_C$ to R_CA is TT_FCARCA_E_VIN in [2]. All these parameters are (Size_E_VIN/Data_TR) secs. Data_TR is the data transmission rate and is assumed as 6 Mbps [25]. Hence all these parameters are proportional to Size_E_VIN.

The waiting time of $E\_VIN_v$ at $BS_B$_VIN_Queue ($WT\_BSB\_E\_VIN_v$) is $\sum_{i=1}^{J}(ST\_BSB\_E\_VIN_i)$, where $ST\_BSB\_E\_VIN_i$ is the searching time of $VIN\_BS_B$ for $E\_VIN_i$ of $i^{th}$ vehicle and J is the number of encrypted VIN waiting in $BS_B$_VIN_Queue in front of $E\_VIN_v$. $ST\_BSB\_E\_VIN_i$ depends upon the size of $VIN\_BS_B$. $VIN\_BS_B$ contains the encrypted VIN and digital signature pair of authentic vehicles. So the size of $VIN\_BS_B$ depends upon the maximum number of authentic vehicles in VANET, Size_E_VIN, and Size_D_Sig.

The decryption time of $E\_VIN_v$ (D_Time) depends upon the size of secret key in RSA algorithm.

The time to check the validity of $D\_VIN_v$ (VT_D_VIN) depends upon the size of $D\_VIN_v$. So it is constant as the size of $D\_VIN_v$ is constant to 17 characters.

As $D\_Sig_v$ is generated using SHA-1 algorithm, so the digital signature generation time (D_Sig_Time) is constant, and it is 15 msec which has been observed during simulation.

The waiting time of $E\_VIN_v$ at CA_VIN_Queue ($WT\_CA\_E\_VIN_v$) in [1] is $\sum_{i=1}^{T} (WT\_CA\_E\_VIN_i)$, where $WT\_CA\_E\_VIN_i$ is the waiting time of $E\_VIN_i$ at CA_VIN_Queue and T is the number of encrypted VIN waiting in CA_VIN_Queue in front of $E\_VIN_v$. $WT\_CA\_E\_VIN_i$ is the sum of D_Time, VT_D_VIN, and D_Sig_Time.

The waiting time of $E\_VIN_v$ at R_CA_VIN_Queue ($WT\_RCA\_E\_VIN_v$) in [2] is $\sum_{i=1}^{T} (WT\_RCA\_E\_VIN_i)$, where $WT\_RCA\_E\_VIN_i$ is the waiting time of $E\_VIN_i$ at R_CA_VIN_Queue and T is the number of encrypted VIN waiting in R_CA_VIN_Queue in front of $E\_VIN_v$. $WT\_RCA\_E\_VIN_i$ is the sum of D_Time, VT_D_VIN, and D_Sig_Time.

The transmission time of $B_v$ from CA to all the BSs under CA is B_CA_BS in [1]. The transmission time of $B_v$ from R_CA to $F\_CA_C$ is B_RCA_FCA and from $F\_CA_C$ to all the BSs under $F\_CA_C$ is B_FCA_BS in [2]. All these parameters are (Size_B/Data_TR) secs where Size_B is the size of $B_v$ and it is (Size_E_VIN + Size_D_Sig) bits. Hence all these parameters are proportional to Size_B.

The transmission time of $D\_Sig_v$ from $Current\_BS_v$ to $V_v$ (V_BS_D_Sig) is (Size_D_Sig/Data_TR) secs, and it is constant.

#### 4.4.1.2 Qualitative Analysis

The qualitative performance of both the schemes is evaluated on the basis of communication overhead per vehicle per initial registration phase and storage overhead per vehicle per initial registration phase.

Communication Overhead per Vehicle

The communication overhead of $V_v$ (COMM_OH) is due to the following:

- Transmission of $E\_VIN_v$ for initial registration phase
  The communication overhead of sending $E\_VIN_v$ from $V_v$ to CA through $BS_B$ in [1] is 2×Size_E_VIN bits, whereas from $V_v$ to R_CA through $BS_B$ and $F\_CA_C$ in [2] is 3×Size_E_VIN bits.
- Reception of $B_v$ after initial registration phase

The communication overhead of sending $B_v$ from CA to Current_BS$_v$ in [1] is Size_B bits. The communication overhead of sending $B_v$ from R_CA to Current_BS$_v$ through F_CA$_C$ in [2] is 2×Size_B bits.

- Assignment of D_Sig$_v$ by Current_BS$_v$ to $V_v$
  The communication overhead of tracking $V_v$ is due to the assignment of D_Sig$_v$ by Current_BS$_v$. So it is Size_D_Sig bits for both the schemes.

So COMM_OH in [1] (COMM_OH_I) is [(2×Size_E_VIN) + Size_B + Size_D_Sig]/Data_TR secs and in [2] (COMM_OH_II) is [(3×Size_E_VIN) + (2×Size_B) +Size_D_Sig]/Data_TR secs.

Figure 4.2 shows the plot of COMM_OH vs. Size_E_VIN for both the schemes. It can be observed from Fig. 4.2 that both COMM_OH_I and COMM_OH_II increase with Size_E_VIN.

Storage Overhead per Vehicle

The CA in [1] and R_CA in [2] use VIN_CA to gather knowledge about the available pattern of VINs of the vehicles that are already manufactured. As VIN_CA is not required during the initial registration phase of $V_v$, the storage overhead of both the schemes for $V_v$ (STO_OH) is assumed as independent on the size of VIN_CA.

The storage overhead of $V_v$ (STO_OH) is due to the following: storage of $B_v$ in VIN_BS of NO_OF_BS number of BSs under CA in [1] and under F_CA$_C$ in [2] after the initial registration phase of $V_v$.

So, STO_OH is NO_OF_BS×Size_B bits for both the schemes.

Figure 4.3 shows the plot of STO_OH vs. Size_E_VIN for both the schemes. It can be observed from Fig. 4.3 that STO_OH increases with Size_E_VIN.

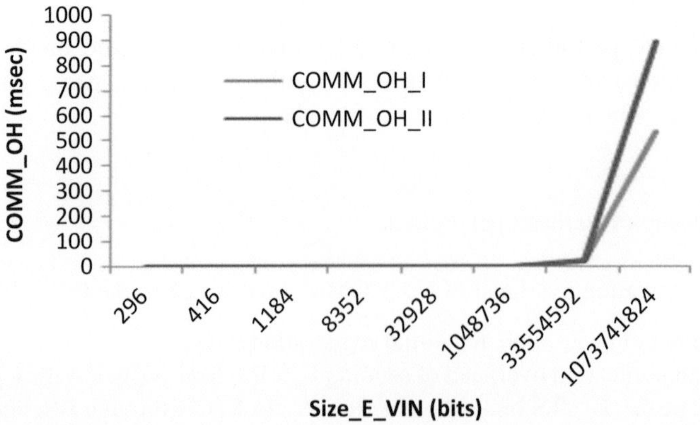


**Fig. 4.2** COMM_OH vs. Size_E_VIN

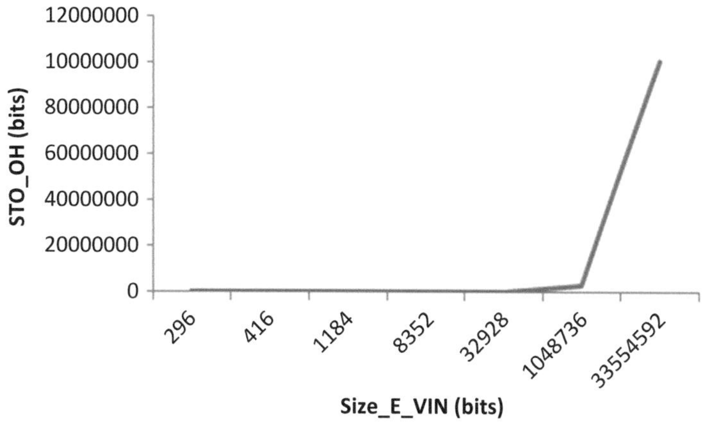


**Fig. 4.3** STO_OH vs. Size_E_VIN

#### 4.4.1.3 Quantitative Analysis

The effectiveness of the schemes mentioned in [1, 2] is evaluated through quantitative analysis in this section. The experiment is conducted to observe the variation of the VIN processing time (VIN_P_Time) and block of service (BL_SE) as a function of the number of vehicles for both the schemes.

VIN_P_Time: The VIN_P_Time of $V_v$ (VIN_P_Time$_v$) is the time to assign D_Sig$_v$ to $V_v$ after receiving its E_VIN$_v$. The VIN_P_Time$_v$ in [1] (VIN_P_Time_I$_v$) is the sum of TT_VBS_E_VIN, WT_BSB_E_VIN$_v$, ST_BSB_E_VIN$_v$, TT_BSCA_E_VIN, WT_CA_E_VIN$_v$, D_Time, VT_D_VIN, D_Sig_Time, B_CA_BS, and V_BS_D_Sig.

The VIN_P_Time$_v$ in [2] (VIN_P_Time_II$_v$) is the sum of TT_VBS_E_VIN, WT_BSB_E_VIN$_v$, ST_BSB_E_VIN$_v$, TT_BSFCA_E_VIN, TT_FCA_RCA_E_VIN, WT_RCA_E_VIN$_v$, D_Time, VT_D_VIN, D_Sig_Time, B_RCA_FCA, B_FCA_BS, and V_BS_D_Sig.

Figures 4.4 and 4.5 show the plot of VIN_P_Time_I$_v$ and VIN_P_Time_II$_v$ vs. number of vehicles, respectively. Both VIN_P_Time_I$_v$ and VIN_P_Time_II$_v$ increase with the number of vehicles as observed from Figs. 4.4 and 4.5, respectively.

BL_SE: The BL_SE in [1] is BL_SE_I and in [2] is BL_SE_II. In both the schemes, block of service occurs at a BS due to the unavailability of channels. Figures 4.6 and 4.7 show the plot of BL_SE_I and BL_SE_II vs. number of vehicles, respectively.

The COMM_OH_II and VIN_P_Time_II$_v$ are higher than COMM_OH_I and VIN_P_Time_I$_v$ due to an extra level in the VANET hierarchy in [2]. Moreover [2] provides service to more vehicles than in [1]. So the size of VIN_BS$_B$ and R_CA_VIN_Queue in [2] is higher than the size of VIN_BS$_B$ and CA_VIN_Queue in [1] which increases ST_BSB_E_VIN$_v$ and WT_RCA_E_VIN$_v$ in [2] than

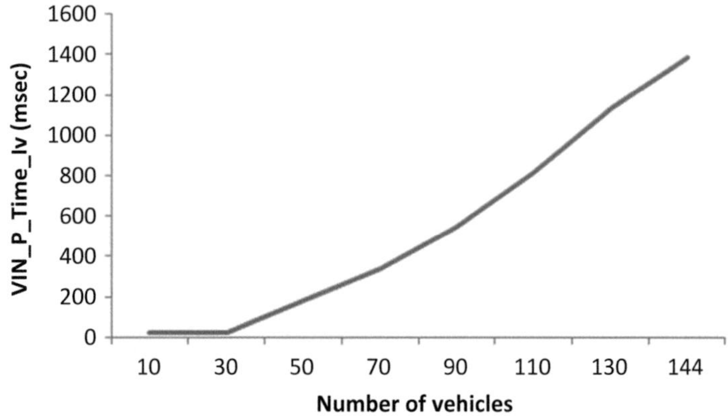


**Fig. 4.4** VIN_P_Time_$I_v$ vs. number of vehicles

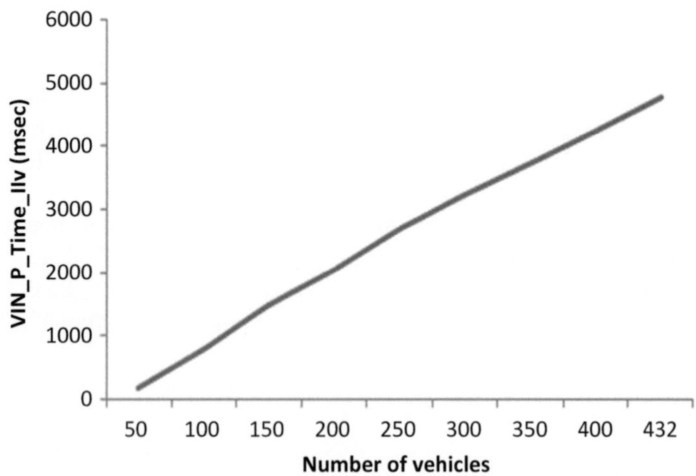


**Fig. 4.5** VIN_P_Time_$II_v$ vs. number of vehicles

ST_BSB_E_$VIN_v$ and WT_CA_E_$VIN_v$ in [1]. BL_SE_II is higher than BL_SE_I due to the increase in number of vehicles. Moreover as [2] can accommodate more vehicles than [1], BL_SE_II starts to increase from number of vehicles greater than 100, whereas BL_SE_I starts to increase from number of vehicles greater than 40.

### *4.4.2 Simulation Results of Phase_II*

The simulation parameters are considered for discussion. The performance of [3, 4] is evaluated and compared qualitatively and quantitatively.

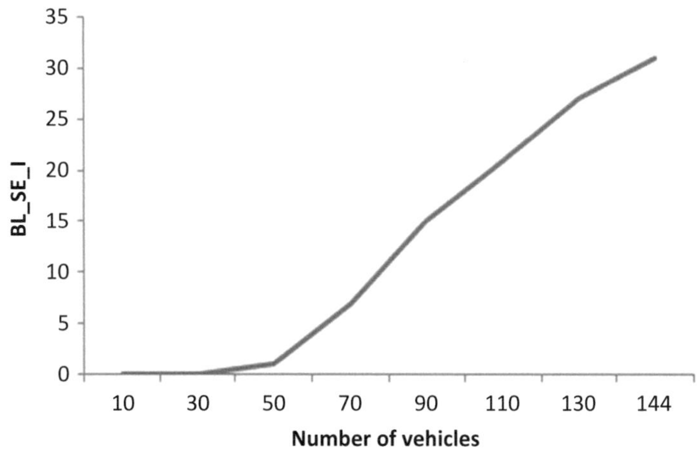


**Fig. 4.6** BL_SE_I vs. number of vehicles

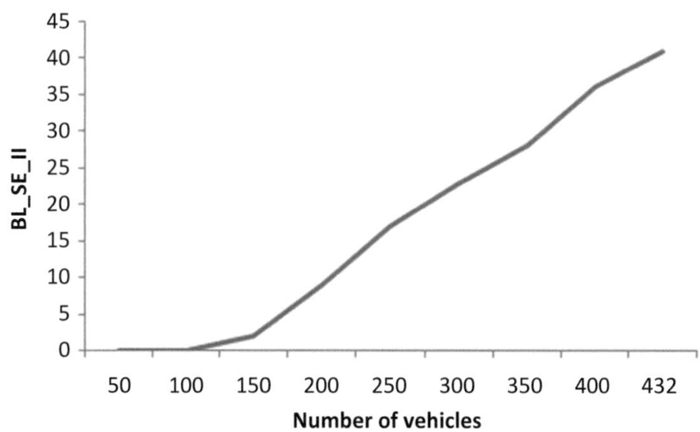


**Fig. 4.7** BL_SE_II vs. number of vehicles

#### 4.4.2.1 Simulation Parameters

The Size_E_VIN is 136 bits as discussed in Sect. 4.3.2. The bit-wise operation is performed among H_MSG and E_VIN to retrieve MESS from H_MSG. Hence the size of H_MSG (Size_H_MSG) and the size of MESS (Size_MESS) are 136 bits. The size of S_MSG (Size_SMSG) is (Size_D_Sig + Size_E_VIN + Size_H_MSG + Size_O_MSG) bits. The value of $\tau_v$, $\tau_B$, $\tau_C$, NO_OF_BS, NEVIN_CRL$_v$, NEVIN_CRL$_B$, NEVIN_CA_CRL, NO_OF_V$_B$, NS_MSG$_v$, and Size_SMSG are assumed as 30 s, 20 s, 20 s, 3, 400, 400, 1200, 144, 400, and 3232 bits. The Data_TR is assumed as 6 Mb/s.

### 4.4.2.2 Qualitative Analysis

The qualitative performance of both the schemes is evaluated on the basis of communication overhead (COMM_OH), storage overhead (STO_OH), and computation overhead (COMP_OH). The qualitative performance is evaluated by considering the maximum length of $Q_v$, $Q_B$, and $Q_C$, i.e., $Q_v$ has $NS\_MSG_v$ number of S_MSGs, $Q_B$ has $NO\_OF\_V_B$ number of CRLs, and $Q_C$ has NO_OF_BS number of CRLs. The qualitative performance of the proposed scheme is compared with [26] on the basis of STO_OH.

Communication Overhead

The COMM_OH of the schemes as mentioned in [3, 4] is $\sum_{B=1}^{NO\_OF\_BS} (COMM\_OH_B)/Data\_TR$ sec where $COMM\_OH_B$ is the communication overhead of $BS_B$ in bits.

$COMM\_OH_B$

It is due to the following:

- Reception of CRLs from $NO\_OF\_V_B$ number of vehicles within its coverage area
  Size of $CRL_v$ in [3] is ($NEVIN\_CRL_v \times Size\_E\_VIN$) bits and in [4] is ($Size\_DP \times \lceil NEVIN\_CRL_v/M_v \rceil$) bits in the worst case. Hence $COMM\_OH_B$ due to the reception of $NO\_OF\_V_B$ number of CRLs in [3] is $\sum_{v=1}^{NO\_OF\_V_B} (NEVIN\_CRL_v \times Size\_E\_VIN)$ bits and in [4] is $\sum_{v=1}^{NO\_OF\_V_B} (Size\_DP \times \lceil NEVIN\_CRL_v \times M_v \rceil)$ bits.
- Transmission of $CRL_B$ to CA
  $COMM\_OH_B$ due to the transmission of $CRL_B$ in [3] is ($NEVIN\_CRL_B \times Size\_E\_VIN$) bits and in [4] is ($Size\_DP \times \lceil NEVIN\_CRL_B/M_B \rceil$) bits.
- Reception of CA_CRL from CA
  $COMM\_OH_B$ due to the reception of CA_CRL in [3] is ($NEVIN\_CA\_CRL \times Size\_E\_VIN$) bits and in [4] is ($Size\_DP \times \lceil NEVIN\_CA\_CRL/M_{CA} \rceil$) bits.
- Transmission of CA_CRL to $NO\_OF\_V_B$ number of vehicles within its coverage area
  Hence $COMM\_OH_B$ due to the transmission of CA_CRL in [3] is ($NO\_OF\_V_B \times NEVIN\_CA\_CRL \times Size\_E\_VIN$) bits and in [4] is $NO\_OF\_V_B \times$ ($Size\_DP \times \lceil NEVIN\_CA\_CRL/M_{CA} \rceil$) bits.

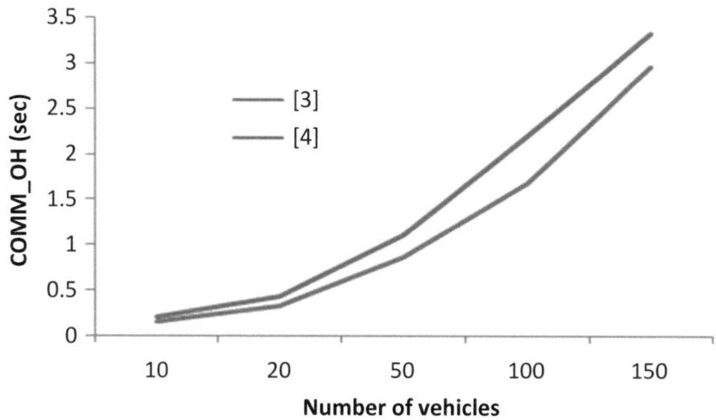


**Fig. 4.8** COMM_OH vs. number of vehicles

Hence, $COMM\_OH_B$ in [3] is $\sum_{v=1}^{NO\_OF\_V_B}(NEVIN\_CRL_v \times Size\_E\_VIN) + Size\_E\_VIN \times (NEVIN\_CRL_B + NEVIN\_CA\_CRL\ (1 + NO\_OF\_V_B))$ bits, and in [4], it is $\sum_{v=1}^{NO\_OF\_V_B}(Size\_DP \times \lceil NEVIN\_CRL_v \times M_v \rceil) + (Size\_DP \times \lceil NEVIN\_CRL_B / M_B \rceil) + (1 + NO\_OF\_V_B) \times (Size\_DP \times \lceil NEVIN\_CA\_CRL / M_{CA} \rceil)$ bits.

Figure 4.8 shows the plot of *COMM_OH* vs. number of vehicles for [3, 4].

Storage Overhead

The STO_OH of both the schemes [3, 4] is the sum of STO_OH of CA (STO_OH_CA) and STO_OH of NO_OF_BS number of BSs under CA (STO_OH_BS).

STO_OH_CA is due to the following:

- Maintenance of NO_OF_BS number of $CRL_B$ in $Q_C$

  Hence STO_OH_CA is $\sum_{B=1}^{NO\_OF\_BS}(NEVIN\_CRL_B \times Size\_E\_VIN)$ bits.

STO_OH_BS is $\sum_{B=1}^{NO\_OF\_BS}(STO\_OH_B)$ bits where $STO\_OH_B$ is STO_OH of $BS_B$ and $NO\_OF\_V_B$ number of vehicles under $BS_B$.

$STO\_OH_B$ is due to the:

- Maintenance of $Q_B$
- Maintenance of $NO\_OF\_V_B$ number of $Q_v$
- Maintenance of $NO\_OF\_V_B$ number of $DT_v$

Now $Q_B$ has $NO\_OF\_V_B$ number of CRLs, and hence size of $Q_B$ ($Size\_Q_B$) is $\sum_{v=1}^{NO\_OF\_V_B}(NEVIN\_CRL_v \times Size\_E\_VIN)$ bits.

$Q_v$ has $NS\_MSG_v$ number of S_MSGs, and hence the size of $Q_v$ ($Size\_Q_v$) is $\sum_{j=1}^{NS\_MSG_v} Size\_SMSG_j$ bits, where $Size\_SMSG_j$ is the size of $S\_MSG_j$.

$DT_v$ has $NS\_MSG_v$ number of records. The size of REMARK attribute in each record is 1 bit and the size of $R_j$ ($Size\_R_j$) is ($Size\_E\_VIN+Size\_MESS_j+1$) bits.

Hence the size of $DT_v$ ($Size\_DT_v$) is $\sum_{j=1}^{NS\_MSG_v} Size\_R_j$ bits.

Hence $STO\_OH_B = Size\_Q_B + \sum_{v=1}^{NO\_OF\_V_B} (Size\_Q_v + Size\_DT_v)$ bits.

Figure 4.9 shows the plot of STO_OH vs. number of vehicles. STO_OH in [3, 4] is less than [26] as observed from Fig. 4.9.

### Computation Overhead

The COMP_OH is the sum of COMP_OH of CA (COMP_OH_CA) and COMP_OH of NO_OF_BS number of BSs under CA (COMP_OH_BS).

COMP_OH_CA in [3] is for:

- Updating NC_CRL
- Performing union operation among the received CRLs from NO_OF_BS number of BSs

COMP_OH_CA in [4] is for:

- Updating NC_CRL
- Performing union operation among the received CRLs from NO_OF_BS number of BSs
- Regeneration of NO_OF_BS number of CRLs from the received data packets
- Fragmentation of CA_CRL among the number of data packets

Now COMP_OH for updating NC_CRL for NO_OF_BS times is O (NO_OF_BS), for performing union operation among NO_OF_BS number of

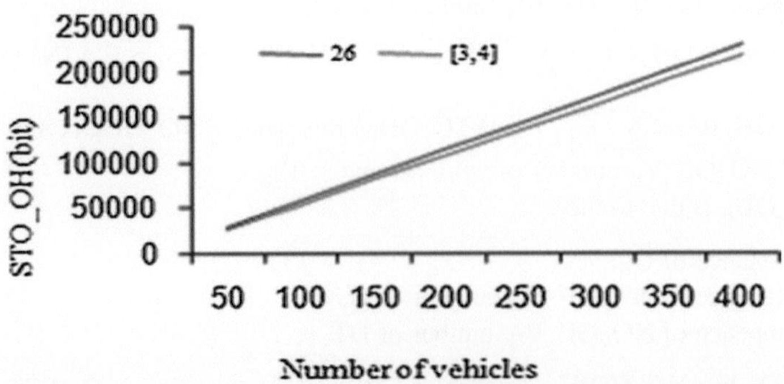


**Fig. 4.9** STO_OH vs. number of vehicles

CRLs is O(⌈log (NO_OF_BS)⌉), for regenerating NO_OF_BS number of CRLs is $O\left(\sum_{B=1}^{NO\_OF\_BS}(NEVIN\_CRL_B)\right)$, and for fragmentation of CA_CRL is O (NEVIN_CA_CRL).

Hence COMP_OH_CA in [3] is O(NO_OF_BS+⌈log (NO_OF_BS)⌉) and in [4] is $O(NO\_OF\_BS + \lceil\log(NO\_OF\_BS)\rceil + \sum_{B=1}^{NO\_OF\_BS}(NEVIN\_CRL_B) + NEVIN\_CA\_CRL)$.

COMP_OH_BS is $O\left(\sum_{B=1}^{NO\_OF\_BS}(COMP\_OH_B)\right)$ where $COMP\_OH_B$ is the sum of COMP_OH of $BS_B$ and $NO\_OF\_V_B$ number of vehicles under it.

COMP_OH of $BS_B$ in [3] is for:

- Updating NB_CRL
- Performing union operation among the received CRLs from $NO\_OF\_V_B$ number of vehicles

COMP_OH of $BS_B$ in [4] is for:

- Updating NB_CRL
- Performing union operation among the received CRLs from $NO\_OF\_V_B$ number of vehicles
- Regeneration of $NO\_OF\_V_B$ number of CRLs from the received data packets
- Fragmentation of $CRL_B$ among number of data packets

Now COMP_OH of updating NB_CRL for $NO\_OF\_V_B$ times is O ($NO\_OF\_V_B$), for performing union operation among $NO\_OF\_V_B$ number of CRLs is O(⌈log ($NO\_OF\_V_B$)⌉), for regenerating $NO\_OF\_V_B$ number of CRLs is $O\left(\sum_{v=1}^{NO\_OF\_V_B}(NEVIN\_CRL_v)\right)$, and for fragmentation of $CRL_B$ is O ($NEVIN\_CRL_B$).

Hence COMP_OH of $BS_B$ in [3] is O($NO\_OF\_V_B$+⌈log ($NO\_OF\_V_B$)⌉) and in [4] is $O(NO\_OF\_V_B + \lceil\log(NO\_OF\_V_B)\rceil + \sum_{v=1}^{NO\_OF\_V_B}(NEVIN\_CRL_v) + NEVIN\_CRL_B)$.

COMP_OH of $V_v$ ($COMP\_OH_v$) in [3] is the sum of:

- Searching overhead of CA_CRL for $NS\_MSG_v$ number of E_VINs
- Execution overhead of ALGO_MESS and ALGO_V

$COMP\_OH_v$ in [4] is the sum of:

- Searching overhead of CA_CRL for $NS\_MSG_v$ number of E_VINs
- Execution overhead of ALGO_MESS and ALGO_V
- Regeneration overhead of CA_CRL
- Fragmentation overhead of $CRL_v$

Now, COMP_OH to search CA_CRL for $NS\_MSG_v$ number of E_VINs corresponding to $NS\_MSG_v$ number of received S_MSGs in $Q_v$ is O ($NS\_MSG_v \times NEVIN\_CA\_CRL \times Size\_E\_VIN$), to execute ALGO_MESS

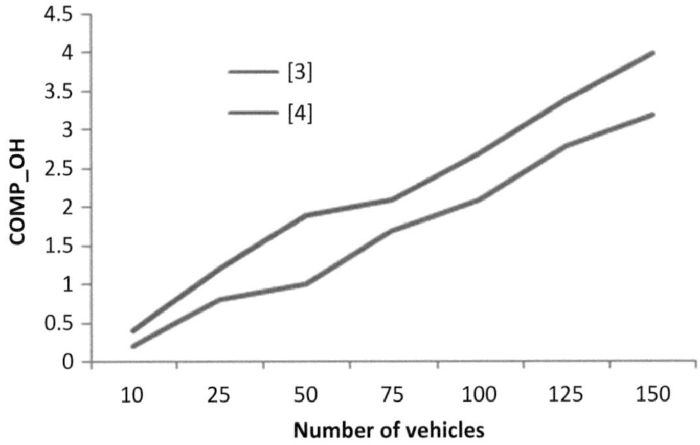


**Fig. 4.10** COMP_OH vs. number of vehicles

algorithm for $NS\_MSG_v$ number of S_MSGs is O (Number_BWO×Size_H_MSG×$NS\_MSG_v$), to execute ALGO_V algorithm for $NS\_MSG_v$ number of records in $DT_v$ is $O(NS\_MSG_v{}^2)$, to regenerate CA_CRL is O (NEVIN_CA_CRL), and to fragment $CRL_v$ is $O(NEVIN\_CRL_v)$.

Hence $COMP\_OH_v$ in [3] is $O((NS\_MSG_v \times NEVIN\_CA\_CRL \times Size\_E\_VIN) + (Number\_BWO \times Size\_H\_MSG \times NS\_MSG_v) + (NS\_MSG_v{}^2))$ and in [4], it is $O((NS\_MSG_v \times NEVIN\_CA\_CRL \times Size\_E\_VIN) + (Number\_BWO \times Size\_H\_MSG \times NS\_MSG_v) + (NS\_MSG_v{}^2) + NEVIN\_CA\_CRL + NEVIN\_CRL_v)$. COMP_OH of $NO\_OF\_V_B$ number of vehicles under $BS_B$ is $\sum_{v=1}^{NO\_OF\_V_B} (COMP\_OH_v)$. Figure 4.10 shows the plot of COMP_OH vs. number of vehicles.

#### 4.4.2.3 Quantitative Analysis

The performance of both the schemes [3, 4] is studied quantitatively on the basis of CA_CRL generation time (CA_CRL_GT) and CA_CRL distribution time (CA_CRL_DT). Both the parameters are determined during simulation. The performance of [4] is evaluated for two cases. The number of blocks at $V_v$, BS, and CA is 5, 4, and 3, respectively, in case 1 (Case_1) as discussed in Sect. 4.3.2. In case 2 (Case_2) the number of blocks reduces to four at vehicle by merging Block_3 and Block_4 into Block_3, to 3 at BS by merging Block_3 and Block_4 into Block_3, and to 2 at CA by merging Block_2 and Block_3 into Block_2. The simulation experiment of [4] is done by considering five threads at each vehicle, four threads at each BS, and three threads at CA in Case_1, whereas four threads at each vehicle, three threads at each BS, and two threads at CA in Case_2.

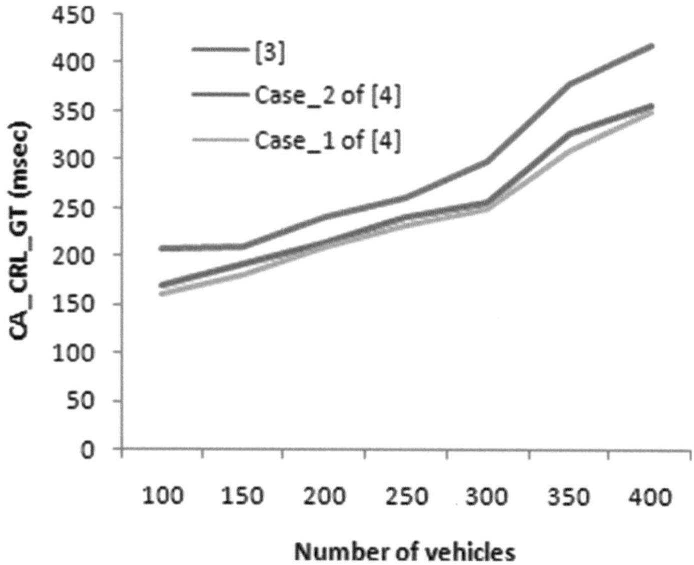


**Fig. 4.11** CA_CRL_GT vs. number of vehicles

CA_CRL_GT

It is the time required by CA to generate CA_CRL. It is the sum of the time required to generate CRL by vehicles, BSs and CA. Figure 4.11 shows the plot of CA_CRL_GT vs. the number of vehicles in VANET. The waiting time of S_MSGs in FIFO queue at vehicles and CRLs in FIFO queue at BS and CA increases with the number of vehicles which in turn increase CA_CRL_GT as observed from Fig. 4.11. CA_CRL_GT in both the cases of [4] is less than [3].

CA_CRL_DT

It is the time required to distribute CA_CRL by CA among the vehicles under it. Figure 4.12 shows the plot of CA_CRL_DT vs. the number of vehicles in VANET. CA_CRL_DT depends upon the size of CA_CRL (Size_CA_CRL). The Size_CA_CRL depends upon the number of misbehaving vehicles which in turn depends upon the number of vehicles in VANET. Hence CA_CRL_DT increases slowly with the number of vehicles in both the schemes as observed from Fig. 4.12. CA_CRL_DT is almost identical in [3] and in both the cases of [4] but it is less than [27].

Figure 4.13 shows the plot of CA_CRL_DT vs. Size_CA_CRL. The Size_CA_CRL is computed as NEVIN_CA_CRL $\times$ Size_E_VIN bits. It can be observed from Fig. 4.13 that CA_CRL_DT increases with Size_CA_CRL in [3, 18]

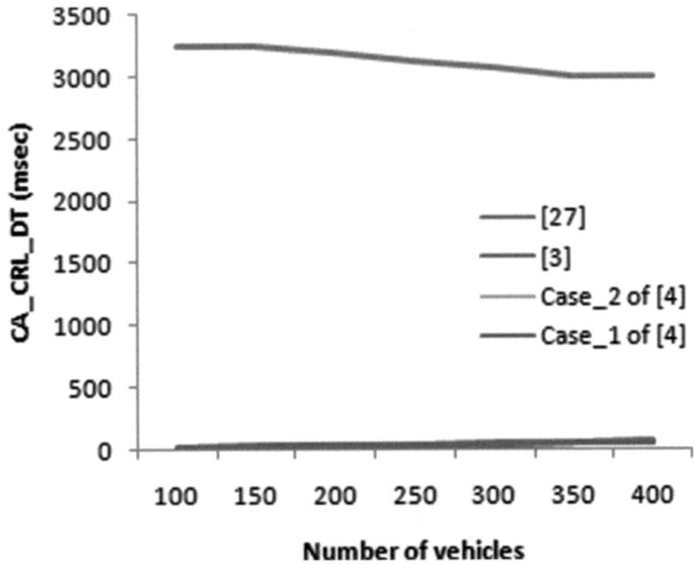


**Fig. 4.12** CA_CRL_DT vs. number of vehicles

and also in the two cases of [4]. In [18] Size_CA_CRL is 1 Mbyte and CA_CRL_DT is around 300 s (Fig. 4.13i). Both in [3] and [4], Size_CA_CRL varies dynamically with NEVIN_CA_CRL, and hence CA_CRL_DT increases slowly (Fig. 4.13ii) with Size_CA_CRL but it is less than [18].

## 4.5 Conclusion

In this chapter, vehicle authentication and misbehaving vehicle revocation schemes are elaborated in two phases. The unauthentic vehicles are identified in Phase_I of the experiment by CA and BS, whereas misbehaving vehicles are detected and revoked jointly by vehicles, BSs and CA in Phase_II of the experiment.

The BS allocates the available channels among authentic vehicles randomly in [1, 2]. Each BS can allocate channels among authentic vehicles depending upon their residing probability within its coverage area which helps to reduce block of service. The CA in [3, 4] may revoke misbehaving vehicles by not allowing them to access the service channel but allowing them to access the control channel until the owner of those vehicles is penalized. It helps to eliminate CA_CRL distribution overhead among vehicles, CA_CRL storage overhead at vehicles, and CA_CRL searching overhead of the vehicles after receiving any S_MSGs.

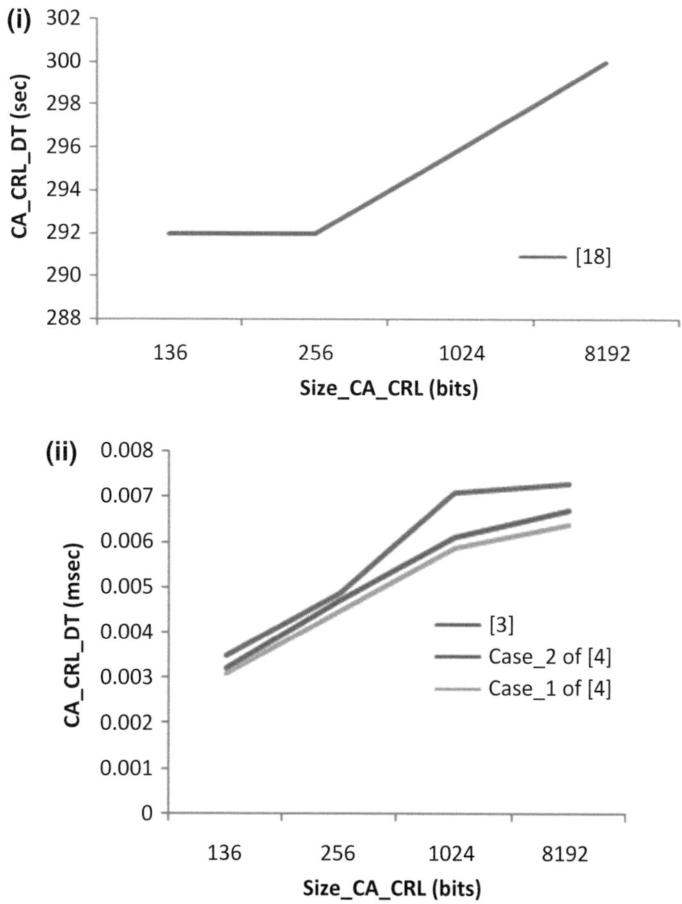


**Fig. 4.13** **i** CA_CRL_DT vs. Size_CA_CRL for [18]. **ii** CA_CRL_DT vs. Size_CA_CRL for [3, 4]

# Appendix

| Parameter name | Parameter description |
|---|---|
| BS | Base station |
| $BS_B$ | $B^{th}$ base station |
| $BS_B$_VIN_Queue | VIN queue at $BS_B$ |
| $B_v$ | ($E\_VIN_v$, $D\_Sig_v$) pair |
| B_CA_BS | Transmission time of $B_v$ from CA to BSs |
| B_RCA_FCA | Transmission time of $B_v$ from R_CA to $F\_CA_C$ |
| B_FCA_BS | Transmission time of $B_v$ from $F\_CA_C$ to BS |
| BL_SE | Block of service |

(continued)

| Parameter name | Parameter description |
|---|---|
| BL_SE_I | BL_SE in [1] |
| BL_SE_II | BL_SE in [2] |
| CA | Certifying authority |
| CRL | Certificate revocation list |
| CA_CRL | CRL generated by CA |
| $CRL_v$ | CRL generated by $V_v$ |
| $CRL_B$ | CRL generated by $BS_B$ |
| CCTV | Closed-circuit television |
| Current_$BS_v$ | Current BS of $V_v$ |
| $CH_v$ | Channel assigned to $V_v$ |
| CA_VIN_Queue | VIN queue at CA |
| COMM_OH | Communication overhead |
| COMM_OH_I | COMM_OH in [1] |
| COMM_OH_II | COMM_OH in [2] |
| COMM_$OH_B$ | COMM_OH of $BS_B$ |
| COMP_OH | Computation overhead |
| COMP_OH_CA | COMP_OH at CA |
| COMP_OH_BS | COMP_OH at BS |
| COMP_$OH_B$ | COMP_OH at $BS_B$ |
| COMP_$OH_v$ | COMP_OH at $V_v$ |
| CA_CRL_GT | CA_CRL generation time |
| CA_CRL_DT | CA_CRL distribution time |
| DSRC | Dedicated short-range communication |
| Dist_V_BS | Distance from vehicle to BS |
| Dist_BS_CA | Distance from BS to CA |
| Dist_BS_FCA | Distance from BS to FCA |
| Dist_FCA_RCA | Distance from FCA to RCA |
| D_Sig | Digital signature |
| D_$Sig_v$ | D_Sig of $V_v$ |
| D_$Sig_j$ | D_Sig of $V_j$ |
| $DT_v$ | Data table at $V_v$ |
| D_$VIN_v$ | Decrypted VIN of $V_v$ |
| DoS | Denial of Service |
| DDoS | Distributed DoS |
| Data_TR | Data transmission rate |
| D_Time | Decryption time of E_VIN |
| D_Sig_Time | D_Sig generation time |
| ELP | Electronic license plate |
| E_VIN | Encrypted VIN |
| E_$VIN_j$ | E_VIN of $V_j$ |
| E_$VIN_v$ | E_VIN of $V_v$ |
| E_MARK | Identify last data packet associated with a CRL |
| F_CA | First-level CA |

(continued)

| Parameter name | Parameter description |
|---|---|
| $F\_CA_C$ | $C^{th}$ F_CA |
| GPS | Global positioning system |
| $H\_MSG_j$ | Hidden message part of $S\_MSG_j$ |
| IoT | Internet of Things |
| IoV | Internet of Vehicles |
| IVC | Inter-vehicle communication |
| $M_B$ | Maximum number of E_VINs of misbehaving vehicles in each data packet of $CRL_B$ |
| $M_{CA}$ | Maximum number of E_VINs of misbehaving vehicles in each data packet of CA_CRL |
| $M_v$ | Maximum number of E_VINs of misbehaving vehicles in each data packet of $CRL_v$ |
| $MESS_j$ | Message after retrieval from $H\_MSG_j$ |
| $NEVIN\_CRL_v$ | Maximum number of E_VINs in $CRL_v$ |
| $NEVIN\_CRL_B$ | Maximum number of E_VINs in $CRL_B$ |
| NEVIN_CA_CRL | Maximum number of E_VINs in CA_CRL |
| NO_OF_BS | Number of BSs under CA |
| NO_OF_FCA | Number of F_CAs under R_CA |
| NC_CRL | Counter at CA |
| NB_CRL | Counter at $BS_B$ |
| $NS\_MSG_v$ | Number of S_MSGs in $Q_v$ |
| $NO\_OF\_V_B$ | Number of vehicles under $BS_B$ |
| Number_BWO | Number of bit-wise operations |
| $Number\_BWO_j$ | Number_BWO among $H\_MSG_j$ and $E\_VIN_j$ |
| $O\_MSG_j$ | Operational part of $S\_MSG_j$ |
| P | Prime number used in RSA algorithm |
| Q | Prime number used in RSA algorithm |
| $Q_B$ | FIFO queue at $BS_B$ |
| $Q_C$ | FIFO queue at CA |
| $Q_v$ | FIFO queue at $V_v$ |
| R_CA | Root CA |
| RSU | Road side unit |
| RSA | Rivest Shamir Adleman |
| $R_j$ | $j^{th}$ record in $DT_v$ |
| $REMARK_j$ | Remark field value in $R_j$ |
| R_CA_VIN_Queue | VIN queue at R_CA |
| S_MSG | Service message |
| $S\_MSG_j$ | $j^{th}$ S_MSG |
| $ST\_BSB\_E\_VIN_v$ | Searching time of $VIN\_BS_B$ for $E\_VIN_v$ |
| SHA-1 | Secret hash algorithm-1 |
| SLNO | Serial number |
| Size_E_VIN | Size of E_VIN |
| Size_B | Size of $B_v$ |
| Size_SLNO | Size of SLNO field |

(continued)

| Parameter name | Parameter description |
|---|---|
| Size_O_MSG$_j$ | Size of O_MSG$_j$ |
| Size_BWO | Size of each bit-wise operator |
| Size_D_Sig | Size of D_Sig |
| Size_DP | Maximum size of data packet |
| Size_H_MSG | Size of H_MSG part of S_MSG |
| Size_MESS | Size of message after retrieval |
| Size_SMSG | Size of S_MSG |
| Size_Q$_B$ | Size of Q$_B$ |
| Size_Q$_v$ | Size of Q$_v$ |
| Size_SMSG$_j$ | Size of S_MSG$_j$ |
| Size_R$_j$ | Size of R$_j$ |
| Size_DT$_v$ | Size of DT$_v$ |
| Size_CA_CRL | Size of CA_CRL |
| STO_OH | Storage overhead |
| STO_OH_CA | STO_OH of CA |
| STO_OH_BS | STO_OH of BS |
| STO_OH$_B$ | STO_OH of BS$_B$ |
| TOT_V | Total number of vehicles in VANET |
| $\tau_v$ | Timer at V$_v$ |
| $\tau_B$ | Timer at BS$_B$ |
| $\tau_C$ | Timer at CA |
| TT_VBS_E_VIN | Transmission time of E_VIN from vehicle to BS |
| TT_BSCA_E_VIN | Transmission time of E_VIN from BS to CA |
| TT_BSFCA_E_VIN | Transmission time of E_VIN from BS to FCA |
| TT_FCARCA_E_VIN | Transmission time of E_VIN from FCA to RCA |
| VANET | Vehicular ad hoc network |
| V2V | Vehicle to vehicle |
| V2I | Vehicle to infrastructure |
| V2H | Vehicle to human |
| VIN | Vehicle identification number |
| VIN_CA | Database at CA |
| VIN_BS | Database at BS |
| VIN_BS$_B$ | VIN_BS at BS$_B$ |
| VDS | Vehicle Description Section |
| VIS | Vehicle Identifier Section |
| V$_v$ | v$^{th}$ vehicle in VANET |
| VT_D_VIN | Time to check the validity of decrypted VIN |
| V_BS_D_Sig | Transmission time of D_Sig$_v$ from Current_BS$_v$ to V$_v$ |
| VIN_P_Time | VIN processing time |
| VIN_P_Time$_v$ | VIN_P_Time for V$_v$ |
| VIN_P_Time_I$_v$ | VIN_P_Time in [1] |
| VIN_P_Time_II$_v$ | VIN_P_Time in [2] |
| WMI | World Manufacturing Identification |

(continued)

| Parameter name | Parameter description |
|---|---|
| $WT\_BSB\_E\_VIN_v$ | Waiting time of $E\_VIN_v$ in $BS_B\_VIN\_Queue$ |
| $WT\_CA\_E\_VIN_v$ | Waiting time of $E\_VIN_v$ in CA_VIN_Queue |
| $WT\_CA\_E\_VIN_j$ | Waiting time of $E\_VIN_j$ in CA_VIN_Queue |
| $WT\_RCA\_E\_VIN_v$ | Waiting time of $E\_VIN_v$ in R_CA_VIN_Queue |
| $WT\_RCA\_E\_VIN_j$ | Waiting time of $E\_VIN_j$ in R_CA_VIN_Queue |

## References

1. Mondal A, Mitra S (2012) Identification, authentication and tracking algorithm for vehicles using VIN in centralized VANET. In: International conference of communication, network and computing, proceedings published by Springer LNICST, vol 108, pp 115–120
2. Mitra S, Mondal A (2012) Identification, authentication and tracking algorithm for vehicles using VIN in distributed VANET. In: International conference on advances in computing, communications and informatics, proceedings published in ACM digital library, pp 279–286
3. Mondal A, Mitra S (2015) Detection and revocation of misbehaving vehicles from VANET. In: International conference on communication and computer engineering (2014), published in Lecture notes of Electrical Engineering, vol 315, pp 767–778
4. Mitra S (2015) Cooperative revocation of misbehaving vehicles from VANET. In: Information systems design and intelligent applications, proceedings published by Springer Series of Advances in Intelligent Systems and Computing (AISC)
5. Calafate CT, Fortino G, Fritsch S, Monterio J, Kano JC, Manzoni P (2012) An efficient and robust content delivery solution for IEEE 802.11p vehicular environments. Journal of Network and Computer Applications 35(2):753–762
6. Besari ARA, Patil MDM, Zamri R, Prabuwono AS (2008) A review of novel sensing techniques for automatic polishing robot system. National conference design and concurrent engineering, pp 353–357
7. Parliamentary Office of Science and Technology, postnote, no. 175, April 2002
8. Electronic Vehicle Identification Executive Summary, 11 Apr 2005. http://ec.europa.eu/transport/roadsafety_library/publications/evi_executive_summary.pdf. Accessed 26 Jan 2015
9. Balon GN (2006) Vehicular Ad-hoc networks and dedicated short range. University of Michigan, Dearborn
10. Papadimitratos P, Gligor V, Hubaux JP (2006) Securing vehicular communications – assumptions, requirements, and principles, ESCAR, 2006
11. Raya M, Padimitratos P, Hubaux JP (2006) Secure vehicular communications. IEEE Wireless Communications, 2006
12. Calandriello G, Padimitrators P, Hubaux JP, Lioy A (2007) Efficient and robust pseudonymous authentication in VANET. Montreal Quebec, Canada, VANET, ACM
13. Studer A, Bai F, Bellur AB, Perrig A (2008) Flexible, extensible and efficient VANET authentication, CyLab, Carnegie Melon University
14. Samara G, Ramadas S, Al-Salihy WAH (2010) Design of simple and efficient revocation list distribution in urban areas for VANETs. International Journal of Computer Science and Information Security 8(1)
15. Kherani A, Rao A (2010) Performance of node-eviction schemes in vehicular networks. IEEE Transaction on Vehicular Technology 59:550–558
16. Samara G, Al-Salihy WAH, Sures R (2010) Efficient certificate management in VANET. Second international conference on future computer and communication, vol 3, pp 750–754

17. Nowatkowski ME, Owen HL (2010) Certificate revocation list distribution in VANETs using most pieces broadcast. IEEE SoutheastCon, pp 238–241
18. Nowatkowski ME, Owen HL (2010) Scalable certificate revocation list distribution in vehicular Ad Hoc networks. IEEE Globecom, workshop on seamless wireless mobility
19. Scully J, Fildes B, Logan D (2005) Use of vehicle identification number for safety research. Monash University Accident Research Centre, Melbourne, Australia
20. Vehicle Identification Number, 3 Apr 2003, http://www.angelfire.com/ca/TORONTO/VIN/VIS.html. Accessed 25 Jan 2015
21. Wikipedia, List of Car Brands, 10 Jan 2015. http://en.wikipedia.org/wiki/List_of_cars. Accessed 25 Jan 2015
22. Kahate A (2010) Cryptography and network security, 2ND Edition, TMH
23. Papadimitratos P, Mezzour G, Hubaux JP (2008) Certificate revocation list distribution in vehicular communication systems. In: Proceedings of the fifth ACM international workshop on vehicular internetworking, pp 86–87
24. Duque OFG, Hadjiantonis AM, Pavlou G, Howarth M (2009) Adaptable misbehavior detection and isolation in wireless Ad Hoc networks using policies. IFIP/IEEE international symposium on integrated network management
25. (2004) Towards effective vehicle identification. The NMVTRC's strategic framework for improving the identification of vehicles and components
26. Huang JL, YehL Y, Chien HY (2011) ABAKA: an anonymous batch authenticated and key agreement scheme for value−added services in vehicular Ad Hoc networks. IEEE Transaction on Vehicular Technology 60:2011
27. Kargl F, Papadimitrators P, Buttyan L, Muter M, Wiedersheim B, Schoch E, Thong TV, Calandriello G, Held A, Kung A, Hubaux JP (2008) Secure vehicular communication systems: implementation, performance and research challenge. IEEE Communication Magazine 46:110–118

# Part II
# Architecture and Frameworks for the Internet of Things

# Chapter 5
# A Resource-Oriented Architecture for the Internet of Things (IoT)

**Ricardo Souza and Eleri Cardozo**

## 5.1 Introduction

The Internet of Things (IoT) is considered the driving force behind the next Internet revolution, the reason why the major Internet corporations are investing expressively in research and development in this area. The overall field of IoT is commonly broken into smaller aspects or focus points, for instance, networking, environments, low-end "things," and semantic aspects. This chapter addresses one of these aspects: networks for supporting IoT-based smart environments.

The networking solution for IoT proposed in this chapter assumes that the addressable objects (the "things") are discovered and accessed following the REST (Representational State Transfer) architectural style. The network is responsible for keeping track of the addressable objects as they join, leave, or change their points of attachment (migrate) across the network. The key element of this resource-oriented architecture (ROA) for IoT is a novel advertising and discovering mechanism for tracking the addressable objects. At the edge of the network, object discovery relies on protocols for detecting their presence according to the network technologies they employ. Examples of such technologies include Wi-Fi, Bluetooth, and IEEE 802.15.4. At the core of the network, the objects detected at the edges have their identification propagated in a standardized way through the OPSF (Open Shortest Path First) routing protocol. OSPF Opaque messages are employed for resource advertisements. As a consequence, regular IP (Internet Protocol) routing and IoT resource routing are two totally decoupled activities over the same protocol. Edge routers advertise objects they discover, eventually performing resource aggregation in order to favor scalability. These routers keep a

R. Souza (✉) • E. Cardozo
Department of Computer Engineering and Industrial Automation, School of Electrical and Computer Engineering, University of Campinas, Campinas, SP, Brazil
e-mail: rssouza@dca.fee.unicamp.br



Z. Mahmood (ed.), *Connectivity Frameworks for Smart Devices*,
Computer Communications and Networks, DOI 10.1007/978-3-319-33124-9_5

table of resources containing the edge routers from where the resources were advertised. This allows the advertising of objects connected to edge routers through non-IP networks such as wireless sensor networks (WSN). In this case, these edge routers act as IP gateways to the networks behind them.

A client discovers "things" using the standard REST interface, that is, by querying any edge router with the URI (Uniform Resource Identifier) path assigned to the object. The result can be the object's current full URI or, recursively, a list of more specific objects the requested URI path aggregates. The URI's address part is always the address of the edge router from which the object is reached (the object's gateway). This address is the object's presence in the Internet no matter what the technology of the network the object is attached to.

An interesting behavior of the proposed resource-oriented architecture is during object migration. When an object changes its point of attachment to the network, its new location information is propagated via OSPF Opaque LSAs as soon as a new edge router discovers it. If a client attempts to interact with a migrating "thing" using the URI containing its previous edge router's address, the client receives an HTTP response indicating the object's reachability status. Object migration is detailed in a later section of this chapter.

This resource-oriented network architecture is illustrated in a smart environment for assisted living scenario. In this scenario, a robotic wheelchair conducting a person with locomotion impairments dislocates within an environment, finding and interacting with "things" present in the environment. Example of such "things" is sensors and services that aid the locomotion of the robotic wheelchair. As the wheelchair moves through the environment, it continues to be accessible through the Internet by the applications running outside the environment. An example of such application is a remote interface to the robotic wheelchair operated through the Internet by a caregiver. Such interface can access information from the environment as provided by the ambient sensors, from the robotic wheelchair as provided by the sensors installed on the vehicle, and from the person her or himself as provided by body sensors. All of these sensors (resources) are discovered and accessed in exactly the same way.

The remaining of the chapter is organized as follows: Section 5.2 presents a brief overview of the IoT current state of the art and some key aspects of the fundamental technologies addressed in this chapter. Section 5.3 addresses the technologies relevant to the IoT architecture presented in this chapter. Section 5.4 details the proposed resource-oriented architecture for the Internet of Things. Section 5.5 presents a case study and experimental results. Finally, Sect. 5.6 concludes the chapter.

## 5.2 Internet of Things: A Brief Overview

One of the main concepts behind the Internet of Things is that of ubiquitous computing. This concept was first introduced by Mark Weiser as a vision of both people and environment being augmented with computational resources providing information and services at any place and any time. He states that *ubiquitous computing enhances computer use by making computers available throughout the physical environment, while making them effectively invisible to the user* [1]. This vision was further developed in his famous article titled "The Computer of the 21st Century," where he points out *that the most profound technologies are those that disappear. They weave themselves into the fabric of everyday life until they are indistinguishable from it* [2]. With the latest growth of connected devices, the large amount of data made available every day, and how the Internet is already incorporated into our lives, it is easy to notice that the Mark Weiser's vision is becoming a reality.

The concept of IoT has been around for more than 10 years, but there are still different definitions and visions of what this system actually is or will become. Most of these differences arise from the fact that researchers tend to devise solutions that are driven by their specific interests, objectives, and backgrounds [3].

One definition is that IoT is a worldwide network interconnecting uniquely addressable objects, based on standard communication protocols [4]. A less pragmatic and more futuristic definition is that of a global infrastructure of physical objects that know what we like, what we want, and what we need and act accordingly without explicit instructions [5]. This definition assumes that, in the future every daily life, devices will be able to dynamically join the network and start to collaborate and cooperate efficiently with other devices in order to perform different tasks for our benefit [6].

The lack of a clear understanding, of what IoT might become, leads to little consensus about how to actually turn it into reality [7]. Most current developments tend to apply existing technologies in different ways based on specific characteristics and demands of a particular IoT vision and/or application. These visions can be classified into three different overlapping categories: Internet, things, and semantics [3].

In short, the thing-oriented vision focuses on technologies that allow devices to communicate. These technologies include Bluetooth, RFID (radio-frequency identification), and NFC (Near Field Communication). The Internet-oriented vision addresses how the things can be integrated into today's and future Internet. IPSO (IP over Small Objects), CoAP (Constrained Application Protocol), WoT (Web of Things), and 6LoWPAN (IPv6 over Low Power Wireless Personal Area Network) are examples of technologies relevant to this vision. Finally, the semantic-oriented vision deals with the technologies for reasoning about the data the connected "things" produce. IoT can be viewed as the convergence of these three visions.

No matter what social aspects are generally assigned to IoT, from the technology standpoint, it is considered the natural evolution of the Internet already deployed in conjunction with the latest developments on ubiquitous and ad hoc networks [8]. The integration of such technologies is usually pointed as one key factor for the growth and success of the IoT [8, 9]. But as these systems become more integrated, some issues arise that should be properly addressed.

One of these issues refers to the nature of endpoints. Nowadays there is a person behind the vast majority of endpoints but the dominant landscape in the IoT will be different [10]. The IoT is expected to encompass millions of connected "things," both providing and requesting data at all times, in such a way that humans may become the minority in terms of traffic generation in a more distant future [11]. In that sense, several machine-to-machine (M2M) platforms have been proposed for this IoT scenario [12]. However, thanks to mobile and wearable devices, human-centric applications still will dominate the Internet in the short- and midterm horizons.

A long debate in computer science has been whether to build centralized or distributed systems. In the 1980s, a wave of decentralization shifted from mainframes to mini- and microcomputers connected via local area networks. This trend culminated in decentralized systems employing mainly the client-server architectural style. In late 2000s, thanks to virtualization technologies, we faced a wave back towards centralization, where control, data, and intelligence of computing systems moved to cloud-based infrastructures. Now we are beginning to see the emergence of a new shift towards decentralization with paradigms like Fog [13] and Edge Computing [14]. In these paradigms, the complexity and management of applications have moved towards the edges of the network, closer to the end users. The objective here is to avoid the long delays in data exchanging between end users and far away data centers. This is a counterpoint of the vision that all the data generated by the "things" will be stored and processed in the cloud.

As cloud-based resources have the potential to provide nearly unlimited processing power and storage capacities, some authors argue that it should be the ideal platform for the IoT [15]. However, it is not clear that such centralized approach is in fact the most suited model [16] as it is not universally applicable [17]. In practice, any hardware that can connect directly to the Internet would require a network access technology that increases the device's cost and power consumption. It is easy to see that not all endpoints in the IoT will be suited for direct connection to the Internet, and therefore the use of gateways becomes necessary as shown in Fig. 5.1. In this scenario, paradigms like Fog and Edge Computing become relevant for IoT deployments.

Since the IoT is a combination of highly heterogeneous devices, we argue that its architecture should also encompass this heterogeneity, employing a combination of technological solutions when and where they are most suited. In this sense, technologies such as Cloud, Fog, and WSN should aim at complementing each other instead of replacing one another. Furthermore, if the IoT is in fact the evolution of the current Internet, it is imperative that legacy systems not only be a part of it but also contribute to this evolution. The easiest way to support the integration of those legacy systems, as well as a multitude of heterogeneous devices, is by employing IoT gateways [18].

As the IoT matures, a variety of architectural models are being proposed but these proposals are still far from converging to a stable and accepted reference model. The most basic model is a three-layer architecture [19] consisting of the application, network, and perception layers. In addition, some authors have added more specialized layers such as a business layer, a service composition layer, and a

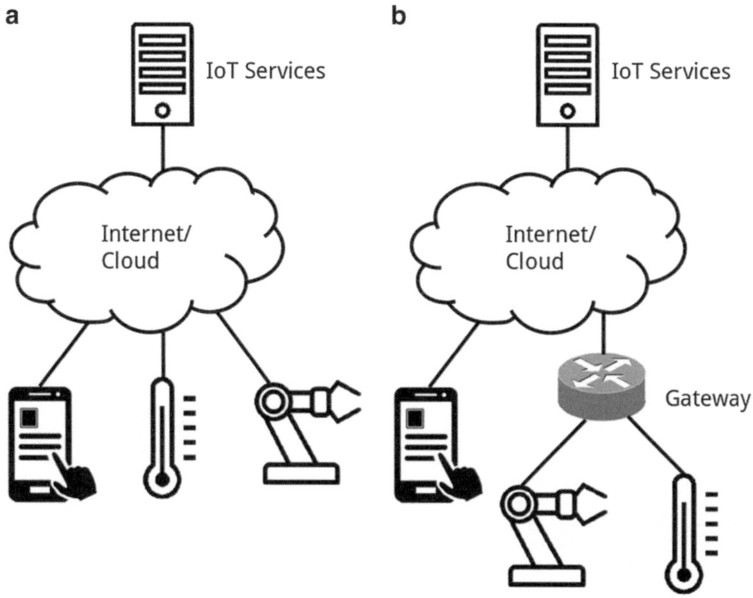


**Fig. 5.1** Two approaches for device connection: direct network connection (**a**) and connection through gateway (**b**)

service management layer [11, 19, 20]. However, such complex layers do not always fit on constrained devices, becoming unfeasible on such devices [21].

Another relevant topic for IoT is mobility, specially mobility in IP networks [22]. Standards such as Mobile IP [23] and Proxy Mobile IPv6 [24] have been proposed to address this issue but their strong drawbacks have prevented the widespread of such standards [25, 26].

The architecture proposed in this chapter focuses on the network layer and supports IoT as an overlay network over the existing Internet. This overlay network is synthesized by a set of gateway nodes connecting both IP and non-IP devices, e.g., wireless sensors communicating with the IEEE 802.15.4 protocol. The gateways turn these non-IP devices into Internet-addressable devices by allowing their discovery and access through a convenient RESTful mechanism. Mobility also is supported, but at the application (HTTP) level instead of the network (IP) level.

## 5.3 Relevant Technologies

This section presents the technologies relevant to the proposed IoT architecture, namely, the Representational State Transfer (REST) architectural style as a basis for resource-oriented architectures and the Open Shortest Path First routing protocol.

### 5.3.1 Representational State Transfer (REST)

The Representational State Transfer architectural style was proposed in 2000 by Roy Fielding in his PhD thesis [27]. Being an architectural style, REST is not tightened to any particular technology or protocol, but imposes some constraints to the architectures that comply with the style, usually referred as *RESTful* architectures. An important restriction is that servers are stateless and session states are kept entirely on the client, meaning that servers have no control over the clients' behavior. As a consequence, requests must carry all the information necessary to perform an operation on the server.

REST also favors a layered system where clients may connect to servers through intermediary network functions such as proxy functions performing request forwarding, protocol translation, and security checking. Another intermediary function is caching, but this function has limited application when the resources change their state continuously.

Although not mandatory, RESTful architectures are usually implemented over Web protocols. Such implementations employ HTTP/HTTPS for message transferring between clients and servers. Resources are identified by URLs (Uniform Resource Locators) and their representations (states) are usually expressed in XML (Extensible Markup Language) or JSON (Javascript Object Notation). Self-descriptive messages require metadata for understanding the meaning of the representations they carry. Metadata can be present either in the HTTP header (e.g., in the Accept and Content-Type header fields) or in the message body (e.g., a link to an XML Schema in a returned XML document).

REST is a basis for building resource-oriented architectures. In RESTful ROAs, every functional component of the architecture is a network-addressable resource maintained in a stateless server and manipulated through a set of REST interfaces. Commonly, such interfaces are based on the HTTP methods PUT, GET, POST, and DELETE for, respectively, to create, access, modify, and remove resources kept by the servers and their corresponding representations.

Resource-oriented architectures must provide ways for resource registration and discovering. Resource registration is usually a matter of configuration on the server, while resource discovering is performed by querying a URI path in a server. The query returns the resources that match the supplied path. Although resource registration and discovering are straightforward in ROA implementations where resources are software components kept in Web servers, these activities are more complex when resources are "things" in IoT scenarios. The reason is that resources are now self-contained physical devices that may connect, detach, and change their points of attachment (migrate) in the network during their lifetime.

REST has been employed to provide services in IoT deployments. For instance, a REST proxy can be used to simplify the interaction with devices employing either HTTP [28] or CoAP [29]. In addition to provide a convenient access to the resources, in the IoT architecture proposed in this chapter, REST has a key role in resource discovering, advertising, and migration.

### *5.3.2 Open Shortest Path First (OSPF)*

The Open Shortest Path First is an interior routing protocol. It provides routing functionality within a domain or autonomous systems (AS) [30]. It was designed to optimize the propagation of topological changes in the network, e.g., when a network link goes down. OSPF is a link-state protocol, which requires that each router on the network maintains a database describing the AS topology. OSPF has been in existence now for over 20 years, and today, link-state protocols like OSPF and IS-IS [31] are the most deployed interior routing protocols.

One of the main characteristics of OSPF is that it allows the routing domain to be split into multiple areas. Each area runs its own instance of OSPF. Therefore, routers only need to know the topology of the areas which they are connected to. This allows for route summarization where routes inside each particular area are invisible from the outside, resulting in a reduction of the inter-area routing traffic.

With the network split into areas, the routers are also divided according to the functions they perform [32]. Internal routers are those connected to networks belonging to the same area. Area border routers (ABR) are those connected to networks belonging to multiple areas. These routers run multiple instances of the OSPF protocol, one for each area they are connected to. ABRs perform summarization of topological information of their attached areas for distribution through the backbone. Backbone routers are those connected to the backbone area, including ABRs. Autonomous system boundary routers (ASBR) are those that exchange routing information with routers belonging to other autonomous systems. Figure 5.2 presents a typical OSPF network.

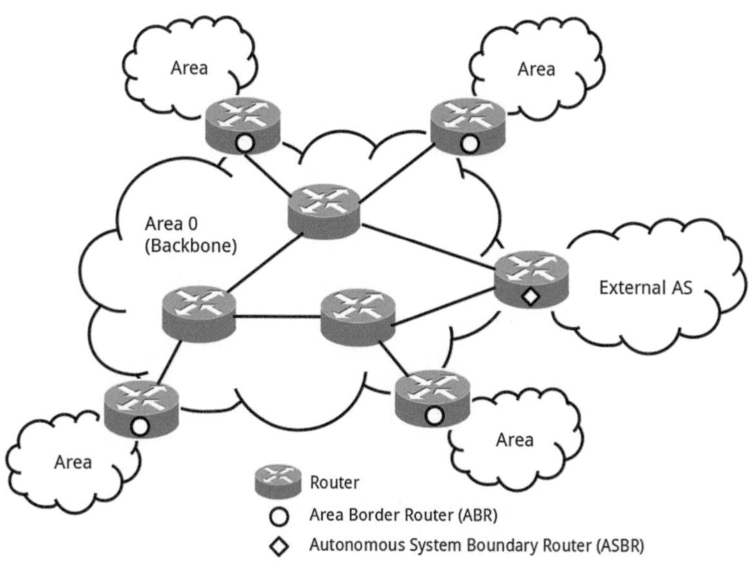


**Fig. 5.2** A typical OSPF network

All data exchanged between OSPF routers is in the form of link-state advertisements (LSA). There are six main LSA types employed for advertising link states that allow the routers to derive the overall network topology. The OSPF routing algorithm is very efficient regarding LSA propagation, minimizing the elapsed time necessary for all the routers to be aware of changes in the network topology. Aside from these LSAs, there are also Opaque LSAs with three different scopes according to the portion of the network they are allowed to traverse: link, area, and autonomous system. The data carried in Opaque LSAs may be standardized independently of the OSPF standards. Routers must forward Opaque LSAs, even if they do not inspect or understand their contents.

The proposed IoT architecture described in the sequence employs Opaque LSAs to propagate the resources discovered by an IoT edge router (gateway) to the remaining IoT edge routers. Only these routers are programmed to interpret the contents of the Opaque LSA. It is possible to employ the concept of OSPF area to aggregate the resources that are physically or logically interrelated, for example, deployed in the same place, network, or apparatus. These resources can be propagated to the remaining areas in an aggregated form, for instance, aggregated around a resource category within the area.

## 5.4 A Resource-Oriented Architecture for IoT

This section presents the proposed architecture for the Internet of Things. Firstly, a high-level description of the architecture is provided along with a brief background of previous research conducted by the authors in resource-oriented architectures. Then, some key implementation aspects of the architecture are presented.

### *5.4.1 Architecture Description*

The core element in the proposed architecture is an embedded server called *RESTthru*. Originally, this server was developed as a server for networked mobile robotics where the robot's resources (hardware and software) were accessible through a RESTful interface [33]. Also, in a previous work, it was presented how the server could be integrated into a cloud architecture [34] or be extended to provide an HTTP interface to an IEEE 802.15.4 wireless sensor network employed to route messages to a mobile robot [35]. Figure 5.3 presents these scenarios.

Currently, *RESTthru* was extended to support IoT developments following a resource-oriented architecture. *RESTthru* instances can act as edge routers connected to an existing IPv4 or IPv6 network core. These instances are connected to addressable objects employing any communication technology such as Bluetooth or ZigBee. Figure 5.4 illustrates this network infrastructure. *RESTthru* instances are aware of the resources they directly connect or they can reach as gateways. The

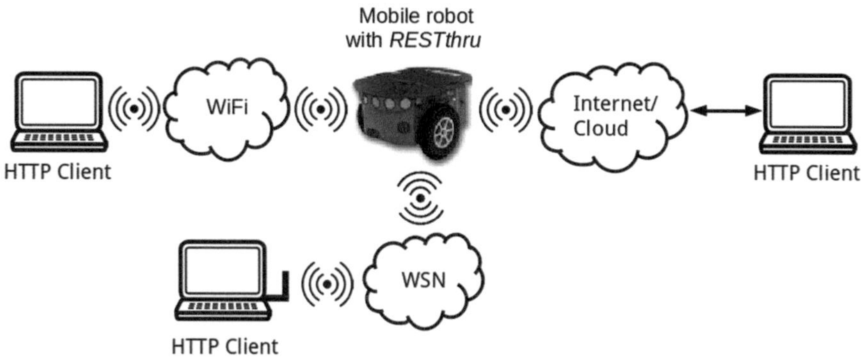


**Fig. 5.3** Different access to a mobile robot as provided by *RESTthru*

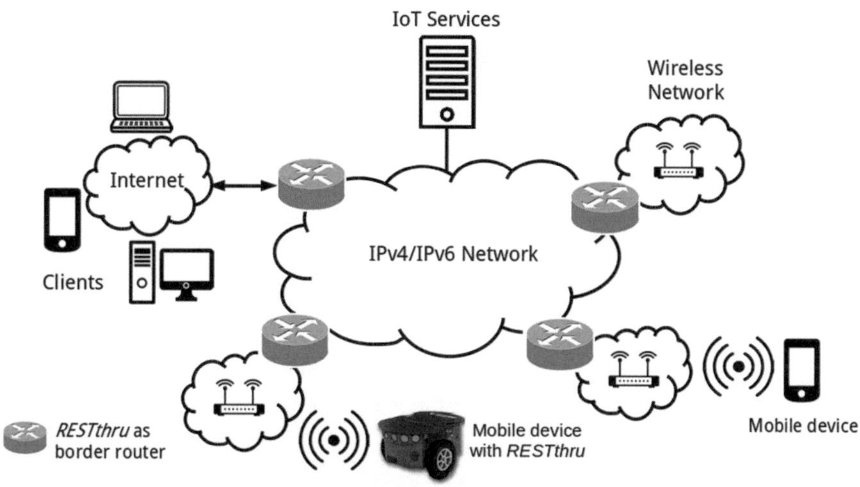


**Fig. 5.4** IoT network infrastructure

connected resources can be informed via configuration or detected via specific discovery protocols such as UPnP (Universal Plug and Play). *RESTthru* instances acting as edge routers exchange information about the resources they discover using OSPF Opaque LSAs as discussed previously. In this way, edge routers become aware of all the resources advertised by these routers.

Information about resources is propagated on Opaque LSAs and consists of three data elements: a network endpoint, a hierarchical name, and a unique identifier. The network endpoint is the IP address of the edge router propagating the LSA. This makes the resource visible on the Internet even if it employs a private IP address or a non-IP addressing scheme. The hierarchical name is a human readable name assigned to the resource, similar to a file path name. The edge router must be able to infer this name hierarchy based on the information exchanged during the discovery process, e.g., from the *service* tag present in the XML UPnP service description. Resource names refer to services offered by the resource or, recursively, to an aggregate of more specialized resources with their own services. A particular IoT deployment can define an ontology to derive this naming scheme. Finally, the unique identifier is an array of bytes uniquely assigned to the resource. This identifier can be computed by the edge router based on certain resource's permanent attributes, e.g., its MAC address, or extracted from the resource discovering messages, e.g., the UDN (Unique Device Name) present in the UPnP response messages.

Upon receiving an Opaque LSA, the edge router updates its resource table, by adding, dropping, or updating resource entries. The resources' unique identifiers are the indexes in the resource table. This allows a resource that changed its network point of attachment to be tracked. As soon as the new edge router discovers the attached resource, it advertises the resource with the same unique identifier, but with the new network endpoint. After a short period of time, all the remaining edge routers will have updated their resource tables. As routes in OSPF, resource table entries are soft state, meaning that the edge routers must keep advertising the resources periodically. Resources no longer advertised have their entries removed from the resource tables by timeout.

Clients employ a REST discovering scheme. A client can query any *RESTthru* instance (via an HTTP GET message) passing a complete or partial resource path. It may receive a list of full URIs of the resources kept by the instance that matches the path or an error response message, for instance, an HTTP Not Found response. Clients now can interact with the resources, either directly or through their corresponding gateways. Figure 5.5 shows two devices with *RESTthru* embedded instances and two *RESTthru* instances acting as edge routers. Clients querying a device with an embedded *RESTthru* instance receive only the matching resources local to the device, while clients querying the instances acting as edge routers receive the matching resources kept by both devices.

Resource migration is handled at the application level by employing the standard HTTP status codes. The following situations can happen when interacting with a

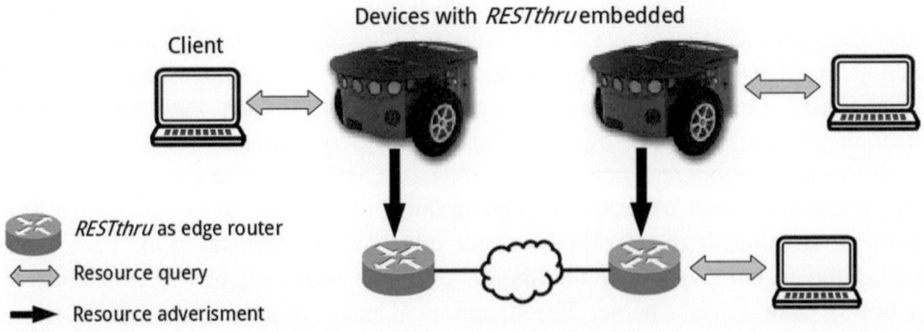


**Fig. 5.5** Resource visibility in RESTthru

migrating resource. When an edge router receives an HTTP request for a resource but there is no matching entry on the router's resource table, the edge router issues an HTTP reply with the 404 status code (Not Found). This situation can happen when the resource has permanently detached from the network. If the resource is in the router's table but the router cannot forward the request to the resource, the edge router issues an HTTP reply with the 503 status code (Service Temporarily Unavailable). This can happen when the resource becomes temporarily unreachable or is in the course of a migration process. Finally, when an edge router finds the requested resource in its resource table but with different network address, it performs an HTTP proxy operation towards the new resource location. Such operation is transparent to the client. This can happen when the resource already completed its migration process and its new location (edge router) was already propagated via OSPF to the overall network.

### *5.4.2 Implementation*

The proposed architecture requires a local resource discovering mechanism. We implemented such mechanism with a modified version of the SSDP (Simple Service Discovery Protocol) [36]. SSDP is used as part of the discovery mechanism for the UPnP specification, and it was designed to provide service (resources, in our case) discovering on local networks, like a home-area network. SSDP employs HTTP messages on a multicast address to discover connected resources running this protocol. SSDP defines two new HTTP methods: NOTIFY, used by resources to announce themselves on the network, and M-SEARCH, used to query resources on the network. Our implementation also uses a well-known multicast address to perform local discovery, but instead of defining new HTTP methods, it employs the standard POST and GET methods to perform analogous operations.

A resource announcement is typically a POST message sent to the *RESTthru* multicast address. A resource registers to the *RESTthru* multicast group at IP address 224.0.0.250:49500, and, from this point on, it will be able to receive and send discovery messages. The *RESTthru* resource discovering process is presented in Fig. 5.6. Each *RESTthru* server keeps a table with the local resources it has discovered, updating this table each time a resource announcement is received. If the server is an edge router, an Opaque LSA is injected on the network announcing the discovered resource. OSPF handles internally the periodic propagation of Opaque LSAs for resources an edge router has discovered. As previously mentioned, the local discovery mechanism is soft state, meaning that the resources must keep sending periodic announcement messages to the multicast address. The lack of such messages causes the resource to be removed from the edge router's resource table and the propagation of an OSPF Opaque LSA informing that the resource is no longer available.

*RESTthru* was designed with modular and extensible software architecture. Resources are manipulated by independent dynamic libraries that are mapped into URL patterns. Such libraries are loaded into memory when a request matches its associated pattern. The discovery process adds one step before this matching process by verifying if the resource is kept by (or reached from) this server. In this case, the request is processed locally. Otherwise, the request is forwarded via an HTTP proxy operation to the address associated with the resource. *RESTthru* instances can announce resources they hold to other instances acting as edge routers as shown in Fig. 5.5. An overall view of the *RESTthru* architecture is presented in Fig. 5.7.

OSPF routing capabilities in *RESTthru* is provided by the Quagga Routing Suite client API [37]. This client was included as an extension of the server's architecture, making the OSPF routing functionality totally decoupled from the other

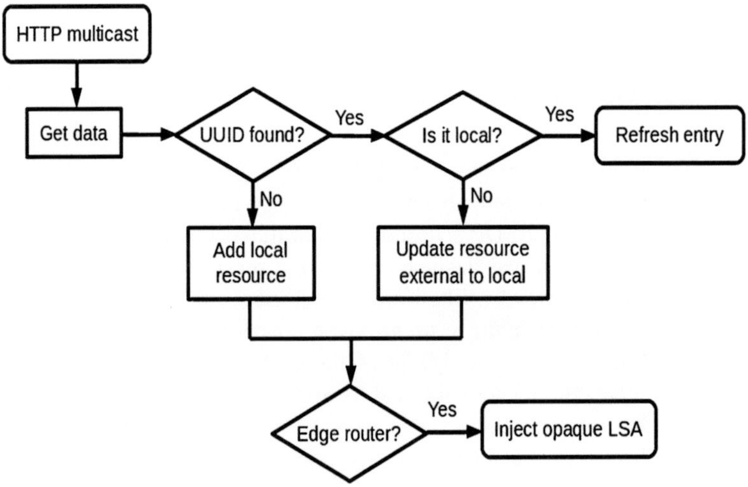


**Fig. 5.6** *RESTthru* resource discovering process

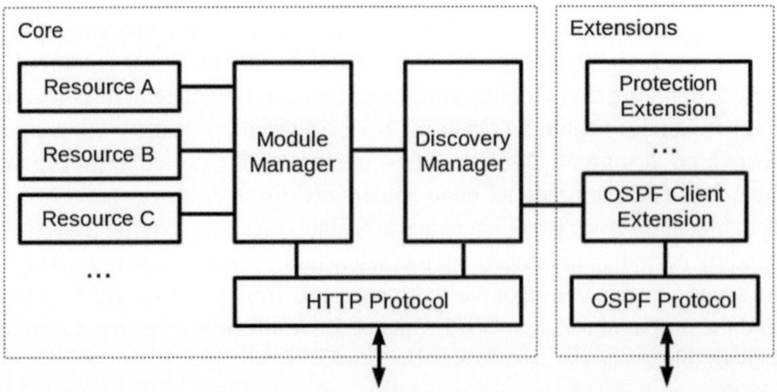


**Fig. 5.7** *RESTthru* embedded server architecture

*RESTthru* functionalities. When the OSPF extension is loaded and is able to successfully connect to an OSPF daemon, the *RESTthru* server becomes an edge router of the IoT architecture.

Clients can be standalone applications connecting to an instance of *RESTthru* from the local host (i.e., colocated with *RESTthru*) or connecting from a local network infrastructure or even from the Internet. A client can also be implemented as an extension of the *RESTthru* server, running embedded on the networked device. For instance, a protection algorithm can be easily implemented to run embedded on a mobile robot as shown in Fig. 5.7.

## 5.5 Case Study

The proposed architecture was deployed in a lab-size environment where a robotic wheelchair is teleoperated by a remote caregiver. The robotic wheelchair is fitted with several sensors such as encoders, cameras, laser and sonar rangefinders, cliff and collision detectors, and body sensors. The wheelchair employs two Arduino microcontrollers for the low-level functions and two Raspberry Pi (R-Pi) boards for providing high-level functions. A Wi-Fi router/access point connects these processors to the network infrastructure. The *RESTthru* server was embedded on each R-Pi boards providing the wheelchair with a RESTful interface. One R-Pi is responsible for providing most of the "robotic" functions such as locomotion and sensoring. The second one connects body sensors monitoring the wheelchair's user. One R-Pi also acts as a border router. With this configuration the wheelchair can be seen as a mobile network. This network is responsible for its own internal addressing scheme as well as resource discovering and management.

The *RESTthru* instances on the wheelchair perform their own discovering for the resources installed on the wheelchair. Once a resource is discovered, the *RESTthru* instance posts a resource announcement on the multicast address. The edge router listening to this address receives this message and propagates the discovered resource via OSPF as stated before.

The OSPF network configured inside our lab consists of four subnetworks (with private and public address) and two wireless local area networks (WLAN). In total, the network has eight nodes, three of these are edge routers, three standard static nodes, and two mobile nodes. One of these mobile nodes is the wheelchair, a network on its own. Figure 5.8 illustrates this scenario.

As the robotic wheelchair moves through the environment, it performs handovers between access points and networks while interacting with the client applications. One client application interacts with the wheelchair from the Internet. This application accesses the network infrastructure from an edge router acting as a gateway between the IoT infrastructure and the Internet. From this edge router, all the resources discovered on the network are made available to the client applications.

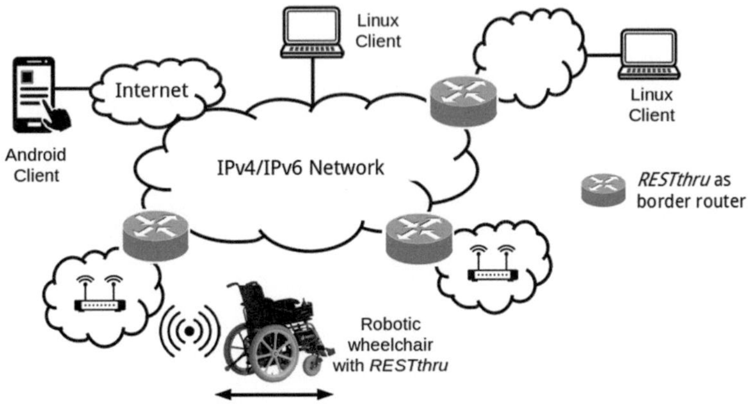


**Fig. 5.8** Network topology for the case study

Another scenario is when a client application runs on a device located within the infrastructure. In this case resources can be accessed either directly or through an edge router. A client application can also run a local instance of *RESTthru* as an edge router in order to discover resources propagated via OSPF without the need to query an edge router.

## 5.5.1 Experiments and Results

An experimental scenario was deployed on our lab employing different client applications. The first client application is a teleoperation interface employed by a remote caregiver assisting the wheelchair user. This application executes on an Android device and has the interface shown in Fig. 5.9. The application presents the image of the wheelchair's camera and a joystick for driving the wheelchair.

While the wheelchair is driven via teleoperation, a different application was used to read the data from the body sensors embedded on the wheelchair, emulating a distributed healthcare application. This application queries the URL of the resources it wishes to interact with and periodically requests data from these resources (more precisely, reads their state). In this application, the resources are an air flow sensor, used to evaluate the user's breathing, and the galvanic skin response (GSR) sensor, employed to evaluate the user's level of stress. A third client application was added in order to increase the communication rate in the network. This application reads the laser rangefinder installed on the wheelchair and plots a local map showing nearby obstacles. These two applications execute on different Linux machines, accessing the data through different edge routers.

An experimental session consisted of a random tour within our lab where the first client application drives the wheelchair remotely while the other two applications capture data simultaneously from the body sensors and from the robotic vehicle.

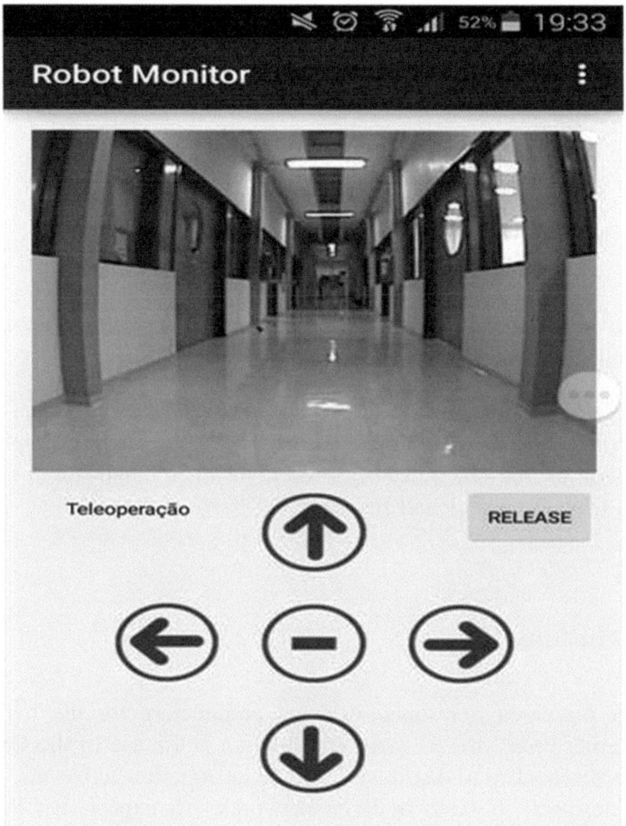


**Fig. 5.9** Android client application

During the session the wheelchair traveled about 50 m, performing the handover process two times. In total there were approximately 700 requests performed by the client applications. From those about 60–70 requests were answered with either a Service Temporarily Unavailable or a Not Found HTTP replies, resulting in a rate of approximately 90 % successful requests. During the handovers the client applications were unable to communicate with the wheelchair in periods of time ranging from 5 to 9 s.

A partial set of the acquired body sensor data is presented in Fig. 5.10a. During the experiment, the emulated user showed some breathing difficulties at some points. The majority of the readings were close to zero indicating that the subject was breathing normally, and the higher readings indicate an abnormal breathing. These sensor readings could be used to determine the level of stress of the wheelchair user.

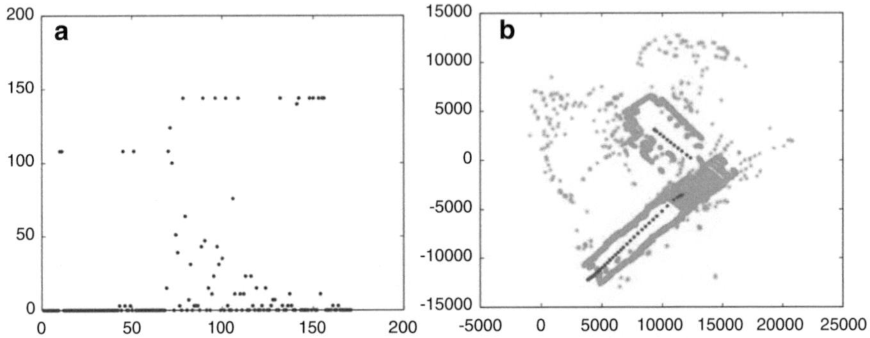


**Fig. 5.10** Air flow sensor data (**a**) and mapping application plot (**b**)

Finally, Fig. 5.10b shows a handover moment on the mapping application (the discontinuity on the red line trajectory), where the client application was unable to recover data from the wheelchair for about 6 s.

## 5.6 Conclusions

This chapter presented a resource-oriented architecture for the IoT, based on standard Internet Protocols. Its main contribution is the use of the OSPF routing protocol as a mechanism to distribute resource information across the network. As OSPF was designed to scale in large networks, we expect that the proposed architecture scales in large IoT deployments as well.

The proposed architecture was built upon *RESTthru*, a RESTful server originally developed for networked mobile robotics. By extending *RESTthru* with resource advertising and discovering capabilities, it becomes the main building block for a highly distributed smart environment without a single point of failure. For example, if a *RESTthru* instance crashes or disconnects from the network, the OSPF soft state scheme will remove the resources reached from this instance in all the remaining instances. In our use case scenario, the architecture was able to propagate resource information throughout the network and to perform dynamic proxy forwarding to migrating resources.

The network architecture was employed to provide access to a robotic wheelchair moving around our lab, switching between networks and access points. In order to test the architecture, different client applications were used. The first one controls remotely the wheelchair, the second one monitors the user of the wheelchair, and the third one maps the surrounding environment. Each client application runs on a different device, all accessing the wheelchair's resources regardless of which network the wheelchair is currently attached to.

At this stage the architecture can be seen as a framework for developing distributed applications and integrating different technologies, as required by IoT deployments. It provides mobility support at the application (HTTP) level for resources that change their network points of attachment. Future work includes the specification and implementation of an ontology for resource description. We are also investigating the integration of other protocols into the architecture such as MQTT (MQ Telemetry Transport), XMPP (Extensible Messaging and Presence Protocol), and CoAP. Finally, we are evaluating the deployment of the architecture on Linux-based router firmwares such as DD-WRT and OpenWrt.

## References

1. Weiser M (1993) Some computer science issues in ubiquitous computing. Commun ACM 36 (7):75–84
2. Weiser M (1999) The computer for the 21st century. ACM SIGMOBILE Mob Comput Commun Rev 3(3):3–11
3. Atzori L, Iera A, Morabito G (2010) The internet of things: a survey. Int J Comp Telecommun Netw 54(15):2787–2805
4. Santucci G, Lange S (2008) Internet of things in 2020: roadmap for the future. http://www.smart-systems-integration.org/public/documents/publications/Internet-of-Things_in_2020_EC-EPoSS_Workshop_Report_2008_v3.pdf. Accessed on Aug 2015
5. Dohr A, Modre-Opsrian R, Drobics M, Hayn D, Scheier G (2010) The internet of things for ambient assisted living. Int Conf Inf Technol New Gener (ITNG), pp 804–809, April 2010
6. Christin D, Reinhardt A, Mogre P, Steinmetz R (2009) Wireless sensor networks and the internet of things: selected challenges. In: Proceedings of the 8th GI/ITG KuVS Fachgespräch Drahtlose Sensormetze, 2009
7. Kortuem G, Kawsar F, Fitton D, Sundramoorthy Y (2010) Smart objects as building blocks for the internet of things. IEEE Internet Comput 14(1):44–51
8. Perera C, Zaslavsky A, Christen P, Georgakopoulos D (2014) Context aware computing for the internet of things: a survey. IEEE Commun Surv Tutor 16(1):414–454
9. Mainetti L, Patrono L, Vilei A (2011) Evolution of wireless sensor networks towards the internet of things: a survey. In: IEEE international conference on software, telecommunications and computer networks, 2011
10. Bonomi F (2011) Connected vehicles, the internet of things and fog computing. ACM international workshop on vehicular inter-networking, September 2011
11. Lu Tan, Neng Wang (2010) Future internet: the internet of things. IEEE international conference on advanced computer theory and engineering, 2010
12. Casto M, Jara A, Skarmeeta A (2012) An analysis of M2M platforms: challenges and opportunities for the internet of things. International Innovative Mobile and Internet Services in Ubiquitous Computing (IMIS), July 2012
13. Bonomi F, Milito R, Zhu J, Addepalli S (2012) Fog computing and its role on the internet of things. MCC workshop on mobile cloud computing, 2012
14. Lopez P, Montresor A, Epema D, Datta A, Higashino T, Iamnitchi A, Barcelos M, Felber P, Riviere E (2015) Edge-centric computing: vision and challenges. ACM SIGCOMM Comput Commun 45(5):37–42
15. Botta A, Donato W, Persico V, Pescape A (2014) On the integration of cloud computing and the internet of things. In: IEEE international conference on future internet of things and cloud, 2014
16. Want T, Shilit B, Jenson S (2015) Enabling the internet of things. IEEE Comput 48(1):28–35

17. Bonomi F, Milito R, Natarajan P, Zhu J, Bessis N, Dobre C (2014) Fog computing: a platform for the internet of things and analytics. Big data and the internet of things: a roadmap for smart environments, 2014
18. Datta S, Bonnet C (2014) Smart M2M gateway based architecture for M2M device and endpoint management. In: IEEE international conference on internet of things (iThings) and green computing and communications (GreenCom), 2014
19. Miao Wu, Ting-Jie Lu, Fei-Yang Ling, Jing Sun, Hui-Ying Du (2010) Research on the architecture of internet of things. International conference on advanced computer theory and engineering (ICACTE), 2010
20. Khan R, Khan S, Zaheer R, Khan S (2012) Future internet: the internet of things architecture, possible applications and key challenges. International conference on Frontiers of Information Technology (FIT), 2012
21. Al-Fuqaha A, Guizani M, Mohammade M, Aledhari M, Ayyash M (2015) Internet of things: a survey on enabling technologies, protocols and applications. IEEE Commun Surv Tutorials 17 (4):2347–2376
22. Ahlgren B et al (2008) Design considerations for a network of information. In: Proceedings of the ACM international conference on emerging networking experiments and technologies, December 2008
23. Perkins C (1996) RFC2002 IP mobility support. 1996
24. Gundavelli S, Leung K, Devarapalli K, Chowdhury K Patil B (2008) RFC5213 proxy mobile IP, 2008
25. Kafle V, Fukushima Y, Harai H (2014) New mobility paradigm with ID/Locator split in the future Internet. In: IEEE consumer communications and networking conference: mobility management in the network of future world. 2014
26. Hong K, Lillethun D, Ramachadran U, Ottenwänder B (2013) Mobile fog: a programming model for large-scale applications on the internet of things. In: Proceedings of the second ACM SIGCOMM workshop on mobile cloud computing, 2013
27. Fielding R (2000) Architectural styles and the design of network-based software architectures, PhD thesis, 2000
28. Han S, Park S, Lee G, Crespi W (2015) Extending the devices profile for web services standard using a REST proxy. IEEE Internet Comput 19(1):10–17
29. Castellani A, Gheda M, Bui N, Rossi M, Zorzi M (2011) Web services for the internet of things through CoAP and EXI. In: IEEE international conference on communications workshops, 2011
30. Goyal M, Soperi M, Baccelli E, Choudhury G, Shaikh A, Hosseini H, Trivedi K (2012) Improving convergence speed and scalability in OSPF: a survey. IEEE Commun Surv Tutorials 14(2):443–463
31. ISO 11589:2002 (2002) Telecommunications and information exchange between systems
32. Moy J (1998) RFC2328 OSPF Version 2
33. Souza R, Pinho F, Olivi L, Cardozo E (2013) A RESTful platform for networked robotics. In: International conference on Ubiquitous Robots and Ambient Intelligence (URAI). November 2013
34. Agostinho L, Feliciano G, Olivi L, Cardozo E, Guimarães E (2011) A bio-inspired approach to provisioning of virtual resources in federated clouds. In: IEEE international conference on dependable, automatic and secure computing (DASC), December 2011
35. Souza R, Agostinho L, Guimarães E, Cardozo E (2011) Control of mobile robots through a wireless sensor network. In: XXIX Brazilian symposium on computer networks and distributed systems. May 2011
36. Goland Y, Cai T, Leach P, Gu Y (1999) Simple service discovery protocol, http://tools.ietf.org/html/draft-cai-ssdp-v1-03. Accessed on Aug 2015
37. Jakma P, Lamparter D (2014) Introduction to the quagga routing suite. IEEE Network, Apr, 2014

# Chapter 6
# Integration Approaches for the Internet of Things (IoT) Era

**S. Rajaraajeswari, R. Selvarani, and Pethuru Raj**

## 6.1 Introduction

Not only everyday instruments, machines, appliances, wares, utensils, etc. but also common, cheap, and casual articles such as cots, chairs, cups, tables, pipes, doors, sofas, windows, etc. in our personal, professional, and social environments are being technically tuned and turned to exhibit hitherto unforeseen smart behavior and to join in the mainstream computing. These transitions are being enabled through the systematic leverage of hugely powerful edge technologies such as disposable and diminutive sensors [1, 2], actuators, chips, codes, stickers, pads, tags, labels, specks, smart dust, etc.

The technologically inspired capability of instrumenting and interconnecting powerful as well as resource-constrained devices (physical, mechanical, electrical, and electronics) with one another in the vicinity as well as with cloud-hosted software applications and data sources over any network is to make the devices smarter in their operations and outputs. Further on, the environments wherein those empowered and connected devices are being deployed in large numbers ultimately become smart in their contributions for the occupants and owners of the environment.

S. Rajaraajeswari
Department of Computer Applications, Raja Rajeswari College of Engineering, Bangalore 560074, India
e-mail: s.raja.raajeswari@gmail.com

R. Selvarani
Computer Science and Engineering Department, Alliance University, Bangalore 562106, India
e-mail: selvarani.riic@gmail.com

P. Raj (✉)
Infrastructure Architect, IBM Global Cloud Center of Excellence, IBM India, Bangalore, India
e-mail: peterindia@gmail.com



Z. Mahmood (ed.), *Connectivity Frameworks for Smart Devices*,
Computer Communications and Networks, DOI 10.1007/978-3-319-33124-9_6

As per the various reports being released by market watchers, analysts, and researchers, the future Internet, by the year 2020, is to comprise millions of software applications and services but also billions of connected devices and trillions of digitized entities. It is an overwhelmingly accepted statement that the fast-emerging and evolving IoT idea is definitely a strategic and highly impactful vision to be decisively and deftly realized and passionately sustained with "the smart adaption and adoption of cutting-edge technologies, the state-of-the-art infrastructures, synchronized processes, integrated platforms, enabling tools, enabling patterns, key metrics and guidelines, best practices, innovative products, industry-strength standards, and futuristic architectures." Industry professionals and academic professors are constantly looking out for appropriate use, business and technical cases in order to confidently and cogently proclaim the transformational value and power of the IoT concept to the larger audience of worldwide executives, end users, entrepreneurs, evangelists, and engineers.

A growing array of open standards are being formulated, framed, and polished by domain experts, industry consortiums, and standard bodies to make the IoT idea more visible, viable, and valuable. National governments across the globe are setting up special expert groups in order to come out with pragmatic policies and procedures to take forward the solemn and sublime ideals of IoT and to realize the strategic significance of the IoT paradigm in conceiving, concretizing, and providing a bevy of context-aware and citizen-centric services to ensure and enhance peoples' comfort, choice, care, and convenience. Research students, scholars, and scientists are working collaboratively towards identifying the implementation challenges and overcoming them via different means and ways especially standard-sticking technological solutions.

In this chapter, we aim to describe the connectivity technologies as well as tools and their contributions for setting up and sustaining smarter environments (smarter homes, hospitals, hotels, transport vehicles, etc.) and ultimately the smarter planet.

## 6.2 IoT for Smarter Enterprises and Environments

The Internet of Things (IoT) concept is an intellectual and inspirational idea gaining immense momentum these days as it has the inbuilt power to bring enhanced care, choice, convenience, and comfort for us. While the implementation technologies and tools are being unearthed and sustained by worldwide product vendors and research professionals collectively and cognitively, the days of the IoT era are all set to beckon the world decisively. Apart from the people empowerment, the raging IoT paradigm is gripping every kind of industry verticals. Industry experts and business executives are very keen to embrace the IoT advancements in order to be ahead of their competitors. The national governments are strategizing viable and value-adding strategies and plans in order to bring forth spectacular and sparkling benefits to their constituents and citizens. The social implications are being systematically expounded in order to articulate the IoT-sponsored advantages for the human society. Thus every segment, sector, and situation in our everyday life is to get sagacious benefits with the faster maturity and stability of IoT technologies, platforms, infrastructures, and services. The personal as well as professional lives are to be impacted significantly in the days ahead with the surging popularity, pervasiveness, and persuasiveness of the IoT paradigm. All kinds of industry verticals are to be transformative and disruptive with the adoption of the pragmatic advancements and innovations happening in the IoT field.

Worldwide enterprises yearn for remarkable and resilient transformations on two major aspects: business operation model and business information leverage. Another vital point not to be lightly taken is to sharply enhance the user experience of business offerings. It is an overwhelmingly accepted statement that the desired enterprise transformation happens through the following five things:

- Infrastructure optimization
- Process excellence
- Architecture assimilation
- Technology adaption and adoption
- Leveraging data (internal as well as external) for deriving insights

The ensuring era of IoT is to play a very stellar role in shaping up world organizations. The IoT concept is an engrossing and essential disruption for everyone in this extremely connected world. In this section, we are to discuss the prime and paramount shifts sweeping the human society.

It is an important point to note that there are a number of noteworthy transitions and trends brewing in the IT field. The abovementioned fifth aspect is gaining a lot of ground these days with the faster maturity and stability of data management solutions and services. At the fundamental and foundation level, a variety of nimbler technologies and tips are evolving in order to bring in delectable transformations in data capture, representation, transmission, enrichment, storage, processing, analysis, mining, visualization, and virtualization tasks. The reasons for the surging popularity of data science and engineering are articulated below for the benefits of readers.

The device ecosystem is embracing a bevy of miniaturization technologies to be slim and sleek yet smart in their operations, outlooks, and outputs. That is, multifaceted devices are hitting the market in plenty. For example, highly miniaturized yet mesmerizing smartphones are being produced in billions these days. Smartphones are not only connecting people with people but also turning out to be capable of operating machines locally as well as remotely.

Digitization and distribution are gaining a lot of ground nowadays, thereby all kinds of tangible items in our home, social, and office environments are getting transfigured to be sensing, communication enabled, display attached, actuation, etc. That is, ordinary articles become extraordinary, and casually found objects in our working, walking, and wandering places become seamlessly connected with one another and hence cognitive enough to seamlessly and spontaneously join in the mainstream computing process. In short, every tangible thing gets emboldened to be smart, every electronics becomes smarter, and every human being is set to become the smartest in his or her actions, reactions, and decision-making with the pervasive, unceasing, and unobtrusive assistance of service-oriented and smartness-ingrained devices, game consoles, media players, consumer electronics, business as well as IT services, and communication networks.

Extreme and deeper connectivity is another well-known phenomenon in order to establish and sustain ad hoc connectivity among different and distributed devices to share their unique capabilities. Further on, it is all about the purposeful integration with remote, off-premise, on-demand, and online applications. These days, devices are accordingly instrumented in the factory itself to collect or generate data to be transmitted to centralized control systems. That is, lately devices are empowered by embedding a number of newer modules internally. In addition, devices are enabled to connect with the outside world.

Data becomes big, fast, and streaming and the IoT data due to multiple transformations such as newer data sources emerging, data collection, and transmission technologies are maturing, data storage and management systems are flourishing, and above all, there is a greater awareness and realization that data brings forth intelligence. Not only the data volume but also the data velocity, viscosity, variability, and variety are seeing a remarkable climb. As the tactical as well as strategical value of data is equally growing, the field of data science, engineering, management, and analytics has grown considerably nowadays.

### 6.2.1 Meteoric Rise of Device Ecosystem

While innumerable devices, sensors, controllers, and actuators are getting fervently deployed in distributed and decentralized fashion in important locations such as offices, manufacturing floors, retail stores, food joints, shopping plazas, nuclear installations, forest and border areas, critical junctions, malls, entertainment centers, etc., the amount of data getting generated and collected goes up tremendously. The machine-generated data is far larger than man-generated data.

### 6.2.2 Growth of Operational and Transactional Systems

With the continued penetration of IT into every aspect of human living, the number of business and IT systems automating and accelerating business operations, fulfilling mobile users, etc. is growing steadily. This is bound to result in a huge amount of log, performance/throughput metrics, security attacks, and transaction data.

### *6.2.3 Emergence of Pioneering Analytics (Generic and Specific)*

The IT infrastructures, platforms, processes, patterns, programming languages, middleware solutions, and databases are getting spruced up for the ensuing challenge of multi-structured and massive data. There are deep learning and knowledge engineering algorithms coming up fluently to speed up the process of knowledge discovery and dissemination. With these advancements, there are newer analytical capabilities such as diagnostic, predictive, prescriptive, and personalized analytics. Real-time analysis is another interesting development enabling a variety of newer possibilities through a nice and neat realization of actionable insights in time with the emergence of centralized and even federated cloud infrastructures.

### *6.2.4 State-of-the-Art Data Science Tools*

There are powerful algorithms and tools for empowering data scientists in scanning data and spitting out useful information quickly. The language R is turning out to be a powerful paradigm in helping data scientists immensely. Data mining and statistical computing algorithms, text analytics, natural language processing (NLP), and various mathematical concepts come handy in facilitating fine-tuned data analysis.

A family of futuristic and flexible architectural paradigms, patterns, and principles such as service-oriented architecture (SOA), event-driven architecture (EDA), model-driven architecture (MDA), resource-oriented architecture (ROA), microservice architecture (MSA), etc., have arrived to consume data-driven insights and to build sophisticated systems.

The much-discussed and discoursed "cloudification" is bringing forth high optimization and organization to ICT infrastructures; therefore clouds are being touted as the one-stop IT solution for all the needs of people in the days ahead.

According to IT experts, there will be a seamless and spontaneous merger of everyday technologies to create a kind of technology cluster to fulfill our personal as well as professional requirements instantly and instinctively. That is, there comes the possibility of transparent merging of our minds with machines. Learning will be everywhere and an every time affair because we will have intimate and real-time access to the world's information assets and knowledge base using any of our accompanying electronic gizmos, and on the reverse side, we will have an unfailing backup of our brains on massive-scale digital storages. Massive research endeavors and efforts are concertedly put into these seemingly magical and leading-edge technology themes, which will led to connect our nervous systems to computers beneficially in the days ahead.

Disruptive and transformative technologies with the smart synchronization of a galaxy of information and communication technologies will emerge to realize revolutionary applications and to accomplish hitherto unheard social networking

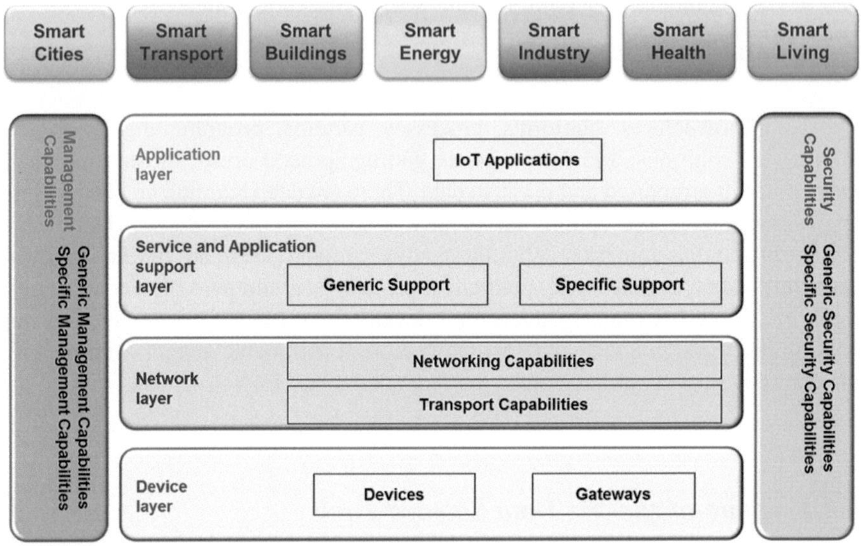


**Fig. 6.1** The IoT applications reference architecture

and digital knowledge societies. Auto-identification tags carrying our personal profile and preferences digitally will map, mix, merge, and mingle with others in realization of novel human aspirations. Our daily tools and products can be converted into smart products by attaching ultra-small computers. For example, our coffee cups, dinner plates, tablets, and clothes will be empowered to act smart in their operations and interactions with other products in the vicinity or even with the human beings. Finally all the tangible and worthy things, objects, materials, and articles will be transitioned into smart and sentient digital artifacts. This will result in the Internet of Things in the decades to come. It is hence no doubt that future generations will experience and realize complete and compact digital and technology-enabled living. The impact of IT in our life becomes bigger and deeper yet calmer as days go by. Figure 6.1 presents the IoT layered architecture.

## 6.3 IoT Device Integration Concepts, Standards, and Implementations

There are several standards for device integration especially for consumer and industry devices. That is, these standards are compactly and constantly optimized towards integrating a wide variety of distributed, decentralized, and disparate devices. However, the ultimate target is to establish smarter environments that link cross-domain automation modules ranging from home, building, and industry automation, manufacturing execution systems, healthcare systems, consumer electronics, kitchen utensils, appliances, instruments, machines, robots, sensor and actuator networks, personal devices, energy grids, etc. In addition, enterprise applications and cloud services will have an ad hoc linkage with diverse and distributed devices resulting in deeply integrated and intelligent applications. There are two groups: IP and non-IP. We are majorly focusing on IP-based technologies for device integration.

From this perspective, it is clear that DPWS [3, 4] and OSGi standards are very much competent, prominent, and dominant. That is, there will be a pervasive, smart, on-demand, and dynamic collaboration among embedded, enterprise, and cloud spaces. In this chapter, we have tried to express the unique qualities and features of the popular connectivity concepts and standards. As expressly indicated above, the device variety and volume are on the consistent climb. Freshly designed devices are hitting the market in large quantities these days. A sample pictorial representation of smart homes illustrating different devices with specific capabilities is given in Fig. 6.2. A variety of device-enable use cases are also indicated in the picture. For example, the use case of motion detection is for enabling lighting for people who are entering into a hall or room within the home. Similarly if any unknown person enters into the house, immediately the security alarm will go off reminding the security personnel to plan and proceed with the plan with authority to mitigate any kind of incursion-induced damages to people as well as properties.

Service-oriented architecture (SOA) has been a proven architectural style, approach, and pattern for designing and developing next-generation distributed systems. SOAs are often used to improve flexibility and reusability of components

**Fig. 6.2** A connected home

in complex distributed applications. This is achieved by modeling functional blocks as independent and self-sufficient services. There are several standards emerging and evolving fast fully subscribing to the game-changing SOA paradigm. There are around 50 well-established Web service (WS) standards to realize new-generation service-oriented systems. The open service gateway initiative (OSGi) standard is the one for realizing modular Java applications. DPWS is a set of a few mandatory WS standards. That is, DPWS [5] is a shrunken version of the WS standards for catering to resource-constrained embedded devices and for building device services. There are other well-known device integration standards such as uPnP, Jini, etc. There are implementations such as device service bus (DSB) for seamlessly integrating different devices. That is, DSBs are the stripped down version of enterprise service bus (ESB) platforms. While the number of distinct devices goes up remarkably, the device broker/middleware solutions are acquiring special status in establishing seamless linkage among devices to enable them to share their specific capabilities with one another, thereby better and bigger device services can be built and delivered to their users.

## 6.4 Device Integration Methods

As sensors and actuators are the new and promising elements and entities in producing and populating data in business and IT application workloads, there has to be a deeper connectivity between ground-level devices and remotely held applications. This is being touted as device-to-cloud (D2C) integration. Also for realizing actionable insights, devices need to be connected (device-to-device (D2D) integration) with one another. There are multiple data formats and protocols. For extracting usable and unambiguous information, devices need to talk the same language. There are specifications from standard organizations and implementations as products to enable seamless and standardized interactions among varied devices. In this section, we are to discuss all, which are facilitating device enablement and collaboration.

### *6.4.1 Device Profile for Web Services (DPWS)*

Services provide a standard and interoperable means for machine-to-machine (M2M) communication on the Internet. The two major classes of services are (a) Representational State Transfer (REST)-compliant services, in which resources are manipulated using a uniform set of "stateless" operations, and (b) arbitrary services, which expose an arbitrary set of operations and use SOAP messages. Both strictly go with the service-oriented architecture (SOA) architectural pattern. From SOA, there came a number of vertical-specific architectural patterns. For example, service-oriented device architecture (SODA) is one serious derivative.

DPWS is a device-specific [6] and SODA-compliant standard that comprehensively addresses discovery, description, security, and control of devices and services on local as well as remote networks. Messaging is the connecting mechanism. DPWS defines a set of implementation constraints to provide a secure and effective mechanism for describing, discovering, messaging, and eventing of services for resource-constrained devices. There are two types of services in DPWS: hosting service and hosted service. The former is a special service representing a device to participate in discovery and to describe other services hosted in it. These services present the functionalities of each device and are called hosted services. DPWS uses SOAP, WS-Addressing, and MTOM/XOP for messaging and supports SOAP-over-HTTP and SOAP-over-UDP bindings. It uses WS-Discovery for discovering a hosting service (device) and WSDL to describe the hosted service (device service). It uses Web Services Metadata Exchange to define metadata about the device, Web Services Policy to define a policy assertion to indicate compliance of the device with DPWS, and WS-Transfer to retrieve service description and metadata information about the device.

DPWS is based on several other Web service (WS) specifications, e.g.:

- WS-Addressing for advanced endpoint and message addressing
- WS-Policy for policy exchange
- WS-Security for managing security
- WS-Discovery and SOAP-over-UDP for device discovery
- WS-Transfer/WS-Metadataexchange for device and service description
- WS-Eventing for managing subscriptions for event channels

The widely articulated OSI model for the DPWS standard is given in Fig. 6.3.

DPWS is evolving fast in order to facilitate developing device services and for orchestration of composite services that are more tuned to peoples' everyday needs. Not only service-oriented applications but also event-driven applications can be realized with the appropriate leverage of any one of the DPWS implementations. DPWS is an important component in realizing and sustaining the ideals of the IoT goals.

The Devices Profile for Web Services (DPWS), promoted by OASIS, enables the realization of services leveraging both resource-constrained and intensive devices.

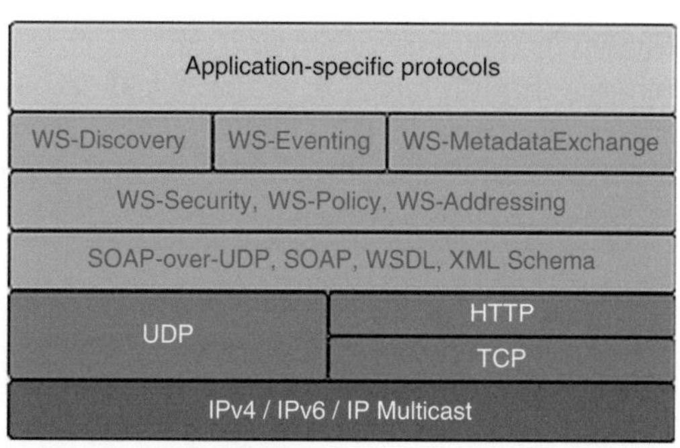


**Fig. 6.3** The IT stack for the DPWS standard

That is, connected devices and digitized objects are the key causes for the flourishing of the Internet of Things (IoT) idea. The widely accepted DPWS standard is being positioned as the cornerstone for the realization of service-oriented and event-driven IoT applications on top of these empowered devices. Further on, the DPWS standard takes care of the integration with Web-based applications and services via the open and public Internet communication infrastructure.

The DPWS standard is based on Web Service Description Language (WSDL) and Simple Object Access Protocol (SOAP) to describe and communicate device services. The major difference is that there is no insistence for a centralized registry repository such as Universal Description, Discovery, and Integration for service discovery. Instead, it relies on SOAP-over-UDP binding and UDP multicast to dynamically discover services. DPWS offers a publish-subscribe eventing mechanism for clients to subscribe for device events. For example, a device switch is on/off or sensing when temperature reaches a predefined threshold. Similarly, when an event occurs, notifications are delivered to subscribers via separate TCP connections.

## *6.4.2 DPWSim Development Toolkit*

As indicated above, DPWS is a widespread standard for service design, development, deployment, and integration for all kinds of devices that are much deviated from standard compute machines. Due to its immense popularity, there came a number of implementations. Especially the European consortium has invested heavily in this promising and potential technology in conceptualizing and concretizing a number of projects to promote the awareness and usage of device integration tools and tips. Those projects could solve many technical problems and successfully released several implementations of DPWS stacks for resource-constrained devices, which preliminarily enables the adoption of the DPWS technology. However, there are currently very few development tools for applications using DPWS. The DPWSim (http://sourceforge.net/projects/dpwsim/) is a simulation toolkit to support the development of such applications. DPWSim allows developers to prototype, develop, and test their IoT applications using the DPWS technology without the presence of physical devices. It also can be used for the collaboration between manufacturers, developers, and designers during the new product development process. DPWSim mimics all the software and protocol features of DPWS under an intuitive graphical user interface to provide an efficient way to simulate and manage DPWS devices.

### 6.4.2.1 Reference Architecture for Smarter Hospitals

In this segment, we are creating a prototype of a smarter hospital and simulating it using DPWSim toolkit. In this hospital design, we have an ICU and many hospital wards. If a critical patient is admitted to the hospital, he is taken to the ICU and a request is sent to the head physician to attend to the patient, who is in critical condition. Similarly if a patient who is not so critical is admitted to the hospital, he is taken to the general ward where a general practitioner is requested to attend to the patient. Also if the condition of a patient in the general ward becomes critical, he is shifted to the ICU and request is sent to the head physician. If any patient in the hospital needs special care, a nurse or caregiver is instructed to attend to the patient. In case there is a discharge of a patient in the hospital, the room in which the patient was present needs to be cleaned and a janitor is ordered for room cleaning.

The beds in the hospital are fixed with pressure sensors that are used to detect the presence of the patient. As the flow diagram presented in Fig. 6.4 depicts, if the patient is admitted to the hospital and is laid on the bed, pressure sensors activate and the system sets a timer to 2 h. This timer is used for regular care taking every 2 h. The patient's condition is assessed using a set of monitoring systems that include heart rate monitor and blood pressure monitor. If the patient condition is assessed to be critical, then the head physician is requested to attend to the patient, and if patient condition is not critical, then a general practitioner is requested to attend to the patient. The timer keeps on decreasing, and when the timer becomes zero, an appropriate message is sent to the medical orderly to attend to the patient. The patient is continuously checked for any emergency situation. If there is an emergency situation, the patient's condition is assessed and a corresponding care is taken. If the pressure sensor resets, it indicates that the patient has been discharged which orders the janitor to clean the room, and the whole process starts from the beginning where pressure sensors are checked for presence of a patient.

As we are simulating the hospital environment using DPWSim, there must be some middleware application that carries out the communication between different devices. For this sake, we use DPWS Explorer, which is a generic DPWS client implementation using the WS4D Java Multi Edition DPWS Stack (JMEDS). In this simulation of smart hospital, all the devices are virtually created using DPWSim which is controlled using DPWS Explorer. DPWSim which is built upon WS4D JMEDS stack is the simulation toolkit for DPWS devices. The JMEDS DefaultDevice class is inherited by DPWSDevice class, which in turn acts as the master class for all the DPWS devices that are being created. Also, DPWSim has the graphical user interface which illustrates device functionalities and operations.

### *6.4.3 Messaging Methods: Pub/Sub and Point to Point*

The WS-Eventing specification is a publish-subscribe (pub/sub) event-handling protocol that allows consumers to subscribe to one or more topics and be asynchronously notified by events generated by a Web service. This is a simple thing to implement in a service-oriented system. However, the resulting architecture is quite complex. On the other hand, the point-to-point mechanism is where producers insert their message in a queue for it is to be read by only one consumer. A queue may

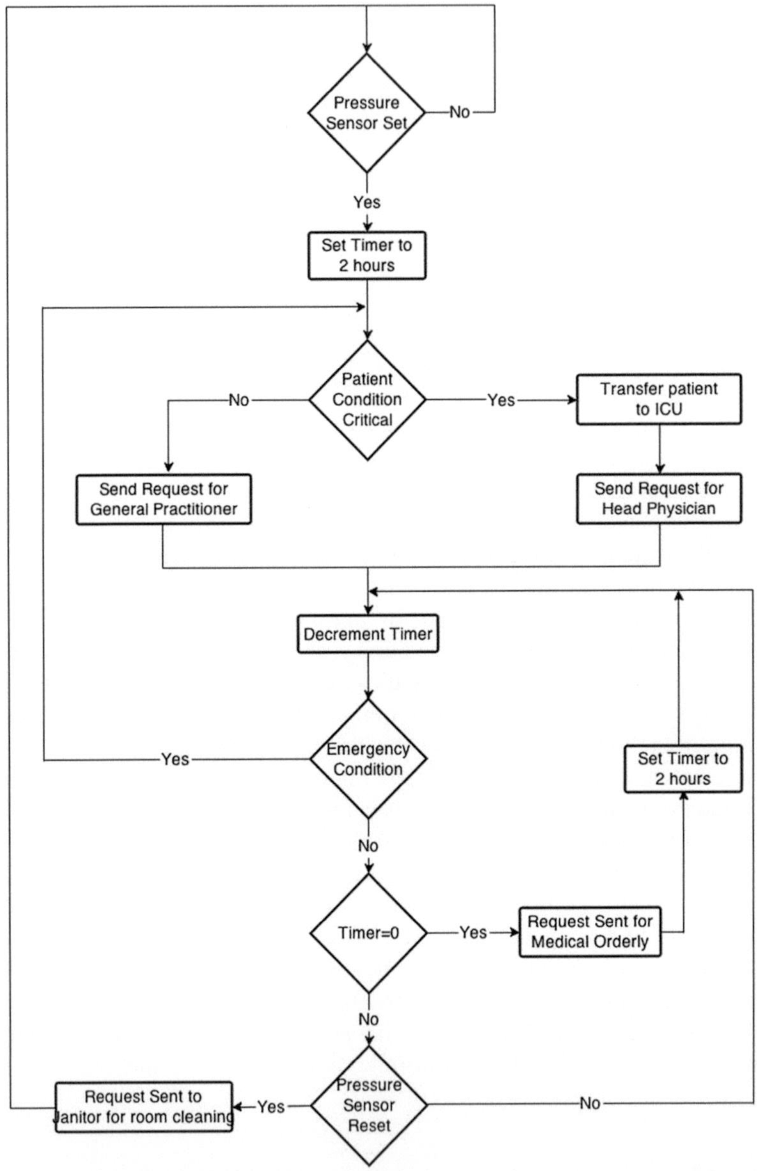


**Fig. 6.4** A data flow diagram

contain more than one consumer, but the message is delivered to only one consumer. This has several advantages over pub/sub as it is more efficient, reliable, and scalable as load balancing between consumers is inherently taken care of. It is especially to transmit large amounts of high-frequency data, thus is more appropriate to transmit sensor readings. JMS supports both pub/sub mechanism and point to point. Unfortunately, DPWS does not use a queuing mechanism and supports WS-Eventing.

WS-Eventing is useful for sending data across very different hardware and software platforms. However, the pub/sub method is a very inefficient method when implemented on low-power devices. A viable alternative is to use an intermediate machine that does the distribution of events to their subscribers.

When implementing DPWS based on a Web service toolkit, the choice of which toolkit to use should be made carefully. A toolkit should support at least transmitting SOAP-over-UDP messages in the form of unicast as well as multicast and support one-way, request-response, and solicit-response message exchange patterns. Further the underlying IP stack must support IP multicast.

Before using a service on a device, a client has to be aware of the service's description and endpoint. Assuming a high dynamical environment, a client needs to do a maximum of three steps for accessing this description: (1) device discovery by device type and scope, (2) device description transfer, and (3) service description transfer. In case the client knows all its needs in advance to communicate with a service (static case), the abovementioned steps can be simply ignored. In all other cases only, the needed steps have to be performed. So the discovery task is only used for device discovery. To determine the capabilities and the endpoint of a requested service, the service description must be acquired with WS-Transfer.

There are also technical pitfalls when implementing the discovery for DPWS. WS-Discovery uses a special message exchange pattern that is comparable to the request-response message exchange pattern. The request is sent by the client by UDP multicast and the response is sent by the device by UDP unicast. The destination of the request is defined by WS-Discovery. The destination of the response is corresponding to the source address of the request. This means that a discovery client, sending a request over UDP multicast to a device, must listen to the same UDP port, and the request was sent for receiving the unicast response. Another technical issue for a device is to obtain its IP address. A device can announce its real address with discovery or must be able to resolve its logical address to its real address. Implementations relying on DNS to obtain its IP address will only work in a network where DNS is set up correctly.

The OASIS standard Devices Profile for Web Services (DPWS) enables the use of Web services on resource-constrained devices, which are the cornerstone for the ensuing era of the Internet of Things (IoT). The DPWS is being positioned as the key one for building service-oriented and event-driven IoT applications on top of these devices with secure Web service capabilities. Thus in short, DPWS is the device-centric SOA standard being prescribed for device integration and orchestration. Having stripped off all the flabs, the DPWS standard is made nimble and fit for the growing device ecosystem to build a growing collection of connected and embedded services. There are several DPWS standard implementations. We have talked about only one implementation (DPWSim), which is a simulation toolkit to support the development of next-generation people-centric applications. DPWSim allows developers to prototype, develop, and test IoT applications using the DPWS technology without the presence of physical devices. It also can be used for the collaboration between manufacturers, developers, and designers during the new product development process. It has been shown that DPWS is a promising technology to seamlessly integrate device functionalities and events into plenty of services and applications on the Web. DPWS thus far has been widely used in automation industry, home entertainment, and automotive systems.

## 6.5 Open Services Gateway Initiative (OSGi) Standard

OSGi [7] is an independent, nonprofit corporation working to define and promote open specifications for the delivery of managed services to networked environments, such as homes and automobiles. These specifications define the OSGi service platform, which consists of two pieces: the OSGi framework and a set of standard service definitions. The OSGi framework, which sits on top of a Java virtual machine, is the execution environment for services. The OSGi framework was originally conceived to be used inside restricted environments, such as the set-top box, and now the standard is being prescribed as the best course of action for all kinds of resource-constrained as well as heavy devices.

OSGi is an industry standard for building Java applications out of modular units loosely connected through services. OSGi brings in the built-in support for describing and handling modules and their dependencies. Traditionally, OSGi has been used to decompose and loosely couple Java applications into easily manageable software modules. These modules encapsulate different parts of the whole functionality, and their life cycle can be individually controlled at runtime. For instance, each single functional module can be updated with a newer version without restarting the application. This key differentiation makes OSGi popular for developing long-running applications such as the firmware of hardware devices or extensible applications. Modules typically communicate through services, which are ordinary Java classes published under a service interface in a central service registry. Through the service registry, service consumers can retrieve a direct reference to the service object of interest. Hence, OSGi provides a very lightweight communication model that avoids performance-adverse indirections known from container systems such as EJB runtimes.

Universal Plug and Play (UPnP) and DPWS [8] require devices to communicate using SOAP or other XML-based communication protocols. Supporting non-binary protocols on the device calls for adequate computational power, and this is resulting in higher cost and power consumption. If it is feasible to implement the necessary functionality on the devices, they can be accessed directly by other network participants. For a device to participate in a Jini network, it needs to support Java and to execute a JVM. This is not feasible for small devices. But as services provide a form of abstraction, we have a second possibility. So-called proxies can be used which implement the middleware-compliant services on behalf of a device and interact with the device using proprietary protocols. These proxies can be outsourced to network nodes with higher computational capabilities like PC and fixed devices (Wi-Fi gateway, etc.). Thus, even small devices can participate in a Jini network via their proxies. As the abstract idea of services is inherent to every SOA middleware, UPnP and DPWS also allow a proxy approach.

In the case of OSGi, all services need to be executed as Java bundles on the central gateway. The bundles then communicate to the devices using proprietary means. Thus, the proxy approach is mandatory in OSGi. The topology, which describes the network setup of a device-centric SOA, is another key characteristic to be taken into consideration. As already indicated above, OSGi networks consist of a central gateway that hosts proxies which then communicate directly with devices. This results in a star topology. Such a topology is favorable, for example, in a home environment, where usually at least one full-featured device, e.g., a PC or a Wi-Fi router, exists that acts as gateway to which home appliances with relatively small computational capabilities are connected to.

For Jini and DPWS (in a certain mode), services can be distributed in the network but need a central service registry to allow dynamic device discovery. This means that a far more open network topology is possible in comparison to OSGi, but still these networks rely on a central component to function. In UPnP and DPWS (in another mode), the network is created on a peer-to-peer basis without the need for any centralized responsibilities. Although Jini, UPnP, and DPWS favor a distributed network, it is still possible to use proxies which are executed on a single machine. This way, a star topology is possible for these SOA device middleware as well. The chosen topology has impact on the scalability and robustness of the system.

## *6.5.1 Scalability*

Scalability refers to the capabilities of a system to compensate an increase or decrease in the number of participants in the network. In this respect, an OSGi network with only a central gateway is not able to scale with the number of participants. The gateway is a dedicated piece of hardware. When the number of services to be executed on the gateway exceeds its capacity, the typical compensation mechanism is not possible during runtime. The only chance to adjust to the needs is to shut down the network and to replace the current gateway with more powerful hardware.

For Jini, UPnP, and DPWS, this is different, as they inherently base on distributed communication. The scalability of these networks primarily relies on the scalability of the underlying physical network like Ethernet, WLAN, etc. Fortunately, the scalability of physical networks has been well addressed in the past. Applying extensible network topologies including switches and routers allows company intranets to scale to the number of employees. Thus Jini, UPnP, and DPWS are able to scale gracefully. One exception for Jini and DPWS (in a certain mode) is the central lookup registry. Just like in the case of the OSGi gateway, exceeding the capabilities of the registry is a problem. But unlike OSGi, the registry is only queried to look up a service and does not need to conduct expensive computing. Thus, the extension of the network has less impact on the service registry than on an OSGi gateway.

### *6.5.2 Robustness*

Here, we will take a look at what will happen if devices are not available to the system due to a component failure or outage. For the chosen SOA realizations, the failure of a single service has only to be compensated by depending services but has no effect on the SOA system as a whole. In OSGi, the necessary OSGi gateway is a single point of failure. As the services are executed on the gateway, a failure of the gateway will prevent any further system activity.

In Jini, a failure of the central service registry is less severe. Without service registry, it is no longer possible to find a new service. But as devices in a Jini network communicate directly with each other, already connected services without any disturbance can continue to interact. A DPWS network is even more fault tolerant, as mechanisms are defined by which it is dynamically decided whether to use a service registry or do decentralized lookup. Thus, failure of the service registry in DPWS can be compensated by the network. For an UPnP network, a failure of a service has no additional effects, as interaction is completely done on a peer-to-peer (P2P) basis.

## 6.6 REST Paradigm

Today everything is fitted with one or more APIs in order to connect and collaborate with everything else. With the overwhelming success of APIs, these days APIs are pervasive. Especially for the impending connected era, the rise and relevance of APIs are grandiosely significant. We have embedded, mobile, Web, cloud, and enterprise applications and services in plenty, and all are fitted with apt APIs for enabling seamless and spontaneous integration and interactions. REST (Representational State Transfer), being synonymous with XML/ JSON over HTTP, is the one standout for the forthcoming IoT days [9, 10]. In the recent past, JSON has supplanted XML as the data format of choice for the Web.

At its core, REST [11] is an architectural pattern for uniformly accessing and modifying a resource. One entity (the server) is the authority over the current state of an object. Other entities may request a "representation" of the current object and may also send requests to create, modify, or delete the object. The current popular REST model uses URIs to identify objects ("/lamp/1234"), HTTP verbs to specify an action, and JSON to represent the object. To fetch an object, a client may send an HTTP request to "GET /lamp/1234." The server may respond with an HTTP 200 and a body containing JSON data.

With DPWS, it is possible to develop and deploy service-oriented device applications that are satisfying and sticking to the service-oriented device architecture (SODA) [12] architectural pattern. However, it still has a big overhead due to many expensive bidirectional message exchanges and data representation in XML. Hence, there is a surging popularity for RESTful architecture, which complies with the resource-oriented architecture (ROA), a distinct architectural style. Representational State Transfer (REST) is a resource-oriented software architecture style for building Internet-scale distributed applications. Typically, the REST triangle defines the principles for encoding (content types), addressing (nouns), and accessing (verbs) a collection of resources using Internet standards. Resources, which are central to REST, are uniquely addressable using a universal syntax (e.g., a URL in HTTP) and share a uniform interface for the transfer of application states between client and server (e.g., GET/POST/PUT/DELETE in HTTP). REST resources may typically exhibit multiple typed representations using, for example, XML, JSON, YAML, or plain text documents. Thus, RESTful systems are loosely coupled systems which follow these principles to exchange application states as resource representations. This kind of stateless interactions improves the resource consumption and the scalability of the system. Therefore, the implementation of a RESTful service can be more simple and lightweight than in other architectures.

REST services can be developed as easy machine readable service interaction with the Web Application Description Language (WADL). The resource-based handling of methods allows a simple and easy scalable service description. WADL is based on XML and describes applications based on HTTP. It supports the automatic description of RESTful services with machine processable service descriptions. The SA-REST is an open, flexible, and standard-based approach for adding semantics to RESTful services.

In the context of the IoT, the RESTful services have many advantages over arbitrary Web services (i.e., SOAP), such as less overhead, low parsing complexity, statelessness, and tighter integration with HTTP. In addition, applications supporting RESTful services perform better on wireless sensor nodes with limited resources as well as are considered easier to learn and implement.

Thus we have shown that DPWS, OSGi, uPnP, and Jini are the prominent standards for device integration. Let us now plunge into the data transmission protocols that are part and parcel of the above device integration standards.

## 6.7 Device Integration Protocols

Devices are originally instrumented to generate and communicate their internal data and/or to capture external data from their operating environments. Devices are also instrumented to be seamlessly integrated with one another in the vicinity and with remote ones over any network in order to share their distinct capabilities and data points. Device data then must be collected and sent to the faraway server infrastructure. That server infrastructure in association with appropriate analytics engine has to crunch the captured and cleansed data in order to produce actionable insights, which are then fed into devices and people to consider the next course of action with all the confidence and clarity. The renowned data transmission protocols are:

- MQTT—a protocol for collecting device data and communicating it to servers (D2S)
- XMPP—a protocol best for connecting devices to people, a special case of the D2S pattern, since people are connected to the servers
- DDS—a fast bus for integrating intelligent machines (D2D)
- AMQP—a queuing system designed to connect servers to each other (S2S)
- CoAP [13]—an optimized protocol

### 6.7.1 MQTT (Message Queue Telemetry Transport)

MQTT was originally developed and released by IBM. Over the past couple of years, the protocol has been moved into the open-source community. This has seen a significant growth in popularity as smartphone applications have taken off on a strong note.

The design principles and aims of MQTT are much more simple and focused. It provides publish-and-subscribe messaging. And it was specifically designed for resource-constrained devices and low bandwidth, high latency networks such as dial-up lines and satellite links. Basically, it can be used effectively in embedded systems. One of the crucial advantages MQTT has over more full-featured "enterprise messaging" brokers is that it is intentionally low footprint and hence is ideal for today's mobile and developing IoT applications. In fact, companies like Facebook are using it as part of their mobile applications because it has such a low-power draw and is light on network bandwidth.

Some of the MQTT-based brokers support many thousands of concurrent device connections. It offers three qualities of service: (1) fire-and-forget or unreliable; (2) "at least once" to ensure that it is sent a minimum of one time, but might be sent more than one time; and (3) "exactly once." MQTT targets device data collection. As its name states, its main purpose is telemetry or remote monitoring. Its goal is to collect data from many devices and transport that data to the IT infrastructure. It targets large networks of small devices that need to be monitored or controlled from the cloud. Figure 6.5 vividly illustrates the uniqueness of MQTT.

MQTT implements the much-published hub-and-spoke model. It makes neither enabling device-to-device (D2D) transfer nor fanning the data to many recipients. A hub-and-spoke architecture is natural for MQTT. All the devices connect to a data concentrator server like IBM's new MessageSight appliance. As the protocol works on top of TCP, which provides a simple and reliable stream, the data loss is not there. Since the IT infrastructure uses the data, the entire system is designed to

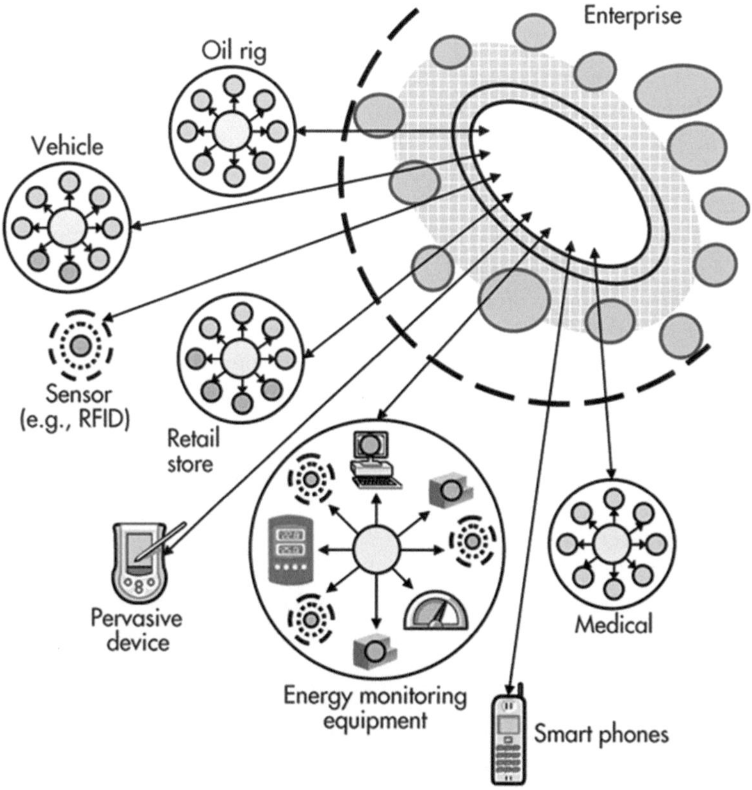


**Fig. 6.5** The MQTT-enabled messaging mechanism

easily transport data into enterprise technologies like ActiveMQ and enterprise service buses (ESBs).

MQTT's main strengths are simplicity (just five API methods), a compact binary packet payload (no message properties, compressed headers, much less verbose than something text-based like HTTP), and it makes a good fit for simple push messaging scenarios such as temperature updates, stock price tickers, oil pressure feeds, or mobile notifications. It is also very useful for connecting machines together, such as connecting an Arduino device to a Web service with MQTT. MQTT enables applications like monitoring a huge oil pipeline for leaks or vandalism. Those thousands of sensors must be concentrated into a single location for analysis. When the system finds a problem, it can take action to correct that problem. Other applications for MQTT include power usage monitoring, lighting control, and even intelligent gardening. They share a need for collecting data from many sources and making it available to the IT infrastructure.

#### 6.7.1.1 VerneMQ

VerneMQ is a high-performance distributed MQTT message broker. It scales horizontally and vertically on commodity hardware to support a high number of concurrent publishers and consumers while maintaining low latency and fault tolerance. As indicated above, the pioneering MQTT protocol connects virtually everything. Client libraries are available for most programming languages and environments. A built-in plug-in mechanism allows to connect custom message stores (SQL and NoSQL databases), rule engines, and complex logging and event processing infrastructures. VerneMQ can be deployed on a wider variety of platforms for reliable and fault-tolerant operation. This platform is to access smart meters over a lightweight, secure, and bidirectional communication link. It is being positioned as the one for enabling connected cars, smarter lighting, public transportation, and smarter homes.

#### 6.7.1.2 ThingMQ

ThingMQ is a carrier-grade multi-protocol message broker for IoT that runs on the cloud. Any device can be easily connected to their cloud using MQTT, CoAP, REST, or WebSockets and ThingMQ handles the rest. To get started, one can use the free shared instance of ThingMQ. You simply connect your device to mq.thingmq.com using the M2M protocol of your choice. For higher security, you can connect your device to one of the dedicated instances. But here devices need to be authenticated. Once you are connected, you need to choose a unique identifier for your device, for example, my-thing-id. Data can be published under my-thing-id via MQTT, CoAP, REST, or WebSockets protocols using JSON, plain text, XML, BSON, MsgPack, or any other payload format.

### *6.7.2 XMPP (Extensible Messaging and Presence Protocol)*

XMPP is primarily for understanding the presence as articulated in Fig. 6.6. That means humans are intimately involved here.

XMPP uses the XML text format as its native type, making person-to-person communications natural. Like MQTT, it runs over TCP. Its key strength is a name@domain.com addressing scheme that helps connect the needles in the huge Internet haystack. In the IoT context, XMPP offers an easy way to address a device. This is especially handy if that data is going between distant and mostly unrelated points just like the person-to-person case. The most implementations use polling or checking for updates only on demand. A protocol called BOSH (bidirectional streams over synchronous HTTP) lets servers push messages. XMPP provides a great way to connect your home thermostat to a Web server, so you can access it

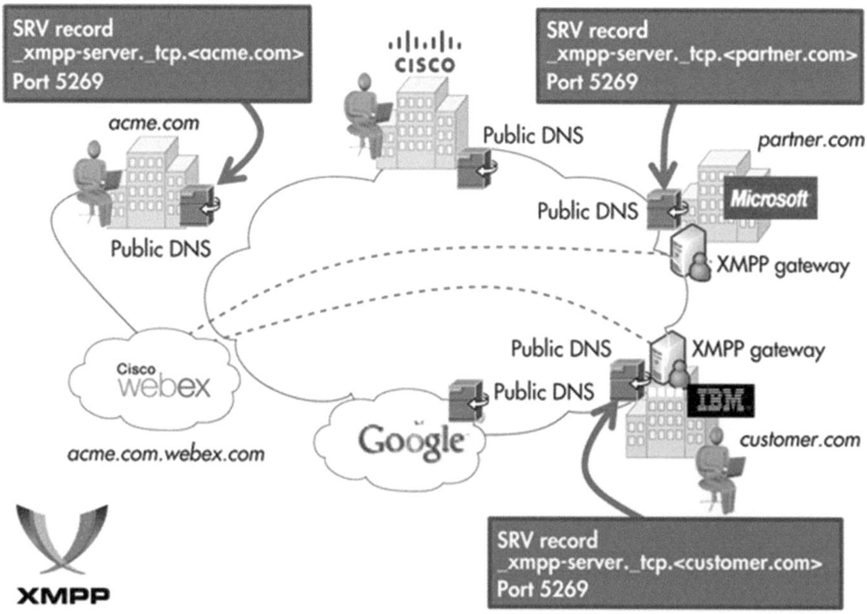


**Fig. 6.6** An XMPP-enabled connected environment

from your phone. Its strengths in addressing, security, and scalability make it ideal for consumer-oriented IoT applications.

### *6.7.3 DDS (Data Distribution Bus)*

DDS targets devices that directly use device data. It distributes data to other devices. While interfacing with the IT infrastructure is supported, DDS's main purpose is to connect devices to other devices. It is a data-centric middleware standard with roots in high-performance defense, industrial, and embedded applications. DDS can efficiently deliver millions of messages per second to many simultaneous receivers. DDS implements the pub/sub pattern as vividly depicted in Fig. 6.7.

Devices need to communicate with many other devices, and TCP's simple and reliable point-to-point streams are far too restrictive. Instead, DDS offers detailed quality-of-service (QoS) control, multicast, configurable reliability, and pervasive redundancy. In addition, fan-out is a key strength. DDS offers powerful ways to filter and select exactly which data goes where, and "where" can be thousands of simultaneous destinations. Some devices are small, so there are lightweight versions of DDS that run in constrained environments.

Hub-and-spoke is completely inappropriate for device data use. DDS implements direct device-to-device "bus" communication with a relational data model.

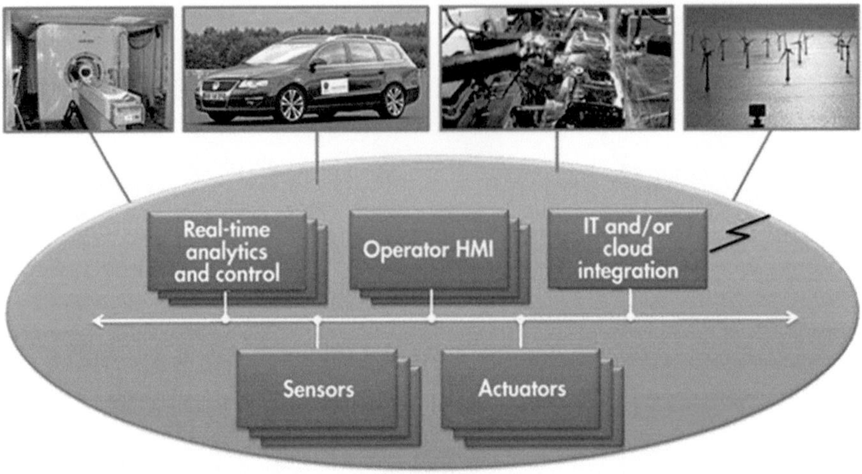


**Fig. 6.7** The reference architecture for the DDS solution

Similar to the way a database controls access to stored data, a data bus controls data access and updates by many simultaneous users. This is exactly what many high-performance devices need to work together as a single system. High-performance integrated device systems use DDS. It is the only technology that delivers the flexibility, reliability, and speed necessary to build complex, real-time applications. Applications include military systems, wind farms, hospital integration, medical imaging, asset-tracking systems, and automotive test and safety. DDS connects devices together into working, distributed applications at physics speeds.

#### 6.7.3.1 DDS

DSS is a middleware protocol and API standard for data-centric connectivity from the Object Management Group (OMG). It integrates the components of a system together, providing low-latency data connectivity, extreme reliability, and a scalable architecture that business and mission-critical Internet of Things (IoT) applications need. Many real systems include devices, servers, mobile nodes, and more. They have diverse communication needs, but it is better and easier to use a single communication paradigm when possible. System designers should determine which of the protocols meets the primary challenge of their intended applications. Then, if possible, extend that primary choice to all aspects of the system.

For example, inter-device data use is a different use case from device data collection. Requirements for turning on your light switch (best with CoAP) are much different than the requirements for managing the generation of that power (best with DDS), monitoring the transmission lines (best with MQTT), or communicating power usage within the data center (best with AMQP).

Overall, DDS is the most versatile of these protocols. It can manage tiny devices; connect large, high-performance sensor networks; and close time-critical control loops. It can also serve and receive data from the cloud. DDS communication is peer to peer. Elimination of message brokers and servers simplifies deployment, minimizes latency, maximizes scalability, increases reliability, and reduces cost and complexity. Using DDS does require building a data model and understanding data-centric principles. It is ideal for IoT applications that require a lasting, reliable, and high-performance architecture.

### *6.7.4 AMQP (Advanced Message Queuing Protocol)*

AMQP was designed as an open replacement for existing proprietary messaging middleware. Two of the most important reasons to use AMQP are reliability and interoperability. As the name implies, it provides a wide range of features related to messaging, including reliable queuing, topic-based publish-and-subscribe messaging, flexible routing, transactions, and security. AMQP exchanges route messages directly by topic and also based on headers.

There's a lot of fine-grained control possible with such a rich feature set. One can restrict access to queues, manage their depth, and more. Features like message properties, annotations, and headers make it a good fit for a wide range of enterprise applications. This protocol was designed for reliability at the many large companies who depend on messaging to integrate applications and move data around their organization.

AMQP is a binary wire protocol which was designed for interoperability between different vendors. Where other protocols have failed, AMQP adoption has been strong. Companies like JP Morgan use it to process one billion messages a day. NASA uses it for Nebula cloud computing. Google uses it for complex event processing. Here are a couple of additional AMQP examples and links:

- It is used in one of the world's largest biometric databases: India's Aadhaar project—home to 1.2 billion identities.
- It is used in the Ocean Observatories Initiative—an architecture that collects 8 terabytes of data per day.

AMQP is all about queues. It sends transactional messages between servers. As a message-centric middleware (Fig. 6.8) that arose from the banking industry, it can process thousands of reliable queued transactions.

AMQP is focused on not losing messages. Communications from the publishers to exchanges and from queues to subscribers use TCP, which provides strictly reliable point-to-point connection. Further, endpoints must acknowledge acceptance of each message. The standard also describes an optional transaction mode with a formal multiphase commit sequence. True to its origins in the banking industry, AMQP middleware focuses on tracking all messages and ensuring that each is delivered as intended, regardless of failures or reboots.

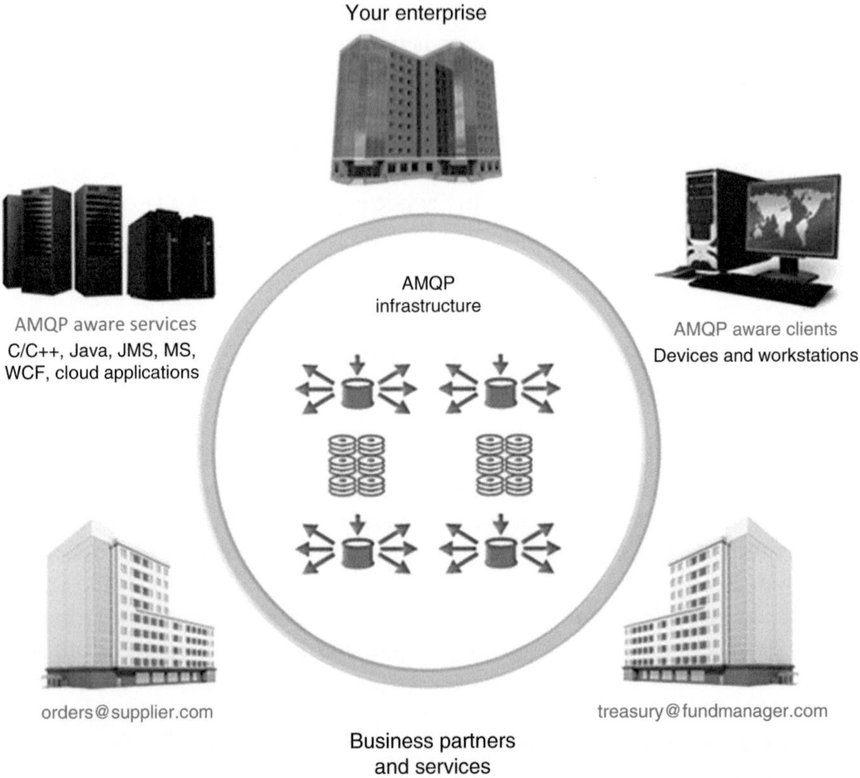


**Fig. 6.8** The AMQP-enabled connected enterprise architecture

robomq.io connects devices, systems, clouds, and things to create smart and context-aware applications. It provides cloud-hosted message queue as a service platform bundled with management interface, dashboards, analytics, and SDK. AMQP message broker is at the core, fully managed and hosted on the cloud. Highly scalable message queue clusters with built-in redundancy, failover, and elastic scaling to add resources as the message traffic increases. robmoq.io brings the messaging platform in a fully managed and hosted message queue as a service SaaS model offering reliability, scale, and manageability required by today's cloud, mobile, M2M, and IoT. robomq.io is an end-to-end IoT middleware platform that can connect any device to any system, application, or cloud through its suite of connectors and adapters. It has an IoT gateway that allows devices and device mesh networks to connect to the cloud over cellular or wired connectivity. This also comes with real-time analytics engine, data-driven alerts and device diagnostics, and management capabilities to help you manage your IoT ecosystem effectively.

The Constrained Application Protocol (CoAP) is a specialized Web transfer protocol for use with constrained nodes and constrained networks in the IoT space. The protocol is designed for machine-to-machine (M2M) applications such as smart energy and building automation. CoAP includes several HTTP functionalities which have been redesigned for M2M applications over constrained environments on the IoT, meaning it takes into account the low processing power and energy constraints of small embedded devices, such as sensors. In addition, CoAP offers a number of features that HTTP lacks such as built-in resource discovery, IP multicast support, native push model, and asynchronous message exchange. There are many implementations of CoAP in various languages, such as libcoap1 (an open-source C-implementation) and Sensinode's NanoService2:

- Physical Layer and Data Link Layer—Wireless networks are essential for the IoT. The IEEE 802.15.4 standard specifies the physical layer (PHY) and media access control (MAC) for low-rate wireless personal networks (LR-WPANs), which focuses on low-power consumption, low cost, and low data transfer rate communication between constrained devices.
- Network Layer—IPv6 over low-power wireless personal area networks (6LoWPAN) standard defined by the IETF brings the Internet Protocol (IP) to small embedded devices (e.g., sensors) in even the most constrained networks such as IEEE 802.15.4. In addition to 6LoWPAN, the IETF routing over low-power and lossy networks (ROLL) working group has defined IPv6 routing protocol for low-power and lossy networks (RPL) for smart object Internetworking. Together these networking technologies provide means for small embedded devices to integrate into the Internet.
- Transport Layer—HTTP typically relies on TCP, which has performance problems over low-power and lossy networks (LLNs), is sensitive to mobility, does not provide multicast support, and has high overhead for short-lived transactions. CoAP, on the other hand, is built on top of the User Datagram Protocol (UDP), which provides significantly lower overhead and supports multicast.
- Application Layer—CoAP provides RESTful services optimized for resource-constrained networks and devices and thus makes the protocol suitable to the IoT and M2M applications. In addition, it provides reliability (with default time-out and exponential back-off retransmission) mechanisms even without the use of TCP as transport layer. One of the most important design goals of CoAP has also been to keep the message overhead as small as possible. HTTP can also be used over 6LoWPAN. However, the results show that the power consumption and bytes transferred per transaction are drastically lower when using CoAP over 6LoWPAN compared to HTTP over 6LoWPAN and thus increasing the battery lifetime of constrained devices.
- Payload—The W3C Efficient XML Interchange (EXI) format is a very compact, high-performance Extensible Markup Language (XML) representation, which significantly reduces bandwidth requirements without compromising efficient use of other resources, such as battery life, code size, processing power, and memory.

In summary, CoAP is a software protocol intended to be used in very simple electronic devices that allows them to communicate interactively over the Internet. It is particularly targeted for small low-power sensors, switches, valves, and similar components that need to be controlled or supervised remotely, through standard Internet networks. CoAP is an application layer protocol that is intended for use in resource-constrained Internet devices, such as WSN nodes. CoAP is designed to easily translate to HTTP for simplified integration with the Web while also meeting specialized requirements such as multicast support, very low overhead, and simplicity. Multicast, low overhead, and simplicity are extremely important for Internet of Things (IoT) and machine-to-machine (M2M) devices, which tend to be deeply embedded and have much less memory and power supply than traditional Internet devices have. Therefore, efficiency is very important. CoAP can run on most devices that support UDP or a UDP analog.

## 6.8 Protocol Landscape for the IoT

There are new protocols for enabling device integration. As the multiplicity and heterogeneity of devices are on the climb, the resulting complexity is to shoot up significantly. There are device middleware and a host of adaptors to translate between one protocol to another in order to ensure unambiguous and uncluttered data consumption and processing of data being transmitted by devices. The matured OSI model is tweaked and twisted a bit for various device protocols. Here is a description for data-centric OSI layers.

- *Connectivity Layer*—RJ45 (the physical connector, usually for Ethernet), PLC, RS-232, RS-485, ModBus, USB (as a connector type, not the communication protocol), SPI, ODB2 (in cars), and wireless (no connector!). There are gateways that will convert any of those physical connectors into wireless.
- *Link Protocol*—Ethernet 802.3, Wi-Fi 802.11a/b/g/n, Bluetooth, BLE, Dash 7, ZigBee, RFID, GSM, 6LoWPAN, and 802.14.5e are the widely used protocol to send data across. The last two are really focused on the IoT use case.
- *Transport*—IPv4 and IPv6 are the ones for the transport layer. Due to the dazzling growth of devices, the adoption of IPv6 is accelerated.
- *Session/Communication*—MQTT and CoAP (Constrained Application Protocol), a kind of REST protocol but more efficient than HTTP, DDS, XMPP, and AMQP, are the prominent ones in the IoT space today.
- *Data Aggregation/Processing*—There are a number of data aggregation, transformation, and processing solutions. Apache Spark, Storm, Kafka, etc. are the most visible ones.
- *Data Storage/Retrieval*—There are SQL, NoSQL, and NewSQL database solutions to store IoT device data. Hadoop HDFS is the file system for IoT data.

Due to the burgeoning nature of devices and the data being generated by those devices, the IoT space needs many powerful data protocols. We have discussed the key protocols in the above section.

## 6.9 Conclusion

Every kind of enterprises ranging from small to large in size are to be immensely benefited out of this game-changing concept. Smarter environments are to be realized with ambient intelligence in order to be situation aware, people centric, event driven, and service oriented. IT will be typically virtual, computing is set to be pervasive, goals such as activity and environment sensing are to be grandly ubiquitous, communication is unified and blessed with reliable and resilient connectivity, network topologies are varying and empowered by ultrahigh bandwidth, and knowledge extraction and engineering are common. Digitalization and distribution are set to be deeper in the sense that there will be billions of connected devices and trillions of digital objects. Every tangible thing in our homes, offices, hotels, hospitals, and manufacturing floors is enabled to be service providing, consuming, and brokering in a purpose-specific manner. Ordinary things get digitized to exhibit adaptive behavior. The expected changes are really fascinating and fabulous with the adoption and adaption of the IoT platforms, patterns, processes, and practices.

The IoT conundrum is capable of touching every facet of our lives. It lays down a stimulating environment for conceiving and concretizing scores of smart and sophisticated applications for enabling knowledge workers, common people, decision-makers, scientists, etc. Every kind of people is to be empowered with a lot of capabilities and competencies in order to shine in their daily works and walks. This chapter is being specifically planned and produced for expounding the connectivity approaches, device integration standards and implementations, and data transport protocols in the fast-evolving IoT space.

## Glossary

**Devices Profile for Web Services (DPWS)** Is for the device world, that is, creating, consuming, connecting, and controlling Web services for the resource-constrained embedded devices. A key concept is the creation of a distributed SOA within heterogeneous environments. DPWS defines a minimal set of standards and specifications in order to provide Web service-based communication for embedded devices. It identifies a core set of Web service specifications comprising the following areas: secure message transmission, dynamic discovery, description, subscription, and event notification.

**OSGi** Caters for the integration of the pre-built reusable and collaborative components, reducing maintenance costs by delivering and updating provided services dynamically. The core of the OSGi specification comprises the OSGi framework which provides an execution platform for Java-based components, called bundles. The platform allows install, uninstall, start, stop, and update bundles at runtime without restarting the entire system. Attaching a fragment bundle to its host bundle provides the ability to extend the host bundle's class path with classes or additional resources. Bundles offer their functionality in the form of services by means of a publish-find-bind mechanism. For this purpose, a service registry is used where bundles can register their services under one or more interfaces and search for other services. Moreover, the OSGi framework contains a service tracker which notifies registered listeners about service registration changes. A generic mechanism to subscribe and receive events from services or the framework itself is provided through the event admin service. OSGi runs in a Java virtual machine (JVM) and offers an intra-JVM SOA.

**Service Component Architecture (SCA)** Is a set of specifications which describe a model for building applications and systems using a SOA. SCA models solutions as sets of service components offering services and making references to services supplied by others, which are combined together by composites which wire references to services and which declaratively apply bindings for communication methods and also apply policies for aspects such as security and transactions. SCA extends and complements prior approaches to implementing services, and SCA builds on open standards such as Web services.

**Service-oriented architecture (SOA)** SOA is an emerging architectural style to achieve high interoperability of heterogeneous software components and systems. Web services implement this principle and provide a convenient way of creating flexible service-oriented solutions.

**WS-Addressing** The main objective of WS-Addressing is to provide an addressing mechanism for Web services as well as messages in a transport-neutral matter. By introducing both concepts, endpoint references (EPR) and message information headers (MI), WS-Addressing overcomes the lack of SOAP's independence of underlying protocols and secondly support of asynchronous message exchange. Both limitations are historically caused by the default SOAP to HTTP binding.

**WS-Discovery** Is a discovery protocol based on IP multicast for enabling services to be discovered automatically. Discovery introduces three different endpoint types: target service, client, and discovery proxy. Target services are Web services offering themselves to the network. Clients may search for target services and discover them dynamically. Discovery proxy is an endpoint enabling discovery in spanned networks since simple discovery is limited to a multicast group and hence to local managed networks only. WS-Discovery defines four operations or messages to discover target services in a network. To explicitly discover target services in a network, a client can use the Probe operation and send as multicast message. Matching target services will answer with the Probe matches operation sent as UDP unicast message to the client. To implicitly discover target services, a client can listen for hello and bye messages. A target service announces its availability with these messages sent as UDP multicast. To resolve logical addresses introduced with the endpoint structure in WS-Addressing, a client can use the resolve operation sent as UDP multicast message. The corresponding target service responds with the resolve matches operation sent as UDP unicast to the client. The discovery proxy does not need any additional operations.

**WS-Eventing** Defines a protocol for managing subscriptions for a Web service-based eventing mechanism. This protocol defines three endpoints: subscriber, event source, and subscription manager. Subscribers request subscriptions on behalf of event sinks to receive events from event sources. Subscription requests contain an event delivery mode and event filter mechanism to negotiate event delivery mechanisms and event filter mechanism. Subscription managers are responsible of holding subscriptions of event sources.

**WS-MetadataExchange/WS-Transfer—WS-MetadataExchange** Is a specification that defines data types and operations to retrieve metadata associated with an endpoint. This metadata describes what other endpoints need to know to interact with the described endpoint. WS-MetadataExchange defines the MetadataSection that divides the metadata into separate units of metadata with a dialect specifying its type. Until the latest version of DPWS, only WS-MetadataExchange was used for service and device description and retrieval. In the latest DPWS version of February 2006, WS-Transfer is used to retrieve the metadata. The structure of the metadata is still as specified in WS-MetadataExchange. The main difference is that WS-MetadataExchange defined operations to retrieve all or parts of the metadata of an endpoint, whereas WS-Transfer only can be used to retrieve all metadata of an endpoint.

# References


1. Hassan MM, Song B, Huh EN (2009) A framework of sensor-cloud integration opportunities and challenges. In: Proceedings of the 3rd International conference on Ubiquitous Information Management and Communication (ICUIMC), ACM, pp 618–626
2. Raj P (2012) Cloud enterprise architecture. CRC Press, Boca Raton
3. Samaras I, Hassapis G, Gialelis J (2013) A modified DPWS protocol stack for 6LoWPAN-based wireless sensor networks. IEEE Trans Ind Inf 9(1):209–217
4. Yang X, Zhi X (2012) Dynamic deployment of embedded services for DPWS-enabled devices. In 2012 international conference on computing, measurement, control and sensor network, pp 302–306
5. Moritz G, Timmermann D et al (2010) Encoding and compression for the devices profile for web services. In 2010 I.E. 24th international conference on advanced information networking and applications workshops, pp 514–519
6. Lerche C, Laum N, Moritz G et al (2011) Implementing powerful web services for highly resource-constrained devices. In: 2011 I.E. international conference on pervasive computing and communications workshops, pp 332–335
7. Dohndorf O (2010) Towards the web of things: using DPWS to bridge isolated OSGi platforms. Published in: Pervasive computing and communications workshops (PERCOM workshops), 8th IEEE International conference
8. Huang C-M (2011) Design and implementation of a web 2.0 service platform for DPWS-based home-appliances in the cloud environment. Workshops of international conference on advanced information networking and applications

9. Han SN (2014) DPWSim: a simulation toolkit for IoT applications using devices profile for web services, IEEE World Forum on Internet of Things (WF-IoT)
10. Cubo J (2014) A cloud-based internet of things platform for ambient assisted living. Sensors 14:14070–14105. doi:10.3390/s140814070
11. REST Without JSON (2013) The future of IoT protocols. https://dzone.com/articles/json-http-and-the-future-of-iot-protocols
12. Lee NK, Lee HW, Ryu W (2015) Considerations for web of object service architecture on IoT environment. Int J Smart Home 9(1):195–202
13. Shelby Z, Hartke K, Bormann C (2013) Constrained application protocol (CoAP)., IETF Internet Draft, https://tools.ietf.org/html/draft-ietf-core-coap-18

# Chapter 7
# Cooperative Device Cloud: A Resource Management Framework for the Internet of Things

**Andreas Kliem and Odej Kao**

## 7.1 Introduction

Following the ubiquitous computing (UC) [1] and Internet of Things (IoT) [2] visions, connected and embedded devices are finding their way into more and more areas of our everyday lives. The technologies and applications we rely on are heavily influenced by their presence, regardless whether we think of the smartphones most of us use every day, heating control in our homes, or computer-aided assistance systems in our cars. Arising from the capability to interconnect and collect data in an ad hoc and ubiquitous fashion, new applications, such as smart grids, traffic congestion, or seamless vital sign monitoring, become viable [3]. This results in a mutual reinforcement of the development of connected and embedded devices and the corresponding applications. Well-known IoT application domains are E-health [4], transportation, logistics [5], automation, and smart homes and cities [6].

Two basic assumptions build the foundation of the UC and IoT visions. First, it is assumed that users are no longer supported by a single monolithic computer system (e.g., a PC). Rather, a set of embedded devices surrounding them constantly provides the necessary resources and applications to fulfill their everyday needs. The term "resources" refers to both data and infrastructure (e.g., storage). The second important assumption is that so-called things or entities are uniquely identifiable and linked to virtual representations using an information network similar to the Internet. The term virtual representation constitutes that a thing is connected to an information network and that it can be accessed through a communication protocol or an interface/service (e.g., a sensor providing data about a user's environment).

A. Kliem (✉) • O. Kao
Complex and Distributed IT Systems, Faculty of Engineering and Computer Science, Technische Universität Berlin, Berlin, Germany
e-mail: andreas.kliem@tu-berlin.de



Z. Mahmood (ed.), *Connectivity Frameworks for Smart Devices*,
Computer Communications and Networks, DOI 10.1007/978-3-319-33124-9_7

Apparently, taking advantage of the seamless integration of these things requires a huge amount of technical infrastructure to be developed, deployed, and maintained.

Apart from the capability of treating things like individuals by assigning globally unique identifiers to them, a variety of supporting technologies needs to be considered. Examples are communication and networking, data processing, or security and privacy technologies. However, as discussed by Uckelmann et al. [7], it has to be noted that these technologies are not to be considered as synonyms when discussed individually. In particular, visions and technologies like UC, embedded devices, wireless sensor networks (WSN), or the Internet Protocol (IP) have a strong relation to and partial overlap with IoT. However, only considering them together as an overall integrated technology framework covers the whole topic IoT is about.

Aiming for an integrated technology framework requires overcoming the heterogeneity challenge, caused by the various involved technologies and components. As a remedy, solutions are often dedicated to specific application domains, which reduce the set of involved technologies to a manageable amount. However, these isolated solutions barely interact. Moreover, application domain-specific IoT resources (e.g., sensors, actuators, gateways) are deployed and statically bound to small groups of users, instead of being allocated and utilized on demand. This is basically motivated by the fact that the IoT misses concepts for on-demand resource allocation, resource sharing, resource pooling and provisioning, or pay-as-you-go (PAYG) pricing models, which became popular with regard to cloud computing [8]. Compared to cloud computing, the set of resources is much more heterogeneous. This makes it difficult to introduce the abstraction of a resource pool that can be accessed on demand using homogeneous APIs. As a result, one of the major challenges to be solved is the IoT resource management challenge. Appropriate IoT resource management concepts enable developers and users to implement, deploy, and operate IoT solutions that seamlessly facilitate and manage the large amount of IoT resources (things, devices, sensors, actuators).

In general, IoT resources provide knowledge (i.e., data) about an entity environment. The question is how efficient knowledge and resource dissemination can be achieved in the scope of IoT-based applications. Basically, as shown in Fig. 7.1, two options to target this dissemination problem exist. Both are likely to coexist depending on the application domain. Looking at an example from the E-health application domain yields a deeper understanding of these two options. They can be characterized as provisioning the data and provisioning the data sources.

E-health applications use sensors to monitor the vital signs of a patient. Sensors are often integrated using gateway devices (e.g., smartphones). The data collected are usually forwarded to the clinical information system of the medical facility responsible for the patient's treatment. Nowadays, especially in case of emergencies, several medical facilities can be involved in the treatment process. In order to get a meaningful survey of the patient's condition, each participant needs access to the data collected from the medical sensors. Provisioning the data refers to the concept of electronic health record (EHR) clouds. EHRs are based on linked clinical information systems of different medical facilities. Data is exchanged

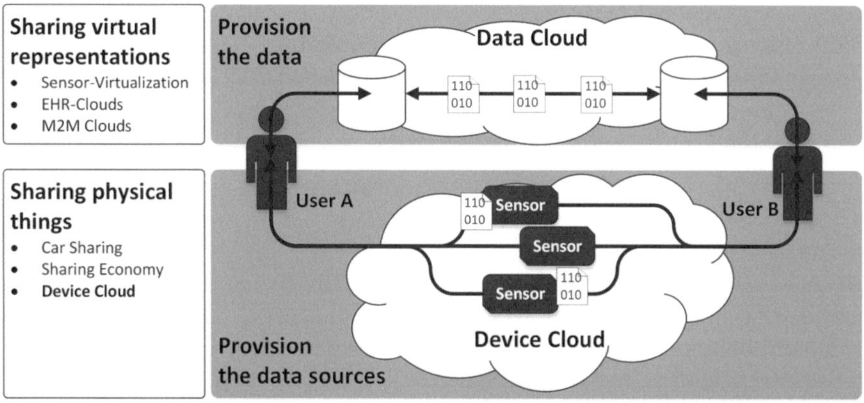


**Fig. 7.1** Two basic approaches for data dissemination in IoT applications—sharing and provisioning the data or the data sources

(provisioned) on the basis of a priori defined legal contracts. This is an important approach, because it allows exchanging data about the treatment history of a patient. However, considering the delay introduced by exchanging real-time data through EHR clouds, interoperability issues and the static nature of how participants are interlinked (resulting from legal contracts), provisioning the data sources (i.e., the medical sensors) becomes reasonable. Instead of exchanging the data by linking the clinical information systems, each clinical information system directly accesses the medical sensors a patient is equipped with. Therefore, the medical sensors must be shared by the participants.

This notion of sharing IoT resources among interested users is in line with several well-established cloud computing paradigms and upcoming concepts like the sharing economy [9] (e.g., car sharing). However, sharing embedded devices in IoT applications not only targets efficiency and resource utilization. It also enables new applications, by giving users the possibility to share the access to physical resources that move in space. Throughout this chapter, a generic architecture approach for sharing embedded devices in various IoT application domains is presented. Foundational issues like interoperability, device integration, and abstraction, as well as security and access right management, are discussed and targeted by the specification of respective backend and middleware components. However, it is important to note that the device cloud does not aim to implement a new IoT protocol or middleware approach. Instead it is about tackling the IoT resource management challenge.

This chapter is organized as follows: Sect. 7.2 provides an introduction to foundational concepts and technologies such as cloud computing, sensor-cloud integration, or OSGi. Additionally, related work is discussed. Section 7.3 presents the device cloud architecture. Starting with a general definition of sharing physical IoT resources, the section presents the five main pillars of the device cloud: data model, interaction model, security model, communication model, and application integration. Section 7.4 discusses possible application scenarios and use cases. In particular, an application of the generic device cloud architecture to the E-health domain is described. Finally, Sect. 7.5 concludes the chapter.

## 7.2 Background

Based on the motivation and problem definition, this section aims at providing an introduction to concepts that constitute the foundation of the device cloud approach. Based on a brief introduction to the subject cloud computing, state-of-the-art concepts that target the integration of IoT resources (e.g., sensors) into cloud computing environments are presented. Afterwards, the challenge of integrating IoT resources into information networks and defining appropriate measures for abstraction is discussed. OSGi is introduced as an enabling technology. Finally, a brief overview of related work and research projects is given.

### *7.2.1 Cloud Computing Fundamentals*

Cloud computing is the commercial reality of a concept called utility computing [8]. Utility computing [10] refers to techniques and business models a service provider uses to offer computing resources and infrastructure management to its customers, usually on demand. According to the National Institute of Standards and Technology (NIST) cloud definition [11], the model behind cloud computing consists of deployment models, service models, and five essential characteristics. The deployment model refers to the set of users that may access the cloud. Private clouds, for instance, are only provisioned to a single organization, while public clouds like Amazon EC2 [12] are accessible by the general public. Service models refer to the well-known paradigms IaaS, PaaS, and SaaS. The essential characteristics, which the device cloud aims to apply to the IoT domain, can be described as follows:

- *On-demand Self-service*: A consumer is enabled to allocate and access computing resources (e.g., server time or network storage) as required without the need for human interaction with a service provider.
- *Broad Network Access*: Computing resources are made available over a network based on standard mechanisms. These allow accessing the resources using heterogeneous client devices (e.g., PCs, smartphones).
- *Resource Pooling*: Providers pool and dynamically provision computing resources to multiple consumers, which increases utilization. A key driver for resource pooling is virtualization. Pooling implies that the consumer usually has no knowledge about the location of a provided resource.

- *Rapid Elasticity*: The cloud establishes the illusion of an endless resource that can be accessed from anywhere at any time. Resources are elastically provisioned and released on demand to achieve a high degree of scalability.
- *Measured Service*: The resource consumption is monitored in order to provide transparency for cloud service providers and consumers. Some cloud services may automatically adapt and optimize the resource consumption to fit the current requirements.

An important paradigm or business model not explicitly mentioned but resulting from these characteristics is pay as you go (PAYG). Based on monitoring the resource consumption and the ability to elastically release resources, PAYG enables the consumer to pay only for the resources actually utilized. Moreover, there is no need for long-term contracts to be given. Another important characteristic, which is already part of the utility computing definition, is the infrastructure management that is implicitly provided to the consumers alongside with the computing resources. These characteristics and paradigms address the major obstacles currently found in the IoT domain: provisioning resources on demand through standard mechanisms (i.e., in a homogeneous fashion) and hiding the complex task of infrastructure management.

### 7.2.2 Sensor-Cloud Integration

Wireless sensor networks (WSNs) can consist of several and up to thousands of nodes. They usually underlie serious resource constraints and are often designed towards specific requirements of the application domain. Sensor access nodes, used to connect external entities to the WSN, hide the complexity of the protocol stack required for (ad hoc) networking, communication, and data aggregation. In contrast to cloud computing, consumers usually have to be aware of the location, the resource constraints, and the infrastructure management requirements of the sensor nodes. This often limits the set of consumers being able to access the WSN. As a remedy, concepts like sensor-cloud integration [13, 14] and sensor virtualization were introduced [15]. These approaches basically aim to overcome the resource constraints of traditional WSNs by integrating cloud resources. Furthermore, access to physical sensors is provided to multiple users based on virtual representations. The latter one is related to sensor virtualization and the concept of M2M clouds. Management and access to the sensors are simplified using standard cloud-based interfaces that hide the location and diversity of the sensors from the consumers (e.g., abstraction from technical details, focus on the semantics, grouping of functional identical sensors as shown in Fig. 7.2) [16]. In contrast to M2M cloud solutions, sensor-cloud infrastructures usually follow the public cloud deployment model and do not limit access to a certain company or group of consumers.

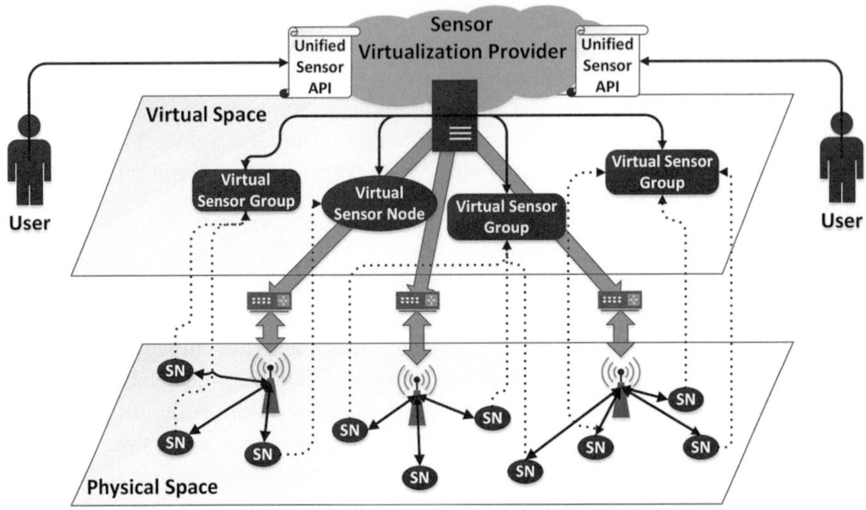


**Fig. 7.2** Sensor virtualization as an enabler for unified access to heterogeneous resources

The term sensor virtualization is ambiguous with the term virtual sensor networks (VSN), but has to be distinguished. VSNs deal with resource sharing, logical grouping, and collaboration of physical sensor nodes, while sensor virtualization is about provisioning the virtual representation (i.e., the cloud interface) of a physical sensor node. Section 7.3.1 discusses the differences between the device cloud approach and sensor virtualization or sensor-cloud Infrastructures, respectively.

Motivated by the increasing capabilities of the nodes participating in WSNs, cloud characteristics like pooling and allocating a subset of the resources to certain tasks on demand are applied to sensor networks. VSNs assume that the overall set of nodes in a WSN can be virtually grouped into subsets and dedicated to specific applications or tasks [17, 18]. Unlike traditional WSNs, where usually all nodes perform similar tasks, a subset of nodes can be allocated for a given time period to perform specific tasks or react to external events. A sensor network deployed in an area recovering from a disaster may, for instance, observe specific events in a certain region. Using VSN, nodes close to that region can be grouped in order to further investigate the situation by executing specific tasks.

Another related concept is called cyber-physical cloud computing [19, 20]. By applying lightweight virtualization capabilities to sensor nodes, sensors basically act as servers that move in space and host virtual sensors. Virtual sensors can migrate between physical ones, which is referred to as cyber mobility (i.e., moving between sensor hosts). Additionally, virtual devices can move with their current sensor host (if the sensor node is mobile), which is referred to as physical mobility. Similar to regular cloud computing, this allows for efficient resource utilization that is achieved by applying virtualization techniques.

## *7.2.3 Device Integration and Abstraction*

Prior to be able to access a physical IoT resource using a possibly cloud-based homogeneous virtual representation, a link between physical resource and virtual representation needs to be established. Thus, each IoT-based solution needs to provide components that take care of integrating the physical resources. Furthermore, these components should provide appropriate measures in order to abstract technical details away.

The integration of sensors or actuators involves several steps like discovery, connection establishment, data transmission, data aggregation, and processing as well as storage or visualization. All these steps in turn involve several hardware and software components and usually depend on protocols spanning all layers of the OSI reference model. In general, device integration in context of IoT or M2M applications is the challenge of achieving interoperability among a heterogeneous set of interacting systems. More precisely, according to Kindberg et al. [21], two principles need to be considered when developing systems that deal with ubiquitous or pervasive devices: physical integration and spontaneous interoperability arising from the integration of nomadic physical devices. The following subsections discuss some of the ancillary challenges.

### 7.2.3.1 The Standardization Problem

Integrating devices and exchanging information requires some kind of communication. Both the sender and the receiver need to agree on a common language (usually based on a canonical or external data representation). A standard can be used as a common language. Standards can be defined as a set of rules that provide the necessary basis for interaction between two systems [22]. The standardization problem is a decision problem that deals with choosing the set of communication standards appropriate for an application. Especially with regard to the IoT domain, it is difficult to make this decision because a huge variety of competing standards like 6LoWPAN, Bluetooth, CoAP, DPWS, ZigBee, or Z-Wave exist. The dissemination of a standard usually depends on the number of authorities and systems using it, which is difficult to estimate in advance [23]. Moreover, standards evolve and sometimes allow for vendor-defined extensions and there are even a lot of entire proprietary solutions. Thus, it is unlikely that the huge set of communication technologies and standards required to achieve interoperability will converge to a set of major standards that can be implemented by single components or applications. Rather, device integration solutions need to be designed flexibly in terms of adaptability towards new or evolving standards. Modularization and generic data representations are key factors for sustainable device integration solutions. These allow clients to request information in a desired format while hiding the complexity of the heterogeneous landscape of communication technologies.

#### 7.2.3.2 Device Integration

The purpose of device integration is the automated exchange of data between two or more devices or systems. With regard to the IoT, device integration is closely related to the topic machine-to-machine communication (M2M). Integrating a device is the process of identifying and loading appropriate control logic (e.g., a driver) for a device that is connected to a system. Connected means that the device is plugged into the system (e.g., in case of USB) or appears on a communication network the system is connected to. According to the M2M Alliance [24], basically three major components can be defined when talking about device integration:

- *Data Endpoint (DEP)*: The DEP (i.e., sender) refers to a device that needs to be integrated. The DEP collects data from the device or waits for control commands. The DEP is usually implemented by an embedded microprocessor linked to the device.
- *Data Integration Point (DIP)*: The DIP (i.e., receiver) refers to a system that hosts monitoring or control applications or acts as a data aggregator. It collects data from connected DEPs or sends control commands to them.
- *Machine Communication Network (MCN)*: DEP and DIP exchange information using a MCN both are connected to. The MCN can refer to a bus system (e.g., USB), an IP-based network, or any other type of communication infrastructure.

Depending on the type of the device the DEP represents (e.g., actuator or sensor), both the DEP and DIP can act as the source or sink of an information flow. In case of M2M, some systems are also for a direct communication between DEPs as well. The variety of device types, DEP platforms, and MCNs make it difficult for DIPs to provide a uniform API to the monitoring and control applications. Therefore, abstraction mechanisms are required.

#### 7.2.3.3 Device Abstraction

In computer science, the abstraction principle [25] is known as a recommendation to programs to avoid duplicity in their program code. In Java, for instance, an abstract class can be used as a skeleton to implement logic that is required by all inheriting classes. An interface can be used to introduce abstract definitions for different implementations which share the same meaning. Basically, abstraction means to introduce different layers of complexity, where each layer is hiding the complexity of the layer below. A prominent example is the OSI model. The transport layer, for instance, abstracts away the technical details and complexity of the physical, data link, and network layer and allows application layer protocols to easily exchange data. In terms of device abstraction, especially the interface concept is of notable importance. It allows developers to define common interfaces, sometimes also called categories or profiles. A category can be used for the devices of the same class/type but based on different implementations (e.g. temperature sensors from different vendors).

Device abstraction is a crucial requirement for device integration solutions because it allows decoupling devices from applications and enhances the portability [26]. Application developers are enabled to focus on the logic, without having to deal with device type or vendor-specific details of the I/O protocol. Devices of the same type can be easily exchanged and the risk of a vendor lock-in is reduced. According to Vaughan et al. [27], three basic levels of abstraction can be defined:

- *Character Device Model*: Originated from Multics and UNIX, this refers to the most basic level of abstraction, where each device can be treated as a data file. The model defines access to the devices by providing five basic operations (open, close, read, write, ioctl).
- *Interface (Driver) Model*: Extending the basic operations offered by the character device model, the interface model offers abstraction by refining the basic operations using knowledge about the structure of a data stream. Thus, device type related operations can be offered. Interface and application developers are no longer required to take care of device-specific protocol or control logic.
- *Client-Server Model*: The third level of abstraction targets the decoupling of the application (i.e., client) and the server that manages the actual device control. Besides platform independence (the client only has to be aware of the protocol offered by the server), this abstraction level simplifies concurrent access to devices. Since session and transaction management can be realized by the server, there is no need for synchronization between multiple applications accessing the same device.

#### 7.2.3.4 OSGi: Enabling Technology for Device Integration

Originating from the embedded system domain, OSGi's capability to design modular applications and middleware solutions which are adaptable at runtime make it a suitable candidate for device integration scenarios. OSGi is a specification of a platform-independent (Java-based) framework for modularized development of applications and services based on the principle of component-based software engineering [28]. A component, sometimes also referred to as a module, is a package of software that encapsulates related functions and data and provides these as services to other components using well-defined interfaces. A component provides the implementation of a certain set of system processes defined by an interface, which is accessible by other components. According to the modularity of a system, an important capability of components is their exchangeability. OSGi allows updating or replacing a component at runtime without breaking the system. Thus, OSGi provides a dynamic service execution environment that is able to deploy and wire services in shape of components at runtime. OSGi consists of a core specification [29], which defines mandatory core APIs, and a compendium specification [30], which defines additional services dedicated to certain use cases.

Proprietary as well as open-source implementations are available. Among the compendium specifications, especially the Device Access Specification (DAS) is of notable importance regarding the topic device integration.

The OSGi DAS describes basic mechanisms regarding the dynamic integration of devices into a service platform without limiting the concepts to any specific type of device or network technology. In particular, it targets the attachment of services to detected devices and the handling of life-cycle issues that arise when devices are plugged or unplugged at runtime. Moreover, it defines mechanisms to dynamically load and attach services from external repositories if new devices appear (i.e., bundles containing device drivers). The following core entities are defined by the DAS to model the dynamic device integration process:

- *Device*: A device service represents any kind of device. It can refer to a single physical device, a network (if the physical device is a gateway or any kind of networking interface), or to a refinement of an already existing device. Refinement means that several device services represent a physical device at different levels of abstraction. A device service must belong to a device category.
- *Device Category*: The device category refers to the introduced interface model abstraction level. The device category specifies the interface needed to communicate with a device (i.e., the interface the device service exposes) and properties that can be accessed to monitor the state of the device (e.g., battery level). Additionally, properties required for matching devices and drivers are defined.
- *Driver*: Driver services provide the control logic. Driver services attach to device services in order to either refine an existing device or to integrate a new device (if, for instance, the device service represents a network). In most cases driver services expose new device services that can be accessed by applications or are again refined by other driver services. The attachment is based on the device category the device and the driver service belong to.
- *Device Manager*: The device manager manages the attachment process. It waits for device services being registered with the framework and searches for suitable driver services. It uses the driver locator and selector to perform the matching and attachment processes. It allows only one driver service to attach to a device service.
- *Driver Locator*: The driver locator provides the bridge to external driver bundle repositories.
- *Driver Selector*: The driver selector provides refinements to the matching algorithm that attaches driver to device services.

### 7.2.4 Related Work

This section provides a brief overview of other topics of IoT-related work, not discussed so far. Especially, the subjects IoT architectures and applications are addressed.

One foundation of the IoT is the communication network that links the virtual representations of the things to the applications. The Internet was basically developed to allow for communication between computers that are located at different sites. As reported by Atzori et al. [31], this host-to-host-based communication paradigm is not likely to be suitable for hundreds of things that will be connected to the Internet in the future. Instead, it has to be considered that the Internet is primarily used as an information dissemination system. Accessing data and not a specific host becomes more and more important. Thus, IoT is an interdisciplinary research domain that requires resolution of challenges in the areas of identification, tracking, distributed intelligence, communication protocols, security and privacy, or information management based on integrated approaches.

One of the core components of IoT architectures are middleware solutions. Since the complexity of the technical layers is hidden from the application developer, more robust and reusable code can be produced. A SOA-based middleware approach for intelligent networked embedded systems was presented by the European research project HYDRA—middleware for networked devices [32]. The resulting LinkSmart middleware [33] focuses on the semantic representation of devices and the possibility to uniformly access each device using semantic Web services. A mechanism called HYDRA enabling that allows wrapping APIs of devices using Web service extensions is provided (i.e., WSDL files extended by semantic descriptions). HYDRA both supports to integrate out-of-the-box HYDRA-enabled devices (i.e., the semantic Web service is hosted by the device) or native devices using proxies. The implementation of the mapping from the Web service to the actual device-specific API has to be provided by the service developer because HYDRA supports different communication technologies (e.g., ZigBee or Bluetooth). A possible foundation for proxies as well as HYDRA-enabled devices is introduced by the Contiki platform [34], which is an operating system dedicated to run on resource-constrained devices in IoT applications and WSNs. Contiki incorporates support for protocols like 6LoWPAN or CoAP. Additionally, it was designed for the dynamic loading and replacement of services and custom program code, which is an important feature for networks of hundreds of resource-constrained nodes that cannot be physically collected and reprogrammed. Prasad et al. [35] presented a hybrid approach between the HYDRA and the ASPIRE middleware, which additionally allows incorporating the development and deployment of RFID-based applications. In general, a lot of research projects conducted in the last years or still ongoing investigate in challenges related to IoT middleware solutions. Further examples are BRIDGE, EBBITS, or SENSEI, most of which are organized within the CERP-IoT research cluster [36].

An overall problem, addressed by the IoT-A project [37], is the lack of a reference architecture. A reference architecture introduces an overall understanding of the entities and their relations within different IoT application domains. Often, devices and applications are designed with respect to a dedicated use case or application, which limits interoperability and leads to island solutions. This is often referred to as the Intranet of Things [38]. The IoT-A project attempts to mitigate this obstacle by defining an IoT reference architecture model (ARM) applicable to different application domains. Each specific architecture is derived and inherits from the ARM with the possibility for own choices regarding design issues like security or real-time requirements. The presence of the basic reference model ensures interoperability. IoT-A describes a set of reference models (e.g., domain model, information model, communication model), an application-independent reference architecture and guidelines that assist in deriving a specific architecture from the reference architecture model.

As already introduced in Sect. 7.1, IoT applications are found in a variety of domains. Examples are smart homes [39], smart cities [40], smart grids [41], building automation, E-health [42], or, due to their origin from RFID-based systems, logistics or object tracking [43]. A detailed discussion of application domains in general and applications in particular is given by Atzori et al. [31] or the CERP-IoT research cluster [36].

Each of these applications basically employs similar architectural patterns while differing regarding specific technologies used. This underlines that IoT architectures can lead to a convergence of these application domains. An example is presented by Li et al. [44]. The described smart community evolves from several smart homes connected to each other. This can be imagined as an ancestor to the smart city. A home domain, referring to the private network of the smart home, a community domain referring to the network of home gateways shielding each home domain, and a service domain referring to a trusted third-party offering service dispatching and emergency services are defined. It is assumed that a wireless ad hoc network exists between the home gateways (i.e., within the community domain). The authors investigate in security and reliability of the networking (e.g., routing) used within the community domain and discuss the detection of home gateways with inaccurate behavior (e.g., incorrect messages, failures while forwarding messages). The authors also discuss the trade-off between security, privacy, and access control, which is of notable importance when dealing with E-health applications and emergency scenarios. Attribute-based encryption schemes are proposed to allow for fine-grained access control to privacy-constrained data dependent on the current situation (i.e., normal vs. emergency).

## 7.3 Device Cloud: Architecture

This section describes the fundamental concepts employed by the device cloud and its resulting architecture. Section 7.3.1 provides a preliminary definition of sharing physical IoT resources. It describes generic models of the resources and participants involved in the sharing/pooling process. Based on these principles of sharing, the architecture is derived and presented with regard to its five main pillars: data model, interaction model, security model, communication model, and application integration. The architecture is discussed in a technology and application domain agnostic manner. Possible application scenarios and a specific mapping are discussed in Sect. 7.4.

### 7.3.1 *Principles of Sharing Devices*

From a technical point of view, the device cloud is about provisioning access to exclusive and non-exclusive resources. Usually, most devices are exclusive resources because there is an exclusive communication link between the device and the system integrating it (e.g., a gateway, a smartphone, or a PC). However, some devices may allow multiple systems to communicate with them simultaneously. These devices are non-exclusive resources. With regard to non-exclusive resources, the device cloud has to be distinguished from approaches like sensor virtualization discussed in Sect. 7.2.2. If the integrating system allows multiple users to access the device through a virtual representation, the representation is shared, not the device itself. For some use cases, sharing the virtual representation fits well. Sharing the virtual representations means that the binding between the device and the integrating system is kept. Accordingly, access is provisioned to the integrating system or a higher level service that exposes the virtual representation. Each sensing device would become a non-exclusive resource in this case. However, there are limitations to this approach, especially regarding security and privacy:

- *Security*: Integrating systems are more vulnerable to attacks because they provide an operating system and allow executing custom code. Some environments may not permit communicating or further integrating such systems. If, for instance, a patient is monitored by medical devices and these devices are integrated by the patient's smartphone, a hospital may not allow communicating with the devices using the patient's private smartphone as a proxy.
- *Privacy*: Provisioning access only to the integrating system relies on trusting the entity having control over the integrating system. Moreover, each node participating in the transmission chain between the device and the integrating system needs to be trusted. Additionally legal issues could be face because the virtual representation is shared. This basically means that the data is shared and not the device.
- *Device Mobility*: Since some devices are mobile, it cannot be guaranteed that the corresponding integrating system is always in range or moves with the device. For instance, a patient may be carried to a hospital in an emergency and his smartphone may not be taken along with him, but the medical sensors monitoring him may still operate.
- *Nonfunctional Constraints*: Accessing the device through its virtual representation may involve several systems (e.g., if the representation is exposed using a backend server system). The resulting delay and loss of control over the participating nodes may not be suitable for all application scenarios.

Thus, the device cloud is about sharing the devices (i.e., the data sources) and not their virtual representations (i.e., the data). It is to be assumed that the integrating systems always belong to an entity and are not shared. However, the concept of sharing the virtual representations can be introduced to the device cloud as an additional feature with minimal overhead. Throughout the rest of the chapter, the following terminology is used for shared and non-shared devices:

- *Device Nodes (DN)*: Device nodes are the device resources (e.g., sensors, actors) that are pooled and shared by the device cloud. According to the M2M definition given in Sect. 7.2.3, DNs refer to data endpoints (DEP).
- *Aggregation Nodes (AN)*: Aggregation nodes refer to the integrating systems used to establish communication links to the shared DNs. Typical examples are routers, smartphones, or PCs. According to the M2M definition, ANs refer to data integration points (DIP).

Since resources are shared and pooled, the device cloud needs to provide locking mechanisms in order to synchronize access to the devices. Similar to read-locks and write-locks, one could distinguish between sensing and actuating devices by introducing functional device classes like exclusive sensing device, non-exclusive sensing device, exclusive actuating device, and so on. However, according to the concept of device categories discussed in Sect. 7.2.3, a more generic classification based on the device categories is defined:

- *Exclusive Transducer Device*: The cardinality between the DN and the AN is 1:1. Only one AN can consume the device based on its category (e.g., a medical sensor). An exclusive lock is applied.
- *Non-Exclusive Transducer Device*: The cardinality between the DN and AN is 1: N. Based on the category, multiple ANs can consume the device simultaneously (e.g., a camera device). A shared lock is applied.
- *Composite Transducer Device*: A generalization of non-exclusive transducer devices. Composite devices can offer multiple categories (e.g., due to multiple sensing devices embedded into one physical device). Categories can be grouped to sets of one or more related ones. Each set either refers to an exclusive transducer device or a non-exclusive transducer device.

In general, the process of device provisioning or sharing can be defined as an owning entity granting a device access lock to a consuming entity. However, sharing can have multiple shapes. For the purpose of an overall sharing definition, we have to consider at least three more roles additional to the already given, owner and consumer:

- *Device Owner*: An entity that owns a device holds this role for the particular device.
- *Device Consumer*: An entity requesting access for the purpose of reading data from the device or controlling it holds the consumer role.
- *Device Integrator*: The entity that integrates the device (i.e., has established a communication link to the device). Either the AN itself or the individual controlling the AN.
- *Device Target*: In most cases this role is similar to the entity that refers to the thing, the being, or the environment sensed by the device.

- *Device Operator*: If an entity exists that operates or manages the device provisioning in charge of the device owner, it holds this role.

The ordinary case just involves the device consumer that requests access from the device owner, while the device target is the same as, belongs to, or is visible to the device consumer without violating any legal regulations. The device integrator role is also held by the device consumer. More complex scenarios involve a device target or a device integrator that does not belong to the device consumer and are likely to include a device operator. In general, all scenarios require the device consumer, upon requesting a certain device, to establish a relation between the device and the device target. Otherwise the recorded data would miss necessary contextual information and could be useless for most of the use cases.

The device cloud architecture, discussed in the following sections, maps this general sharing definition to a specific set of entities, architectural components, and interactions.

### 7.3.2 Overall Architecture: Components and Participants

Besides the basic classification of resources and the definition of roles required to describe the sharing interactions, the device cloud architecture is founded on five major pillars:

- *Data Model*: Describes and defines the state of device resources as well as the knowledge a device provides to other participants of the device cloud.
- *Interaction Model*: Sometimes also referred to as service model, defines primitives and interactions used to access and modify the data model. This, for instance, includes the services and methods participants use to interact with the resource pool and to share, allocate, or provision device resources on demand.
- *Communication Model*: Defines the mapping of the interaction model to a specific technical infrastructure. Emphasis is put on M2M aspects of the device cloud architecture. In particular, it is described how M2M can be realized while staying independent from the application domain or specific protocols and simultaneously provide homogeneous interfaces to access the pooled resources.
- *Security Model*: The security model basically covers the authenticity of the principals involved in the interactions. Moreover, it defines mechanisms to access to the pooled resources. The resources are shared by participants that are likely to be unknown to each other.
- *Application Integration*: Finally, it has to be described how applications can be linked to the resources managed by the device cloud.

Figure 7.3 shows the participants and the major architectural components required to set up the device cloud and implement its five major pillars. The interactions conducted by the participants using the architecture components

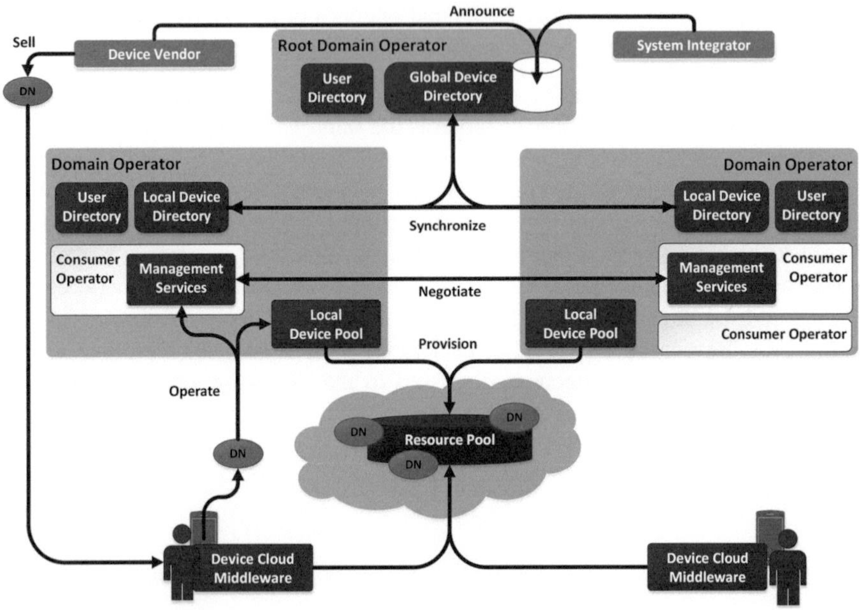


**Fig. 7.3** Device cloud architecture

result in the forming of a "federated device pool." The pool can be transparently accessed by consumers in order to offer and allocate device resources on demand. Related to the concept of cloud federation [45], the federated device pool can be envisioned as the sum of all devices offered by the different participants of the device cloud. According to the IoT definition, it is assumed that each device in the pool has a globally unique identifier. In order to properly manage the devices and the provisioning process, each interaction between the participants needs to be tagged with such an ID. The ID has to be assigned to a device by the device vendor, which usually is the first participant announcing a device to the device cloud.

The following architectural components are defined:

- *Device Directory*: The device directory hosts the device knowledge base and acts as a directory service for devices. Besides device type information, corresponding configurations, or dependent software modules, the directory knows every device in the pool by maintaining their respective IDs. The device knowledge base basically refers to the data model of the device cloud.
  - *Global Device Directory*: The global device directory is used to synchronize the local instances hosted by each domain operator. It maintains all stateless information and software modules available in the device cloud. Furthermore, it allows determining which operator is responsible for which device.
  - *Local Device Directory*: Local directories are partial mirrors of the global instance. They represent all devices a domain operator is responsible for. In

contrast to the global instance, local device directories also maintain stateful or private information like the provisioning state of a device or security credentials required to connect to a device.

- *User Directory*: Similar to LDAP-based directory services, the user directory maintains all users known to a domain operator (i.e., other actors like consumers or consumer operators). It allows for authentication and authorization. Hence, it is an integral part of the security model. The user directory can be implemented as an interface or wrapper around an existing directory service of the operator.
- *Management Services*: Management service is a generic term for services a consumer operator has to provide in order to implement the provisioning process (e.g., decision policies, accounting, device locking algorithms, device access negotiation between operators). In order to enhance modularity, the overall concept separates these services from the directories.
- *Device Cloud* **Middleware**: The device cloud middleware is deployed on aggregation nodes and can be envisioned as an execution environment for software modules provided by the device directory. The device cloud middleware is the consumer's interface to its corresponding operator. It triggers the interactions defined by the interaction model and implements major parts of the communication model.

The following participants are defined:

- *Device Vendor*: The device vendor manufactures and sells the devices provisioned within the device cloud. The vendor provides device descriptions and software modules and is responsible for registering each sold device with the global device directory.
- *System Integrator*: The system integrator provides custom knowledge (i.e., software modules) for devices and device types already registered with the global device directory (e.g., data transformation modules).
- *Domain Operator*: The domain operator can be envisioned as an Internet service provider (ISP) that maintains basic infrastructure and services to set up the device cloud. It serves a device directory and a user directory. Thus, it offers services for device identification, device description, or identity and access management (IAM). Hence, the domain operator acts as a trusted entity for participants registered within its domain and does not participate in the device-sharing and pooling processes. Basically, the domain operator protects access to the resources offered by its device directory. Multiple domains are supported by the device cloud to simplify IAM processes. Similar to the concept of Kerberos realms, cross-domain interactions are possible.
- *Consumer Operator*: The consumer operator provides user level services required to manage, pool, offer, and allocate device resources. Consumer operators act as a bridge between consumers and the federated device pool. Consumer operators can either manage the devices in charge of their customers, own and provision a set of devices themselves, or follow a hybrid approach. Usually, consumers offering devices mandate a consumer operator, which is in charge of

managing and pooling them. Multiple consumer operators can coexist within on domain.
- *Consumer*: The consumer uses one or more instances of the device cloud middleware to interact with consumer operators and access the resource pool. If the consumer owns devices and wishes to offer them to other consumers, a consumer operator has to be mandated. This consumer operator takes the role of the device operator for the particular device.

In summary, the device cloud concept is based on a modular device cloud middleware that is able to load and deploy software modules at runtime. The device knowledge base and other backend information services are managed by a set of cooperating operators that virtually combine their local device pools to an overall pool (i.e., federated device pool). This pool contains all devices shared by the consumers. Apart from the general concept design, an entity may take several roles or act as multiple participants. The consumer operator and the domain operator could be hosted by the same legal entity. A consumer operator could operate an own set of devices and therefore additionally take the device owner role. Moreover, a consumer operator could allocate device resources in charge of its customers and thus act as a consumer from the perspective of the consumer operator managing the device.

## *7.3.3 Architecture: Data Model*

The data model builds the foundation for the device cloud provisioning interactions. It reflects the outcome of each device cloud interaction and in turn affects each following interaction (e.g., is a device compliant to a category, is a device ready to be locked). Therefore, the data model consists of entities that act as virtual representations of the device cloud resources and participants. These entities usually refer to records stored by the device directory or the user directory.

The major part of the data model is served by the device directories, which can be envisioned as directory services for devices. Device directories describe and manage device resources (i.e., DNs) by maintaining two sets of knowledge/device attributes: stateless and stateful device knowledge.

### 7.3.3.1 Stateless Device Knowledge

Stateless device knowledge is used to describe a device resource in terms of its capabilities. This includes its category, its static properties, and the software modules (e.g., device drivers) required to integrate and handle it. As shown in Fig. 7.4, several entities are defined to describe device resources of the device cloud. Basically, a device is represented by a device instance that corresponds to a certain device type. The type complies with a certain device category and requires a

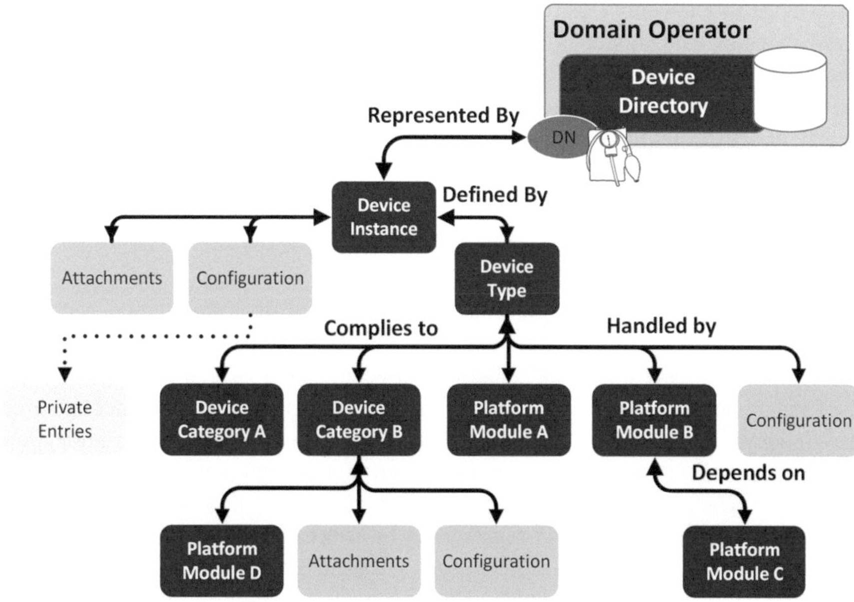


**Fig. 7.4** Simplified example of a knowledge tree representing a device

set of software modules in order to be integrated and handled. The relation between instance, type, and category can be exemplary envisioned as a vendor that sells a blood pressure monitor (category) which has a product number or model code (type) and a serial number (instance) that identifies the concrete physical instance:

- *Device Instance*: The device instance represents a physical device that is part of the device pool and can be provisioned to consumers. It holds information that just apply to the physical instance it represents (e.g., security credentials such as a Bluetooth pin required to connect to the device).
- *Device Type*: The device type refers to a type of devices, which means a set of devices from a certain vendor that comply with the same specifications (i.e., have the same model or product number). It stores information that are applicable to all device instances of that type (e.g., vendor name, description). Each device type corresponds to at least one device category and maintains a set of dependencies on platform modules.
- *Device Category*: The device category as introduced in Sect. 7.2.3.4.
- *Platform Module*: Platform modules refer to the software modules provided by the device directory. Platform modules are executed by the device cloud middleware in order to integrate or handle devices. Examples are device drivers, discovery modules, data transformation, utilization modules, or core modules of the device cloud middleware itself.

Besides attributes such as device vendor or device name, each entity can inherit from the abstract configurable and attachment entities. This allows to attach custom knowledge to each entity using custom formats. Accordingly, it has to be emphasized that the data model is not designed as a replacement for existing device ontologies like FIPA, TEDS, or SensorML. Rather, it is used as a basic description necessary for the device cloud interactions and easily allows embedding existing device or sensor ontologies through its attachments.

#### 7.3.3.2 Stateful Device Knowledge

Stateful device knowledge represents the state model of a device and acts as a foundation for all device allocation and provisioning interactions (e.g., is a device lockable). As already introduced, stateful knowledge is usually only maintained by the local device directory that belongs to the same domain as the consumer operator managing the device. Moreover, except for special cases like a device allocation carried out between two consumer operators, stateful knowledge is usually not subject to synchronization between several device cloud domains. As shown in Fig. 7.5, stateful knowledge is represented by properties attached to the general device description entities. Additionally, a special entity called device lock is defined. A device lock is created each time a device resource was successfully allocated. Hence, it behaves similar to a lock used in mutual exclusion. Each device lock corresponds to a device category. As depicted, multiple device category resources may be offered by a single device instance (e.g., a composite transducer device—a display with an embedded Webcam). Which device categories are offered is defined by the device type. Additionally, the device type specifies if a category belongs to the class of exclusive or non-exclusive transducer devices. The latter case allows multiple device locks to be attached with regard to a single

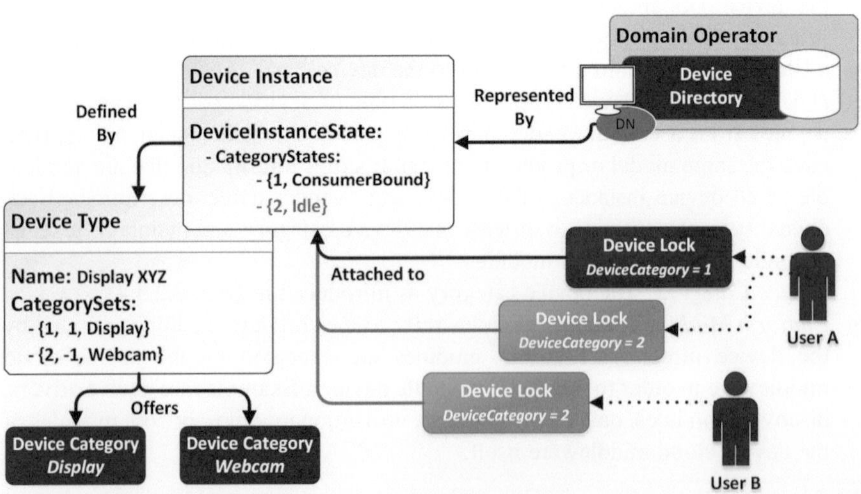


**Fig. 7.5** Device states attached to stateless device description records

category offered by a device resource. Based on the definition of available device categories, the device instance maintains the state of each offered category. The most important states in terms of device provisioning are:

- *Idle*: Further provisioning of the offered category is possible.
- *Consumer Bound*: No further provisioning is possible but the device is not already technically integrated by an aggregator.
- *Aggregator Bound*: No further provisioning is possible and an active communication link between the device and an aggregator exists.

The two-stage locking representation is used to simplify decision-making and handover processes. Section 7.3.4 discusses the state model with respect to the device cloud interactions in more detail.

Due to the domain-based design of the device cloud, multiple device directories exist. However, a vendor usually updates the stateless device description (i.e., device type) only at the global directory. A device owner modifies security credentials of a device instance only at the domain he belongs to. Therefore, knowledge dissemination and synchronization are required between the domains. Otherwise the device pools would be restricted to a single domain.

#### 7.3.3.3 Device Cloud Knowledge Dissemination and Synchronization

Since the device directories are organized hierarchically on a per domain basis, synchronization is required to ensure proper knowledge dissemination. The "DD Sync Protocol" is fundamental to the provisioning capabilities of the device cloud. It ensures that each participant can access knowledge required to integrate and handle devices. Similar to DNS, the consistency model used by the device directories is eventual consistency [46]. This means that a relatively high degree of inconsistency is tolerated. It is ensured that updates are propagated to all replicas, but not immediately.

In order to track changes and control the synchronization, general properties are defined for each entity of the data model. These properties additionally act as enablers for access control or the domain-based federation of the device cloud:

- *EntityType, EntityID, and EntityDomain*: Uniquely identify an entity with respect to its type and origin.
- *EntityVersion*: Allows verifying whether a replica is up to date.
- *EntityOwner*: The owner is able to modify the entity and grant access permissions to other entities. Only the owner is able to define the EntityOperator.
- *EntityOperator*: Manages the entity in charge of the owner (e.g., a consumer operator).

Based on the EntityDomain property, the synchronization protocol defines two types of entity replicas:

- *Master Copy*: The EntityDomain property is equal to the domain the device directory belongs to. Only one master copy can exist. The device directory responsible for the master copy has to coordinate and synchronize modifications.
- *Local Copy*: The EntityDomain property is not equal to the domain of the device directory. The local copy can only be modified, if a lock has been acquired from the master copy. If a local copy has been modified, changes must be immediately propagated to the master copy (before the lock is released).

Synchronization between the device directories is a necessary requirement for the device cloud interactions. Interactions rely on transparent knowledge dissemination, because only one local device directory instance is queried by an application. Moreover, interactions that modify the state of a device require a consistent view.

### 7.3.4 Architecture: Interaction Model

The interaction model covers the interactions performed by the participants in order to dynamically share and allocate device resources. Interactions can be described as the services offered by the device cloud. Basically, two types of interactions are known: interactions that add or request stateless knowledge or interactions that modify stateful knowledge. Interactions operating on stateless knowledge are used to gather descriptions about devices or participants of the device cloud. Interactions operating on stateful knowledge are used to provision devices. Additionally, the interaction model defines the state model for device resources, which is discussed with regard to decision policies and simultaneous attempts to access device resources.

#### 7.3.4.1 Device Cloud Interactions

A device cloud interaction is either triggered by the deployment of a device or by the discovery of a device through an aggregation node. In general, four interactions are known, as follows:

- *Device Deployment*: Announce a device to the device cloud and define its device owner and operator. Operates on stateless knowledge.
- *Device Identification*: Is triggered each time a local device directory is queried for an unknown device ID. Operates on stateless knowledge.
- *Integration Request*: Is triggered by an aggregation node that has discovered a device, which is of interest for the corresponding consumer. Basically, an integration request is an attempt to allocate a device resource from the pool. Operates on stateful knowledge.
- *Integration Offer*: Can be envisioned as a reverse integration request. It is triggered if an aggregation node has discovered a device that is not of interest

for the corresponding consumer. It is tested if there is another consumer that might possibly be interested in the device resource (e.g., if he already allocated the device but owns no suitable aggregation node that is in range of the resource). Operates on stateful knowledge.

Figure 7.6 shows the typical interaction workflow triggered by the discovery of a device. It consists of following steps:

1. *Discovery*: A device resource is moved into the range of an aggregation node.
2. *Identification*: The aggregation node triggers a device identification interaction in order to determine the device category and the responsible device operator.
3. *Checking Interest*: After having identified the category, the aggregation node can check the corresponding consumer profile. The profile defines if the device resource is of interest. Among others, the consumer profile defines which device categories are required by a consumer given certain constraints (e.g., time).
4. *Trigger Interaction*: Depending on the result, an integration request or an integration offer is triggered.
5. *Evaluate Request*: The corresponding consumer operator decides whether the request can be accepted or has to be rejected. This possibly involves additional consumer operators (e.g., if the requested operator is not the operator responsible for the device). This step may involve decision policies: if, for instance, a handover has to be carried out or the device is already allocated by another consumer with less priority.
6. *Issue Access Token*: The consumer operator managing the device in charge of the owner issues an access token, which is transmitted to the middleware. Only a

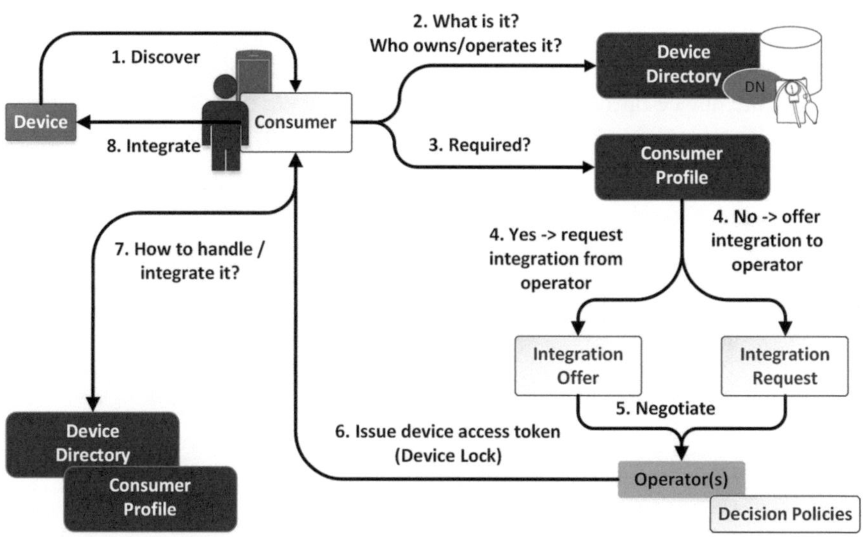


**Fig. 7.6** Device cloud interactions resulting from the discovery of a possibly interesting device resource

valid and signed access token triggers the device cloud middleware to integrate a device.

7. *Load Modules*: The device cloud middleware loads the platform modules required to integrate the device. The modules are deployed at runtime.

#### 7.3.4.2 Device Locking: State Model

As already introduced in Sect. 7.3.3, allocating and provisioning of a device is based on its state (i.e., the state of the corresponding device instance entity). Figure 7.7 shows the possible states and corresponding transitions. As mentioned, one device instance can hold different states for each device category it offers. The following states are defined:

- *Announced*: The vendor has announced the device instance to the device cloud by adding it to the knowledge base of the global device directory. This includes assigning a unique identifier and attaching the device instance to the corresponding device type. Up to this state, the EntityOwner of the device instance refers to the vendor.
- *Owned*: Afterwards, the device is usually sold to a consumer. This refers to the device deployment Interaction. Transitioning to the owned state means that a valid device owner was defined (i.e., the EntityOwner property was set).
- *Operated*: Before the device instance can be added to the federated device pool, the device operator needs to be elected. This results in a transition to the operated state (i.e., the EntityOperator property is set by the owner).
- *Idle*: While the device instance stays in the operated state, it can only be used by the device owner. In order to be added to the device pool, the device owner has to notify the device operator. This leads to a transition to one of the pooled states.

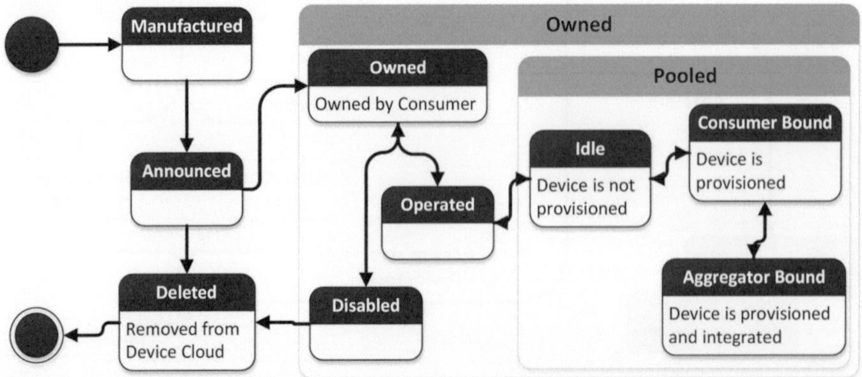


**Fig. 7.7** Device state model

The pooled state contains three sub-states. As long as the device instance is not being provisioned to consumers, it remains in the idle state.

- *Consumer Bound*: If a consumer has successfully requested access to a device, the corresponding device instance transitions to the consumer bound state. This means that a device lock was created, which is not linked to an aggregation node yet. Since devices can be mobile and the lock can span an unspecified period of time, multiple aggregators can be involved in the integration process of a device bound to a consumer. Therefore, locking and integration are separated from each other.
- *Aggregator Bound*: If the device is integrated by an aggregator, the device instance transitions to the aggregator bound state, and the aggregator property of the device lock is set. This means that the device instance is finally provisioned and integrated and all mandatory roles that describe the sharing process are assigned (device owner, device integrator, device operator, device consumer). The definition of the device target role remains optional because it depends on the use aces.

#### 7.3.4.3 Device Locking: Decision Policies

Some application scenarios can require an adaptation of the standard, state-based provisioning behavior described so far. According to the introductory E-health scenario, an example is given by medical sensors used to monitor a patient. Usually, the sensors are integrated by an aggregation node belonging to the patient (e.g., a smartphone). In case of an emergency, the patient's smartphone may not be available while the sensors are still operating. Thus, an aggregation node within the ambulance and an aggregation node at the hospital may successively request access to the sensors while they are still locked by patient's private aggregation node. This results in the requirement to implement handover mechanisms. Basically, two handover types have to be considered:

- *Aggregator Handover*: The aggregator (i.e., device integrator) is changed, while the device consumer remains. Hence, an active device lock granted to the requesting consumer must already exist.
- *Consumer Handover*: The consumer is changed. Usually, the aggregator is changed too, but may also remain. No active device lock granted to the requesting consumer exists.

The E-health scenario sketched above refers to a consumer handover. Both consumer and aggregator change, while an optionally defined binding to the device target (i.e., the patient) remains. An important parameter for handover decisions is given by the location of the device. If a device is in the state aggregator bound, but was discovered at a location out of range of the locking aggregation node, a handover is likely to be reasonable. Additionally, operators may monitor the activity of a device and provide an assessment regarding the connection status of a device. However, the E-health scenario described above can involve situations, where decisions based on the location or the activity are not sufficient. If the patient enters the emergency ward, the aggregation node of the ambulance might still be in range. Thus, the operator has to decide between two or more overlapping sensor access points. As not all communication protocols used by the sensors provide mechanisms to assess the quality of a connection, like mobile telecommunication networks do, traditional handover approaches are difficult to apply. A possible solution would be to introduce classes of device consumers and assign priorities to them. Hospitals or other authorities providing emergency or safety-critical services could belong to a preferred class. In general, this problem is related to the definition of QoS policies for shared resources (e.g., networks). Each application domain must define a set of contextual data items required to implement sufficient decision policies.

As shown in Fig. 7.8, from a formal point of view, making a decision is related to the problem of preemptive multitasking or scheduling. In case of a consumer handover, there are two processes (i.e., consumers) A and B that compete for the exclusive device resource D. Furthermore, a scheduler C (i.e., consumer operator) has to decide whether A can continue consuming D or A has to be interrupted for the purpose of assigning D to B. Similar to priority-based scheduling, C has to dynamically compute a priority given the contextual data provided by A and B. The priority reflects the benefit the device owner of D gains by either assigning A or B to D (i.e., the goal of C—the consumer operator—is to optimize the benefit of the device owner). Thus, C first has to select the active device lock with the lowest priority and subsequently compare it to the priority calculated from the contextual data provided by B. The set of contextual data applicable for a particular device resource D and a function mapping a numerical value to each data item could be defined by the device categories. Possible contextual data items are:

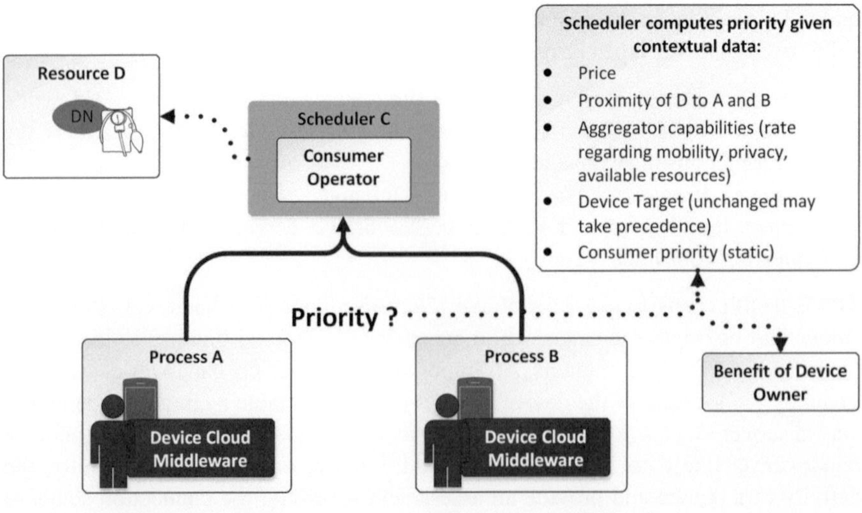


**Fig. 7.8** Generic representation of a device resource access decision-making

- *Price*: The price A and B are willing to offer to the device owner. In case of an integration request, the highest offer wins the competition. In case of an integration offer, the lowest one is preferred.
- *Proximity*: The proximity of D to A and B.
- *Aggregator Capabilities*: Aggregators involved in the provisioning can be rated regarding their mobility, privacy, available resources (e.g., possible platform modules), or reliability.
- *Device Target*: An unchanged device target may take precedence (e.g., the binding to a patient is kept). Composite devices may be able to serve multiple consumers but only monitor one device target simultaneously. Thus, a request including a device target differing from the current one would lead to a revocation of other existing device locks.
- *Consumer Priority*: As mentioned, some use cases (e.g., E-health) are likely to define static priorities for the consumers (e.g., the emergency ward of a hospital takes precedence over a home doctor).

### *7.3.5 Architecture: Communication Model*

Once a device cloud interaction has completed, a device is likely to be integrated by an instance of the device cloud middleware. The device cloud communication model defines a protocol agnostic approach to integrate devices independent from the used communication technology or the dedicated application domain.

The device cloud middleware is an execution engine for platform modules. According to the classification of platform modules, the middleware consists of two major parts: the device layer engine (DLE) and the aggregation layer engine (ALE). While the ALE is mainly dedicated to the integration of applications, the DLE transparently handles the communication with the devices and hides the complexity of the underlying communication protocols and topologies. Its focus lies on modularity, reusability, and automated runtime composition of device control logic.

The device cloud middleware is based on OSGi. As shown in Fig. 7.9, it defines a set of core services required for both, the DLE and ALE part:

- *Aggregator Agent*: The aggregator agent itself acts as the bridge to the device cloud infrastructure by providing a client implementation of the defined device cloud interaction model. It maintains the private key of the aggregator principal and ensures that each request of its sub services is properly authenticated and mapped to the interactions.
- *Device Manager*: The device manager lists the set of physical devices and device categories currently offered by the DLE.
- *Monitoring Manager*: The monitoring manager is used to collect metadata and status information about integrated devices.

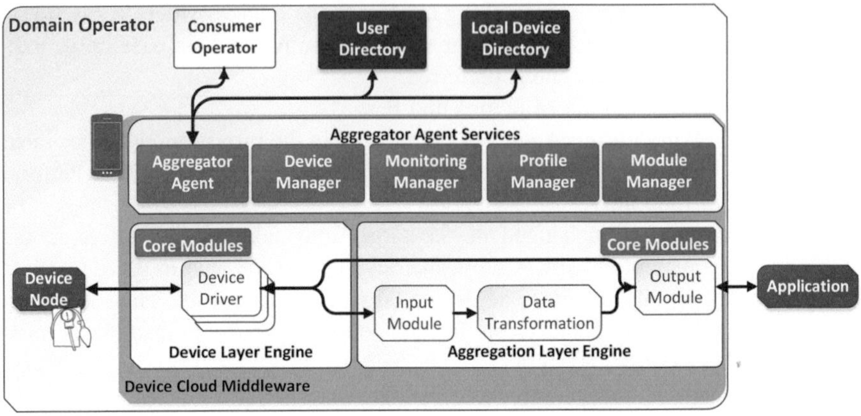


**Fig. 7.9** Overview of the device cloud middleware

- *Profile Manager*: The profile manager maintains the consumers linked to the aggregation node.
- *Module Manager*: The module manager controls the life cycle of the deployed platform modules. It maintains status information about each already deployed module. Additionally it can resolve dependencies if new modules shall be deployed and uninstalls modules in case of resource bottlenecks.

The DLE is based on the OSGi DAS introduced in Sect. 7.2.3.4. Its main capability is to dynamically compose device control logic based on device categories. Figure 7.10 illustrates a typical example found in many application scenarios. It underlines the requirement to represent device control logic in a modular fashion while providing different levels of abstraction. Device B (light switch) is connected to the aggregator based on two different networks that follow different protocols with respect to the OSI layers. However, a light switch usually has the same control semantics regardless whether it is attached using Ethernet or another networking technology. Thus, an application should only recognize the presence of a device compliant to a certain device category. Moreover, the application is usually not interested in the technical details of the integration and the underlying protocols used. However, the challenging issue raised by the use case consists in the fact that a gateway device can introduce a whole network. The network may follow completely different addressing schemes than the network the aggregator is attached to. In order to represent such kinds of topologies, a mechanism which is able to compose several device and protocol drivers in a transparent way is required.

The DAS models the composition of device control logic by establishing a relationship between driver services and device services based on the device category. If a new device service is registered, the driver manager can attach a suitable driver service, which in turn can register new device services. Driver and device services must specify the device category they belong to. The DLE adopts

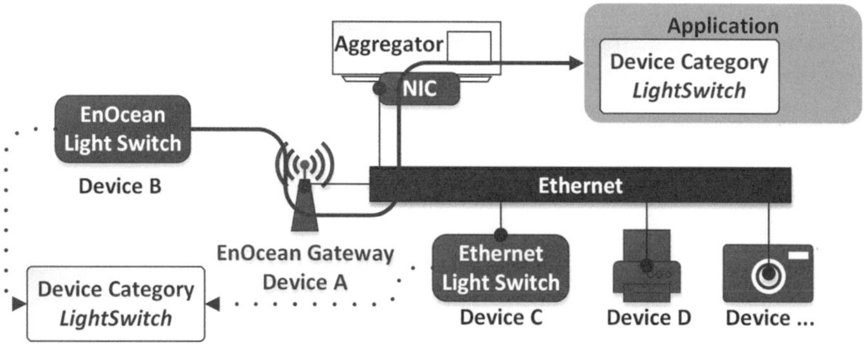


**Fig. 7.10** Two light switches using similar control semantics but requiring different control logic attached to an aggregation node

the standard DAS behavior and extends it by a set of discovery services that specify how base drivers are deployed to the system. Base drivers create the first representation of physical devices (i.e., the first device services). Thus, they initially trigger the DAS attachment process. As shown in 7. 11, the first base driver appears due to a bootstrap discovery module, which is deployed along with the initial device cloud middleware package. The bootstrap discovery module identifies the host device of the aggregation node using the introduced device category-based approach. The resulting category is used to load appropriate modules from the device directory using the default DAS driver attachment process. Additionally, a discovery manager listens for registrations of device services that refer to I/O interfaces (e.g., USB, Bluetooth, ZigBee) and searches for appropriate discovery modules. These are attached similar to device driver modules. Discovery modules create so-called device records, which are a special implementation of device services and thus can be used by the DAS attachments process like regular device services. Device records act as the first representation of a newly discovered physical device.

Before a discovered device can be integrated, the necessary permission needs to be acquired. Therefore, the device cloud middleware must authenticate itself against its consumer operator and request an access token. The process of authenticating principals within the device cloud and acquiring access tokens is defined by the security model of the device cloud.

### *7.3.6 Architecture: Security Model*

Providing authenticity and secure means for gaining access to devices is a mandatory requirement of the device cloud. Therefore, the device cloud defines its own abstract security model.

Based on the IAM capabilities offered by the user directories, the device cloud performs authentication and authorization of its principal entities. The user directory of a domain can be envisioned as a Kerberos realm. It is important to mention that this does not imply that the Kerberos protocol is used for authentication within the device cloud. However, similar to Kerberos, a trusted relationship between the domains (or at least the root and its child domains) needs to exist. This is because provisioning interactions can span domains. Staying with the Kerberos terminology, the user directory stands for the authentication server (AS) and the device directory for the ticket granting server (TGS).

An even more appropriate terminology, fitting the general entity properties defined in Sect. 7.3.3.3, is given by the OAuth 2.0 authorization protocol [47]. OAuth 2.0 defines the role resource owner, resource server, client, and authorization server. A client willing to access a resource protected by the resource server needs to present a valid access token. Only the resource owner can issue the token. Therefore, the authorization server has to authenticate the resource owner and issue an access token to the client. As shown in Figs. 7.11 and 7.12, this model can be easily mapped to the device cloud and the process of provisioning. In simplified terms, provisioning a device requires that the consumer operator, being responsible for provisioning and granting access locks, gets access to a device instance entity and modifies its state. As mentioned, all device-related entities are maintained by the device directory and each entity has an EntityOwner property. Hence, the device directory is a resource server that protects access to device-related entities based on the EntityOwner and EntityOperator properties.

The device cloud security concept is based on asymmetric encryption (i.e., a public and a private key for each principal entity). This technique can be used along with several authentication concepts (e.g., challenge-response methods) and specific protocols (OpenID Connect) and additionally allows ensuring integrity and confidentiality. The public key is stored by the trusted domain operator which is responsible for the principal, while the private key remains private to the principal.

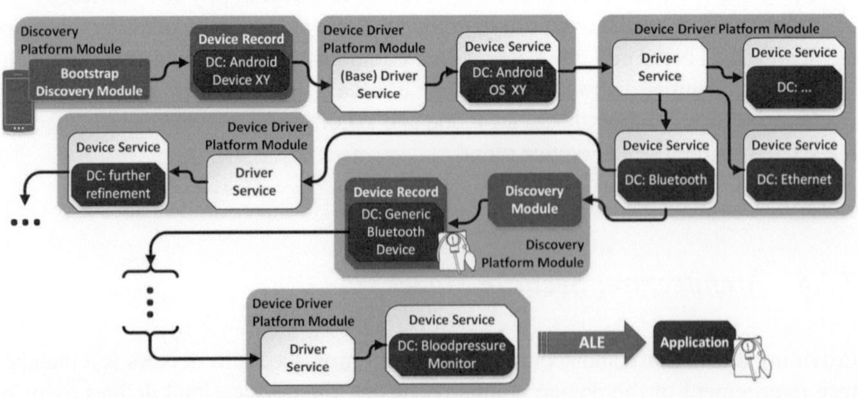


**Fig. 7.11** Runtime composition of device control logic

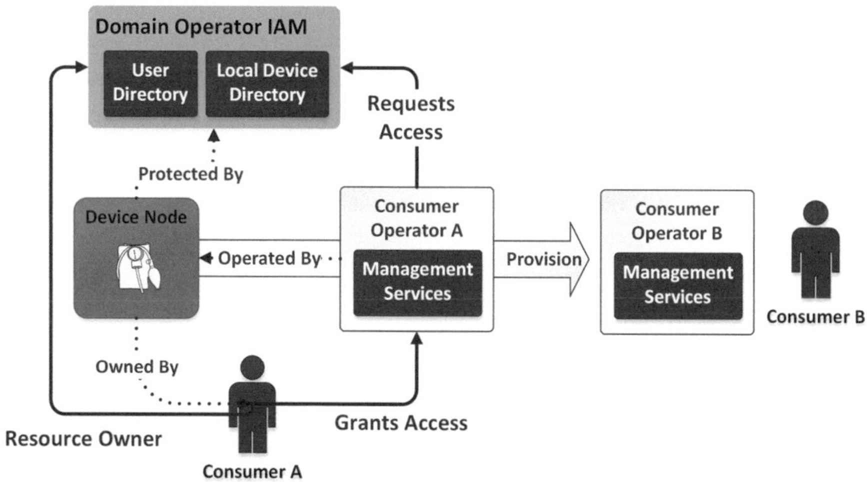


**Fig. 7.12** Domain operator protects access to device data and state model on behalf of the owner

#### 7.3.6.1 Device Access Token

Device access tokens are used to validate that a consumer is allowed to integrate a device. In other words, using the device access token, the device cloud middleware is able to determine that a device was provisioned to the device consumer by the device owner or an entity authorized to do so (e.g., the device operator). Therefore, in addition to regular principals, each device instance maintains a key pair. The public key is stored by the global device directory (i.e., root domain) and is thus accessible by all device cloud participants. The private key is stored by the domain operator the device corresponds to and is only accessible by the device owner. The device owner can authorize a device operator to access the private key. Thus, it is ensured that a device access token signed with the private key of the corresponding device instance was issued by the responsible device operator or device owner. The device access token consists of the following properties:

- *DeviceID*: The EntityID of the device instance the token belongs to.
- *LockID*: The EntityID of the device lock the token belongs to.
- *Issuer*: The EntityID of the operator issuing the token.
- *Validity*: Usually a time span.
- *CategorySet*: The set of device categories this lock is valid for (e.g., if a device offers multiple categories).
- *OperatorManaged*: A flag denoting whether the device integration has to be supervised by the issuing operator. This property is important for withdrawal of access tokens and distribution of private knowledge (e.g., security credentials are required in order to connect to the device).
- *OperatorToken*: Indicates whether this token was issued to another consumer operator or a consumer (i.e., operator token or consumer token). If

OperatorToken is true, the properties PublicKey and AttachedToken become mandatory.

- *PublicKey*: Mandatory in case of an OperatorToken. Refers to the public key of the consumer operator this token was granted to.
- *AttachedToken*: Mandatory in case of an OperatorToken. Used by an intermediary consumer operator to further re-provision the device to its consumers (i.e., further specify the validity). The attached token is added by the intermediary operator and therefore not part of the signature.

#### 7.3.6.2 Open Security Issues

The security model discussed cover principals and components belonging to the device cloud infrastructure. Providing an overall security model would require to adapt the protocols used by the devices (i.e., the protocols used to establish a communication link between a device and an aggregation node), which is not feasible. Hence, the device cloud has to rely on the security measures offered by the devices themselves. The individual measures conducted by each protocol are subject to a huge heterogeneity and sometimes do not even exist. Therefore, the device cloud cannot ensure a higher level of confidentiality or integrity as provided by the protocol an integrated device is based on.

A related issue is given by missing mechanisms to ensure the authenticity of devices and the generated data. If an attacker is able to guess a valid device instance ID, the corresponding device could be simulated. This can result in malicious data inferred to the device cloud. This issue can be mitigated by relying on devices with appropriate security measures in case of application domains with high security requirements. Additionally, the device cloud could monitor if a device instance is discovered while already being integrated and active at the same time. The issue of data authenticity for mobile sensors has been further discussed by Gilbert et al. [48].

### *7.3.7 Architecture: Application Integration*

Once a device has been discovered, identified, an access permission was granted, and a communication link has been established, it needs to be linked to a data sink. A sink is usually represented by an application of the consumer. The task of application integration is handled by the ALE part of the device cloud middleware. The ALE is the execution engine for aggregation platform modules, whose composition is defined by consumer profiles.

As shown in Fig. 7.13, the consumer profile contains a set of entries that enable the device cloud middleware to evaluate whether a particular device is of interest. An entry can be envisioned as a directed acyclic graph, which defines the processing of a data stream. Besides the entries, the profile holds a set of references

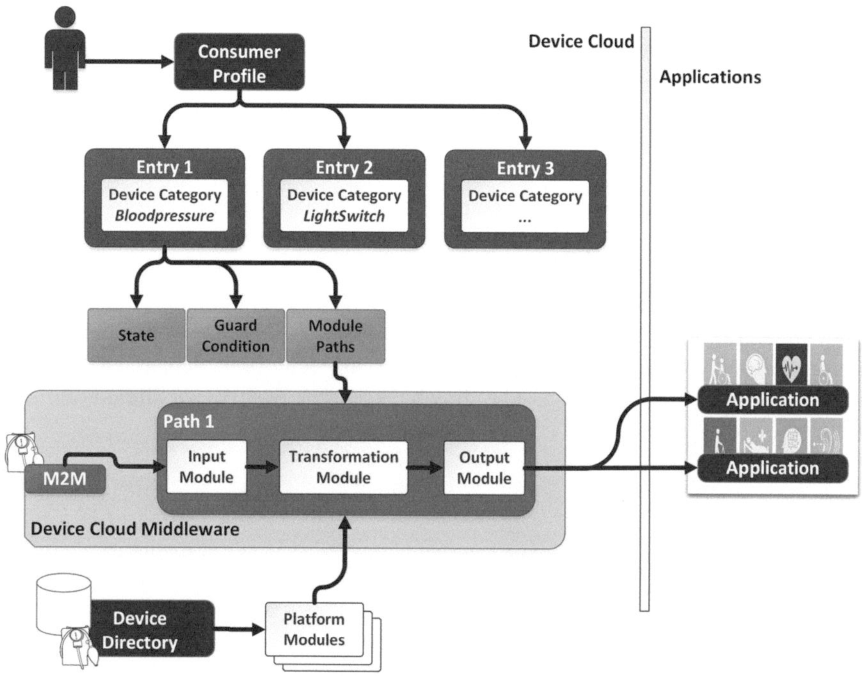


**Fig. 7.13** Consumer profile based application integration

to platform modules maintained by the device directory. The referenced modules are used by the entries. Each entry basically consists of:

- *Device Category*: The device category this entry is applicable for (e.g., a blood pressure monitor). The category is matched against the categories offered by a discovered device.
- *Entry State*: The state of the entry (e.g., is a matching device integrated and linked to the consumer). The state may also include information about the device target.
- *Guard Condition*: The condition allows consumers to specify detailed constraints and has to return true or false in case a device offering a matching category was discovered. The evaluation can include all contextual information available. Examples are costs, an integration schedule (e.g., three times a day), or other constraints like a minimum duration.
- *Module Paths*: A set of module paths defining the processing graph (i.e., a set of referenced platform modules). Additionally, path-specific configurations can be defined for the aggregation platform modules.

The paths define the binding between the DLE (i.e., the integrated devices) and the applications. Based on the requirements of the applications, different types of preprocessing can be performed (e.g., data aggregation or transformation).

Basically, two types of bindings can be configured. A category-based binding and a push (event)-based binding. The binding is realized by an output platform module, which has to be configured appropriately in order to forward the data to the bound application. In case of a category-based binding, the output module simply exposes the device category-based interface of the integrated device to the application. Hence, the output module acts as a service interface to the device and the application can interact with the device as specified by its device category. In case of a push-based binding, data generated by the device is forwarded to the application once generated (i.e., event driven). Therefore, an input module is attached to the device category and pulls data from it (if the category does not support push-based communication natively). In contrast to the category-based binding, the push-based binding allows introducing further preprocessing modules (e.g., data transformation platform modules) to the path. The drawback is that push-based streams do not allow the application to send control commands to the device.

## 7.4 Application Scenarios

This section presents possible application scenarios for the generic device cloud architecture. Based on the introductory assumptions that the amount of devices surrounding us is constantly growing, the need for on-demand provisioning these resources is well motivated from a technical point of view. Having a look at what the term device provisioning can be referred to from the user's perspective and what kind of applications this technical capability renders possible further motivates the concept of sharing physical resources. Use cases can be found in various IoT application domains, such as smart homes, smart cities, or, as already introduced, E-health.

When referring to the term smart home, applications like automated heating or light control, securing our environment with cameras or motion detectors, monitoring the state of our kitchen devices, or managing our entertainment devices are popular examples. Sharing can be used to improve many of these applications. In most of the smart homes, several individuals coexist, regardless whether families, visitors, or apartment sharing communities are considered. Often each individual brings devices that are used by the whole community. Two simple sharing use cases are found when thinking of visitors or entertainment devices. Each visitor usually has its own preferences regarding room temperature and light control. For the period of his stay, the visitor could be allowed to access the respective sensors and actuators in his guest room and use his own smartphone and already stored preferences to control their behavior. The second use case is given by all the display devices available in the smart home. Each resident can temporarily take control over a screen and use it to display preferred contents (e.g., a movie or video game streamed by his smartphone). More complex scenarios evolve out of the interaction of multiple smart homes or a smart home and devices in the public domain, which the term smart city refers to.

### *7.4.1 E-Health Application Scenario*

The E-health use case is based on the introductory assumption that patients are monitored by a body area network of medical devices. Furthermore, multiple care delivery operators (CDOs) are involved in the treatment (e.g., home doctor, medical specialist, hospital). Medical devices are treated as resources of patient-related data. In general, a data resource can be considered as required if it becomes visible to the network of a CDO involved in the treatment of a patient. Thus, the patient takes the role of the device target, while the device consumer role is switched between the participating CDOs. The required data resource can be booked and integrated, based on the PAYG usage model offered by the device cloud. Based on the type of the device cloud deployment, each hospital or other large medical facilities can become consumer operators. The domain operator could be given by an independent third party (e.g., a health ministry or a governing body of CDOs). Regular domains could be organized on the basis of federal states, while the root domain could refer to the country.

According to the general sharing definition given in Sect. 7.3.1, two medical device-sharing principles can be distinguished based on the device target (i.e., the patient):

- *Optimizing Device Utilization*: A medical institution (or even a single individual) can optimize the utilization of owned medical devices. It is assumed that a pool of devices exist and that each device can be provisioned dynamically based on the demands of the patients. A hospital could efficiently pool the medical devices even among several sites. This sharing principle is based on a changing device target (i.e., medical devices are provisioned to multiple patients based on their requirements).
- *Optimizing Data Availability*: In contrast to optimizing the utilization, optimizing the data availability is based on an unchanged device target. A patient, already bound to a set of medical devices, is moving between several CDO involved in the treatment process. The patient holds the device target role, while each CDO is acting as a device consumer. Device owner and device operator can refer to each CDO, the patient himself, or even a third party (e.g., a health insurance or a telemedicine provider). The initial binding of the devices to the patient can be due to participation in a telemedicine program or because of any other type or treatment (e.g., a patient is transferred from a general hospital to a specialized clinic while the devices remain attached).

Accordingly, the definition of a valid device target is of crucial importance for E-health application scenarios. Without a device target defined for a device instance, a CDO would not be able to link an integrated device to a patient. If only one CDO is involved in the treatment, the mapping from devices to patients could be maintained externally (e.g., the clinical information system). However, as soon as multiple CDOs are involved, the mapping has to be maintained by the device cloud. The device target can be attached as configuration entries to the device instance or the device locks. The device target must be expressed as an identifier common to all participating CDOs (e.g., health insurance number or identity card ID).

In case of the E-health application scenario, the device cloud requires that each integration request, resulting in a state transition from idle to consumer bound, contains a definition of the device target. This basically covers the utilization sharing principle. In case of the availability sharing principle, where the medical devices are moved between CDOs but are still bound to the patient, an integration request presumes that the device instance is already in the consumer bound state. Note that the device consumer role differs from the patient (i.e., the device target) in this case. This can be envisioned as follows:

- A set of devices is bound to a patient for a certain period of time by requesting a device lock and defining the device target. The initial device consumer could be the patient himself, a home doctor, or a telemedicine provider.
- A CDO involved in the patient's treatment discovers devices that are either in consumer or aggregator bound state and are linked to the patient through the device target.
- An access request would lead to a temporary revoke of the initial device lock (based on the device operator's decision policies). Subsequently, a new lock is issued to the CDO, which becomes the device consumer.
- The E-health use case requires that the decision policies of the device operator remember the initial device lock that was revoked. If the CDO releases its lock, the device operator has to restore the initial lock.

In summary, deploying the generic device cloud architecture to the E-health domain requires the following steps:

- Define the device categories necessary to describe the interfaces offered by the devices. Device categories can be derived from standardization activities such as ISO/IEEE 11073 [49].
- Provide the platform modules necessary to integrate devices and preprocess the data streams.
- The decision policies used by the management services of a consumer operator must be defined. Multiple decision policies may coexist and can be applied, based on the application domain a device belongs to. In case of medical devices, a decision policy based on static priorities can be applied. This is because emergency wards usually have higher priorities than home doctors.
- Provide tools that integrate into clinical information systems and easily allow the medical staff to modify consumer profiles of the patients.

## 7.5 Conclusion

Following the ubiquitous computing vision, the basic IoT assumption is that people are no longer supported by a single monolithic computing system. Rather they use all the small embedded systems surrounding them to fulfill their needs (e.g., sensors, actuators, smart devices). Currently, most of these smart devices act like closed "boxes" and barely interconnect or collaborate with each other. Moreover, usually an application domain-oriented segmentation of IoT-related solutions can be observed (i.e., one box for entertainment, one box for smart home control, one box for E-health services). Justified by the proliferation of IoT solutions, the increasing amount of devices, and the increasing capabilities offered by them, appropriate measures to dynamically manage and provision these IoT resources in an application domain-independent manner are required.

On-demand allocation and provisioning of resources are key capabilities offered by the cloud computing domain. Users can consume resources on demand on a PAYG basis without having to worry about the details of the underlying physical infrastructure.

The device cloud contributes to the field of IoT research by describing a technology and application domain-independent framework and architecture for on-demand provisioning of physical devices to users, called the device cloud. The device cloud mitigates the problem of static, application domain-dependent bindings between users and devices by applying cloud computing paradigms to the IoT domain. Devices are considered as resources that should be provisioned to users based on their requirements. Thus, the device cloud can be envisioned as a cloud-inspired resource management framework for the IoT. Based on a discussion of related approaches, such as sensor virtualization, and possible application scenarios, a theoretical foundation enabling the provisioning and sharing of physical devices between users is presented. This includes the fundamental principles of sharing physical devices as well as an entity, an interaction, and a security model. A generic, application domain-independent device cloud architecture, consisting of a backend information system and a device cloud middleware, is derived from the models. By employing modularity, abstraction, and spontaneous interoperability features, the middleware is designed in a technology and protocol agnostic manner, being able to adapt to the requirements of the environment at runtime.

## References


1. Weiser M (1999) The computer for the 21st century. SIGMOBILE Mob Comput Commun 3 (3):3–11. doi:10.1145/329124.329126
2. Ashton K (2009) That "internet of things" thing. RFiD J 22(7):97–114
3. Libelium Comunicaciones Distribuidas SL (2014) Top 50 internet of things applications – 50 sensor applications for a smarter world. www.libelium.com/top_50_iot_sensor_applications_ranking/. Accessed 21 Nov 2014

4. Wang YW, Yu HL, Li Y (2011) Notice of retraction internet of things technology applied in medical information. In: Proceedings of Consumer Electronics, Communications and Networks (CECNet), pp 430–433. doi:10.1109/CECNET.2011.5768647
5. Yuqiang C, Jianlan G, Xuanzi Hu (2010) The research of internet of things' supporting technologies which face the logistics industry. In: Proceedings of Computational Intelligence and Security (CIS), pp 659–663. doi:10.1109/CIS.2010.148
6. Chong G, Zhihao L, Yifeng Y (2011) The research and implement of smart home system based on internet of things. In: Proceedings of Electronics, Communications and Control (ICECC), pp 2944–2947. doi:10.1109/ICECC.2011.6066672
7. Uckelmann D, Harrison M, Michahelles F (2011) An architectural approach towards the future internet of things. In: Dieter Uckelmann D, Harrison M, Michahelles F (eds) Architecting the internet of things. Springer, Berlin. doi:10.1007/978-3-642-19157-2_1
8. Armbrust M et al (2010) Above the clouds: a Berkeley view of cloud computing. Commun ACM 53(4):50–58
9. Sacks D (2011) The sharing economy. Fast Company 155. http://search.ebscohost.com/login.aspx?direct=true&db=bth&AN=60036724&site=ehost-live. Accessed 26 Nov 2014
10. Parkhill DF (1966) The challenge of the computer utility. Addison-Wesley Publishing Company, Reading
11. Mell P, Grance T (2011) The NIST definition of cloud computing. Natl Inst Stand Technol 53 (6):50
12. EC Amazon (2010) Amazon elastic compute cloud (Amazon EC2). http://aws.amazon.com/de/ec2/. Accessed 26 Dec 2014
13. Yuriyama M, Kushida T (2010) Sensor-cloud infrastructure – physical sensor management with virtualized sensors on cloud computing. In: Proceedings of Network-Based Information Systems (NBiS), pp 1–8. doi:10.1109/NBiS.2010.32
14. Alamri A et al (2013) A survey on sensor-cloud: architecture, applications, and approaches. Int J Distrib Sensors Netw 2013:1–18. doi:10.1155/2013/917923
15. Alam S, Chowdhury MMR, Noll J (2010) SenaaS: an event-driven sensor virtualization approach for internet of things cloud. In: Proceedings of Networked Embedded Systems for Enterprise Applications (NESEA), pp 1–6. doi:10.1109/NESEA.2010.5678060
16. Aberer K, Hauswirth M, Salehi A (2006) A middleware for fast and flexible sensor network deployment. In: Proceedings of the 32nd international conference on very large data bases, pp 1199–1120
17. Jayasumana AP, Han Q, Illangasekare TH (2007) Virtual sensor networks – a resource efficient approach for concurrent applications. In: Proceedings of information technology ITNG'07, pp 111–115. doi:10.1109/ITNG.2007.206
18. Islam M et al (2012) A survey on virtualization of wireless sensor networks. Sensors 12 (2):2175–2207
19. Craciunas SS et al (2010) Information-acquisition-as-a-service for cyber-physical cloud computing. In: Proceedings of the 2nd USENIX conference on hot topics in cloud computing, p 14
20. Kirsch C et al (2012) Cyber-physical cloud computing: the binding and migration problem. In: Proceedings of Design, Automation Test in Europe Conference Exhibition (DATE), pp 1425–1428. doi:10.1109/DATE.2012.6176587
21. Kindberg T, Fox A (2002) System software for ubiquitous computing. Pervasive Comput IEEE 1(1):70–81. doi:10.1109/MPRV.2002.993146
22. Westarp F et al (2002) The standardization problem in networks – a general framework. In: Jakobs K (ed) Information technology standards and standardization: a global perspective. Idea Group Publishing, Hershey. doi:10.4018/978-1-878289-70-4.ch011
23. Buxmann P et al (1999) The standardization problem – an economic analysis of standards in information systems. In: Proceedings of the 1st IEEE conference on Standardization and Innovation in Information Technology SIIT, pp 157–162
24. M2M Alliance e.V (2007) Machine-to-machine (M2M) – whitepaper. http://www.m2m-alliance.de/uploads/media/Whitepaper.pdf. Accessed 26 Dec 2014

25. Pierce BC (2002) Types and programming languages. MIT Press, Cambridge
26. Ohlenburg J, Broll W, Lindt I (2007) DEVAL – a device abstraction layer for VR/AR. In: Stephanidis C (ed) Universal access in human computer interaction. Coping with diversity. Springer, Berlin. doi:10.1007/978-3-540-73279-2_56
27. Vaughan RT, Gerkey BP, Howard A (2003) On device abstractions for portable, reusable robot code. In: Proceedings of Intelligent Robots and Systems 2003 (IROS 2003), pp 2421–2427. doi:10.1109/IROS.2003.1249233
28. Heineman GT, Councill WT (2001) Component-based software engineering: putting the pieces together. Addison-Wesley Longman Publishing Co, Boston
29. OSGi Alliance (2012) OSGi Core Release 5. Tech. rep. http://www.osgi.org/Specifications/HomePage. Accessed 9 Jan 2015
30. OSGi Alliance (2013) OSGi Compendium Release 5. Technical report. http://www.osgi.org/Specifications/HomePage. Accessed 9 Jan 2015
31. Atzori L, Iera A, Morabito G (2010) The internet of things: a survey. Comput Netw 54 (15):2787–2805. http://dx.doi.org/10.1016/j.comnet.2010.05.010
32. Eisenhauer M, Rosengren P, Antolin P (2010) HYDRA: a development platform for integrating wireless devices and sensors into ambient intelligence systems. In: Guisto D et al (eds) The internet of things. Springer, New York. doi:10.1007/978-1-4419-1674-7_36
33. Kostelnik P, Sarnovsk M, Furdik K (2011) The semantic middleware for networked embedded systems applied in the internet of things and services domain. Scalable Comput Pract Exp 12 (3):307–316
34. Dunkels A, Gronvall B, Voigt T (2004) Contiki – a lightweight and flexible operating system for tiny networked sensors. Proc Local Comp Netw 2004:455–462. doi:10.1109/LCN.2004.38
35. Prasad NR et al (2010) Open source middleware for networked embedded systems towards future internet of things. In: Sundmaker H et al (eds) Vision and challenges for realising the internet of things, CERP-IoT cluster. European Commission, Luxembourg
36. Sundmaeker H et al (2010) Vision and challenges for realising the internet of things, CERP-IoT cluster. European Commision, Luxembourg. doi:10.2759/26127
37. Bassi A et al (2013) Enabling things to talk. Springer, Berlin/Heidelberg
38. Zorzi M et al (2010) From today's INTRAnet of things to a future INTERnet of things: a wireless- and mobility-related view. Wirel Commun IEEE 17(6):44–51. doi:10.1109/MWC.2010.5675777
39. Darianian M, Michael MP (2008) Smart home mobile RFID-based internet-of-things systems and services. In: Proceedings of Advanced Computer Theory and Engineering, 2008. ICACTE'08, pp 116–120. doi:10.1109/ICACTE.2008.180
40. Jin J et al (2014) An information framework for creating a smart city through internet of things. Internet Things J IEEE 1(2):112–121. doi:10.1109/JIOT.2013.2296516
41. Karnouskos S (2010) The cooperative internet of things enabled smart grid. In: Proceedings of the 14th IEEE international symposium on consumer electronics (ISCE2010), pp 7–10
42. Jara AJ, Zamora MA, Skarmeta AFG (2010) An architecture based on internet of things to support mobility and security in medical environments. In: Proceedings of Consumer Communications and Networking Conference (CCNC), pp 1–5. doi:10.1109/CCNC.2010.5421661
43. Li M, Li H (2011) Research on RFID integration middleware for enterprise information system. J Softw 6(2):167–174
44. Li X et al (2011) Smart community: an internet of things application. Commun Mag IEEE 49 (11):68–75. doi:10.1109/MCOM.2011.6069711
45. Celesti A et al (2010) How to enhance cloud architectures to enable cross-federation. Proc Cloud Comput (CLOUD) 2010:337–345. doi:10.1109/CLOUD.2010.46
46. Tanenbaum A, Steen MV (2006) Distributed systems. Pearson Prentice Hall, Upper Saddle River, NJ, USA
47. Hardt D (2012) RFC 6749–The OAuth 2.0 authorization framework. Technical reposrt. The Internet Engineering Task Force (IETF). https://tools.ietf.org/html/rfc6749. Accessed 9 Jan 2015

48. Gilbert P et al (2011) YouProve: authenticity and fidelity in mobile sensing. In: Proceedings of the 9th ACM Conference on Embedded Networked Sensor Systems. SenSys '11, pp 176–189. doi:10.1145/2070942.2070961
49. IEEE (2010) ISO/IEC/IEEE health informatics–personal health device communication–Part 20601: application profile–optimized exchange protocol. ISO/IEEE 11073–20601 2010 (E):208. doi:10.1109/IEEESTD.2010.5703195

# Chapter 8
# Towards Enabling Clouds for IoT: Interoperable Data Management Approaches by Multi-clouds

**Tamas Pflanzner, Roland Tornyai, and Attila Kertesz**

## 8.1 Introduction

Cloud computing offers on-demand access to computational, infrastructure, and data resources operated from a remote source. This novel technology has opened new ways of flexible resource provisions for businesses to manage applications and data responding to new demands from customers. These services are offered at different cloud deployment models ranging from the lowest infrastructure level to the highest software or application level. Within Infrastructure as a Service (IaaS) solutions, we can differentiate public, private, hybrid, and community clouds according to recent reports of standardization bodies [13]. The previous two types may utilize more than one cloud system, which is also called as a cloud federation [14]. One of the open issues of such federations is the interoperable management of data among the participating systems. Another popular family of cloud services is called cloud storage services or Personal Clouds. With the help of such solutions, user data can be stored in a remote location and can be accessed from anywhere. Mobile devices can also benefit from these cloud services: the enormous data that users produce with these devices are continuously posted to online services, which may require the use of several cloud providers at the same time to efficiently store and retrieve these data. The aim of our research is to develop a solution that unites and manages separate Personal Clouds in an autonomous way to provide a suitable solution for these user needs.

The Cluster of European Research Projects on the Internet of Things (CERP-IoT) considers the Internet of Things (IoT) as a vital part of future Internet, and they define it as a dynamic global network infrastructure with self-configuring capabilities based on standard and interoperable communication protocols. *Things* in this

T. Pflanzner • R. Tornyai • A. Kertesz (✉)
Software Engineering Department, University of Szeged, Szeged, Hungary
e-mail: keratt@inf.u-szeged.hu



Z. Mahmood (ed.), *Connectivity Frameworks for Smart Devices*,
Computer Communications and Networks, DOI 10.1007/978-3-319-33124-9_8

network interact and communicate with each other and with the environment by exchanging data and information sensed and react autonomously to events and influence them by triggering actions with or without direct human intervention [1].

Gubbi et al. [3] suggest that to support the IoT vision, the current computing paradigms need to go beyond the traditional mobile computing scenarios and to evolve into connecting everyday existing objects and embedding intelligence into this environment. Furthermore, cloud computing has the potential to address these needs, and it is able to hide data generation, processing, and visualization tasks in order to tap the full potential of the Internet of Things in various application domains. Assuncao et al. [2] also highlight that there are many open challenges in applying clouds for big data management. Our work addresses one of the issues they raised, viz., how to store information in a way that it can be easily shared between cloud providers.

In this chapter, we propose novel solutions for interoperable personal data management in clouds to contribute to the evolution of the Internet of Things. Our approaches enable to manage and process user data produced by mobile devices in different clouds transparently and to share this data among cloud providers in an autonomous way by continuously tracking their performance. The main contributions of this work are (i) envisioning a solution for the data interoperability problem of cloud federations, (ii) providing a way for autonomous data management among Personal Clouds, and (iii) the development and evaluation of an application that is able to measure the performance of the interconnected providers and use this information to distribute user data among them. We also exemplify how to build applications using different clouds in an interoperable way by (i) developing and evaluating an image generator application that interconnects mobile devices, IaaS services, and cloud storage services; (ii) proposing a solution based on a biochemical use case of a real-world application that manages Ubuntu One, Dropbox, OpenNebula, and Amazon; and (iii) evaluating these applications to determine the performance of the proposed solutions.

The remainder of this chapter is organized as follows: Sect. 8.2 summarizes relevant related works. Section 8.3 presents an overview of the addressed cloud storage providers. The section also introduces our motivation for this work and then describes our approach for autonomous data management. Section 8.4 introduces a scenario for managing user data in a cloud produced by mobile devices, and Sect. 8.5 shows the porting of a biochemical application with interoperating infrastructure and Personal Clouds including the performed evaluations. Finally, our discussion and contribution are summarized in Sect. 8.6.

## 8.2 Related Works

The need for data interoperability and the extensive use of cloud storage services have been identified by various research and expert groups, e.g., [4, 6, 13]. Managing user data in the cloud also raises privacy issues [7, 15] that need to be taken into account during data processing. Nevertheless, in this work, we refrain from discussing legal issues and focus mainly on interoperability problems. Dillon et al. [5] gathered several interoperability issues that need to be considered in cloud research and named a new category called Data Storage as a Service to draw attention to the problem of data management in clouds.

Garcia-Tinedo et al. [8] have addressed performance issues of Personal Clouds. They developed a tool for actively measuring three providers: Dropbox, Box.com, and SugarSync. They performed measurements for 2 months with various data transfer load models to search for interdependency among data sizes, transfer quality and speed, and published their measurement data and concluded that these providers have different service levels, and they often limit the speed of downloading. This work also served as a motivation for our research, but we decided to develop a more lightweight and easily extendible measuring tool to support our further research goal of autonomous data sharing among these providers.

Fernando et al. [9] surveyed research relating to integrating the mobile world and clouds. They argue that exploiting the full potential of mobile computing is difficult because of inherent problems such as resource scarcity, frequent disconnections, and mobility. Mobile cloud computing can address these problems by executing mobile applications on resource providers external to the mobile device.

Botta et al. [10] envisioned the integration of IoT and clouds, summarizing the main properties, features, underlying technologies, and open issues. Nastic et al. [12] proposed a solution for merging IoT and clouds. They argue that system designers and operations managers face numerous challenges to realize IoT cloud systems in practice, due to the complexity and diversity of their requirements in terms of IoT resource consumption, customization, and runtime governance.

With this work, we plan to take a step forward in the field by combining cloud computational and data services with mobile device capabilities. This vision brings these technologies closer to users and provides a simple way to use heterogeneous cloud services to ease their lives.

## 8.3 An Approach to Autonomous Data Management Within Personal Clouds

Besides IaaS Cloud solutions, the user-provided data are also stored using cloud storage services, on what is often referred to as Personal Clouds [6, 13]. Their popularity is accounted for easy access and sharing through various interfaces and devices, synchronization, version control, and backup functionalities. The free nature of these services is also helping to maintain a growing user community [16]; the high number of users also implies the development of other higher-level services that make use of their cloud functionalities. To overcome the limits of freely granted storage, users may sign up to services of different providers and distribute their data manually among them, which situation leads to a provider selection problem. In this situation, tracking the amount and location of the already uploaded files and splitting larger files can be a difficult task for everyday users, which leads to the problem of cloud provider selection—not to mention their different capabilities concerning data transfer speeds. These facts serve as a motivation for our research, and one of the main goals of this work is to propose a higher-level service that helps users to better manage their data by providing transparent and automated access to a unified storage over these clouds.

### 8.3.1 *The Considered Providers*

To exemplify the suggested approach, we discuss four providers, namely, Dropbox [28], Google Drive [27], SugarSync [30], and Box.com [31]. Their main properties are shown in Table 8.1. The foundation of Dropbox is originated in a problem we still face nowadays. Drew Houston, one of the founders of the company, kept on leaving his pen drive at home during attending courses at MIT. Since he used several computers simultaneously, he had to email necessary files to stay updated at all devices, which he got tired of, soon. Since no suitable online data sharing solution existed by that time, he invented one. In 2007, he founded Dropbox Inc, and their service started in 2008. By 2011, it reached 14 % market share by having 50 million registered users. According to the latest figures, this number exceeded 200 million in 2013 [29]. Its freemium model grants 2 GB storage for a new registration that can be extended by up to 8 GBs by inviting others or performing certain tasks. Concerning the main properties of the service, it is written in Python, supports version control, and applies the so-called “delta encoding” technique, which only uploads the newly changed parts of a previously uploaded file. It supports a wide range of APIs and has several SDKs, as shown in Table 8.1.

Google Drive is a Personal Cloud solution of Google. It was initiated in 2012, but it has several predecessors such as Google Docs since 2006. It also serves as an in-house data store for several other Google services. It provides 15 GBs freely for a new user. Thanks to the coupled services of Google, its Web interface is capable of previewing numerous file formats in a browser.

SugarSync was launched in 2009, but its predecessor Sharpcast Photos dates back to 2006. It provided 5 GB free storage for a newly registered user till December 2013, when the owners announced to close freemium services till February 2014. Since then its free service is only valid for 30-day trial period.

Box.com was founded as a start-up company in 2005. Since 2010, it has been providing its built-in file preview functionality. It provides 10 GBs of free storage for a new user.

**Table 8.1** The main properties of the chosen providers

| Provider | Initial storage (GB) | Bonus (GB) | Max. storage (GB) | Supported OS | Mobile platforms |
|---|---|---|---|---|---|
| Google drive [27] | 15 | – | 15 | Win, Mac | iOS, Android |
| Dropbox [28] | 2 | 0.5 | 8 | Win, Mac, Linux | iOS, Android |
| SugarSync [30] | 5 | – | 5 | Win, Mac | iOS, Android |
| Box.com [31] | 10 | – | 10 | Win, Mac | iOS, Android |

| Provider | Version control | Encryption | Num. of devices | APT | SDK |
|---|---|---|---|---|---|
| Google drive [27] | + | – | – | + | Java, Python, PHP, NET, Ruby iOS, Android, Ruby, OS X |
| Dropbox [28] | + | + | – | + | |
| SugarSync [30] | + | + | 1 | + | Java |
| Box.com [31] | + | + | – | + | iOS, Android, Python, Win, Java, C# |

### 8.3.2 *Proposed Solution for Managing Multiple Personal Clouds*

Now that we have stated our motivation and introduced the considered cloud providers, we describe our proposed solution as shown in Fig. 8.1. Our approach is demonstrated with an application written in Java, which uses the OAuth [17, 24] standard to authenticate users. By using this protocol, client tools can act on behalf of certain users to access certain files without knowing their passwords, they use so-called tokens instead with limited lifetime. Its version 2.0 is the latest since 2012. It is only a framework and not a clearly defined protocol, so it can be regarded as guideline. The application consists of three components:

- MeasureTool component—for performing monitoring processes
- DistributeTool component—for splitting and distributing files
- CollectTool component—for retrieving split parts of a required file

The MeasureTool component implements three basic functions: connecting to a user account at a certain provider, uploading, and downloading certain files to and from the storage of this account. It has a plug-in-based structure to separate methods for different providers and to enable further provider support.

A monitoring process for measuring the performance of a provider consists of generating a file of a predefined size with randomized content, uploading this file to the provider's storage under a given user account, and then downloading this file back to the host of the application. The monitoring output and the measured performance data for the mentioned providers are shown and discussed later.

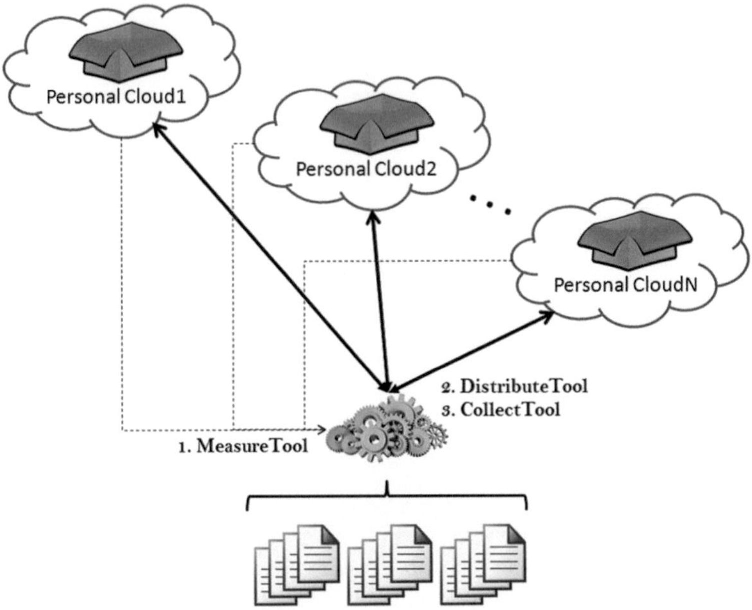


**Fig. 8.1** The proposed solution for mobile data management across Personal Clouds

The main task of the DistributeTool component is to apply certain policies for splitting up and packaging files to be distributed among the participating cloud providers in an efficient way. The file to be uploaded to the providers' storages is first split to a predefined number of files, what we call chunks, with equal sizes (large files are also supported, since only parts of a file are in memory at a time using buffering). The second step decides where to upload these file chunks. Once it has been determined and a chunk is uploaded, the DistributeTool component stores chunk identifiers (e.g., name, user token, file ID) to a local metadata cache file. By using this metadata file, the CollectTool component can later fetch the required chunk files from the different providers.

The provider selection in the second step is made upon the information gathered by the MeasureTool component. Historical performance values are also stored and taken into account, and it is the role of the application administrator to set the relevance (i.e., ratio) of historical and latest performance results for provider selection. The measured performance values are converted to the following format (denoting percentage shares—the sum of these values represent 100 %) taking into account the aggregated historical performance values ($h$), the latest performance values ($l$), and their ratio ($r$) by evaluating ($h+l*r$), e.g.:

{"googledrive": 5392, "dropbox": 1615, "box": 1085, "sugarsync": 292]

According to these configuration numbers, the DistributeTool component takes the sum of these values (*sum*) and generates a random number independently drawn from the range [*0*, *sum*] for each chunk by using Gaussian distribution. The given number will determine the provider to be used for the actual chunk (e.g., the randomly generated number 4,537 denotes Google Drive, while 7,509 selects Box.com according to the example above (5,392 + 1,615 + 502)). This selection criteria can be easily expanded later if needed, e.g., incorporating the experienced number of failures during the measurements. Our further goal is to support scenarios, where not only freemium storages are considered. In this way provider selection could be optimized by payment minimization.

The CollectTool component is able to collect the previously uploaded user files from the cloud providers by using the metadata description file. Once the chunks of a required file are retrieved, they are unified with an optimized buffering technique.

### 8.3.3 Evaluation of the Proposed Solution

We have performed evaluations on a private IaaS Cloud based on OpenNebula. It has been developed by a national project called SZTAKI Cloud [18], which was initiated in 2012 to perform research in clouds and to create an institutional cloud infrastructure for the Computer and Automation Research Institute of the Hungarian Academy of Sciences. Since 2013, it has operated in experimental state, and since 2014, it is in production state available for all researchers associated with the institute. It runs OpenNebula 4.4 with KVM and controls over 440 CPU cores, 1,790 GBs of RAM, 66 TBs shared, and 35 TBs local storage for serving an average of 250 Virtual Machines (VM) per day (considering the data taken in an average month).

The application consisting of the previously discussed components has been deployed in a VM started at SZTAKI Cloud. The evaluation architecture is depicted in Fig. 8.2.

For users, the most important metric for measuring provider performance is the data transfer speed. Therefore, we used this metric to monitor the providers and to use as a base for autonomous file sharing. To perform an evaluation of the MeasureTool component, we uploaded and downloaded files to each Personal Cloud with the following data sizes, 5, 10, 50, and 100 MBs, considering the following scenarios, (i) transferring two 5 MBs files or a 10 MBs file, (ii) transferring five 10 MBs files or a 50 MBs file, and (iii) transferring ten 10 MBs files or a 100 MBs file.

In this way, we arrived at six different cases, and we could also measure data transfer performance for handling many small and few big files. We went through all cases systematically and performed the same measurements several times. Once the limit of the freemium storage of a provider got exceeded, we halted the measurement and deleted all files on that storage to start following tests. We performed the same measurements on different periods of a week, i.e., on weekdays and at weekends. For measuring failures, we omitted failed transactions caused by server-side errors. Finally, the measured time taken to upload and download the files incorporates the writing of the files to the storage discs at the providers' side (in case of Google Drive, we could have omitted this interval, if we wanted to).

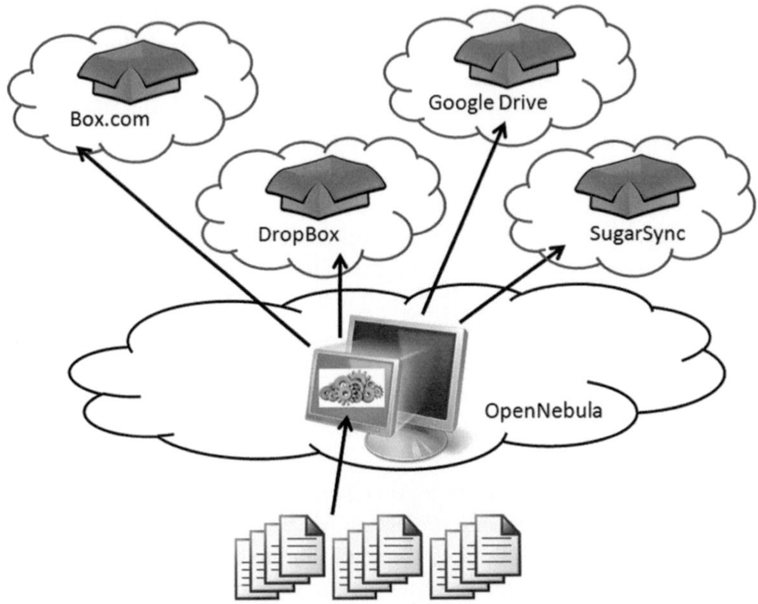


**Fig. 8.2** Evaluation architecture for mobile data distribution

The evaluation results showed that Google Drive has the best performance values followed by Dropbox and Box.com, while SugarSync has the worst values. While the difference between Google Drive and SugarSync is slight, it is not easy to compare Box.com and Dropbox. Many small files are better handled by Dropbox, while bigger files are transferred faster by Box.com. It is also an interesting observation that transfer speeds are accelerating for larger files. This is caused by the fact that during transferring a small file, the connection won't "speed up" in time, but for bigger files, it can utilize most of the available bandwidth. As mentioned before, the evaluation has been performed at different days of a week, but we experienced no major differences in these cases.

Concerning the amount of data transferred to and from the utilized providers, though the same cases have been executed for all providers, we measured different amounts. The differences among the providers lie in transaction restarts caused by failures or storage limit exceeding (though "delta encoding" and similar techniques could save some amount of data transfers). The total amount of data moved to and from these providers for the whole evaluation was more than 100 GBs by utilizing freemium storages. Regarding reliability of the considered cloud services, we also measured the number of failures experienced during up- and downloading the files. For Box.com we experienced a relatively high number of failures by downloading big files resulted in abortion of the transactions. On the other hand, SugarSync was proved to be the most reliable provider without a single failure.

Based on the results of the evaluation of the MeasureTool component, our initial hypothesis that service quality levels differ for various cloud providers has been proven. Now we continue with the evaluation of our proposed autonomous file distribution solution.

Earlier in this section, we briefly discussed how the DistributeTool component works for a sample configuration based on aggregated historical performance values, latest performance values, and their predefined ratio. Next, we evaluated the performance of our proposed application with four different configurations (i.e., $r = \{0, 0.1, 0.5, 0.9\}$) for user data distribution over the interconnected Personal Clouds. During these measurements, the DistributeTool component performed the splitting and packaging of the user files, selecting providers for the created file chunks based on the performance values and configurations, and uploading the files to these providers. The retrieval of the files was performed by the CollectTool component by using the metadata description file created by the DistributeTool component. The average transfer speeds during the evaluation for the considered providers are shown in Fig. 8.3—which correlates to the ones experienced in the MeasureTool evaluation. Furthermore, we can also observe that transfer speeds achieved by our application by utilizing all providers are faster than single utilization of three providers (only Google Drive performs better alone).

The evaluation results for the different configurations are shown in Fig. 8.4. As we can see on this diagram, slight modifications on the ratio of historical and latest

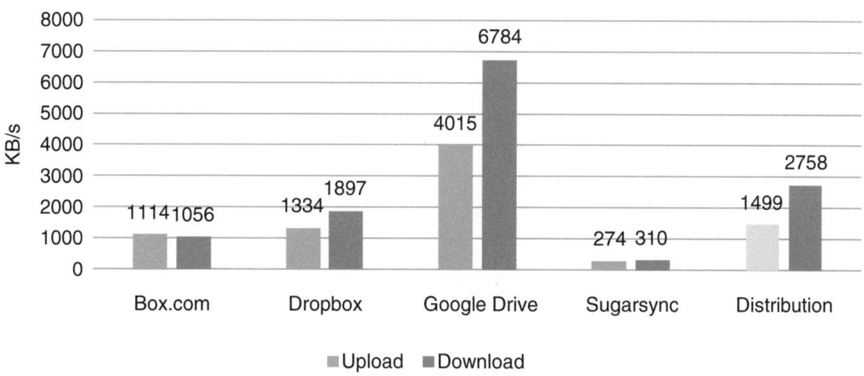


**Fig. 8.3** The measured speed of cloud providers during the evaluation

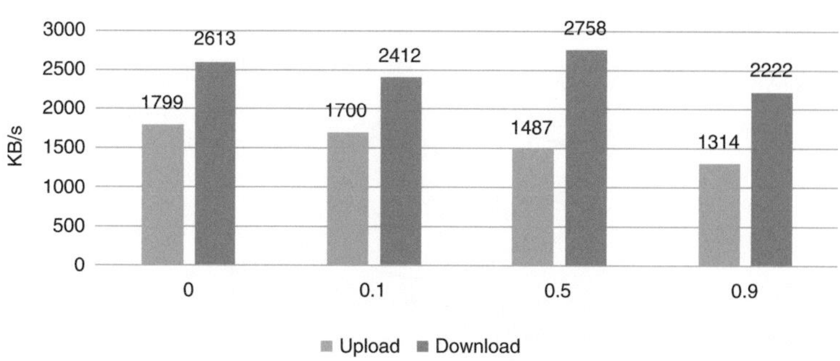


**Fig. 8.4** Evaluation results for the proposed application with different configurations for data distribution

performance values (e.g., changing $r$ from $0$ to $0.1$) do not imply big differences, but relying more on the latest performance values (i.e., using $r = 0.9$) results in faster up- and downloading times for the overall user data.

## 8.4 Managing Mobile Data in Clouds

Mobile devices, which play an important role in IoT, can also benefit from cloud services. The enormous amount of data that users produce with these devices is continuously posted to online services, which may require the modification of these data. As a use case, we have identified a real-world scenario that requires interoperable data management among cloud infrastructures to manage user data produced by mobile devices. Though the computing capacity of mobile devices has rapidly increased recently, there are still numerous applications that cannot be solved with them in reasonable time. Our approach is to utilize cloud infrastructure services to execute such applications on mobile data stored in Personal Clouds. The basic concept of our solution is as follows: services for data management are running in one or more IaaS systems that keep tracking the cloud storage of a user and execute data manipulation processes when new files appear in the storage (see Fig. 8.5).

The service running in the IaaS Cloud can download the user data files from the cloud storage, execute the necessary application on these files, and upload the modified data to the storage service. Such files can be, for example, a photo or video made by the user with his/her mobile phone to be processed by an application unsuitable for mobile devices. In our solution, currently developed for Android devices, there is a possibility to configure the processes to be performed on the data

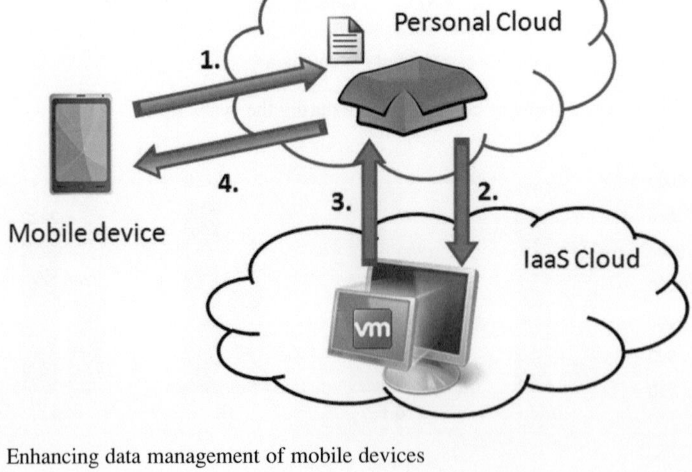


**Fig. 8.5** Enhancing data management of mobile devices

with a separate configuration file, which is automatically created and managed by a mobile application running on the user's device. This application is also responsible for communicating with the cloud storage, which is Dropbox in our case. The file manipulation applications have been created as a virtual appliance and have been pre-deployed in our SZTAKI cloud infrastructure based on OpenNebula, to perform our evaluations.

## 8.4.1 A Mobile Application for Image Generation

In order to exemplify the usability of this generic approach, we have developed an Android application called *FolderImage*, which can be used to manipulate pictures produced by mobile devices. This program creates thumbnails of each image of the appropriate folder and then ensembles them into a single image (called as *Folderimage*) that represents the folder and gives an overview of its contents to the user. This app can be really useful by providing a glimpse of a directory, when a user has thousands of pictures spread over numerous directories, and she is looking for a specific one. It can be used in two modes: (i) in local operation when the folder image is generated by using the computing resources of the actual device and (ii) in cloud operation where the application communicates directly with Dropbox; in this case, the pictures can be uploaded on demand or synchronized continuously, and the folder image is generated in the cloud, which is downloaded to the device after completion. These modes can be triggered by clicking on the appropriate button in its graphical interface (refer to Fig. 8.6). After installing and starting the

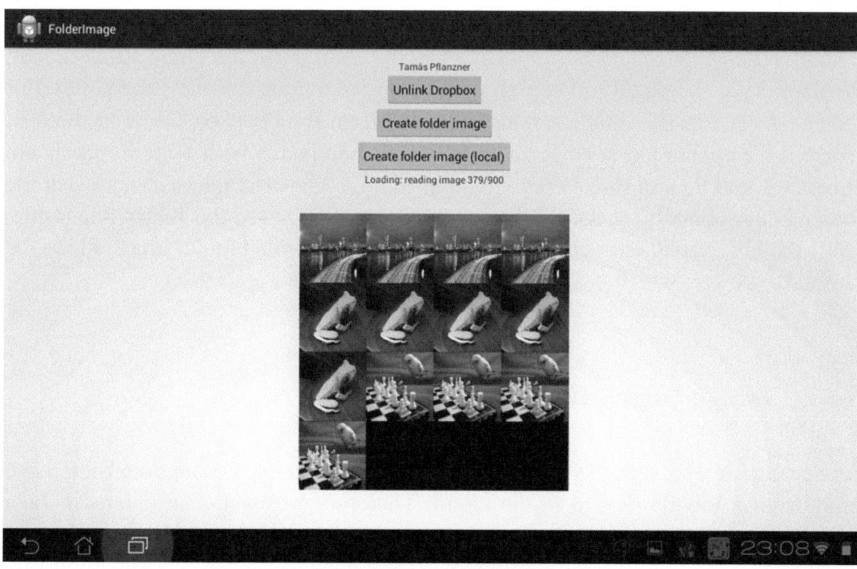


**Fig. 8.6** A screenshot of the FolderImage Android application

FolderImage application, the user will see a similar look with three buttons. Clicking on the first, top button, it will automatically log in to Dropbox, and after the successful login, the name of the account holder is displayed above the button. The second button can be used to trigger a folder image creation in the cloud, and the third one to perform the folder image generation locally. For simplicity, this prototype uses the "Photos" directory and creates a file called "folder_image_Photos.jpg". (This prototype can be easily extended to handle any directories on the device storage.) This generated image is also shown in the application GUI, under the buttons. Status messages and updates on image upload and download and image generations are also shown between the buttons and the folder image. Though this GUI is relatively simple, it is not an easy task to show proper look on devices having different display resolutions.

As mentioned earlier, the second and third buttons can be used to generate the folder image. These events trigger the "createFolderImage" and "createFolderImageLocal" methods, respectively. These methods comprise five steps as follows:

1. List: to generate a list of the images the actual folder contains
2. Download: to access the images of the folder
3. Resize: to generate thumbnails of the images
4. Create: to ensemble the thumbnails
5. Upload: to save the created folder image

These steps are time stamped; therefore, comparison between the local and cloud computation can be easily done. The second step of the local computation (when each image is loaded to the memory) had to be optimized for the local version, because most Android device has a relatively small internal memory for this purpose (e.g., 32 MBs). Therefore in this step, it is not the transfer time that needs to be considered, but the loading of the pictures to the internal memory one by one to generate separate thumbnails (on the contrary to the cloud version, here the memory is too small to keep all pictures in the memory at the same time). For the cloud version, the images are downloaded from the Dropbox folder to the VA, where the computation is performed. In step 3 thumbnails with $50 \times 50$ pixels are generated, and then in step 4 they are organized into a matrix that will represent the folder image. Finally, in step 5 the local version only saves the folder image file, while the Java application in the cloud uploads the generated folder image file to the Dropbox storage, which will be retrieved by the device application.

### *8.4.2 Image Generation in the Cloud*

As depicted in Fig. 8.5, the idea of our scenario is to move computation-intensive tasks from a mobile device to the cloud. Therefore we have also created a Java application called *ImageConverter* that is capable of performing the five steps discussed in the previous subsection. We have encapsulated this application to a virtual appliance (VA), deployed, and started it as a Web service running in a local cloud. It also has a direct connection with the user's Dropbox storage. It can continuously synchronize the image directory and perform the folder image generation once a new image is added to the folder. It can also be set to listen to a specific configuration file that instructs it to execute certain methods (e.g., performing different kinds of image manipulation processes). Once the "createFolderImage" method is called from the Android application, the configuration file is refreshed, and the Web service running in the cloud is notified about this change, which triggers the folder image generating and uploading processes.

If we deployed Web services of similar VAs into different IaaS providers, we could execute a set of cloud services that can access the same data storage under a Dropbox account. In this way we could handle and manage data in an interoperable way among different IaaS solutions.

### *8.4.3 Evaluation of the "FolderImage" Application*

As already mentioned, we performed our evaluations by using a private IaaS Cloud based on OpenNebula [23]. It has been developed by a national project called SZTAKI Cloud [18], which was initiated in 2012 to perform research in clouds and to create an institutional cloud infrastructure for the Computer and Automation Research Institute of the Hungarian Academy of Sciences. Since 2013, it has operated in experimental state, and since 2014 it is in production state available for all researchers associated with the institute. It runs OpenNebula 4.4 with KVM and controls over 440 CPU cores, 1,790 GBs of RAM, 66 TBs shared, and 35 TBs local storage for serving an average of 250 Virtual Machines (VM) per day, considering a typical month.

To perform the measurements, we deployed the *ImageConverter* VA to this IaaS Cloud. We have deployed them to two different types of virtual images: one having one processor and one GB memory (VM1) and the other four processors with 4 GBs of memory (VM2). Meanwhile, we have also tested the *FolderImage* application on two different Android devices: on a phone and a tablet. Table 8.2 summarizes the resources used during the evaluations. Table 8.3 shows the evaluation results corresponding to the five steps of the executed methods introduced in the previous section for a folder containing 900 images.

**Table 8.2** Capabilities of the used devices in the evaluation

| | Samsung Galaxy Mini (phone) | Asus Slider SL101 (tablet) | Cloud VM1 | Cloud VM2 |
|---|---|---|---|---|
| OS | Android 2.2 | Android 4.0 | Ubuntu 12 | Ubuntu 12 |
| CPU | 600 MHz | 1 GHz (dual core) | 1 CPU | 4 CPUs |
| RAM | 384 MBs | 1 GB | 1 GB | 4 GBs |

**Table 8.3** Evaluation results for 900 images

| Device | 1. List (ms) | 2. Down (ms) | 3. Resize (ms) | 4. Create (ms) | 5. Up (ms) | Sum (ms) |
|---|---|---|---|---|---|---|
| Android phone | 2,972 | 401,312 | 1,496 | 21,643 | 3,173 | 430,596 |
| Android tablet | 971 | 133,575 | 509 | 6,957 | 998 | 143,010 |
| Cloud VM1 | 44 | 220 | 300 | 575 | 702 | 1,841 |
| Cloud VM2 | 24 | 191 | 73 | 541 | 239 | 1,068 |

Results from the evaluation clearly show the differences among the different types of executions. Regarding the Android devices, the tablet performed the generation three times faster than the phone in both rounds of experiments. The Web service running in VM2-type virtual machine performed two times faster than the other deployment at VM1. The local executions on the Android devices are significantly slower (more than 100 times) than the image generations performed in the cloud. These measurements fulfill our expectations; therefore, it is worth, both in terms of computation time and energy efficiency, to move computation-intensive tasks to clouds from mobile devices.

Nevertheless, we have to mention that file transfer times can also affect these execution times. When a significant amount of data should be moved from a mobile device with slow internet connection may result in much worse performance, but if the new images are occasionally uploaded to Dropbox by using high speed Wi-Fi connection, still good results can be achieved.

## 8.5 Multi-cloud Evaluation of Data Management with a Biochemical Use Case

In order to evaluate our approach in a multi-cloud scenario, we ported a biochemical application called the TINKER Conformer Generator (TCG) to an environment consisting of academic and commercial IaaS Clouds. This application generates conformers by unconstrained molecular dynamics at high temperature to overcome conformational bias and then finishes each conformer by simulated annealing and energy minimization to obtain reliable structures by using the TINKER package [11]. The conformer generation algorithm in its present form comprises five different conformer finishing methods:

1. Minimizing the initial conformational states generated at high temperature (TM)
2. Performing a short low-temperature (e.g., 300 K) dynamics with the high-temperature conformations to simulate a low-temperature thermodynamic ensemble (TD)
3. Minimizing the above low-temperature states (TDM)

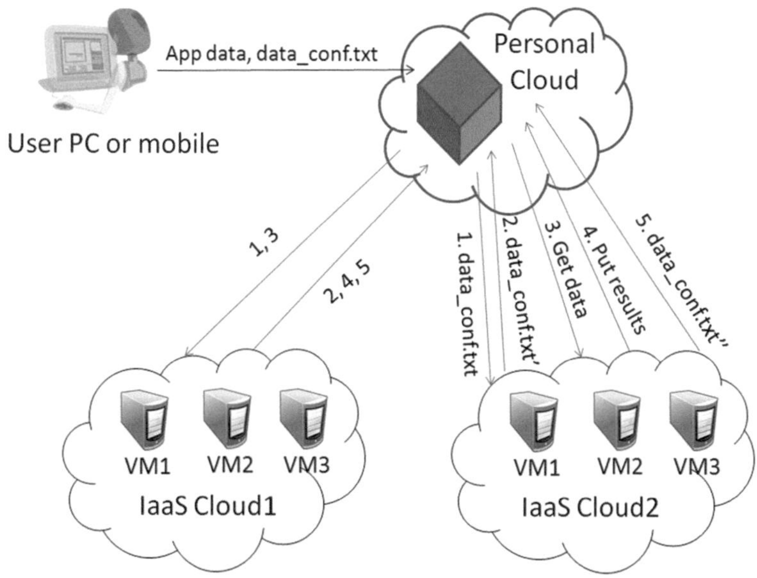


**Fig. 8.7** The proposed solution for interoperating IaaS and Personal Cloud services

4. Cooling the high-temperature states by simulated annealing, e.g., to 50 K or completely to 0 K (TSA)
5. Minimizing the annealed states (TSAM)

The end users of this application are biologists or chemists, who need to examine molecular modeling for QSAR studies for drug development, and the execution of the whole application in a single PC takes around 5–8 days.

Our proposed solution is shown in Fig. 8.7. By using this approach, users only need to make available his/her data in a Personal Cloud and to specify with a configuration file the order of data processing (by linking VM methods to data). Once this configuration file is available and at least one VM (executing the necessary service for processing user data) is running in an IaaS Cloud, the autonomous data processing starts and goes on till all data is processed. Steps 1–5 (in Fig. 8.7) denote communication between an infrastructure and a Personal Cloud:

- In Step 1, the configuration file is downloaded to a VM, and the first yet not reserved task is selected.
- In Step 2, the modified configuration file is uploaded back to the storage containing the new reservation.
- In Step 3, the VM downloads the data to be processed in the selected task.
- In Step 4, once the data processing is finished, the results are uploaded to the storage.

- And finally in Step 5, the configuration file is refreshed denoting the successful execution of the selected task.

### 8.5.1 A Ported TCG Application for Clouds

In the following, we describe our proof-of-concept implementation using the TCG application as a use case. We used three scripts managed by a Java Web application to execute TCG in a VM: the master script (*master.sh*) to perform the initial conformer generation, the worker script (*worker.sh*) to perform additional conformer finishing methods for 1,000 conformers at a time (including TM, TD, TDM, TSA, and TSAM tasks, selection is based on the input data), and the uploading script (*upload.sh*) to compress the sub-results to a single result file. In this way the execution of the ported TCG consists of the execution of a master task in the first phase, followed by running 50 worker tasks for processing the 50,000 conformers (possibly in parallel) in the second phase, finally calling the uploading script to create the final result in the third phase.

Initially we chose Ubuntu One [19] as a Personal Cloud to store application data in our proof-of-concept implementation. This cloud service is available primarily for Ubuntu users and is able to store, synchronize, and share user data in the cloud. It is operated by Canonical [20], and a newly registered user can use 5 GBs free storage. It also provides a Web-based graphical interface called Ubuntu One Dashboard, accessible by a Launchpad account.

The greatest challenge in porting TCG to this environment was to manage the configuration file properly for the maximum 50 competing parallel workers. A synchronization problem occurs when more than one VM try to modify properties of our configuration file (typically for reserving a task). This problem is exemplified in Table 8.4 for two competing threads A and B that both try to increment the value of a variable. Thread A reads the value of the variable in Step 2, while Thread B in Step 3. In Steps 4 and 5, they increment the read value in parallel and write it back in Steps 6 and 7. After two increments, the value of the variable should be 2 instead of 1.

To solve this issue, first we used the *listDelta* method provided by Ubuntu One to track file changes denoted by incremental generation numbers (instead of time

**Table 8.4** Synchronization problem

| Time | Thread A | Thread B | Value |
|---|---|---|---|
| 1 | – | – | 0 |
| 2 | Read | – | 0 |
| 3 | – | Read | 0 |
| 4 | Increment | – | 0 |
| 5 | – | Increment | 0 |
| 6 | Write | – | 1 |
| 7 | – | Write | 1 |

stamps)—this is a unique capability of Ubuntu One. In this way we could synchronize VM access to the configuration file by locking it for Steps 1, 2, and 5 (to avoid the selection of the same task by multiple VMs). Unfortunately this solution gave a poor performance according to our evaluations (caused by unexpected delays of the *readLine* method of the U1FileAPI library [26]); therefore, we have chosen a different solution that can be used by any Personal Clouds, not only by Ubuntu One.

In order to find a better solution for synchronization, we turned our attention to Amazon SimpleDB [21]. It provides access to a non-relational database running in the Amazon cloud. We used its free service providing up to 1 GB data transfer over 25 h of usage. With this solution we could easily manage concurrent access to our configuration file now moved to this cloud service. The value of a variable stored in SimpleDB can be incremented in three steps:

1. Get the value of the variable from SimpleDB.
2. Increment this value.
3. And finally put the new value instead of the old one in the database.

In order to avoid the abovementioned synchronization problem, we use the so-called conditional put or conditional update of SimpleDB in the third step. With this update before writing back the incremented value, we can check if the value has been modified since we read it. If this is the case, we won't update the value; otherwise, we do write it back. Of course, if the value has been changed by someone else, we need to perform the first two steps again (reading out and incrementing the correct value) till we are able to write our modification back to the database. The next section details our performed evaluations.

### *8.5.2 Evaluation of the Ported TCG Application*

We have performed our evaluations by using the SZTAKI Cloud, again. The ported TCG application has been deployed in VMs started at SZTAKI Cloud by a desktop application using the Amazon AWS API [22]. With this tool we can deploy a certain number of VMs in the SZTAKI Cloud that start the TCG application in a Web service. First these TCG instances (capable of behaving as masters, workers, or uploaders) connect to Ubuntu One and to the Amazon SimpleDB service and query the configuration parameters stored there in a loop till there is any task to perform. We could also follow the changes of the configuration parameters of the ported TCG application with the SdbNavigator interface tool, which is a free and open-source Amazon SimpleDB Administration Interface [25]. To reserve a task, an instance writes its VM identifier and the time of reservation to SimpleDB (to the *LockedBy* and *LockedAt* fields, respectively). After reservation, depending on the type of the actual task (*TaskType*), the instance downloads the input files from Ubuntu One and runs the corresponding script.

We have performed the evaluations in three rounds by deploying three, six, and nine VMs at SZTAKI Cloud each having four virtual CPUs and 4 GBs of memory. In the first phase, a master task is executed by one VM (the rest of the VMs are waiting for worker tasks), and then worker tasks are started in parallel in the second phase; finally an upload task is performed in the third phase to create the final result file. The evaluation results are shown in Fig. 8.8. From these results we can clearly see that by increasing the number of deployed VMs, the total execution time is decreasing.

To increase heterogeneity and to show a scenario when academic and commercial IaaS Clouds are interoperated through a Personal Cloud, we created another evaluation by using Dropbox, OpenNebula, and Amazon. We used the same template configuration for OpenNebula (denoted by ONe in the figure) to start three VMs in SZTAKI Cloud, and for Amazon (denoted by AM) we also started three VMs with Linux Micro instances. It took around 10 min to perform the initial input data transfers and to deploy the IaaS VMs to start with Phase 1. We measured nearly the same performance as in the previous round with six OpenNebula VMs. The result is shown in Fig. 8.9. Detailed measurement results for Phase 2 of this experiment are depicted in Fig. 8.10. In these diagrams we can see how the VMs of

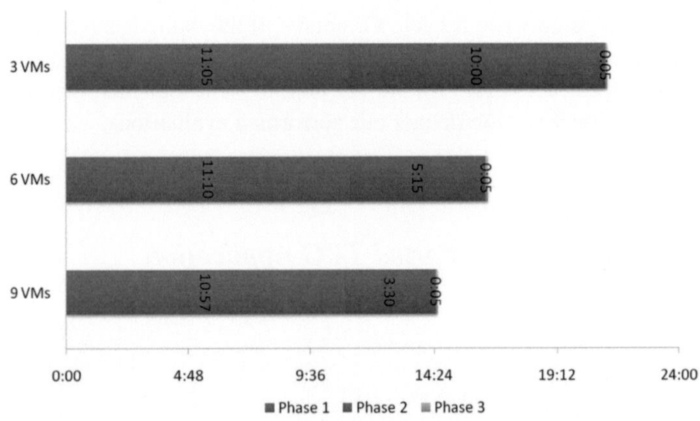


**Fig. 8.8** Evaluation results with Ubuntu One and OpenNebula

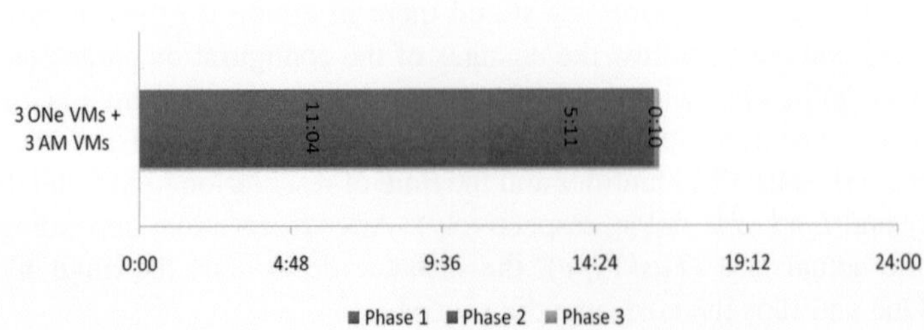


**Fig. 8.9** Evaluation results with Dropbox, OpenNebula, and Amazon

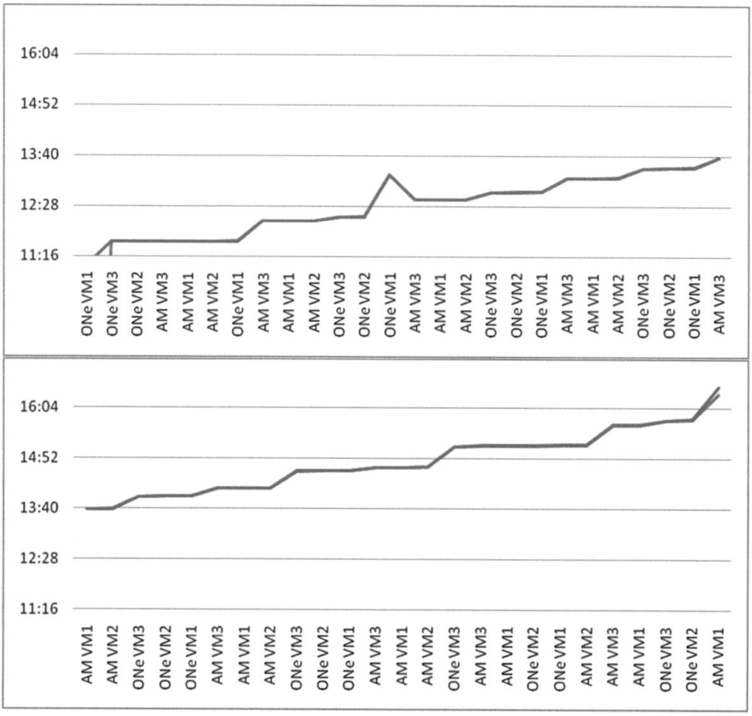


**Fig. 8.10** Detailed evaluation results for Phase 2

different IaaS systems competed for tasks, and how long it took them to compute these tasks in total (the curve marks the start time of task computations by VMs—except for the first task, which started at 0:00). In both evaluations, the data transfer time between the Personal and the IaaS Clouds were negligible (up to 1 or 2 min).

## 8.6 Conclusions

Enormous amount of data that users produce using mobile devices is continuously posted to online services, which may require the use of several cloud providers at the same time to efficiently store, process, and retrieve these data. The aim of our research was to develop solutions that contribute to the evolution and proliferation of the Internet of Things.

In this chapter, we introduced solutions for the data interoperability problem of cloud federations. Our approach enables us to manage and process user data produced by mobile devices in different clouds transparently and to share this data among cloud providers in an autonomous way. First, we have shown an approach for autonomous data management among Personal Clouds and discussed the development and evaluation of an application that is able to measure the performance of the interconnected providers and use this information to distribute user data among them. Second, we have shown how to build applications for mobile devices using different clouds in an interoperable way. We also developed and evaluated an image generator application that stores user data produced by mobile devices in Personal Clouds and processes them in IaaS Clouds.

Finally, we have exemplified how to build applications using different IaaS Clouds in an interoperable way by developing and evaluating an image generator application that interconnects mobile devices and cloud services. This solution is based on a biochemical use case of a real-world application that manages various cloud providers to store and process user data. We have also evaluated the ported biochemical cloud application and found that significant performance gains can be achieved by our multi-cloud approach besides the user-friendly, interoperable, and autonomous operation that this solution provides.

**Acknowledgments** The research leading to these results was supported by the European Union and the State of Hungary, cofinanced by the European Social Fund in the framework of TAMOP 4.2.4. A/2-11-1-2012-0001 "National Excellence Program" and by the European COST program under Action identifier IC1304 (ACROSS).

## References

1. Sundmaeker H, Guillemin P, Friess P, Woel S (2010) Vision and challenges for realising the Internet of Things. CERP IoT – Cluster of European Research Projects on the Internet of Things, CN: KK-31-10-323-EN-C
2. Assuncao MD, Calheiros RN, Bianchi S, Netto MAS, Buyya R (2013) Big data computing and clouds: challenges, solutions, and future directions. arXiv:1312.4722
3. Gubbi J, Buyya R et al (2013) Internet of Things (IoT): a vision, architectural elements, and future directions. Futur Gener Comput Syst 29(7):1645–1660
4. Bozman J (2010) Cloud computing: the need for portability and interoperability. IDC Executive Insights
5. Dillon T, Wu C, Chang E (2010) Cloud computing: issues and challenges. In: Proceedings of the 24th IEEE international conference on advanced information networking and applications. pp 27–33
6. Fraunhofer Institute for Secure Information Technology (n.d.) On the security of cloud storage services. SIT technical reports. Mar 2012. Online: http://www.sit.fraunhofer.de/content/dam/sit/en/documents/Cloud-Storage-Securitya4.pdf. Accessed 28 Jan 2014
7. Gagliardi F, Muscella S (2010) Data confidentiality and interoperability challenges. In: Book: cloud computing, computer communications and networks. Springer, London, pp 257–270
8. Garcia-Tinedo R, Sanchez-Artigas M et al (2013) Actively measuring personal cloud storage. In: The 6th IEEE international conference on cloud computing (Cloud'13). pp 301–308
9. Fernando N, Loke SW, Rahayu W (2013) Mobile cloud computing: a Survey. Futur Gener Comput Syst 29(1):84–106
10. Botta A et al (2014) On the integration of cloud computing and internet of things. In: Proceedingsof the 2nd Int'l Conference on Future Internet of Things and Cloud (FiCloud14)
11. Tinker molecular modelling package. Online: http://dasher.wustl.edu/tinker/, May 2011

12. Nastic S et al (2014) Provisioning software-defined IoT cloud systems. In: Proceedings of the 2nd Int'l Conference on Future Internet of Things and Cloud (FiCloud14)
13. Jeffery K, Neidecker-Lutz B (2010) The future of cloud computing, opportunities for European Cloud Computing beyond 2010. Expert Group Report
14. Kertesz A (2014) Characterizing cloud federation approaches. In: Mahmood Z (ed) Book: cloud computing – challenges, limitations and R&D solutions. Springer series on computer communications and networks, pp 277–296, Springer International Publishing Switzerland.
15. Kertesz A, Varadi S (2014) Legal aspects of data protection in cloud federations. In: Nepal S, Pathan M (eds) Book: security, privacy and trust in cloud systems. Springer, Signals & Communication. pp 433–455, Springer-Verlag Berlin Heidelberg.
16. Wikipedia, Freemium (2014) Online: http://en.wikipedia.org/wiki/Freemium. Accessed 4 May 2014
17. Wikipedia (2014) OAuth. Online: http://en.wikipedia.org/wiki/Oauth. Accessed 4 May 2014
18. The SZTAKI Cloud project (2014) http://cloud.sztaki.hu/en/home. Accessed 10 Sept 2014
19. Ubuntu One (2014) Online: https://one.ubuntu.com/dashboard/. Accessed 4 May 2014
20. Canonical Ubuntu website (2014) Online: http://www.canonical.com/products. Accessed 4 May 2014
21. Amazon SimpleDB (2014) Online: https://aws.amazon.com/simpledb/. Accessed 4 May 2014
22. Amazon AWS documentation (2014) Online: https://aws.amazon.com/documentation/. Accessed 4 May 2014
23. OpenNebula website (2014) Online: http://opennebula.org/documentation. Accessed 4 May 2014
24. Oauth standard documentation (2014) Online: http://oauth.net/documentation/. Accessed 4 May 2014
25. SdbNavigator interface (2014) Online: http://www.kingsquare.nl/sdbnavigator. Accessed 4 May 2014
26. Ubuntu One Files Java library (U1FileAPI) (2014) Online: https://one.ubuntu.com/developer/_les/store_les/android. Accessed 4 May 2014
27. Google Drive (2014) Online: https://drive.google.com/. Accessed 4 May 2014
28. Dropbox (2014) Online: https://www.dropbox.com/. Accessed 4 May 2014
29. Wikipedia – Dropbox (2014) Online: http://en.wikipedia.org/wiki/Dropbox%28service%29. Accessed 20 April 2014
30. SugarSync (2014) Online: https://www.sugarsync.com/. Accessed 4 May 2014
31. Box.com (2014) Online: https://www.box.com/. Accessed 4 May 2014

# Chapter 9
# Performance Optimization of Intelligent Home Networks

**K'Obwanga M. Kevin, Okuthe P. Kogeda, and Manoj Lall**

## 9.1 Introduction

Computer networks have been in existence for over the past four decades worldwide. Different environments including offices, campuses, military bases, governmental institutions, etc. have their electronic devices connected to enable both communication and sharing of different devices. In the recent past, home environments have created a niche as an area that equally requires networking of its devices for sharing, communication, and accessibility purposes, thus enhancing on control, scheduling, and monitoring of the home and its devices both locally and remotely. The intelligent home networks comprise subnetworks such as smart grid, Bluetooth, Wireless Fidelity (Wi-Fi), ZigBee, Ultra Wide Band (UWB), and Body Area [1]. Each subnetwork has devices connected to the Subnetwork Gateway (SNG), which are further connected to the Home Network Gateway (HNG). However, home devices, as well as the supported application services, continue to grow in numbers. These growths are attributed to rapid developments in the manufacturing and start-up business enterprises. Moreover, there are constant technological evolutions especially among the networking standards. These increases and technological changes, therefore, affect quality of service (QoS) of the home networks, thereby resulting in unreliable, unavailable, inefficient, and poor performing home network.

In this chapter, we present an Intelligent Home Network Optimization (OIHN) model. The model classifies and prioritizes the various subnetworks within the home network through virtual local area network (VLAN) protocol, prioritizes and classifies the various devices in each subnetwork via the use of weighing factors,

K.M. Kevin • O.P. Kogeda (✉) • M. Lall
Department of Computer Science, Faculty of ICT, Tshwane University of Technology, Pretoria, South Africa
e-mail: kogeda@gmail.com



Z. Mahmood (ed.), *Connectivity Frameworks for Smart Devices*,
Computer Communications and Networks, DOI 10.1007/978-3-319-33124-9_9

and further classifies and prioritizes the home network-supported services into six classes based on Differentiated Services Code Points (DSCP). Each network device can support a minimum of one Class of Service (CoS) and a maximum of six CoSs. Moreover, the number of packets on transmission per CoS in every iteration has been increased, in which CoS 6, which has the highest priority, is scheduled to transmit a maximum of seven packets for each iteration, as CoS 5 transmits a maximum of six packets, with CoS 4, 3, 2, and 1 transmitting a maximum of five, four, three, and two packets, respectively, in each iteration. This has yielded an average network packet throughput of 99.74 % in the entire network, made an optimal allocation of the available network bandwidth, and also reduced packet delay and loss to 3.02 s and 1.59 %, respectively, for the entire network as per the OMNET++ simulation, testing, and evaluation output results. This has provided an available, reliable, efficient, and optimized performing home network both locally and remotely irrespective of increase in number of devices and services and technological evolutions that the home network may support.

The rest of this chapter is organized as follows: In Sect. 9.2, we present an overview of intelligent home network. Sect. 9.3 presents an overview of the standard QoS mechanisms. In Sect. 9.4, we provide a discussion on the related works. The system design and architecture of the proposed intelligent home network is discussed in Sect. 9.5. In Sect. 9.6, we present modeling and simulation of the developed framework, with results and discussion being presented in Sect. 9.7. In Sect. 9.8, we suggest a way forward to extend the development of intelligent home network performance and conclude the chapter.

## 9.2 Intelligent Home Networks

An intelligent home network is an example of a network prescribed for use within homes. It deploys the use of intelligent systems in its operations, with most of the connected devices having the capability to monitor, control, and prompt a given user, on real-time basis, of any malfunction, elasticity reach, need for recharge, etc. An intelligent home network limits the users from constant configurations since they are able to self-heal and allow for dynamic re/configurations. An intelligent home network, therefore, provides comfort, enhances on security and health, helps in energy conservation, etc. both locally and remotely [3]. Devices within home networks continue to grow in numbers; most of these devices come with newer services that they are capable of supporting besides the existing supported services. These new services can only be supported by specific new technological standards.

### *9.2.1 Overview of Intelligent Home Networks*

An intelligent network provides services independent of both the network owners and equipment vendors and enables users to introduce self-tailored services within their devices. An intelligent network is a combination of both the knowledge modules and intelligent models and structures. The model has four basic information processing models [2], control, data, demand, and information driven, and has logical, temporal, and topological structures embedded together. In home network context, it is defined as an application of ubiquitous computing that is able to provide user automated or assistive services in the form of ambient intelligence, remote and local home control, management, and automation [3].

For an intelligent network to operate, a decision has to be made in which the decision model collects data/information, which is analyzed by the intelligent systems before a hypothesis is made to produce a report analysis that helps in the generation of policy needs. This process is iterated for any incoming data/information [4]. The essential characteristics of services supported by intelligent home networks include [5]:

- Extensive use of information processing techniques
- Delivery of data, voice, and other services over the same infrastructure
- Ability to guarantee the identity of a user
- Ability to prevent unauthorized users from gaining access into the network and Denial of Service attacks
- Efficient use of the network resources
- Guaranteeing quality of service
- Reusability of network functions
- Integration of network services
- Flexible network function allocations and standardized management
- Ability to self-heal (whenever a fault is experienced within the entire network, the network is able to reconfigure itself)

Intelligent networks support services such as tele-voting, call transfers, call queuing, seamless Multimedia Messaging Service (MMS) message access, mass calling services, private number plans, Virtual Private Networks (VPN), telephone number portability, call screening, toll free calls, etc.

Most network technologies including Global System for Mobile (GSM) communication, broadband, General Packet Radio Service (GPRS), EDGE, and Code Division Multiple Access (CDMA), 2G/3G/LTE, Wi-Fi, WiMAX, and many other technologies support intelligent networks and systems within their infrastructure. ITU-T standards differentiate most networks by coverage distances, number of network devices supported, and user's authentication and authorizations.

#### 9.2.1.1 Benefits of Intelligent Networks

The benefits of intelligent networks include [6–10]:

- Provision of information on real-time basis, thus minimizing delay between the network and the devices.

- Provision of dynamic configurations of network devices, e.g., the Wi-Fi network where several users can log into the system, road traffic robots that grants access to different vehicles in different places instantly.
- Minimal human errors in setups and configurations.
- Provision of security to its users, e.g., the CCTV cameras for monitoring.
- Saving of lives in hospitals and at homes: the devices monitor patients' health progress in real time and transmits the information promptly to the relevant doctor for diagnosis.
- Provision of remote connectivity and monitoring of network's devices.

#### 9.2.1.2 Demerits of Intelligent Networks

The demerits of intelligent networks include [9]:

- The network devices and the software for setting up an intelligent network are currently slightly expensive.
- Setting up an intelligent network requires highly skilled personnel who are expensive to hire and maintain.
- Some intelligent networks are prone to errors and external attacks.
- Most intelligent networks require constant power supply.

In the intelligent home network perspective, provision of comfort, safety, energy conservation, healthcare, and security are realized as follows [3]:

- Comfort—is enhanced by identifying human-related activities and event automation locally, thus helping in distinguishing location, identity, activity, and time. Moreover, remote management is made possible via the use of Internet or telecommunication infrastructure that provides bidirectional communication between the homes and the owners, enabling monitoring and control of the home appliances.
- Healthcare—is enhanced by providing healthcare services to the elderly, patients, and healthy people through an onsite stand-alone machine that generates health reports locally; the information can be sent to the remote practitioners for analysis and prescriptions.
- Security—is managed both locally and remotely through the locally installed HNG which implements user authentication and authorization schemes.

### *9.2.2 Features of Intelligent Home Network Applications*

There are several application services (apps) that help in the automation of home, home devices, and appliances. Some of these apps include Loxone, Smart Things, Control4, Incontrol, Vivint, Creston, Savant, Via International, etc. and contain security, control, monitoring, and management features. These features include [10]:

- Digital gate with an inbuilt camera, button, and voice recognition device and systems.
- Digital doors that have biometric detection devices and numeric keypad. Each door is configured with unique encrypted password and each user provided authorization to specific rooms. The doors help in either turning on or off of the room lights as one walks in or out, respectively.
- Light control in which lights can be turned on/off in any of the rooms. Further, user's preference on light dimming is enabled. Security lights are dynamically configured to turn on/off at specific times of the day.
- Appliance control in which high-definition television (HDTV), amphitheater, stove, fan, microwave, refrigerators, etc. can be monitored both locally and remotely. A user can regulate the volumes of various sound systems, change channels or movies to watch in HDTV, shut down the entire electricity usage in the home, monitor foods in the fridge, and automatically order for more food products.
- Controlling both the window and door curtains.
- Temperature and ventilation controls.
- Vehicle detection system and plant and pet monitoring system.
- Health monitoring devices and apps that check on the heart rate beats, pressure, weight, temperature, cardiac arrest, etc. This information is transmitted on real-time basis to family doctors for effective actions. The elderly and home patients are monitored in real time via the use of either object mounted onto the body or at specific locations within the house/home.

## 9.3 Standardized QoS Mechanisms

In this section, we discuss various mechanisms used in achieving QoS in both frames and packets. The various QoS classification fields in frames and packets are also outlined.

### *9.3.1 Classification Fields of Frames and Packets*

Both frames and packets are divided into three categories as shown in Fig. 9.1a. Each of the categories has fields used for classification when implementing QoS. The three categories are IP Packet, Transmission Control Protocol/User Datagram Protocol (TCP/UDP) segment, and Data Payload.

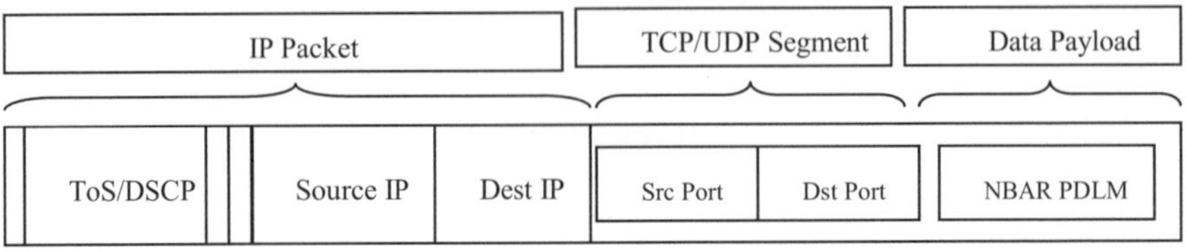


**Fig. 9.1a** Frame/packet classification fields

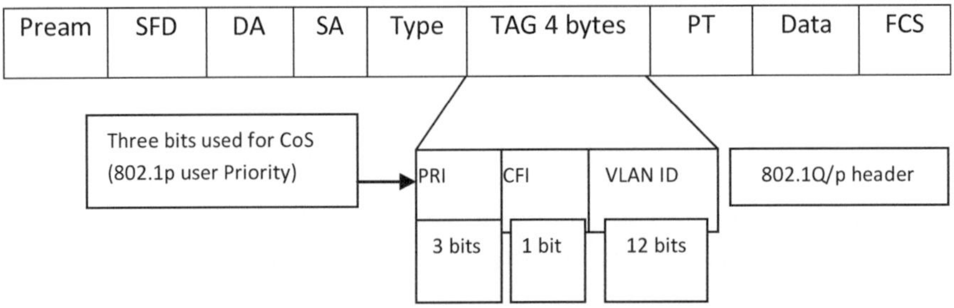


**Fig. 9.1b** Fields in Ethernet 802.1Q frame

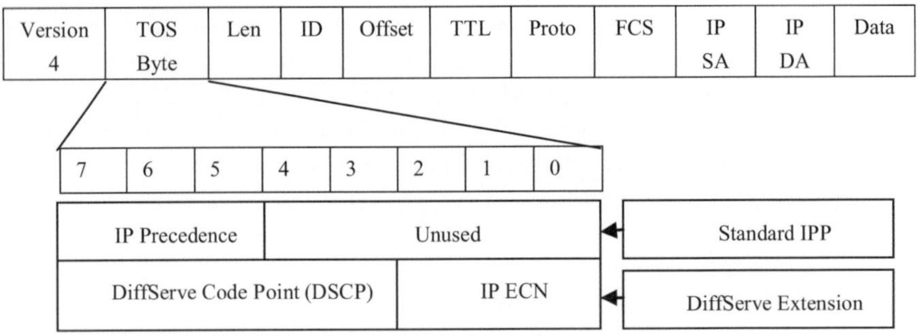


**Fig. 9.1c** IPv4 Packet Type of Service (TOS) Byte

### *9.3.2 Marking of Frames and Packets*

Class-based marking and marking using class-based policing are the two majorly used tools for marking packets and frames. The data link layer marking field is 802.1Q/p Class of Service (CoS), while those for network layer include IP Precedence and DSCP fields as shown in Fig. 9.1b, 9.1c, respectively.

802.1Q standard is an IEEE specification for implementing VLANs in layer 2 switched networks and defines two byte fields: Tag Protocol Identifier (TPID) and Tag Control Information (TCI), grouped as TAG 4 bytes as shown in Fig. 9.1b.

In Fig. 9.1c, both IP Precedence (IPP) and DSCP are used, making it widely acceptable since it has end-to-end network significance and can easily be translated

| | | | | | | |
|---|---|---|---|---|---|---|
| Version 6 | Traffic Class | Flow Label | Payload Length | Next Header | Source address | Destination address |

**Fig. 9.1d** IPv6 packet header fields

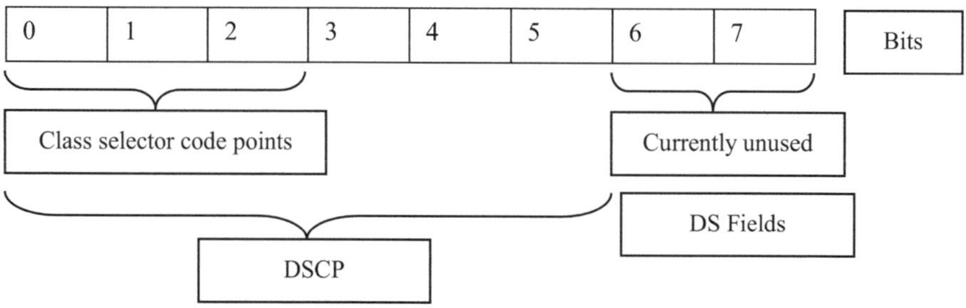


**Fig. 9.2** DSCP in IPv6 packet

to the layer 2 frame marking. Each packet comes with a new header. The IPP bits are similar to 802.1Q CoS bits in Ethernet frame. The IPP values 6 and 7 are reserved for network control traffic and routing; IPP value 0 is the default marking value. The remaining values 1–5 are used to differentiate non-best traffic, in which IPP 5 is used for voice, IPP 4 is shared by both conferencing and streaming videos, and IPP 3 is used for call signaling. The IPP values 1 and 2 are used for all data application marking options.

The packet header for IPv6, which is the newest technological addressing scheme, has fewer fields as compared to IPv4 as shown in Fig. 9.1d. DSCP is implemented at the Traffic Class field. The information provided herein helps in identification of the various and maximum CoS that can be supported by the intelligent home network.

### *9.3.3 Differentiated Service Code Points (DSCP)*

DSCP, which aids in classification and prioritization of the Classes of Services, uses the same 3 bits as IPP, but combines them with the 3 bits in Type of Service (ToS) byte, therefore providing a 6-bit field for QoS marking. The bit values range from 000000 (0) to 111111 (63), which is a better range for marking granularity as shown in Fig. 9.2.

The eight classes of traffic applications in 802.1p and DSCP for IPv6 addressing are shown in Table 9.1. Values 6 and 7 are reserved with value 0 being for best effort traffics.

**Table 9.1** CoS/IP precedence values by application types

| CoS value | Application |
|---|---|
| 7 | Reserved |
| 6 | Reserved |
| 5 | Voice |
| 4 | Video conferencing |
| 3 | Call signaling |
| 2 | High-priority data |
| 1 | Medium-priority data |
| 0 | Best effort |

## 9.4 Related Work

Several researches have been ongoing currently on various ways to optimize the performance of home networks. In this section, we discuss briefly some of these works.

### *9.4.1 QoS Harmonization for Home Networks*

Bhatti et al. [11] presented a home network QoS harmonization model which had class-based communication protocol. The model helped in differentiating priorities in both third and second layers. Differentiated Service Code Points (DSCP) was used to change the signal state, priority level, and protocol identification (ID) of the classified and marked packets in layer 3 from standard to harmonize, with the protocol IDs from the mapping table being used by layer 2 in recovering DSCP values as shown in Figs. 9.3a and 9.3b. This enabled bandwidth allocation. Our model uses DSCP too in service classification and prioritization; however, we have increased the number of CoS being used and packets being transmitted per each CoS as opposed to their approach.

### *9.4.2 A Simple Packet-Classifier Algorithm for QoS Control in Home Networks*

Takabatake [12] has presented a simple packet-classifier algorithm model for QoS control in home networks. The model classified packets into Non-Real Time (NRT) and Real Time (RT) and clients into ordinary and high priority. The RT packets, which were the first in priority within the media, were transmitted to high-priority clients, resulting in least delay and maximum throughput, whereas NRT packets, which had the last priority within the media, were assigned and transmitted to respective ordinary clients, resulting in high packet delays and loss and unavailable

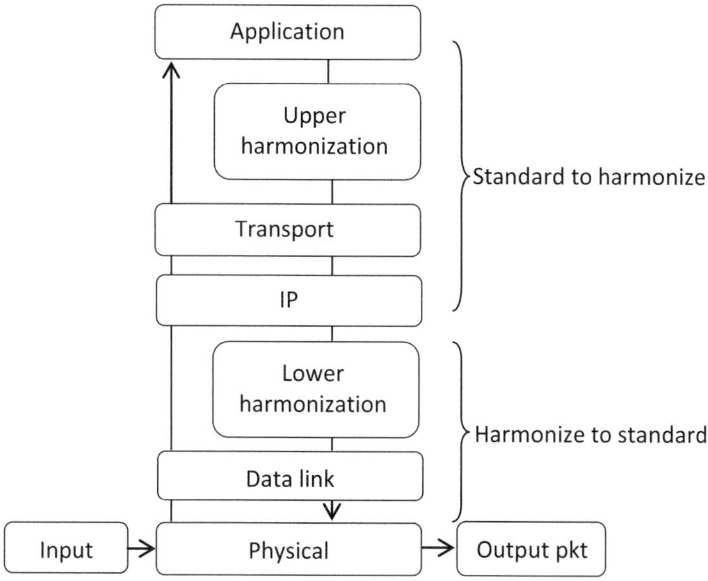


**Fig. 9.3a** Two harmonization layers of the communication protocol

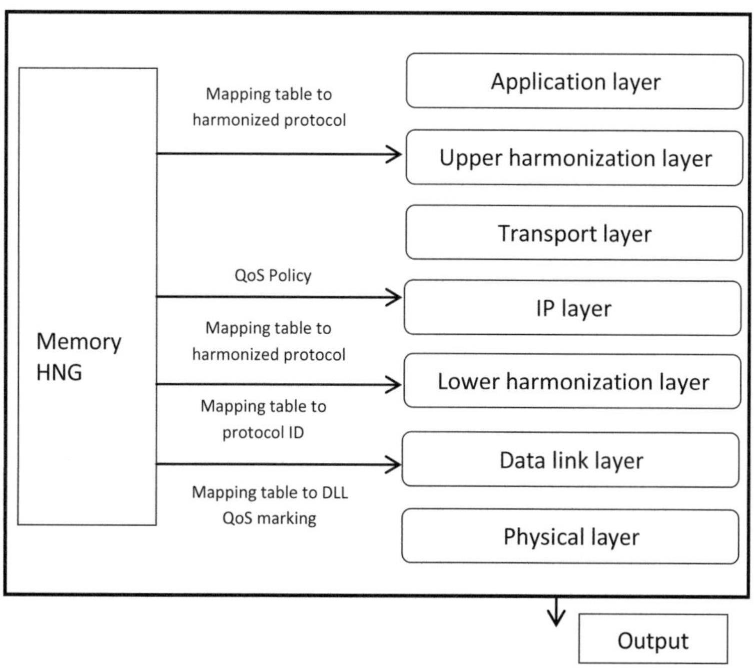


**Fig. 9.3b** Harmonization of protocols

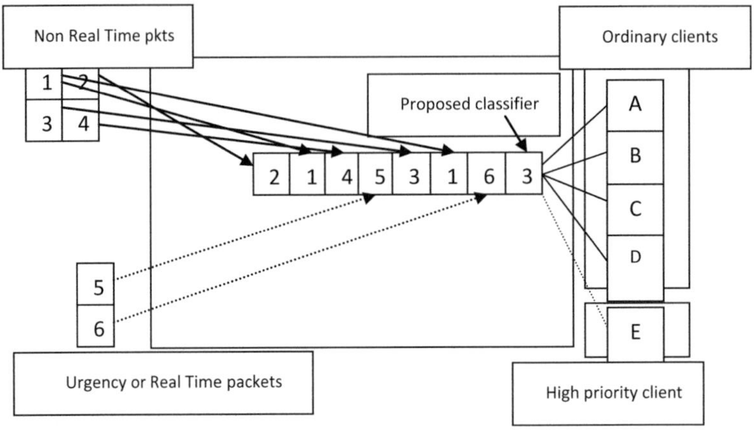


**Fig. 9.4** Harmonization of protocols (Adopted from [12])

bandwidth as shown in Fig. 9.4. However, our model has identified and prioritized six CoS and increased the number of transmitted packets in each CoS as opposed to the approach. This has enabled maximum packet throughput and minimum packet loss and delay in each CoS.

### 9.4.3 *Supporting Real-Time Traffic with QoS in IEE 802.11e-Based Home Networks*

Chen and Zhang [13] have presented a Hybrid Coordination Function (HCF) model. The HCF is an IEEE 802.11e standard that operates on the Wi-Fi networks as the MAC scheme. It combined the contention-based access method, Enhanced Distributed Channel Access (EDCA), and the contention-free access method, where EDCA provided differentiated and distributed access to the wireless media with access categories. The HCF allocated the Transmission Opportunities (TxOP) to wireless stations by polling and took control of the media after sensing idleness for some time; thereafter, it grabbed the media and polled the stations on its polling list in the order of entry. The given polled station would either respond with QoS null packet, showing no data to send, or with a QoS + ACK packet, showing availability of data to send; this was iterated during a single TxOP, and in the end, the HCF released the media if there was unavailability of more stations to poll or send QoS poll to the next station in the polling list. This helped in achieving both minimum delay and maximum throughput especially for video applications. However, the scheme did not address other services such as voice and data applications, which are equally important within home networks. Our model has defined six Classes of Services and given each an allocation within the media, besides increasing the number of transmitted packets in each Class of Service. This has presented an available, reliable, and optimized intelligent home network irrespective of increase in number of devices, services, and technological evolutions.

### 9.4.4 Smart Home M2M Architecture

Wang and Xu [14] presented a smart home machine-to-machine (M2M) architecture model that deployed cloud computing. The model used Internet of Things (IoT) in its infrastructure to gather, store, and upload processed information into the cloud for analysis and processing. The stored information at the cloud helped in processing and controlling of the network's events and resources, resulting in real-time interaction and saving of bandwidth. However, in our model, all the network's resources and operations are based locally, with a central HNG as the main operation unit. Classification and prioritizations of the SNGs ensure availability of network's bandwidth.

### 9.4.5 Class-Based Weighted Fair Queuing Model

Fischer et al. [15] developed a CBWFQ model that converged data, voice, and video signals together. In the model, two classes of packets, each having weighing factor and buffer, were used. The first class was served before the proceeding class. Packet arrival rates, average time to serve a given class, and probability to select a given class when both are in waiting were collected. This necessitated competition for the limited network resources thus meeting QoS. Higher throughput and least delay were observed in the first class than the second class. However, in our model, we have used DSCP in classifying and prioritizing home network services into six classes. We have further increased number of transmitted packets in each CoS per iteration. This we have done in order to optimize home network performance irrespective of upsurge in numbers of devices and services. We have yielded an optimized network performance in our model.

### 9.4.6 Priority Scheduling Model

Rajput and Gupta [16] developed a priority scheduling model which assigns fixed priority to every process. The model scheduled five processes. Lower priority processes had larger waiting and response time and got interrupted by incoming higher priority processes. This made them to be starved. Moreover, least waiting time and packet loss were observed in higher priority than lower priority processes. However, in our model, we have used DSCP to classify, prioritize, and schedule each CoS in the network. We have increased number of transmitted packets in each

CoS and iteratively scheduled each in the media. This has eliminated starvation and ensured optimized performance of intelligent home network irrespective of increase in number of devices and services into the network.

## 9.5 System Design and Architecture

The developed intelligent home network architecture consists of six different subnetworks as shown in Fig. 9.5a. These subnetworks include ZigBee, UWB, Wi-Fi, smart grid, Bluetooth, and Body Area with their respective devices mounted onto them. The network has been designed in star topology format to aid in configuration from a central point. Various devices have been connected to the SNGs which have further been connected to the HNG. Connections to both the home server and secure router have been done at the HNG too.

In setting up the home network, various resources such as Multi-Layer 3 switch (NETGEAR M4100, Cisco SG300 series, SG500-28P, Cisco 3650, 4500, and 6500), Access Gateway Switches (DES – 3200 series, S3610 series, S3100 series, etc.), Linksys wireless routers or Access Points, cables, a secure server, a secure router, Digital Subscriber Line (DSL), or Internet Service Provider (ISP) have been pooled together as shown in Fig. 9.5a.

Any of the Multi-Layer 3 switches is configured as the HNG, since it has the capacity to handle large amounts of traffic, different interface ports including Gigabit interface that connects to the secure server, is easy to configure, supports hardware-based packet switching, allows inter VLAN routing and prioritization, prioritizes packets by the 6 bits in IP DSCP, is able to implement QoS DiffServe, and is cost effective as compared to purchasing and installing a router. The SNGs are configured with VLAN numbers and names and Dynamic Host Control Protocol (DHCP) pool that dynamically allocates Internet Protocol (IP) addresses to the subnetwork devices.

The segmentation of the entire network into six different subnetworks aids in prioritization. This ensures adequate distribution of the various network resources. The network segmentation has been done at the Multi-Layer 3 switch, HNG, which consequently doubles up as the VLAN Trunking Protocol (VTP) server. The VLAN configuration has enabled identification and prioritization of subnetworks through numbering and naming. Further, it has enabled port bandwidth capacity specification and allocation of interfaces to respective VLANs within the network from the HNG. A total of seven VLANs, 10, 20, 30, 40, 50, 60 for respective subnetworks in descending order of classification and priority and 100 for home network's management purposes, have been configured. Each VLAN has been assigned an IP address, which doubles up as the default gateway, and aids in easier identification of the subnetworks during management. Consequently, DHCP pool has been configured on wired VLANs to foster dynamic allocation of IP addresses to the subnetwork connected devices, thus limiting users' involvement.

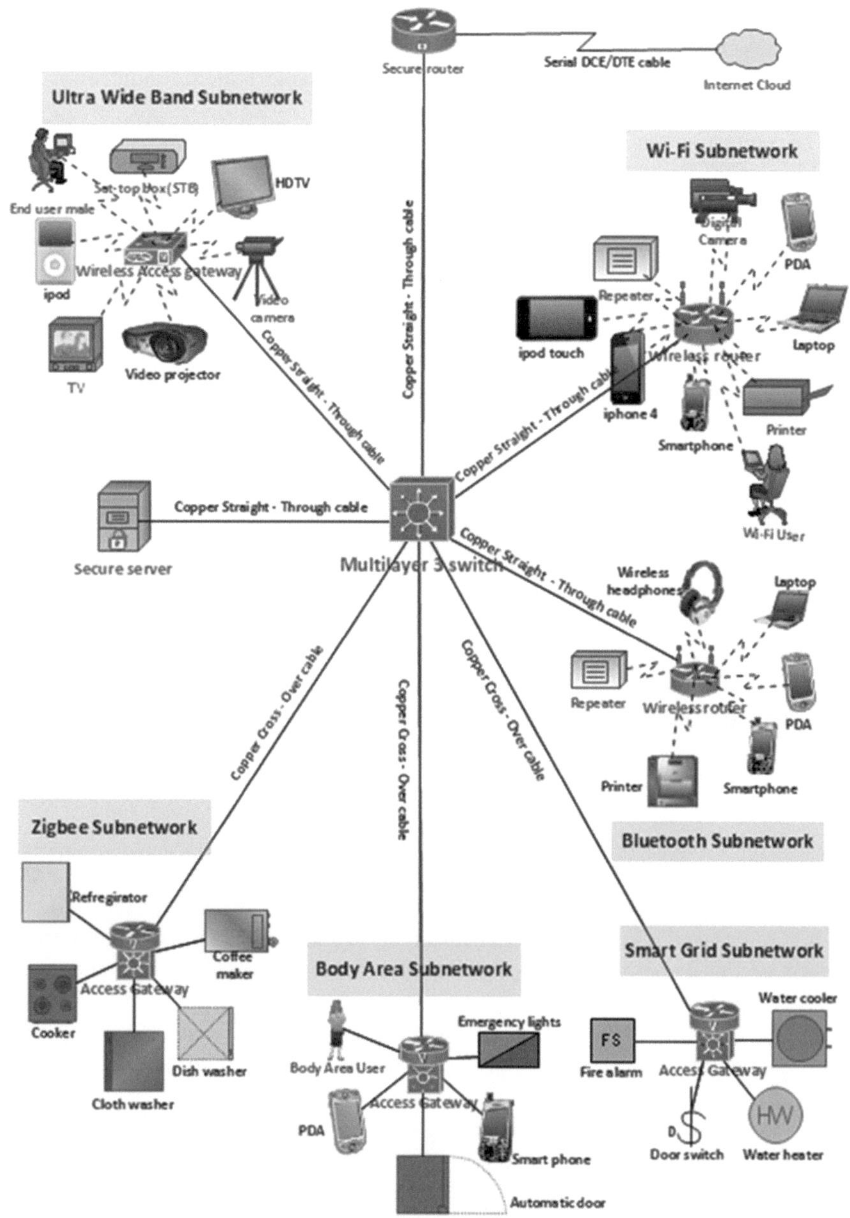


**Fig. 9.5a** Proposed home network system architecture

The layer 2 switches are configured as VTP clients. Any additional layer 2 switches to any of the subnetworks have to be configured within the designated VLAN; this enables access to the services of the particular subnetwork. Inter VLAN routing (IP routing) is configured at the HNG to allow for communications among the subnets. Routing protocols, Open Shortest Path First, OSPF, has been configured between the HNG and the access router to enable intercommunication and communication to the remote networks.

The secure server is statically configured with an IP address and contains databases, files, mails, configurations, management, and security features that aid in timely and available operations of the home network. The network's server IP address is also used as the domain name system (DNS) address that can be accessed by all the network's devices. We would have configured DHCP at the server to allocate addresses to the devices on the wired subnetworks if we did not configure VLANs with DHCP pool. The services that the server can perform are activated and the domain name is set up to enable email addresses configuration and file transfers. Virtual Private Network (VPN) is also configured in the HNG to enable remote connectivity and management.

All the subnetworks have wired connections between the HNG and the respective SNGs except Wi-Fi, Bluetooth, and Ultra Wide Band (UWB) that use either Access Points (APs) or Linksys wireless routers in their connections. The Linksys wireless routers have been renamed with the subnetwork names and router passwords and each statically configured on the Internet Interface with one of the reserved IP addresses to aid in connections to the rest of the network. The subnetwork addresses for the Linksys routers have been configured with an IP address, DHCP enabled and the starting IP address, and the maximum number of users supported provided. The wireless network names (SSID), network mode, are configured; Wi-Fi Protected Access (WPA) 2 Personal enabled as the security mode and Media Access Control (MAC) address filtered for specific users. This makes the wireless subnetworks secure, available, and reliable to specific users only.

The secure router is statically configured with an IP address to the HNG, and it aids in remote connectivity either via Internet Service Provider (ISP) or Digital Subscriber Line (DSL). The VLAN database is reconfigured with the assigned VLAN names and numbers at the secure router to aid in identification and prioritization of the incoming remote signals. The single gateway at the secure router helps in traffic management from and or to the VLANs.

The SNGs of the ZigBee, smart grid, and body area networks have been prioritized by assigning each port a VLAN number. This aids in device classification and prioritization.

The secure access router is in the core layer of the network design and allows for QoS implementation. The Multi-Layer 3 switch works at the distribution layer of the network design and allows for QoS implementation. The access switches work at the access layer, with the end devices representing the endpoint layer of the network design. The developed OIHN model has been implemented at the distribution layer, HNG.

### 9.5.1 System Flowchart

Any signal arriving at the HNG from the remote location has its contents validated with the device's database information. However, all locally originating signals have to first pass via HNG before being relayed to respective SNGs and to the intended devices as shown in Fig. 9.5b. Correct entry of the authorization credentials permits accessibility into the system, whereas false credentials terminate the authorization process instantly, thus ensuring maximum security.

Upon gaining access, either locally or remotely, various subnetworks, their corresponding devices, and the available bandwidths are displayed to the user. This information is relayed from the subnetworks' database. A user selects the particular subnetwork and the device to be accessed. The subnetworks and their devices have weighting factors to aid in classification and prioritization.

## 9.6 Modeling and Simulation

In this section, we present the proposed developed model and simulations. We also discuss, in depth, the development stages involved.

### 9.6.1 Model Implementation

Using Fig. 9.4, the subnetworks are first identified and prioritized using VLAN protocol. The subnetworks are represented by $i$:

$$\begin{aligned} &i_n \in i \ \text{ in which } i = 1, 2, 3, \ \ldots, 6 \\ &X_i^{(L)} < X_i < X_i^{(U)}. \end{aligned} \tag{9.1}$$

Both $L$ and $U$ represent the lower and upper limits of the subnetworks. The $\min_{i\in 6} i_n = 1$ represents the least prioritized subnetwork and $\max_{i\in 6} i_n = 6$ represents the highest prioritized subnetwork.

Based on Eq. (9.1), devices in each subnetwork are identified and prioritized using weighing factors. The devices are represented by $j$:

$$\begin{aligned} &j_n \in j \ \text{ in which } j = 1, 2, 3, \ \ldots, n \\ &X_j^{(L)} < X_j < X_j^{(U)} \end{aligned} \tag{9.2}$$

Both $L$ and $U$ represent the least and highest prioritized devices in each subnetwork. The $\min_{j\in\infty} j_n = 1$ shows the least prioritized device and $\max_{j\in\infty} j_n = n$ shows the highest prioritized device within the network.

Using Eqs. 9.1 and 9.2, total network bandwidth is arrived at by using Eq. (9.3):

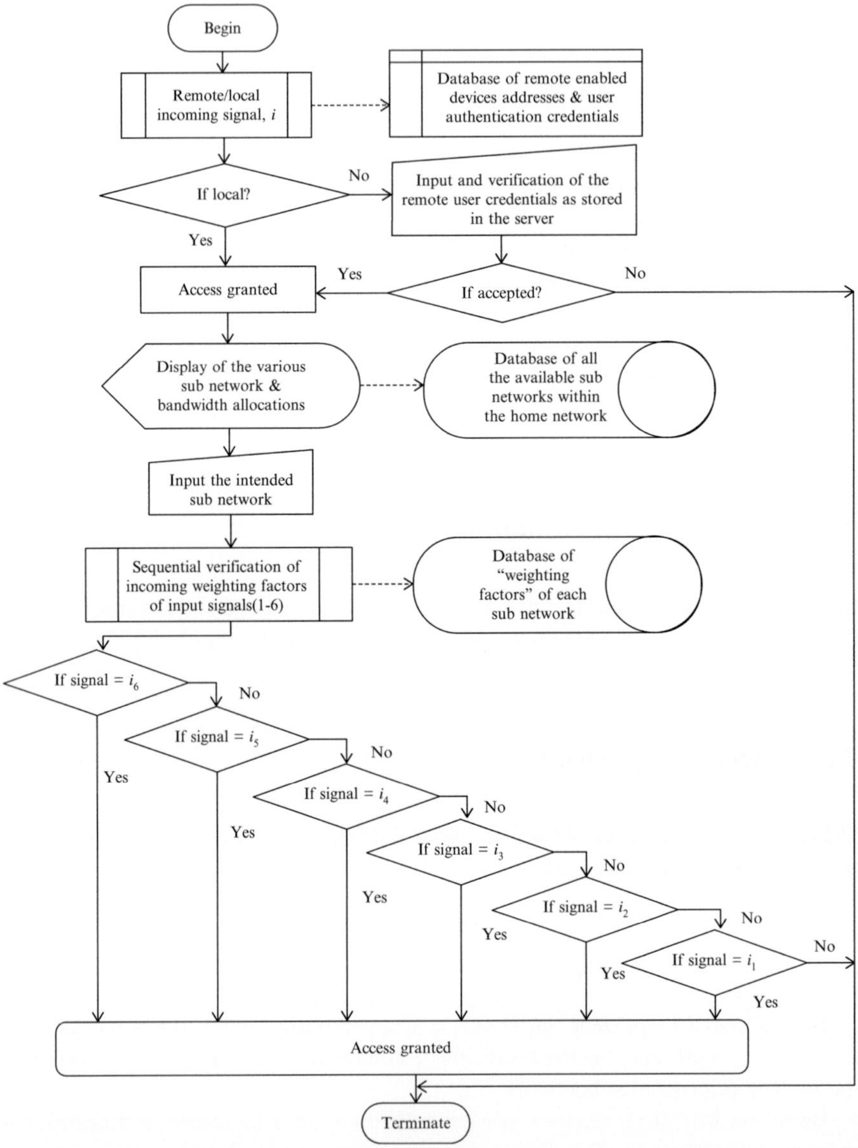


**Fig. 9.5b** Home network gateway system flowchart

$$\begin{aligned} i_6b_6 + i_5b_5 + i_4b_4 + i_3b_3 + i_2b_2 + i_1b_1 &= \sum_{i=1}^{n} b_n \\ i_6j_nl_n + i_5j_nl_n + i_4j_nl_n + \cdots + i_1j_nl_n &= \sum_{i=1}^{n}\sum_{j=1}^{n} l_n \end{aligned} \tag{9.3}$$

The value $b_n$ represents the total bandwidth assigned to each subnetwork, whereas $l_n$ represents the bandwidth assigned to each device within each subnetwork. The total subnetwork bandwidth is computed as $\sum_{j=1}^{n} l_n$

Using Eq. (9.2), different and maximum CoS supported by each device and the entire network is identified, classified, and prioritized using weighing factor:

$$\begin{aligned} &k_n \in k \text{ in which } k = 1, 2, 3, \ldots, 6 \\ &X_j^{(L)} < X_j < X_j^{(U)} \end{aligned} \tag{9.4}$$

The $L$ and $U$ show the least and upper prioritized CoS within the network, with $\min_{k \in 6} k_n = 1$ representing the least prioritized CoS and $\max_{k \in 6} k_n = 6$ representing the highest prioritized CoS.

Based on Eq. (9.4), different numbers of packets are scheduled for each CoS in the network. The packets are placed on a linked list for transmission. The packets $p$ are iteratively transmitted within the media:

$$\begin{aligned} &k_6 \text{transmits } \max_{p=\infty} P = 7 \text{ per iteration.} \\ &k_5 \text{transmits } \max_{p=\infty} P = 6 \text{ per iteration.} \\ &k_4 \text{transmits } \max_{p=\infty} P = 5 \text{ per iteration.} \\ &k_3 \text{transmits } \max_{p=\infty} P = 4 \text{ per iteration.} \\ &k_2 \text{transmits } \max_{p=\infty} P = 3 \text{ per iteration.} \\ &k_1 \text{transmits } \max_{p=\infty} P = 2 \text{ per iteration} \\ &\text{then leaves the media for the first and highest prioritized CoS, } k_6. \end{aligned} \tag{9.5}$$

Based on Eq. (9.5), the total throughput in each CoS is arrived at by

$$\text{throughput} = \sum_{t_1}^{t_n} \text{packetsize} \tag{9.6}$$

where $t_1$ is the start time of the first packet $p_1$ and $t_n$ is the end time of the last packet $p_n$ to be dispatched by each CoS.

Based on Eq. (9.5), arrival/departure time for each CoS is represented by

$$a_i^k \text{ and } d_i^k, \text{ respectively} \tag{9.7}$$

The $i$ shows the route followed by each CoS from source to destination.

Using Eq. (9.7), the waiting duration for each CoS in the medium is arrived at by

$$\{d_i^k - a_i^k\} \geq S_{\min} \text{ for minimum waiting duration and } \{d_i^k - a_i^k\} \leq S_{\max} \text{ for maximum duration.} \quad (9.8)$$

where $S$ represents waiting duration.

Using Eq. (9.8), no single CoS on the network should wait for more than a certain period of time, T, before transmitting its packets. This is enforced by checking all possible differences between departure and arrival times by limiting those values to T. The constraints that may cause these delays can be formulated by introducing a new set of variables:

$$\delta_i^{k,\ k+1} \quad (9.9)$$

between $k - th$ and the next $k + 1 - th$ CoS within the same route, $i$, and take a value of 1, showing that the conditions and transfer are feasible.

Between any two CoS, the following condition must be satisfied for all $i$ and $k$ basing on Eq. (9.9):

$$\{d_i^{k+1} - a_i^k\}\delta_i^{k,\ k+1} \leq T \quad (9.10)$$

But the left side function of Eq. (9.10) is zero for those transfers that are not feasible. Transfers to the next available CoS are assumed; therefore, mathematically we have the total time duration computed by

$$\sum_{k+1} \delta_i^{k,\ k+1} = 1 \quad (9.11)$$

for all $i$, $k$, and $k$+1.

Using Eq. (9.11), the total transfer and the initial waiting times for the entire CoS are computed by the function in Eq. (9.12). The function too represents the complete problem solution:

$$\sum_i \sum_k \sum_{k+1} \delta_i^{k,k+1} \{d_i^{k+1} - a_i^k\} w_i^k + \sum_i \sum_{k+1} \int_0^{a_i^k - a_i^{k-1}} v_{i,k}(t)\left[\left(a_i^k - a_i^{k-1}\right) - t\right] dt \quad (9.12)$$

The parameter $w_i^k$ represents the number of packets being transferred in the kth CoS. The parameter $v_{i,k}$ is the number of packets arriving at the end of the kth CoS at a given time.

Using Eq. (9.12), the following function represents the sum of the initial waiting times for all the packets in each CoS:

$$\int_0^{a_i^k - a_i^{k-1}} v_{i,k}(t)\left[\left(a_i^k - a_i^{k-1}\right) - t\right]dt \tag{9.13}$$

Using Eq. (9.8), the total network delay is arrived at by

$$\text{Delay} = \left\{ \frac{\sum_{t_1}^{t_n} \text{Delivery time} - \sum_{t_1}^{t_n} \text{Arrival time}}{\sum_{t_1}^{t_n} \text{Received packets}} \right\} \tag{9.14}$$

Here, arrival time represents packet arrival at the MAC layer of the source node. Delivery time represents packet delivery to the MAC layer of the destination node. Received packets are total number of packets received between start time $t_1$ of CoS kth and the start time $t_n$ of the next CoS $k{+}1{-}th$.

$$i_6 d_6 + i_5 d_5 + i_4 d_4 + i_3 d_3 + i_2 d_2 + i_1 d_1 = \sum_{i=1}^{n} d_n$$

$$i_1 j_n y_n + i_2 j_n y_n + i_3 j_n y_n + i_4 j_n y_n + i_5 j_n y_n + i_6 j_n y_n = \sum_{i=1}^{n}\sum_{j=1}^{n} y_n$$

The $d_n$ represents the total delay in each subnetwork and $y_n$ represents the delay experienced in each network device.

Network jitter is arrived at by

$$j = \sqrt{\frac{1}{n-1}\sum_{n=1}^{n}(di - D)^2} \tag{9.15}$$

Here $j$ represents jitter, $di$ represents the delay per each flow, and $D$ represents the average delay for all the flows; $n$ represents the total number of flows/measurements.

Based on Eq. (9.5), network packet loss is computed by

$$\text{packet loss} = \left\{ \frac{\sum_{t_1}^{t_n} \text{dropPacket}}{\sum_{t_1}^{t_n} \text{sendPacket}} \right\} * 100 \tag{9.16}$$

### 9.6.2 *Simulation Setup*

The setup consists of seven nodes as shown in Fig. 9.6. The model involves configuration of simple modules, which represents both the sinks and source nodes as shown and network module which groups together both the nodes using

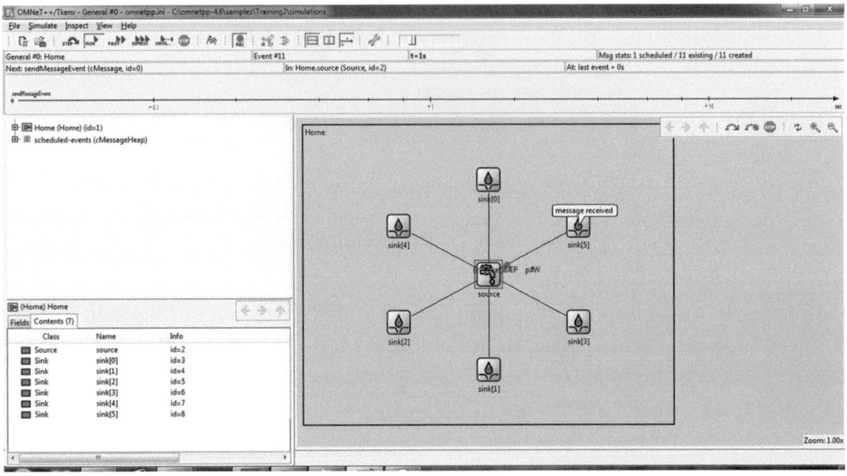


**Fig. 9.6** Classes of Services

the connections. The connections are configured to enable duplex communications between the source and the sink nodes. Delay in the entire network configuration setup is uniform, at 100 ms.

The source node represents a particular device in any of the subnetworks with the capability of supporting all the Classes of Services (CoS); the sink nodes represent the respective CoS, in which Sink [5], Sink [4], Sink [3], Sink [2], Sink [1], and Sink [0] represent CoS 6, CoS 5, CoS 4, CoS 3, CoS 2, and CoS 1, respectively, as discussed in the algorithm implementation.

The source, subnetwork's device, holds the packets for transmissions to respective sinks, CoS. A total of twenty-seven (27) packets, representing the maximum number of packets that can be successfully transmitted from the source and received at the sinks per iteration in every device within the network, were scheduled during the simulation. All the incoming packets either from the remote locations or within the locality first reach the source before being distributed to respective sinks as per the algorithm queuing order.

OMNET++, which is an extensible, modular component-based C++ simulation library and framework for implementing network simulators, has the capability of producing both scalar (bar graph) and vector (line graph) analysis results which complements each other. The algorithm above has generated throughput, packet loss, and delay vector results as shown and discussed in Sect. 9.7.

## 9.7 Results and Discussions

In order to test and evaluate the performance of the above algorithm, we set up the framework that evaluates the factors of QoS in OMNET++. Simulations have been conducted for OIHN, Priority Queuing (PQ), and Class-Based Weighted Fair

Queuing (CBWFQ) models and results recorded to ascertain the objectives of the study.

### *9.7.1 Network Throughput*

An incline in the packet throughput is observed from CoS 1 through to CoS 6 for the OIHN model as shown in Fig. 9.7a. More and steady throughput is observed between CoS 3 and CoS 6 than between CoS 1 and CoS 2. The model has achieved an average network throughput of 99.74 %, thereby representing an available, efficient, and reliable network irrespective of increases in devices, services, and technological evolutions.

The average network packet throughput of our model in comparison to PQ and CBWFQ are shown in Fig. 9.7b. The three models have shown an increase in packet throughput from CoS 1 to CoS 6 from the observations. Both OIHN and CBWFQ models have minimal differences in packet throughput in each CoS from the observations; however, PQ has the least packet throughput in all its CoSs. OIHN, CBWFQ, and PQ have average packet throughputs of 99.74 %, 99.75 %, and 99.47 %, respectively, representing maximum throughput in CBWFQ model than OIHN and PQ models. However, OIHN model has shown an optimal performance than the two despite having higher increases in number of packets being transmitted in each CoS. In resultant, this has yielded an adaptable and scalable model to the various technological changes.

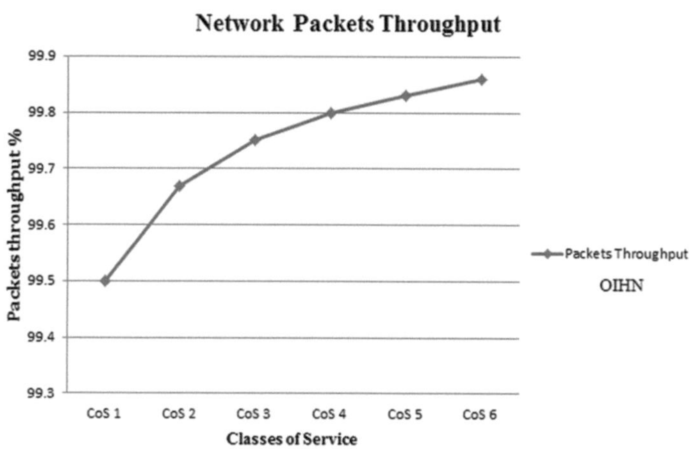


**Fig. 9.7a** Network throughput

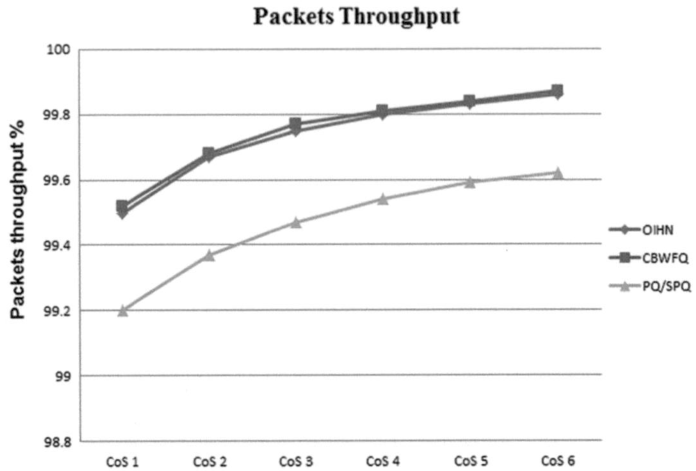


**Fig. 9.7b** Evaluated network throughput

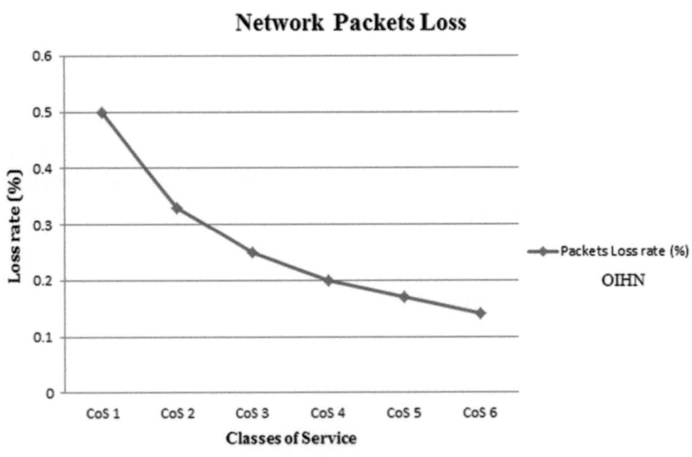


**Fig. 9.7c** Network packet loss

### *9.7.2 Network Packet Loss Rate*

More packets are lost at CoS 1 at 0.50 % which is also the least prioritized CoS; however, at CoS 6, which is the highest prioritized CoS, a loss of 0.14 % is experienced as shown in Fig. 9.7c in the OIHN model. CoSs 2, 3, 4, and 5 have packet losses of 0.33 %, 0.25 %, 0.20 %, and 0.17 %, respectively, realizing a total packet loss of 1.59 %. This shows the difference in need and importance given to each CoS within the network. The packet losses are further attributed to queuing, congestion, bit errors, different hardware platforms of the source and the sinks,

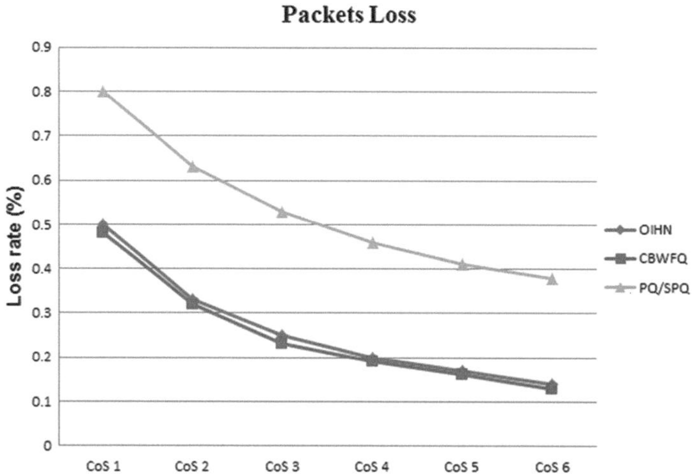


**Fig. 9.7d** Evaluated network packet loss

various configuration and technological standards of the network, and the duration of usage.

The packet losses for the three models, OIHN, CBWFQ, and PQ, are shown in Fig. 9.7d. OIHN and CBWFQ models have almost similar losses among the CoSs, with greater loss being observed at CoS 1 than at CoS 6 of both models. However, higher losses, which sequentially decline from CoS 1 to CoS 6, are observed in the OIHN model as compared to those with the CBWFQ model. PQ has shown higher losses in all the respective CoSs as compared to OIHN and CBWFQ models. The losses are attributed to queuing, serialization, and transmission delays in which PQ has higher value of the attributes than the remaining two, OIHN and CBWFQ. Total packet losses of 1.59 %, 1.51 %, and 3.21 % have been realized for OIHN, CBWFQ, and PQ, respectively. The above results have presented OIHN as a better model since it operates optimally than the two despite having additional number of packets being transmitted in each CoS than the rest.

### *9.7.3 Network Packet Delay*

OIHN model has more delay of 0.71 s being witnessed at CoS 1, which is the least prioritized CoS, as compared to CoS 6, which is the highest prioritized CoS that witnesses low delay of 0.37 s as shown in Fig. 9.7e. CoS 2 has delay of 0.58 s, CoS 3 has delay of 0.50 s, CoS 4 has delay of 0.45 s, and CoS 5 has delay of 0.41 s. The minimum delay in CoS 6 is due to its provision to schedule and transmit its packets first in every successive iteration. A total network delay of 3.02 s is witnessed in the model. The observation is attributed to queuing, propagation, and transmission delays.

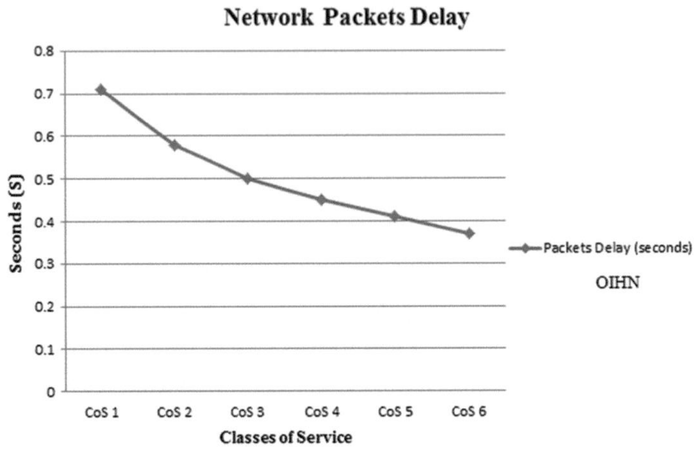


**Fig. 9.7e** Network packet delay

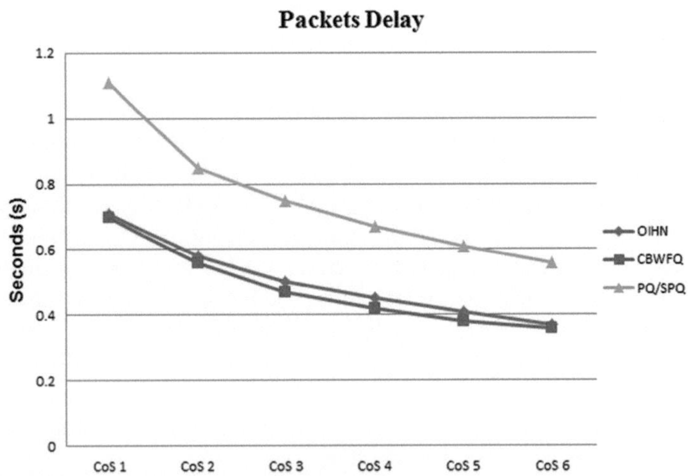


**Fig. 9.7f** Evaluated network packet delay

Total network delays of 3.02 s, 2.89 s, and 4.55 s are observed in the OIHN, CBWFQ, and PQ models, respectively, as shown in Fig. 9.7f. CBWFQ experiences least delay than the rest of the models since it schedules a single packet per transmission in each CoS. PQ has shown maximum delay since it transmits all its packets in a single transmission for successive CoS. However, all the three models have shown more delay at CoS 1 and dynamically reduces as we edge to CoS 6. Consequently, OIHN model has shown tremendous optimization in delay reduction and almost became at par with CBWFQ model despite having an increase in the number of packets being transmitted iteratively per CoS. The total delays for all the models are associated to queuing, processing, propagation, and transmission delays of the packets in respective CoS.

## 9.8 Conclusion and Future Work

Minimum network throughput, high packet error rates and losses, network delays and jitter, and other factors of QoS affect the availability, reliability, efficiency, and performance of the intelligent home networks. The reduction in QoS and performance of intelligent home network are majorly associated with the increasing number of home devices and services from the engineering and telecommunication industries. Moreover, the networking technological standard shifts from Internet Protocol (IPv4) to IPv6 also form a major contribution to the poor performance of these intelligent home networks. Consequently, poor performing intelligent home network hinders comfort, security, health provision, monitoring, scheduling, remote connectivity, etc. of the users, animals, and devices within homes.

In this chapter, we introduced and presented the various factors affecting the performance of intelligent home networks. An overview of intelligent home networks, merits, demerits, and existing models was presented. We implemented model, simulated, tested, evaluated, and discussed the results. Lastly, we presented the challenges and proposed future work.

The implemented model has segmented, classified, and prioritized the various subnetworks using VLAN protocol and classified and prioritized subnetwork devices using weighing factors. Further, the implemented model has identified six Classes of Services based on DSCP maximum usable bits and prioritized different services to respective subnetworks and devices within the network. Each subnetwork and device has the capability to accommodate a maximum of six CoS and a minimum of one CoS. Consequently, the CoS have been classified and prioritized throughout the home network using weighing factors, in which CoS 6 has the first priority within the media, followed by CoS 5, and then CoS 4, CoS 3, CoS 2, and CoS 1 have the least priority. Moreover, an increase in the number of transmitted packets in each CoS per iteration has been implemented; CoS 6 transmits seven packets, CoS 5 six packets, CoS 4 five packets, CoS 3 four packets, CoS 2 three packets, and CoS 1 two packets iteratively.

The model yielded an average network packet throughput of 99.74 %, total packet loss of 1.59 %, and total network delay of 3.02 s from the simulation and testing results in OMNET++. This realized an available, reliable, efficient, and optimized performing intelligent home network both locally and remotely irrespective of increases in the numbers of home devices, services, and technological network standard evolutions.

Further work could be done on bandwidth allocation and management in intelligent home networks. The technological changes may require reprioritization and addition of more Classes of Services to meet the incoming demands. This aspect may also require further work.

## References


1. Zhang Y, Yu R, Xie S, Yao W, Xiao Y, Guizani M (2011) Home M2M networks: architectures, standards, and QoS improvement. IEEE Commun Mag 49(4):44–52, April 2011
2. Nemeth G (2004) Knowledge-based generic intelligent network model. In: Proceedings of the 1st conference on computing frontiers schia, Italy, pp 263–267, Hungary, 2004
3. Raisul M, Reaz M, Ali M (2012) A review of smart homes – past, present and future, IEEE transactions on systems, man and cybernetics – part C: applications and reviews, vol 42, no. 6, November 2012
4. Berbec M (2009) Intelligence networks-the model based methodologies problem, CALITATEA VIETII, XX, nr. 1–2, pp 203–214, 2009
5. Martikainen O, Lipoainen J, Molin K (1995) Tutorial on intelligent networks, Helsinki, Copenhagen, 1995
6. Shunxing C (1999) Intelligent networks. http://www.tml.tkk.fi/studies/Tik-110.300/1998/Essays/in_2.html. Accessed 12 July 2015
7. Juniper Networks (2011) Benefits of intelligent oversubscription in Next-Generation Networks Higher Network Utilization with Careful Planning and Intelligent Network Design, Application note, 2011
8. Intelligent Networks (IN), the international engineering consortium, ftp://comptek.ru/pub/Dialogic/doc/tutorial/in.pdf. Accessed on 9 Feb 2016
9. What are intelligent networks, http://www.wifinotes.com/computer-networks/what-are-intelligent-networks.html. Accessed 12 July 2015
10. (2014) Innovations, The smart home/intelligent home automation. http://www.entrepreneural-insights.com/smart-home-intelligent-home-automation/. Accessed 12 July 2015
11. Bhatti G et al (2010) QoS harmonization for home networks. In: Proceedings of IEEE Broadband and Multimedia Symposium, pp 1–5, March 2010
12. Takabatake T (2007) A simple packet–classifier algorithm for QoS control in home networks. In: Access networks & workshops, 2007. AccessNets'07. Second International Conference on IEEE, pp 1–5, 2007
13. Chen D, Gu, Zhang J (2004) Supporting real – time traffic with QoS in IEEE 802.11e based home networks. In: Consumer Communications and Networking Conference, 2004. CCNC 2004. First IEEE Conference, pp 205–209, 2004
14. Wang Z, Xu X (2013) Smart home M2M networks architecture, 2013 I.E. Ninth International Conference on Mobile Ad-hoc and Sensor Networks (MSN), pp 294–299, 2013
15. Fischer MJ, Masi DMB, Shortle JF (2008) Simulating the performance of a class-based weighted fair queueing system. In Proceedings of the 40th Conference on Winter Simulation, pp 2901–2908
16. Rajput IS, Gupta D (2012) A priority based round robin CPU scheduling algorithm for real time systems. Int J Innov Eng Technol 1:1–11

# Chapter 10
# Network Neutrality in the IoT: A Fuzzy Cognitive Map Extend Technology Roadmap Perspective

**Bo Xing**

## 10.1 Introduction

The Internet of Things (IoT) is fast becoming the essential building block to citizens, consumers, and public services. Currently, there is much interest in the IoT vision and many related topics (e.g., cloud computing, data security, machine-to-machine (M2M) interaction, and communication protocols) and projects, especially in smart home care, access control, logistics, as well as entertainment, are being researched and undertaken. Yet, one worry is real in that the volume of digital traffic will continue to grow exponentially, and the increasing levels of expected traffic will generate significant pressure on the capacity of current networks. In other words, even though there are technology-oriented research studies dealing with Web bandwidth and data analytics, few of them concerned IoT from a comprehensive perspective of the access to the Internet broadband services. As a result, the capacity to develop new services, new solutions, new applications, and new technology of IoT will be limited. Therefore, a question is immediately emerging: what if this infrastructure (i.e., Internet) fails?

The researchers have good reasons to wonder who is responsible for making sure that infrastructure, which society now counts on to carry all this traffic, keeps up. According to the World Economic Forum, an international institution, the digital infrastructure has invested by multiple parties that include Internet service providers (ISPs), content providers (CPs), and hardware and software manufacturers [45]. Because of such a diversity of stakeholders that are in charge, even what one might assume to be a straightforward initiative, such as entrance of new IoT

B. Xing (✉)
Computational Intelligence, Robotics, and Cybernetics for Leveraging E-future (CIRCLE), School of Mathematical and Computer Sciences, Faculty of Science and Agriculture, University of Limpopo, Limpopo, South Africa
e-mail: bxing2009@gmail.com



Z. Mahmood (ed.), *Connectivity Frameworks for Smart Devices*,
Computer Communications and Networks, DOI 10.1007/978-3-319-33124-9_10

application services, serious impediments exist since there is large pressure on the capacity of current networks, and thus it will inevitably undermine the continued rapid growth of the IoT economy.

As a result, network neutrality (NN), which dictates *neither a ISP nor a government nor anyone else should be able to block or discriminate unreasonably* (e.g., *by price, availability, or otherwise*) *against any content carried over the Internet* [45], has direct impact on the IoT due to direct linkages to such issues as anticompetitive behavior, innovation and investment, privacy and data protection, consumer awareness, empowerment and protection, and freedom of expression.

As we know, the central reason for the success of the Internet is that every point on the network can connect to any other point on the network without discrimination. Indeed, in the IoT environment, with much more expanding into M2M communication and applications such as power utilities, it is hard to avoid. But without NN, the freedom of expression and the right to receive and impart information will be destroyed.

The NN debate started in 2002, when evidence of a discrimination problem was clear from several sources, such as end-user complaint about operators who block their voice over Internet Protocol (VoIP) service. To deal with this issue, regulators adopted a set of rules to prevent future extortions of rent from customers or CPs. For example, the US Federal Communications Commission (FCC) proposed several "principles" to govern relations among consumers, ISPs, and CPs [17]. In addition, scholars from diverse range of backgrounds haven't paid attention to this issue. According to [28], NN debates can be categorized into five main topics, i.e., discrimination, vertical integration, reinvestment, innovation, and social welfare. Proponents argued that all types of content (e.g., video, e-mail, messaging, etc.) should be transmitted via communication networks according to the best effort principle. For example, Viviane Reding, the European Commission vice president, once pointed out: "I don't believe that restricting consumers' choice can ever be an appealing driver of more growth. I certainly don't believe that restricting access to the Internet will attract many more innovative European Internet companies. And I don't believe that restricted access to the Internet is the right answer to a faster deployment of next generation access networks." However, a variety of individuals and organizations support non-NN (NNN). They viewed regulation as a hindrance to competition and innovation. For example, the authors of [19] claimed "mandating NN would be inconsistent with sound economic management of the Internet." Inevitably, this is often reflected in arguments made by ISPs. Take, for instance, the CEO of AT&T at the time, Ed Whitacre, who stated: "Now what CPs would like to do is use my pipes free, but I ain't going to let them do that because we have spent this capital and we have to have a return on it."

Nevertheless, some scholars (e.g., [9, 18, 29]), particularly in America, take a different view that the best way for the NN to be beneficial to society is to find the key requirements of a sustainable compromise between investment protection, quality of service (QoS), and the promotion of competition and innovation. To get more insight into the present situation, several authors (e.g., [31, 32, 38]) modeled the Internet as a two-sided market, in which ISPs act as "middle men" between CPs and consumers. Such studies will help governments design more effective regulations on the Internet. But the regulators should recognize that there is a big difference between deregulation on broadband providers in order to improve consumer welfare and indulging in contortion whose only aim is to become monopoly. In this chapter, we will provide a systematic approach for addressing this debate.

With this in mind, the remainder of this chapter is organized as follows: first, the relevant background and literature review on the NN debate are detailed in Sect. 10.2 which is followed by a presentation of the main problem statement in Sect. 10.3; second, Sect. 10.4 elaborates the strong arguments for addressing the NN debate issue via employing the methodology of an extended technology roadmap (eTRM) through fuzzy cognitive map (FCM)-based scenario planning (SP); then, the draft progress of applying the proposed method to NN debate is summarized in Sect. 10.5; then the future works are discussed in Sect. 10.6; and finally, Sect. 10.7 draws the conclusion of this chapter.

## 10.2 Background and Literature Review of Network Neutrality Debate

Nowadays, NN regulations have become a hotly debated topic. However, the discussion has been mainly focused on rhetoric rather than on economic perspective. In this section, we provide some empirical evidence of NN debate that is based on economic theory. In addition, as some researchers have used the idea of two-sided markets to study NN, some related information of two-sided pricing on the Internet will be introduced in this section as well.

### *10.2.1 Network Neutrality (NN)*

Network neutrality (NN) has become the focus of attention in the regulatory debate on the Internet. Scholars from a diverse range of backgrounds offered different ways to understand this issue, ranging from absolute nondiscrimination [49] to limited discrimination without QoS tiering [12] to limited discrimination and with QoS tiering [18]. In addition, stakeholders (such as ISPs and CPs) also hold fundamentally different perspectives and suggestions for remedial action. To clarify how NN is addressed and to whom, this section provides short summaries of the articles covering this issue and their most important findings and suggestions for future research.

#### 10.2.1.1 Network Neutrality on the Internet: A Two-Sided Market Analysis

This paper [12] analyzed a theoretical model designed to assess the welfare effects of NN; particularly, the authors considered two-sided pricing in monopoly and duopoly scenarios (ISPs) with several CPs and customers. Through the examples, the authors observed, under the monopolistic model, consumers and platform operators lose under NN, while content providers gain. Under the duopolistic model, both content providers and platform operators may gain under NN, while consumers are still unambiguously worse off. Finally, the authors concluded that the total welfare may be enhancing or reducing depending on whether certain parameter restrictions are satisfied.

#### 10.2.1.2 Network Neutrality and Congestion Sensitive Content Providers: Implication for Content Variety, Broadband Investment, and Regulations

This article [27] answered and analyzed many of the arguments in the NN debate, such as welfare enhancement, capacity expansion, and best effort. Several conclusions have been reported. First, after considering the effect of new CP entrants and competition between ISPs, the authors did not agree with previous research on capacity expansion, since it may force them (ISPs) to invest in higher capacities. Second, the analysis considered the effect of bad QoS and thus captured the disutility that might be the effect from congestion with traditional BE networks. Third, the article also analyzed different strategic options for policy makers, like minimum quality standards or strategic degradation. The former may be effective but inefficient concerning investments, while the latter may decrease the overall welfare as fewer CPs enter the network. All in all, except for the capacity expansion, the article agreed with much earlier research in that in general the CPs are worse off while the overall welfare in general is higher. However for very congestion sensitive CPs, QoS tiering might put them better off because QoS tiering can allocate congestion-to-congestion insensitive CPs. The article concluded that QoS tiering is the preferred regime for ISPs and that prohibiting this can eventually be harmful to content variety, broadband investment, and welfare.

#### 10.2.1.3 Net Neutrality, Foreclosure, and the Fast Lane: An Empirical Study of the UK

This article [33] analyzed the NN debate using empirical data in which the inceptives for an ISP to break NN empirically are investigated. The data is used in a two-stage consumer demand model of differentiated online content providers and downstream ISPs. The demand estimates were then used to explore two counterfactual simulations of breaking NN, with focus on YouTube in particular. There was one analysis where a fast lane was offered and another where the ISP can foreclose through quality degradation. The results in the article are preliminary. They revealed that a fast lane increases consumers' surplus, industry revenues, and advertising revenues. However, foreclosure reduced the foreclosing ISP's revenues from selling broadband more than it can recuperate through advertising on online content and was therefore an unlikely scenario. The article also showed a summary empirical data: market share among the players, competition in the local exchanges, statistics on households, share of households that consumed different type of only content by speed, and product characteristics. The author was going to expand the preliminary model to allow for more realistic substitution patterns as well as estimate complementary or substitutability between content providers. Future empirical research should look at the long-run effects of net neutrality regulation on investment in the broadband network as well as on innovation among content providers.

#### 10.2.1.4 Empirical Evidence of Network Neutrality: The Incentives for Discrimination

Based on the survey data, this article [29] studied two major issues, i.e., whether ISPs have the incentives to discriminate against CPs and whether those incentives changed according to various conditions. Concerning the first issue, the ISPs have the incentive to provide a low QoS level for costly CPs. Regarding the conditions, it is showed that such conditions are as per the regulatory regimes, the cost of the CPs, the willingness to pay of the end users, and the degree of competition among the ISPs.

#### 10.2.1.5 Net Neutrality and Internet Fragmentation: The Role of Online Advertising

The article in [10] investigated the relation between NN regulation and Internet fragmentation. A simple two-sided market model is considered, in which CPs and consumers interact through ISPs, and CPs sell consumers' attention to advertisers. However, unlike other literature on NN, the authors particularly focused on the advertising side. In the neutral regime, a zero-price rule is enforced (i.e., ISPs have to terminate all traffic free of charge), and under the non-neutrality regime, ISPs are allowed to make access to their subscribers for CPs conditional on payment of a termination fee. Finally, the article showed that, on the one hand, when competition among CPs has a relevant impact on advertising rates, letting ISPs charge termination fees may induce fragmentation of the Internet. On the other hand, when competition among CPs has little impact on advertising rates, Universal Connection emerges in equilibrium regardless of the regulatory regime.

### 10.2.2 Two-Sided Markets

In general, the two-sided markets are characterized by two sets of agents who interact through an intermediary of platform and try to get the two sides "on board" by appropriately charging each side, in order to guarantee each side at least not lose [39]. According to [15], to establish a two-sided market, three necessary conditions must be met: viz, (1) there are two or more distinct groups of consumers; (2) there are externalities associated with customers A and B becoming connected or coordinated in some fashion; and (3) an intermediary is necessary to internalize the externalities created by one group for the other group. An obvious example is the credit cardholders. A credit card benefits both shoppers and merchants, if it can be accepted by many stores. The interactions of distinct groups of entities (men and women, shoppers and retailers, etc.) explain the potential indirect network effects in two-sided markers, such as the value obtained by one kind of customer increases with measures of the other kind of customer. As a consequence, the two-sided platforms emerged. Other examples include newspaper and media industry [13], dating services [16], operating systems industry [40], mobile telecommunication industry [25], and Bitcoin start-ups [3].

Based on these descriptions, inevitably, the NN debate is comprised in essence two-sided platforms, since the network character of the Internet implies a strong tendency that different economic relationships among multiple industry participants can derive different economic results concerning the precise nature of demand, cost, and indirect network effects [20, 50]. In particular, the debate around NN is focused on whether an ISP should operate as a platform in a two-sided market or not, i.e., ISPs can sell broadband Internet access services to consumers and may set fees to CPs on the Internet. Still, the previous research provided important insights on this topic. In this section, a short summary of the current state of the art is presented:

- *Competition in two-sided markets* [4]. This article has discussed two-sided pricing with three different models, a monopoly platform, a model of competing platforms where agents joined a single platform, and a model of competitive bottlenecks where one group joined all platforms. The article provided necessary and sufficient condition for a market-sharing equilibrium to exist and postulated formulas to calculate welfare maximizing and profit maximizing. Small wonder that this model has been considered as standard two-sided market model by several searches, such as [12]. In addition, the article also discussed different pricing schemes, e.g., two-part tariffs or uniform prices. By the way, in the setting, the models were put up with examples from real life, e.g., supermarkets where the customers entered for free and the shops paid a sum to the supermarket (this is a competitive bottleneck).
- *Two-sided markets: a progress report* [39]. Like the article in [4], the authors focused on the definition of two-sided markets and provided sufficient conditions for a market to be two sided. However, these two papers differed from each other in the fact that [4] modeled users' participation on the platform, whereas the authors of [39] analyzed platform usage. For example, in the model by [39],

the product of the number of users on the two-sided represented the potential number of interaction of the platform. For each single interaction, the total price is split between the two members who actually interact. In the model by [4], consumers on the two sides paid for the right to interact on the platform.

- *Strategies for two-sided markets* [14]. Here, the authors analyzed potential business strategies for platform operators to win the battle in a two-sided market. According to them, three challenges are identified: (1) pricing the platform; (2) winner-take-all dynamics, which described the fact that due to the intergroup network effects, two-sided markets often exhibited a tendency that the whole market was served by a single platform; and (3) threat of envelopment, i.e., the danger that other platforms may start to offer the service as part of a bundled product, thereby attracting users of one's own platform.

## 10.3 Presentation of the Key Problem Statements

In this IoT era, NN is a key element required for sustainable development, since new IoT applications (e.g., M2M communication) are placing increasing pressure on the Internet. The key point of NN debate is the treatment of the data by Internet providers, i.e., all Internet traffic should be treated equally. However, from the standard economic point of view, there is nothing nefarious about attempting to introduce NNN, where a specialized service lane can be offered to the CPs that are willing to pay for it. So, it is raising some key questions for main actors within the Internet ecosystem and the policy makers, such as:

- By leaving the NN regime and in favor of the NNN regime, what effects do we have?
- If there is one or more scenarios that exist, which can lead to a beneficial outcome for the key actors and overall social welfare?
- By regulating the QoS in the NNN regime, what effects can be anticipated from the Internet key actors and social welfare point of view?

To summarize, the abovementioned problem statements aim to provide, in this chapter, some deeper insights and possible answers to a general concern involved in the NN debate: how to design different scenarios in both NN and NNN settings; furthermore, how to use a quantitative method to analyze the economic effects that is beneficial to IoT society; and finally, how to analyze the economic impact and recommend policy implications for key network ecosystem participants?

## 10.4 Justification of the Employed Methodology

The objective of this chapter is to argue that a recently proposed eTRM via FCM-based SP (or eTRM-FCM-SP) [1] can be used for dealing with the proposed problem statements arisen from NN debate. The role of this section (as illustrated in

**Fig. 10.1** Network regime roadmap—Stage I: methodology justification

Fig. 10.1) is to justify the suitability of the employed methodology by screening several key building blocks of eTRM-FCM-SP.

In the following, we will introduce SP, FCM, and TRM, respectively. In the literature, SP is a well-known method for coping with future changes in the organization [46]. However, while this approach has yielded some insight about how organizations can deal with uncertainty, it has not proven its ability to inform organization leaders a holistic overview of the pertinent issues surrounding the subject area. Therefore, another key factor has emerged (i.e., FCM-based SP) that indicates a variety of plausible future occurrences. In addition, most FCM-based SP approaches are complicated to apply in practice because it is critical to ensure selection of different aspects both internal and external in regard to the company. As a result, we need one managerial tool (i.e., TRM) to provide a view from different layers (e.g., organization, product, technology, and national levels), in order to help make the business strategy happen.

### *10.4.1 Building Block 1: Scenario Planning (SP)*

Today's successful businesses code is all about successfully coping with uncertainty and ambiguity. However, traditional strategic management frameworks (e.g., Porter's five forces or the market share-growth matrix) fail to provide adequate answers in this context. To help leaders of organizations and governments address this central problem, the use of scenarios as part of strategic planning has taken off. The first case study of using SP can be founded in the 1970s at the oil company Shell [48]. As several authors pointed out, the most advantage of SP is that it integrates uncertainty into the strategy process, taking into consideration volatility and complexity. Since then, based on the Brain & Company annual survey of the most-used management tools [37], SP has risen considerably from 40 % in 1999 to 70 % in 2006.

According to [23], the word "scenario" refers to "a set of hypothetical events set in the future constructed to clarity a possible chain of causal events as well as their decision points." In other words, SP can stimulate strategic thinking and helps us think through options (i.e., multiple scenarios), create insights, and spark innovative ideas. However, beneath those valuable advantages, the hardest part of SP is recognizing our desperate clinging to a single answer and consciously shifting towards an open future of vast potential – both positive and negative. This can best be managed by encouraging the participants to consider options beyond the traditional operational and conceptual comfort zone of the organization [7], i.e., shifting the thinking inside the organization. In addition, SP also certainly involves learning and imagination.

## *10.4.2 Building Block 2: Fuzzy Cognitive Map-Based Scenario Planning (FCM-SP)*

Fuzzy cognitive map (FCM) can be used to develop scenarios, and the strength of this approach lies in that it has the capability of overcoming the weaknesses that the traditional scenario building techniques (i.e., quantitative methods) have suffered. For example, since FCM employs fuzzy logic, both qualitative knowledge and quantitative analysis have an opportunity to be integrated together. In addition, FCM, as a kind of graph model, can directly show the multi-relationships between different concepts and the inference and thus result in robust scenario development.

### 10.4.2.1 Theoretical Background

Fuzzy cognitive map (FCM) refers to a graphical technique of modeling causal knowledge via fuzzy feedback dynamical system [34]. The "causal" component of these maps is defined as the cause-effect relationships, such as the relationships between the decision and the possible diagnosis. The FCM was first proposed by [26] in 1986 as a fuzzy extension of the original cognitive map which was introduced in the 1970s in [5] as a tool to represent social scientific knowledge via an interconnected and directed graph comprising nodes, edges, and arrows [24]. Remarkably, the FCM approach makes a powerful support for the indeterminacy problems of the original cognitive maps which occurs when one concept is influenced by an equal number of negative and positive ingoing arrows. In addition, as an extension and enhancement of a cognitive map, FCM has the additional capability to model the complex chains of the causal relationships through weighted causal links.

In general, each concept (node) in a FCM model may reflect varied system components, such as a state, event, mood, action, goal, trend, objective, and value. These concepts are nonlinear functions and a link between the concepts is assigned weights to quantify the strength of their causal relationships. One merit of FCM is that a finite number of FCMs can be combined together to produce a joint effect and capture opinion of multiple experts together in one collective map [24]. Therefore, the integrated FCM provides a more holistic overview of the pertinent issues surrounding the subject area [43]. In addition, these maps allow systematic integration of multiple perspectives when considering the long-term planning [43].

According to the available literature, the development of FCM involves the following three steps: (1) determination of the key domain issues or concepts, (2) identification of the causal relationships among these concepts, and

(3) estimation of the strength of the causal relationships. Nowadays, the FCM plays a vital role in decision-making process and has been used in a much wider range of applications, such as business, economics, engineering, project planning, robotics, and computer-assisted learning [24, 34].

#### 10.4.2.2 Fuzzy Cognitive Map (FCM)-Based Scenario Development Process

The FCM map building process facilitates and encourages debate and discussion among the key stakeholders regarding the scenario theme [43]. In general, the FCM-based SP process is conducted with the help of an expert panel. Identification of the experts is considered as the first step of the knowledge elicitation process. For example, experts are asked to provide possible scenarios to the concept preparation and formulation. Afterwards, individual causal maps are drawn to express experts' mental models and imagination. Subsequently, the integrated FCM is developed and, then, evaluates and classifies the scenario modeling (e.g., streamline the causal links and assign weights) and refines the scenario selection (e.g., calculate the FCM model for different input vectors). Finally, the integrated FCM will be tested to improve scenario quality and thus it's ideal for making long-term strategic decisions. Overall, the following steps have been proposed for the development of FCM-based scenarios by integrating the SP and FCM modeling processes [22], i.e., scenario preparation, knowledge capture, scenario modeling, scenario development, scenario selection and refinement, and strategic decisions.

Fuzzy cognitive map (FCM)-based SP processes have gained considerable research interest. However, the utility and usefulness of this approach significantly depends on the quality of the underlying individual causal map. Therefore, it is critical to select knowledgeable experts and carefully examine the causal relationships, uncertainties, and assumptions of the FCM model.

#### 10.4.2.3 Augmented Fuzzy Cognitive Map (FCM)-Based Scenario Development

Nowadays, there are some facilities of FCM-based scenario development. For example, the authors of [21] proposed a morphological analysis (i.e., to generate plausible input vectors that are subsequently used to generate the scenarios) to capture expert knowledge in the networks of different variations. Several studies (e.g., the authors of [11]) proved that this process can be used as an improvement to the scenario selection and refinement activities. The following three steps are recommended in the literature to conduct the morphological analysis [36]:

- Step 1: Enter the critical scenario drivers (concepts) at the top of each column.
- Step 2: Identify the number of conceivable development variations (at least two) of each scenario driver.

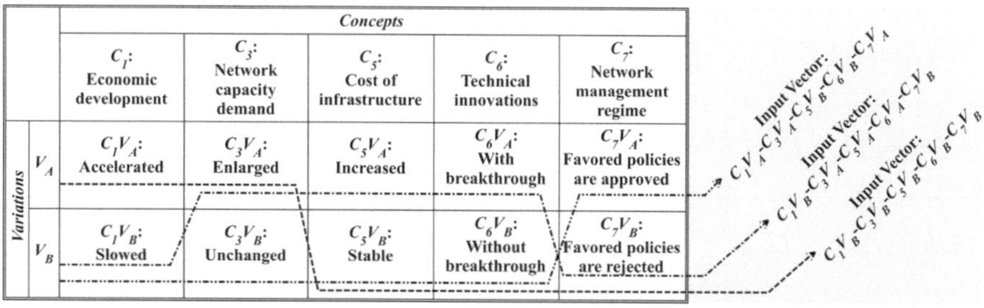


**Fig. 10.2** Morphological analysis to generate input vectors

- Step 3: Combine the development variations into plausible strands.

An example of the morphological analysis for generating three input vectors is presented in Fig. 10.2.

As shown in Fig. 10.2, morphological analysis helps to ensure that there is no contradiction in these combinations denoted by different line types. It is a useful tool and helps to visually analyze the combinations of conceivable development variations and ensure plausibility.

### *10.4.3 Building Block 3: Technology Roadmap (TRM)*

To utilize SP, a framework for strategic management in an uncertain world is the first step a CEO should take; however, most SP approaches are complicated to apply in practice, as it is critical to ensure selection of different aspects both internal and external in regard to the company. As a result, we need another managerial tool that is useful in such tasks, i.e., providing a view from different layers (e.g., organization, product, technology, and national levels), in order to help make the business strategy happen.

One of those useful tools is technology roadmap (TRM). In simple language, a TRM is a supporting technological tool, especially for exploring and communicating the dynamic linkages between different aspects, such as product/service, business, and market perspectives. More specific definition is "a future based strategic planning device that outlines the goals, barriers, strategies necessary for achieving a given vision of technological advancement and market penetrations." To be a good TRM, there are three fundamental questions that must be answered: (a) Where are we going (i.e., what are our vision, mission, objectives, goals, and targets)? (b) Where are we now (i.e., present state of technology, products, markets)? (c) How can we get there (i.e., policy measures, R&D programs, action items, and long-term and short-term strategies)?

Nowadays, there are different types of TRM, in terms of the intended purpose (e.g., product planning, service/capability planning, strategic planning, long range planning, etc.) and format (e.g., multilayers, bars, table, text, graph, etc.) [35]. In

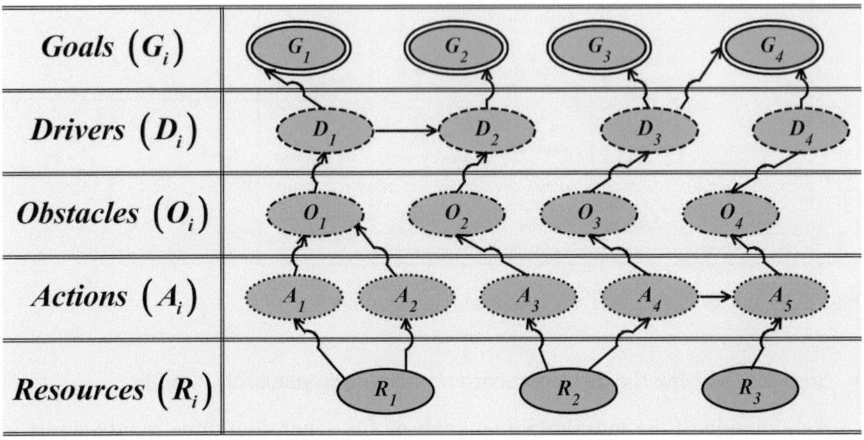


**Fig. 10.3** Generic multilayered graphical roadmap

this chapter, we will use multiple-layer format. Figure 10.3 highlights a generic multilayered roadmap. In fact, it is the most common format of TRM that have information of different functions and perspectives against an agreed timeline.

In Fig. 10.3, the evolution within each layer is explored, together with the interlayer dependencies, facilitating the integration of technology into products, services, and business systems. As a result, it helps to visualize different factors between the technology development, the company's capabilities evolution, and market needs and trends.

### 10.4.4 Benefits of Utilizing Technology Roadmap (TRM) and Scenario Planning (SP) Together

Often, an individual method does not provide a perfect strategy. Literature highlights that both SP and TRM have some strengths and weaknesses (see Table 10.1), which make it more desirable to integrate these two methods [41, 42]. For example, the authors of [30] pointed out that SP technique can improve if it is combined with another research method such as the roadmapping or the Delphi method or both. This paper [44] recommended that the combined use of SP with TRM can enhance the flexibility and vision of the roadmap; meanwhile it can capture and convey the full context of decisions and enable anticipation of a broader range of possible changes. As a result, combining the SP and TRM is beneficial since both methods are complementary, i.e., disadvantages of roadmaps can be addressed by advantages of scenarios and vice versa [42]. For example, SP focuses on consistent and coherent of multiple hypothetical futures, whereas a TRM replies on a single future with a complete action plan. Thus, both methods are better off when they are

**Table 10.1** Scenario planning vs. technology roadmapping: a comparison

| | Scenario planning | Technology roadmapping |
|---|---|---|
| Interactivity and participation degree | ☺ | ☹ |
| Exploration/standardization in terms of examining diverse future | ☺ | ☹ |
| Openness and creative thinking | ☺ | ☹ |
| Connection between the present and the desired future | ☹ | ☺ |
| Offering clear and understandable information | ☹ | ☺ |
| Confirmative actions and strategies | ☹ | ☺ |

integrated. For more details about the benefits of integrating the TRM and SP, refer to [41, 42, 44].

## 10.5 The Draft Progress of Exploiting eTRM-FCM-SP in the Context of NN Debate

### *10.5.1 How to Exploit eTRM-FCM-SP?*

For the purpose of developing network neutrality technology roadmaps and scenarios, expert panels should be created comprising members of varied backgrounds (e.g., public or private sectors). The feasible future roadmaps and scenarios can thus be formed by combining their variety of input. Then, the experts' knowledge can be captured when they express their mental models in the FCM form. Next, one or more promising scenarios can be established via the integrated FCM. Finally, according to [1], a roadmap can be drawn for each particular scenario based on the obtained information at hand. The flowchart of this process is summarized and illustrated in Fig. 10.4.

#### 10.5.1.1 The Development of FCM-SP

In order to develop various FCM-based scenarios, different procedures have been recommended in the literature. Some key steps are extracted from various sources and summarized as follows [1, 22, 47]:

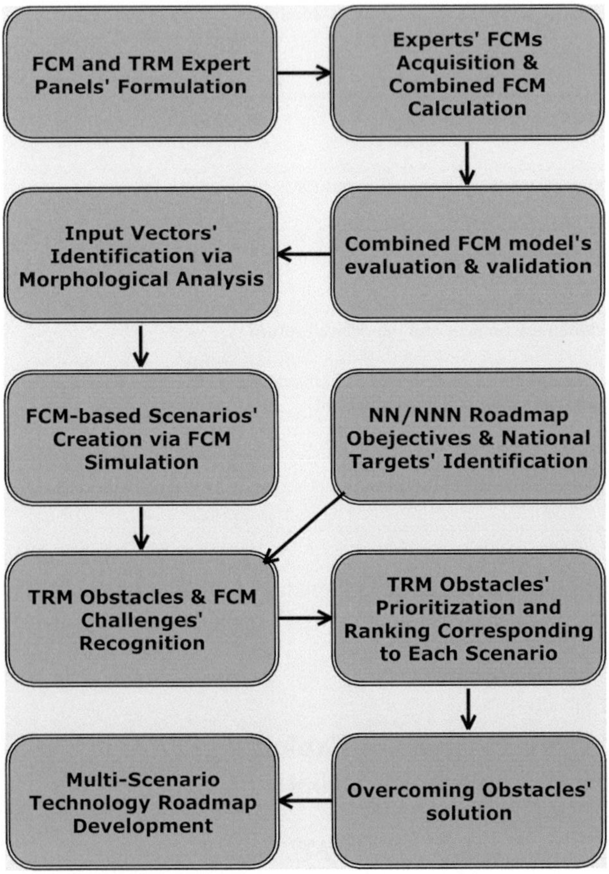


**Fig. 10.4** Flowchart of the proposed methodology

- Crucial factors—investigation and definition:
  - Representative issue brainstorming
  - Issues' classification and prioritization
- Causality between these factors—determination:
  - Interconnected factors' identification
  - Their relationships' determination (positive or negative)
  - The strength of the relationships' quantification a 5-point Likert-type scale casual weight. The values range from 1 to 5, representing relationship between a very weak causal link and a very strong causal link.
- Combined/integrated FCM—review and discussion:
  - FCMs' collection from each individual expert

  - Integrated FCM's formulation
- Most uncertain factors in the integrated FCM—identification:
  - Pinpointing the most uncertain factors
- Input vectors consisting of the most important factors from the integrated FCM—creation:
  - Worksheet distribution among experts with the critical scenario drivers and the associated conceivable development variations highlighted
  - Input vectors' creation

Once all of this has been done, a single map (a joint effect of multiple FCM's combination) can be created for further in-depth analysis. Typically, an individual FCM only contains limited information from single source. The combined FCM thus is often considered more useful by overcoming such weakness. Since the underlying casual map's quality determines the final FCM model's usefulness and utility, the process of selecting suitable experts and combining the resultant cognitive maps plays an important role in FCM-SP development.

There are two methods presented in the literature to combine FCM of multiple experts [1, 22]:

- One approach is built upon expert creditability's assessment (via calculating each expert's creditability weights).
- Another method of generating combined FCM is to make use of the average of expert opinions expressed in all FCMs.

Due to its popularity and simplicity, the second methodology, i.e., averaging multiple FCMs, is employed in the proposed methodology. To illustrate how to use this method, three different fuzzy cognitive maps are shown in Fig. 10.5, represented as $FCM_1$, $FCM_2$, and $FCM_3$ , respectively, and the combined FCM is denoted by $FCM_{\text{combined}}$. Meanwhile, each node represents unique variables, while the directed edges are used to stand for node-to-node weighted relations.

The combined FCM ($FCM_{\text{combined}}$) is a union set of nodes; and average of the causal weights is taken. If a specific node is not shown in an individual FCM map, the edge weight will be considered as zero. For instance, in $FCM_1$, node 4 is no-show and thus there is no connection between variables 1 and 4. Therefore, a zero value is assigned to the edge weight between variables 1 and 4, and the value of edge weights from node 4 to all other nodes is also zero in $FCM_1$. Thus $FCM_{\text{combined}}$ can be easily calculated by combining multiple FCMs.

After the integrated FCM is obtained, the experts will be asked to rank the scenario drivers; the morphological analysis will then be used to develop the input vectors. Subsequently FCM-based scenarios are generated via input vector-led simulation.

The FCM simulation will only terminate when the output vectors reach stable condition. This process is carried out via multiplying matrices, i.e., input vector and

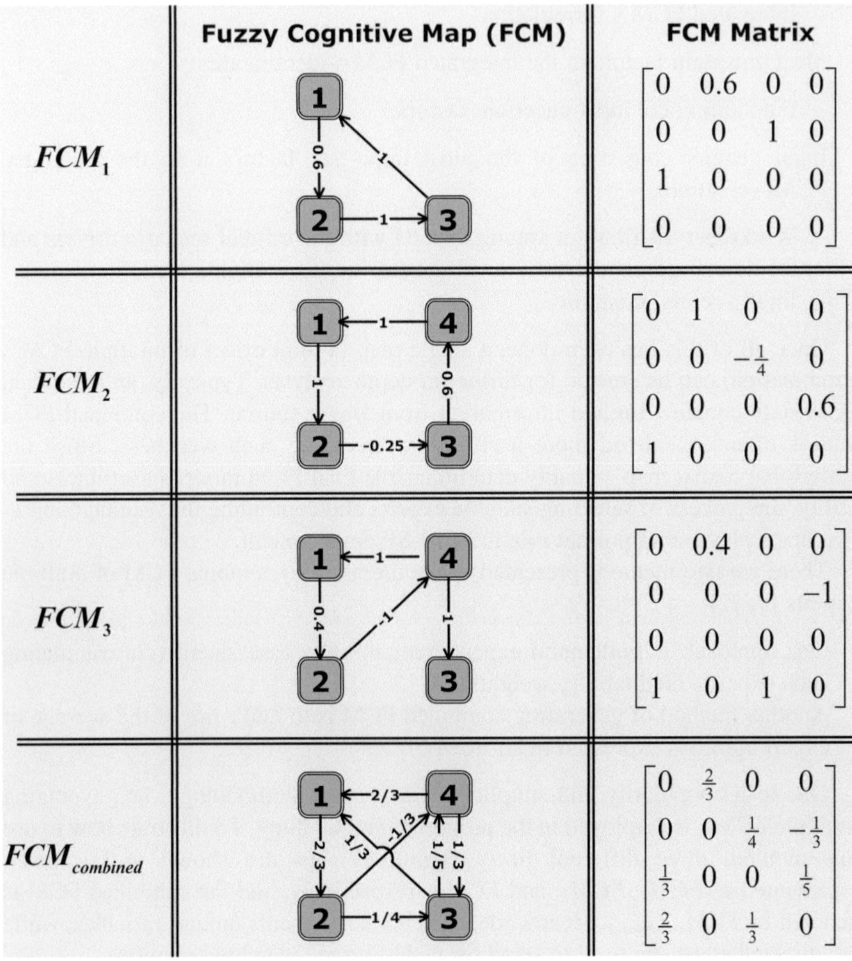


**Fig. 10.5** Combining the FCMs by average method

FCM adjacency matrix. After each multiplication, a squashing function [1] can be applied as a threshold function to the output vector.

In the proposed method, a simple binary squashing function can be used for squeezing multiplication results into the interval of (0, 1). For $n$ variables, the input vector is denoted by $1 \times n$, and the FCM adjacency matrix can be written as $n \times n$, while the output vector is therefore represented by $1 \times n$. The output vector is again multiplied with the FCM adjacency matrix, and the interaction of this process is continued until the multiplication results arrive equilibrium [22]. This vector-matrix multiplication is performed via Eq. (10.1) [1]:

$$S_i = I_j \times E \tag{10.1}$$

where $S_i$ denotes the new state vector (output/inference vector), $I_j$ represents the $j$th inference vector, and $E$ stands for the FCM adjacency matrix.

#### 10.5.1.2 Technology Roadmap Development

The second part of using eTRM-FCM-SP is to develop a technology roadmap which is often regarded as a high-level planning tool used for supporting the development and implementing strategy/plans. According to [1], a roadmap can be developed through a top-down approach by following the steps outlined below:

- Step 1: Roadmap strategic objectives
- Step 2: Roadmap targets
- Step 3: Roadmap obstacles
- Step 4: Roadmap action items

#### 10.5.1.3 Consistency of Expert Judgments

Inconsistency shows the degree to which an individual is inconsistent in his/her own judgment, whereas consistency indicates a situation where the expert's judgment keeps unchanged over time. Therefore the test of individual stability offers very useful information, and it is often used to measure the consistency of between successive responses [1].

In this chapter, a demonstration case, borrowed from [1], is used to illustrate the working principles of a typical stability test. Table 10.2 highlights the outputs by 122 panelists for three response intervals (A, B, and C) in the second and third rounds of a given Delphi study.

According to the assumption that the null hypothesis of independence is true [8], we can calculate the expected frequencies as tabulated in Table 10.2. Here Eq. (10.2) is used [1]:

**Table 10.2** Observed and expected individual frequencies

| **Observed frequencies** | | | | | |
|---|---|---|---|---|---|
| **Response interval** | | **3rd round** | | | **Total** |
| | | A | B | C | |
| **2nd round** | A | 26 | 0 | 0 | 26 |
| | B | 7 | 62 | 2 | 71 |
| | C | 0 | 0 | 25 | 25 |
| **Total** | | 33 | 62 | 27 | 122 |
| **Expected frequencies** | | | | | |
| **Response interval** | | **3rd round** | | | |
| | | A | B | C | |
| **2nd round** | A | 7.0 | 13.2 | 5.8 | |
| | B | 19.2 | 36.1 | 15.7 | |
| | C | 6.8 | 12.7 | 5.5 | |

$$\chi^2 = \sum_{k=1}^{n} \sum_{j=1}^{m} \frac{\left(O_{jk} - E_{jk}\right)^2}{E_{jk}} \tag{10.2}$$

where the observed and expected frequencies (indicating the number of respondents who voted for the $j$th response interval in the $i$th round, but voted for the $k$th response interval in round $i+1$) are denoted by $O_{jk}$ and $E_{jk}$, respectively, and $m$ and $n$ are the number of nonzero response intervals between the rounds $i$ and $i+1$. According to Eq. (10.2), the chi-square ($\chi^2$) value can be calculated, based on the observed and expected frequencies shown in Table 10.2, and the value is 197.5.

For the purpose of testing individual stability in a Delphi study, the following factor (i.e., whether there is a significant difference between the individual responses in two consecutive rounds using the chi-square test) needs to be determined. The following hypotheses can thus be tested:

- $H_0$: Individual responses of rounds $i$ and $i+1$ are independent.
- $H_1$: Individual responses of rounds $i$ and $i+1$ are not independent.

If we find that the same respondent who voted for a given response interval, say, in the round $i$, has also voted for the same response interval in another round, i.e., $i+1$, we can conclude that the individual responses in the consecutive rounds are dependent. Thus, the null hypothesis ($H_0$) is rejected, whereas the alternative hypothesis ($H_1$) is accepted, and it can also be concluded that, between any consecutive rounds, there is an individual stability. Rejection of the null hypothesis means that the individual stability has reached. For the example illustrated in Table 10.2, there is 4-DoF (i.e., degree of freedom) and it is calculated via Eq. (10.3) [1]:

$$\text{DoF} = (m-1)(n-1) \tag{10.3}$$

At a 0.05 level of significance and four (4) DoFs, the critical $\chi^2$ value is 9.488. Since the calculated $\chi^2$ statistic is greater than this critical value, the null hypothesis is rejected and we can conclude that the individual stability has been demonstrated. Therefore, in a follow-up Delphi survey (normally conducted to prioritize the roadmap barriers for each scenario), the $\chi^2$ test can be employed for measuring the group responses' stability.

### 10.5.2 General Assumptions of Using eTRM-FCM-SP

The following assumptions have been made for implementing the proposed methodology:

- The selected experts are knowledgeable in the areas related to the targeted theme.
- Biases of experts can be balanced within each corresponding expert panel.

- The biases of the final judgment made by each panel are in general limited.
- All main factors that may affect the deployment of NN or NNN policy on a national level can be captured by expert panels.
- Only causal link connected factors may affect each other.

## 10.6 Future Research Directions

Although building scenarios with FCM has been proved very useful as a method to combine the benefits of both qualitative and quantitative analysis, questions remain. For example, detailed instructions about how to choose and judge experts' knowledge, how to define appropriate number of scenarios, and how FCM can be verified are also currently lacking. This section attempts to clarify some of these ambiguities when applying eTRM-FCM-SP.

### *10.6.1 Expert Panels' Chosen and Options' Judgment*

As stated earlier, the quality of information obtained from the expert panel significantly depends upon the participants' knowledge and experience. Therefore, members of the expert panels need to be carefully selected for their in-depth knowledge and experience of the relevant fields. In general, expert panels can be classified into two groups, i.e., traditional expertise (e.g., government departments, private sectors, scientists, and engineers) and nontraditional expertise (e.g., customers, journalists, and a range of other stakeholders during participatory planning and discussion). As a result, there may be some degree of overlap or contradiction to inform the decision-making process. For example, in the literature, these conflicts are often demonstrated by the defining of the elicitation objectives (e.g., individual knowledge of group beliefs), the preparation of research questions (e.g., standardizing concepts or free association of concepts), and the process of obtaining the expert options (e.g., collecting individual FCM or facilitating group modeling). Thus, the future research should focus on what trade-offs should be considered in terms of appropriately representing group knowledge.

### *10.6.2 Scenario Selection and Appropriate Number of Scenarios*

It is very important to develop an appropriate number of scenarios for a study, since on the one hand, comparing different outcomes of scenario analyses across several scenarios through "clamping" the same variables may allow for qualitative interpretation of how a domain may react. On the other hand, however, coding different

**Fig. 10.6** Network regime roadmap—Stage II: methodology verification

variables into discrete scenarios may provide the insight into which agreement can be identified and assessed. Unfortunately, there is no precise response to the question of how many future scenarios are optimal in the scenario planning literature. In the literature, some researchers recommend that the ideal set of scenarios consist of three or four narratives, which should be structurally or qualitatively different [7]. Others (e.g., [11]) recommend to develop scenarios around four to six fundamental hypotheses; otherwise the sheer magnitude of possible combinations will be overwhelming. Despite the number dispute, this paper [6] pointed out that scenarios should be developed by considering the most likely (expectable), challenging (what could go wrong), and visionary (surprisingly successful) possibilities. Therefore, the generally recommended number of alternative scenarios ranges from 3 to 6 [2].

### *10.6.3 Verification of the Proposed Methodology*

The ultimate goal of this chapter is to develop a national-level network regime roadmap through the proposed methodology. The present work focuses on justifying the suitability of dealing with the focal question. An immediate research venue for future study would be targeting on Stage II (see Fig. 10.6), i.e., verify the feasibility of the proposed methodology.

For a successful application of the proposed methodology, the following steps are suggested:

- Develop a national network regime roadmap to address various strategic objectives.
- Identify practical insights on the factors supporting and hindering deployment of targeted network policy.
- Propose the action items and plans for the deployment of desired network policy on a large scale, and give recommendations to the stakeholders for a better implementation of such policy.

## 10.7 Conclusion

This chapter presents a possible use of eTRM-FCM-SP as an approach to dealing with the ongoing NN/NNN debate in the era of Internet of Things. eTRM-FCM-SP combines FCM-based scenario planning with technology roadmapping techniques.

Through a careful suitability justification, this chapter examines three main building blocks of the proposed methodology. As illustrated, the usefulness of TRM has been significantly improved, and a wide range of possible future outcomes that may arise in NN debate can thus be anticipated. The advantage of utilizing the proposed systematic approach is manyfold; first, we can get a possibility of gaining insights on the relative benefit of the NNN regime compared to the NN in an end-to-end multi-actor environment. Meanwhile, it also has the potential to show which scenarios are beneficial for the individual actors. Last, but not the least, the proposed technique offers a chance to provide some general recommendations regarding the effects of regulation, and how policy makers could use regulation to improve the relative benefit of the NNN regime for all actors and maximize social welfare with the forthcoming everything connected scenario.

## References


1. Amer M (2013) Extending technology roadmap through fuzzy cognitive map-based scenarios: the case of the wind energy sector of Pakistan. Portland State University
2. Amer M, Daim TU, Jetter A (2013) A review of scenario planning. Futures 46:23–40
3. Arias MA, Shin Y (2013) There are two sides to every coin – even to the Bitcoin, a virtual currency. The Regional Economist, July 2013, pp 1–3
4. Armstrong M (2006) Competition in two-sided markets. RAND J Econ 37:668–691
5. Axelrod R (1976) Structure of decision: the cognitive maps of political elites. Princeton University Press, New Jersey
6. Bezold C (2010) Lessons from using scenarios for strategic foresight. Technol Forecast Soc Chang 77:1513–1518
7. Brabandere L, Iny A (2010) Scenarios and creativity: thinking in new boxes. Technol Forecast Soc Chang 77:1506–1512
8. Celiktas MS, Kocar G (2010) From potential forecast to foresight of Turkey's renewable energy with Delphi approach. Energy 35:1973–1980
9. Choi JP, Kim B-C (2010) Net neutrality and investment incentives. RAND J Econ 41:446–471
10. D'Annunzio A, Russo A (2015) Net neutrality and Internet fragmentation: the role of online advertising. Int J Ind Organ 43:30–47
11. Durance P, Godet M (2010) Scenario building: uses and abuses. Technol Forecast Soc Chang 77:1488–1492
12. Economides N, Tåg J (2012) Network neutrality on the internet: a two-sided market analysis. Inf Econ Policy 24:91–104
13. Ehrlich M, Greiner T (2013) The role of online platforms for media markets – two-dimensional spatial competition in a two-sided market. Int J Ind Organ 31:723–737
14. Eisenmann T, Parker G, Alstyne MWV (2006) Strategies for two-sided markets. Harv Bus Rev 1463:1–12
15. Evans DS (2003) The antitrust economics of multi-sided platform markets. Yale J Regul 20:325–381
16. Evans DS, Passel P (2003) Everything you ever wanted to know about two-sided markets. The Milken Institute Review Second Quarter
17. Federal Communications Commission (2014) Protecting and promoting the open Internet NPRM, retrieved from http://fcc.gov/document/protecting-andpromoting-open-internet-nprm. Accessed on 15 May 2014

18. Fishburn PC, Odlyzko AM (2000) Dynamic behavior of differential pricing and quality of service options for the internet. Decis Support Syst 28:123–136
19. Hahn R, Wallsten S (2006) The economics of net neutrality. Econ Voice 3:1–7
20. Hildebrand T (2012) Estimating network effects in two-sided markets without data on prices and quantities. Econ Lett 117:585–588
21. Jenkins L (1997) Selecting a variety of futures for scenario development. Technol Forecast Soc Chang 55:15–20
22. Jetter A, Schweinfort W (2011) Building scenarios with fuzzy cognitive maps: an exploratory study of solar energy. Futures 43:52–66
23. Kahn H, Wiener AJ (1967) The year 2000: a framework for speculation on the next thirty-three years. The Macmillan, New York
24. Kandasamy WBV, Smarandache F (2003) Fuzzy cognitive maps and neutrosophic cognitive maps. Indian Institute of Technology, Madras
25. Kang J-S, Downing S (2015) Keystone effect on entry into two-sided markets: an analysis of the market entry of WiMAX. Technol Forecast Soc Chang 94:170–186
26. Kosko B (1986) Fuzzy cognitive maps. Int J Man-Mach Stud 24:65–75
27. Krämer J, Wiewiorra L (2012) Network neutrality and congestion sensitive content providers: implication for content variety, broadband investment, and regulation. INFORMS 23:1303–1321
28. Lee D, Hwang J (2011) The effect of network neutrality on the incentive to discriminate, invest and innovate: a literature review. TEMEP discussion paper
29. Lee D, Kim Y-H (2014) Empirical evidence of network neutrality – the incentives for discrimination. Inf Econ Policy 29:1–9
30. Mietzner D, Reger G (2005) Advantages and disadvantages of scenario approaches for strategic foresight. Int J Technol Intell Plan 1:220–239
31. Musacchio J, Schwartz G, Walrand J (2009) A two-sided market analysis of provider investment incentives with an application to the net-neutrality issue. Rev Netw Econ 8:22–39
32. Nijoroge P, Ozdaglar A, Stier-Moses NE, Weintraub GY (2013) Investment in two-sided markets and the net neutrality debate. Rev Netw Econ 12:355–402
33. Nurski L (2012) Net neutrality, foreclosure and the fast lane: an empirical study of the UK. NET Institute 1–31
34. Papageorgiou EI (2014) Fuzzy cognitive maps for applied sciences and engineering: from fundamentals to extensions and learning algorithms. Springer-Verlag, Berlin, 978-3-642-39738-7
35. Phaal R, Farrukh CJ, Probert DR (2001) Characterisation of technology roadmaps: purpose and format. Portland International Conference on Management of Engineering and Technology (PICMET), pp 367–374
36. Pillkahn U (2008) Using trends and scenarios as tools for strategy development. Publicis Corporate Publishing, Erlangen
37. Ramirez R, Selsky JW, Heijden KVD (eds) (2008) Business planning for turbulent times: new methods for applying scenarios. Earthscan, London
38. Rochet JC, Tirole J (2003) Platform competition in two-sided markets. J Eur Econ Assoc 1:990–1209
39. Rochet JC, Tirole J (2006) Two-sided markets: a progress report. RAND J Econ 37:645–667
40. Rysman M (2009) The economics of two-sided markets. J Econ Perspect 23:125–143
41. Saritas O, Oner MA (2004) Systemic analysis of UK foresight results: joint application of integrated management model and roadmapping. Technol Forecast Soc Chang 71:27–65
42. Saritas O, Aylen J (2010) Using scenarios for roadmapping: the case of clean production. Technol Forecast Soc Chang 77:1061–1075
43. Soetanto R, Dainty ARJ, Goodier CI, Austin SA (2011) Unravelling the complexity of collective mental models: a method for developing and analysing scenarios in multi-organisational contexts. Futures 43:890–907

44. Strauss JD, Radnor M (2004) Roadmapping for dynamic and uncertain environments. Res Technol Manag 47:51–57
45. The World Economic Forum (2014) Delivering digital infrastructure: advancing the Internet economy. Hyperconnected World. World Economic Forum, 91–93 route de la Capite, CH-1223 Cologny/Geneva, Switzerland
46. Varum CA, Melo C (2010) Directions in scenario planning literature – a review of the past decades. Futures 42:355–369
47. Vliet M, Kok K, Veldkamp T (2010) Linking stakeholders and modellers in scenario studies: the use of fuzzy cognitive maps as a communication and learning tool. Futures 42:1–14
48. Wack P (1985) Scenarios: uncharted waters ahead. Harv Bus Rev 63:73–89
49. Wu T (2003) Network neutrality, broadband discrimination. J Telecommun High Technol Law 2:141–179
50. Zhang N, Levä T, Hämmäinen H (2014) Value networks and two-sided markets of internet content delivery. Telecommun Policy 38:460–472

# Part III
# Security Mechanisms for the Internet of Things

# Chapter 11
# Data Security and Privacy in the Internet of Things (IoT) Environment

**Vijayaraghavan Varadharajan and Shruti Bansal**

## 11.1 Introduction

Internet of Things (IoT) has become one of the most frequently used keywords in technical space these days. Evolution of the IoT has changed the way we look at devices, with communication between intelligent devices making our lives easier day by day. IoT stands for constellation of sensor embedded/carrying objects known as "things" connected via the Internet.

A smartphone with its range of sensors (accelerometer, gyroscope, video, proximity, compass, GPS, etc.) offering a variety of communication capabilities like Wi-Fi, NFC, Bluetooth, or 3G/4G connectivity is a well-equipped IoT device in our pockets. Consider someone wearing heart rate monitor, wrapped around the chest or a smart watch on the wrist, which is continuously reading and transmitting the heart rate sensor readings to another IoT node. Such smart devices or computing systems constitute Internet of Things network, where day-to-day sensor measurements can be read, processed, and analyzed. Due to widespread Internet connectivity, a number of devices connected to IoT networks have arisen prominently in recent times. Experts approximate an optimistic rise in the number of IoT connected devices in the coming years; Cisco [1] estimates 25 billion of these by the end of 2015 and expects it to double by 2020.

We are in the early stages of creating an IoT world by combining sensors, actuators, and network intelligence. Smart home and healthcare are the biggest potential markets for IoT networks [2]. Consider a typical scenario: Bob goes out

V. Varadharajan (✉)
Infosys Limited, Bangalore, India
e-mail: Vijayaraghavan_V01@infosys.com

S. Bansal
Infosys Limited, Pune, India
e-mail: Shruti_Bansal01@Infosys.com

 
Z. Mahmood (ed.), *Connectivity Frameworks for Smart Devices*,
Computer Communications and Networks, DOI 10.1007/978-3-319-33124-9_11

for a walk wearing a fitness band. The band keeps track of his step frequency and heart rate (HR) and streams the recorded vitals to doctors for health monitoring and to adjust his prescription accordingly. While Bob is 15 min away from reaching home, sensor-driven air conditioning is switched on, and as he walks inside, light intensity is adjusted as per time of the day.

With IoT connectivity transforming businesses and entering our day-to-day lives, data availability in connected space has already grown apace in terms of volume, velocity, and variety. A highly optimistic number has been projected for increasing data volume and traffic. On estimating potential impact of Internet of Everything (IoE) on cloud, Cisco Global Cloud Index: Forecast and Methodology (2013–2018) report [1] predicts data created by IoE devices to reach 403 ZB per year by 2018, with around 40 % increase in usage of personal cloud storage by consumer Internet population.

Alternatively, the presence of heterogeneous consumer data like personal and professional information, medical/fitness data, geographic data, and health data, with varied sensitivity, elevates the necessity for secure and scalable transport mechanisms as well as storage environment. Apart from connected user access, consumer data may be read, analyzed, or even treated with massive computations for research purpose. In such a case, where devices or automated systems have access to sensitive information like vitals and location, security attacks and potential abuse on consumer data is an imminent threat. Hence, IoT security and regulated data access control are more of a necessity than mere added features.

For a widespread uptake of IoT consumer data in the shared space, appropriate security and privacy techniques need to be in place to induce safe data transport and storage. In this chapter, we describe such techniques and their implementations in IoT space for a protected consumer experience and data handling.

The rest of this chapter is organized as follows. Section 11.2 presents the data security evolution and its challenges. Section 11.3 discusses IoT security risks and challenges, as well as data security requirements in IoT. Recommendations for IoT data security are detailed in Sect. 11.4. This section also discusses the context-based data access control, identity masking, authorization using OAuth, and device-based certificates. Section 11.5 concludes the chapter and Sect. 11.6 charts the road ahead.

## 11.2 Background

### *11.2.1 Evolution of Data Security*

Until a decade ago, data available in the Internet space was confined to enterprise or consumer data residing at organizations' physically secure infrastructure and servers. Dedicated servers could be classified based on data sensitivity and hence be secured using simple mechanisms like form-based authentication or selective access control. Users could establish secure connection with server over the network to access data using their login credentials.

With the Internet and Web storage entering our daily lives, data security is enhanced using techniques like two-factor authentication, storage and transport encryption, network firewall, data masking, and access control based on access policies, roles, user profile, or biometrics. These mechanisms are widely accepted for securing and managing volumes of consumer data in Web space and ensuring data security throughout the life cycle, i.e., when stored, while in transit, and when being accessed.

Authentication and authorization mechanisms are based on available user information and assignment of access permissions on requested data resource. Form-based authentication bedecked with alternative techniques like biometrics, grid codes, OTP, security token, or public keys facilitates enhanced Internet security. Based on a set of rule base known as "access policy," access permissions define fine-grained access control [3] and refine authorization mechanisms for securely accessing Web resources.

Encryption ensures that data does not get accessed by unauthorized entities while in storage and also is not altered during transit. A plethora of data encryption methods and options exist in the marketplace. Private-key cryptography (symmetric) and public key cryptography (asymmetric) are basic types of encryption methods [4].

Transport Layer Security (TLS) protocol assures security between two communicating endpoints, computing systems or devices on the Internet. In a client-server architecture, TLS [5] makes sure that no third party may eavesdrop the message in flight. TLS 1.0 is a standardized successor of Secure Sockets Layer (SSL 3.0). Secure HTTP or HTTPS is the most familiar application of SSL.

Advent of intelligent hardware such as RSA secure ids, smart cards, and bar code has brought security and privacy mechanisms to the next level. These objects provide additional security using biometrics chip, secure passwords, and network pin codes. Policy implementation and management in such cases are quite challenging. Web security and privacy techniques thus try to address necessary confidentiality and access control on consumer data throughout the life cycle, from transport to storage and processing.

### *11.2.2 Data Security: A Challenge*

Exponential increase in data availability and sensitivity in recent times has become a challenge for data security and privacy in a connected world. Manyfold technologies, services, and standards embraced in Internet and cloud space suggest security threats may magnify with fleeting time. Figure 11.1 shows the steep growth in security threats observed over the years, following availability of new tools to establish an attack in secure cyberspace. However, with the sophistication of security attacks ever increasing, knowledge needed to launch an attack decreases exponentially [6, 7]. Therefore, privacy protection and security measures must equally be adaptive to offer end-to-end and robust data security.

A static approach for securing data and regulating access is becoming unacceptable as it fails to address the necessity for a scalable data security mechanism. "One

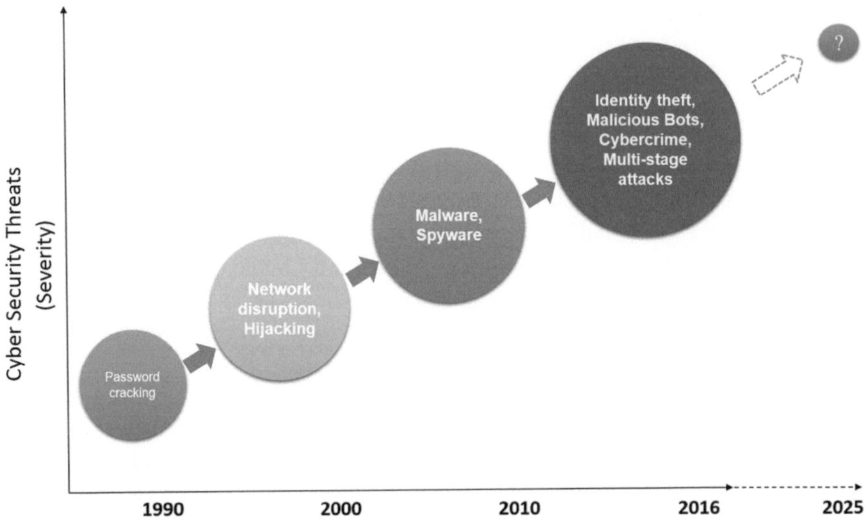


**Fig. 11.1** Evolution of cyber security threats over time

technique fits all" approach does not help in securing current data systems which are highly complex and sensitive in nature. On-demand security and privacy techniques for protecting data in storage or transit, adaptable to varied data usage in current era, are necessary to facilitate robust access control and protection of data in shared space.

Techniques like device programming, storage encryption, and access control lists (ACL) are quite inert in nature. Little attention has been paid to implement effective security and privacy measures for protecting data and access control in accordance to the dynamics of resource, environment, users, or the application. Additionally, increased user intervention in protecting his/her own sensitive data is another challenge. A fine-grained access control and varied privacy options for a user are thus necessary. Hence, it is quite essential to realize that security and privacy techniques have to be more dynamic and robust in nature to be able to address ever-increasing demands of the digital world.

## 11.3 IoT Security

### *11.3.1 Risks and Challenges*

IoT sensor devices such as fitness bands, health monitoring devices, and automated bill payers handle highly sensitive consumer and financial data. Optimistic growth in volume of data and connected devices, e.g., scanables, wearables, or complex systems like smart appliances and vehicles, health monitors, and sensors, triggers equally exorbitant surge in challenges, in terms of data handling, transport, security, and access control.

Connected things, people, and devices represent typical data-driven IoT scenarios. While a completely connected world with intelligent computing systems and smart devices enabling daily lives sounds cool and futuristic, not having appropriate security and privacy mechanisms to protect sensitive data bears potential physical and safety risks. Network of devices records, manages, stores, and transports huge amount of sensitive data. With ever-evolving ways of handling and analyzing generated data, privacy and security challenges are inescapable. While unauthorized access and misuse of sensor data like vitals (glucometers, scales, heart rate, and blood pressure monitors) and devices such as pacemaker can lead to serious health hazard (or even fatal), network devices like home appliances (door locks, cameras, ovens) could be accessed by intruders and abused. Inappropriate access over credit card or vehicular control is dangerous at both physical and financial grounds.

In addition to the volume and heterogeneity, IoT sensing increases identity dependency and hence data sensitivity. This intervention is more situational but tightly coupled. Ownership theft in sensor devices or failure to perform identity verification can lead to serious safety hazards. Consider chip-based smart cards, for example. A miscreant in possession of the smart card may gain unauthorized access to other users' sensitive data in the absence of any identity verification mechanism. Concerns relating to electronic failure, identity thefts, and data abuse are hence relatively higher in IoT and, if not taken care, can have serious implications.

Current Internet security and privacy techniques fail to address IoT-driven data security challenges like varied ownership, key management, security laws and regulations, heterogeneous connectivity, and different device life cycle [8, 9]. - Sensor-embedded devices differ in terms of make, type, and usage. An IoT device may be used by one or more users for sensing, storing, or processing sensitive data; hence, applying an appropriate access control and identity authentication system is quite a challenge.

Unlike traditional data systems, data from IoT devices is heterogeneous and may stream at unpredictable rates. In a classical Web setup, recorded data could be encrypted and sent over secure communication channels for server-side processing. However, in smart IoT devices, server-side operations like data analytics, processing, and inference are more of decentralized. Data traveling across communication channels ranges from sensor readings to inferences and analytic information. This makes data communication channels extra susceptible to breach and attack by intruders.

When compared to a typical client-server or distributed Web infrastructure, IoT architecture is quite different in terms of data volume and variety, connectivity, control management, and computation distribution among various layers. Hence, it is quite essential to understand the security challenges faced by an IoT network with respect to its layered architecture.

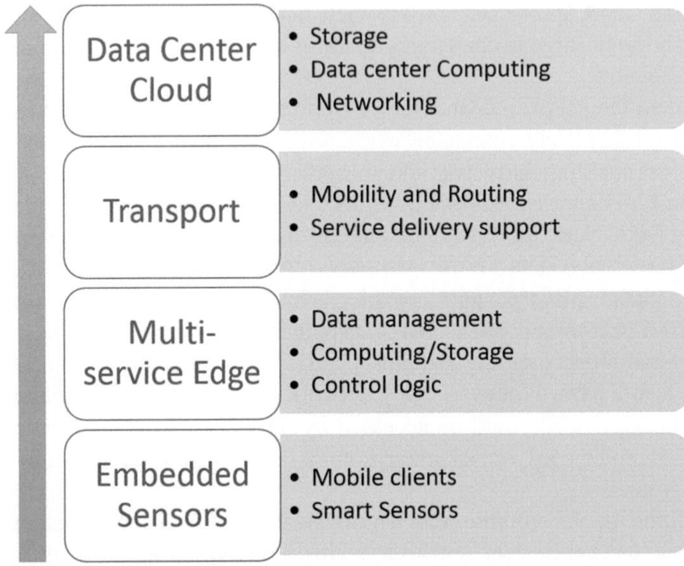


**Fig. 11.2** Layered architecture of IoT

CISCO [10] suggests an IoT/M2M platform architecture as composed of four layers. A modified form of their architecture is shown in Fig. 11.2.

Embedded systems consisting of sensors, actuators, and mobile clients, typically small devices with varying OS, CPU types, and memory, form the lowermost layer in the IoT architecture, where data is collected and sent to secondary systems or network for further processing or transport, respectively. The entities in this layer are primarily single-function devices with rudimentary network connectivity, such as temperature or motion sensor. Identity verification and data validation are the biggest challenges at this layer. Due care must be taken to ensure the authenticity of source data.

Multiservice layer offers local storage, computing, or inference capabilities. This layer should accommodate variety of endpoints and protocols. Hence, achieving scalability to support data volume and variety is again challenging. Additionally, appropriate security services should be in place to protect inherently insecure endpoints.

Transport layer provides path for data and information exchange between multiple subnetworks. Eavesdropping, impersonation, relay, and replay attacks are security threats in IoT at this level.

Data center cloud hosts applications that provide services to manage end-to-end IoT architecture. Security services are critical at this layer to prevent infiltration and endpoint exploitation from attackers. Managing data volume and heterogeneity as well as maintaining data privacy for multiple consumers is vital. Using classical cryptographic encryptions for secure data storage could be difficult to manage because they can be broken in a short time. Appropriate security techniques are required to mitigate threats like compromised systems, transaction replays, or Denial of Services.

To facilitate highly diverse IoT environment and related security challenges, a flexible security framework is thus obligatory. The threats in IoT layers should be addressed through dedicated data privacy and security mechanisms devised upon clear understanding of IoT-specific security requirements.

## *11.3.2 Data Security Requirements in IoT*

Varied sources of data and heterogeneous devices build up an IoT ecosystem. The IoT can be expected to contain a huge number of sensors collecting and passing data about environmental conditions, physiological measurements, machine operational data, etc. In addition to consumer devices (smartphones, tablets, and gaming consoles), smart home appliances and intelligent computing nodes with embedded processors are likely to join IoT brigade sometime soon. Most communications occur automatically without much manual intervention. A smart vehicle control system can renew your car insurance automatically by selecting the best available plan and using your credit card details. Regulating access to highly sensitive information like credit cards is thus a prime necessity in IoT data security.

Research as reported in [11–15] confers IoT-related risks faced by the stakeholders as compared to classical security mechanisms and also outlines recommendations for designing an appropriate security and access control infrastructure for IoT to mitigate possibilities of security breaches and exposure of sensitive consumer data. WIND report [16] identifies how security must be addressed throughout a device life cycle from initial design to operational environment. Security recommendations presented at RSA conference, 2014 [8] discussed how data can be protected while at rest, transit and binding for an end-to-end IoT security solution.

Confidentiality, authentication, privacy, and trust among users and devices are prime concern areas while building secure access control in IoT. Varied standards and communication stacks prevent direct application of traditional security countermeasures to IoT. Moreover, a flexible security and privacy infrastructure is required to deal with scalability issues posed by high volume and variety of interconnected devices in a dynamic IoT environment.

Endpoint identity and authentication are building blocks of securing an IoT infrastructure. Current authentication schemes, majorly based on cryptographic suites for secure storage and transport, require high-compute platform which may not be present in an IoT sensor or embedded end device. User intervention while applying authentication and authorization protocols in IoT endpoints might not also be possible due to limited access. Consequently, authentication and authorization require appropriate reengineering to accommodate new IoT connected world.

Alternatively, privacy preservation is a grave concern in IoT applications and devices particularly in healthcare. Traceable signatures of location, activity behavior, and identity of individuals can be compromised if not protected. It is hence essential to verify device ownership and owner identity before sensor data could be transported to computing or storage layers.

Crucially, IoT space is still growing in terms of size and variety and hence the security risks. For an end-to-end secure infrastructure in the IoT network, consideration of IoT-specific, highly dynamic security and privacy mechanisms is indispensable. Security and privacy techniques for IoT if designed with flexibility shall offer a robust and highly secure IoT infrastructure.

Hence, to summarize, data security in an IoT network has the following characteristics:

- Endpoint authentication and trust management for M2M interactions, i.e., man to machine, machine to machine, or machine to man
- Privacy and access control not only for users but also for things while interacting with a system
- Scalable and flexible access control to accommodate high volume and velocity of sensitive data
- Identity verification for users and devices to regulate sensor data ownership
- On-demand secure access by a third party for computations or analytics
- Fine-grained access control system that accommodates variety of data and is equally dynamic in nature
- Mechanisms that can be applied on the fly, without much device programming or hardening

## 11.4 Recommendations for IoT Data Security

Necessity for a robust and scalable security system to protect data is quite evident in IoT. An equally dynamic security and privacy system that offers secure storage, access, and transport must be in place. Threats in IoT environment may be similar to those in traditional Internet, but looking into magnitude and variety in IoT, overall impact of a security breach is quite significant. The scale and context of IoT make it a compelling target for security attacks which could do significant harm to companies, organizations, nations, and more importantly people. In this section we shall discuss necessary access protection and control techniques suitable for an IoT ecosystem.

Endpoint identity authentication, privacy preservation, and access control for storage and transportation are building blocks for IoT security. A summary of the research status of crucial security technologies like encryption and communication security in the field of IoT can be found at [9].

The following subsections outline recommendations for key security mechanisms for IoT: authentication, confidentiality, and access control, with standard security and privacy mechanisms bedecked with scalability and granularity to facilitate dynamics of an IoT ecosystem. We discuss dynamism and scalability in access control with the help of context, flexibility in security by masking, granularity in third-party access through OAuth, and a reliable device security system to support heterogeneous devices.

### 11.4.1 Context-Based Data Access Control

Authentication mechanisms to gain access to sensitive data or resources have evolved in recent times. Upgrading simple form-based authentication to multifactor mechanism makes an ecosystem relatively secure for handling sensitive data or resources. However, it makes the process equally dependent upon entities (users, devices, or applications) to whom these credentials are assigned.

Consider a banking application, where user authentication for online banking requires card-based information like grid numbers or flash codes along with simple username-password combination, or an employee attendance system, where chip-based smart cards are used to recognize a user via biometric input such as thumbprint. The elevated levels of authentication indeed secure user's sensitive data like banking information, personal, medical, or professional data. However, these mechanisms cater to a very small group of users, who have access to these supplementary parameters.

Similarly, contemporary authorization methods are vastly user centric. Access to a data resource is generally based on user membership/subscription (ACLs), roles, or characteristics (attributes). Refining access using attribute-based authorization does enhance granularity for access control. However, a mere user-centric approach is quite static and non-scalable. Looking into heterogeneity and scale in IoT, data security needs flavor of dynamism in access control and needs to be equally adaptable to leverage the benefits of IoT connectedness to the fullest.

An ecosystem, where static properties of entities like user, device, or network are decked with context information, is more dynamic and adaptable to active application environment. Context-based access control evaluates the access requestor on the basis of information captured automatically from environment, network, or device. Current location, time, user activity, road traffic, network connectivity, and weather forecast are common examples of context-based parameters. Dynamic access control based on context is capable of accommodating varied users, devices, or data, without having to hard code access permissions to a specific user group, codebase, or hardware. Hence, context information is more reliable and safer than user supplied information.

Context-based multifactor authentication is quite popular among domains like banking, social media, and e-commerce where sensitive personal data is in place. However implications of authorization mechanisms based on context information are yet to be explored to the fullest.

Cloud and IoT have become sites for varied types of sensitive consumer data in recent times, like personal, professional, health and medical, geographical, statistical, analytical, or even fitness and workout. This data is just not kept and accessed by a set of known users, but also requested by third parties for research and/or analytics. Hence, to provide a better user control on his/her data at granular level, context-based access control would suffice. Data could be shared or permitted to be accessed on conditional basis with respect to environment, application, network, or device context.

Context parameters are broadly classified as parameters related to physical factors and those related to human factors. Human factor-related context accounts for information on user (habit knowledge, emotional state, or biophysiological conditions), social environment (colocation, social interaction, group dynamics), and activity based (spontaneous activity, engaged tasks, general goals). Likewise, context related to physical environment is structured into three categories: location (absolute position, relative position, colocation, proximity, distance), infrastructure (surrounding resources for computation, communication, task performance), and environmental conditions (noise, light, pressure, air quality, temperature).

Using a variety of context parameters in addition to static properties, users can thus assign a set of generalized permissions for accessing a data set or resources, which are adaptable to dynamic physical or human environment. Consider a user allowing other users to access his/her workout history only when the requester is in proximity of less than 5 km. The access permission here is defined based on a context parameter, i.e., current location. Such permissions are dynamic in nature and hold true for a larger set of user group, assuring scalability as compared to attribute- or role-based permissions which are static in nature.

Similarly, device centric permissions set on persistent device attributes like model number, UUID, and data type are error prone and difficult to manage. In the IoT environment where a wide variety of devices and data are available, maintaining persistent attributes related to devices, users, or networks is highly complex. Thus, for a more adaptive and dynamic access control in IoT, complete potential of context needs to be exploited.

A suggestive layered diagram for context-based access control system is shown in Fig. 11.3. Context awareness layer interacts with IoT device layer to sense context information and pass to inference layer for intelligent implications or computation of values. Access control layer combines available persistent information from user and resource stores with context information obtained from context engine. Access to the protected data resource is thus given to requesting application or device as per permissions defined in access policies.

A hybrid access control system that combines traditional authorization techniques with automatically captured context information, to examine the legitimacy of a user, device, or application to a requested resource, is most fitting for a shared space like IoT. Contextualizing access control in a heterogeneous and distributed IoT system could address challenges posed by varied devices and data in highly dynamic shared space. Security threats like impersonation and identity thefts could also be dealt using context-based access control system as values are recorded in real time with/without user intervention; using context parameters is thus more reliable and secure for privacy and access control.

While access control could be managed on the basis of real-time perspective from user, device, environment, or network, maintenance of trust is also a

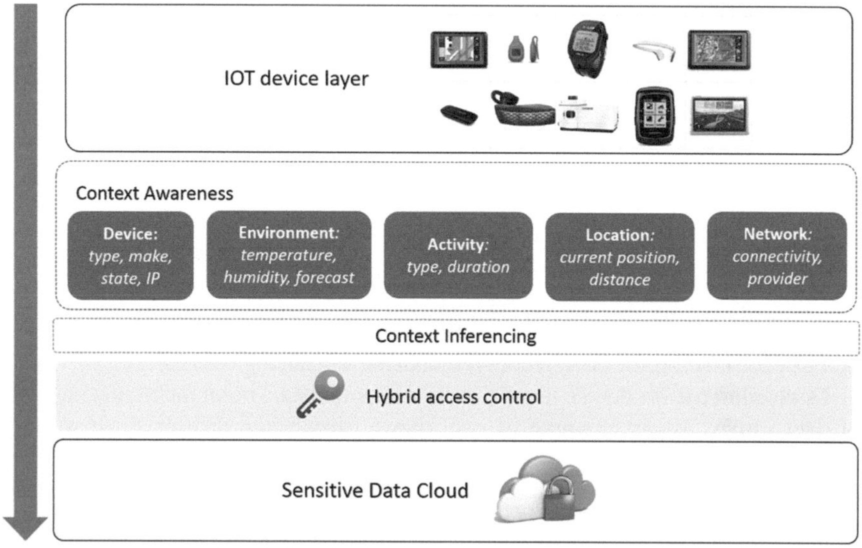


**Fig. 11.3** Context-based access control in IoT

challenge. Permissions on conditional basis using context can be coupled with machine learning techniques like behavior tracking, usage patterns, or simply system dynamics. These techniques make an intelligent computing system more adaptive and secure. For mobile IoT devices or pervasive computing systems, context is the key to dynamism and thus a fluent access control for a variety of devices, users, and data.

### *11.4.2 User Identity Masking for Analytics or Research Purposes*

With connected networks growing interstellar in recent times and consumer data being available and accessed ubiquitously, setting up data privacy and access regulations at granular level for each IoT device or user is indeed a challenge. In addition, to known user/device access, third parties could request access to consumer data for research and analytic purpose. For instance, a recommendation system active on Facebook home page uses information from users' browser or device cookies about one's purchase or browsing history, to provide suggestions for advertisements to be displayed there. The data may be used to evaluate market trends and analyze user activity, auditing, personalized recommendations, tracking, or research. Browser level or device-based privacy in such cases can either deny or permit third parties from accessing user cookies or browsing data, but is unable to keep a watch on how authorized data is being processed or used, thus raising an alarm for possible misuse or security hazard.

Sensitive data such as user stats, location, activity and behavior, device, and network information are susceptible to misuse while being accessed by third parties. Accessed data may be subjected to simple/massive computations or processing depending upon the purpose of usage. Hence, a flexible consumer data retrieval mechanism that is secure and equally useful for analytics or research is vital. Camouflaging sensitive aspects of the requested consumer data, while supplying to a third party, can serve the purpose. Chief implication of sensitive data (personal, demographic, geographic, activity, health/medical) leakage is a revelation of user identity in open space. Similarly, exposing device or network information can be misused for device/network hacking or causing damage.

Unraveling user or device identity from a sensitive data point makes it a mere set of data values. As an example, if one knows (in a given dataset about reading interests of users) that 60 % of them prefer travel journals, it would not be as revealing as if when one says that John and Sana prefer reading romance, whereas Bob, Sonia, and Ed like travel journals. Plus a third-party application which, say, is trying to analyze reading preferences of kindle users would just be interested in usage numbers rather than individual device information. Same could be applied to more sensitive data like health and medical, leakage of which can also lead to legal implications.

IoT devices such as health monitors, smart watch, and mobile phones are closely connected to user demographics and capture their sensor data. When user, device, or network data is accessed by third-party applications for analysis, the data could be masked in such a way that user or device from whom the data has been collected must not be traced or reengineered.

Data masking camouflages sensitive data with information that looks structurally similar to original data but is logically different. Data-masking mechanism is used for concealing personal details enclosed in a data set. This gives the flexibility of using the data for analytics or research without violating user privacy. Masked data gives an identical look and feel as its unmasked counterpart. Hence, data is present but hidden. Figure 11.4 illustrates a data set before and after masking process applied to each of its column using appropriate techniques.

Identity protection is a prime concern when data is accessed by a third party. Data masking is adopted to facilitate secure data access without revealing the true identity of the data owner. The modification of the existing data is done in such a way that the masking removes all identifiable distinguishing characteristics yet the data still remains usable. Data masking prevents sensitive data from malicious or accidental exposures and also abide to data privacy and identity protection laws. A number of data-masking routines are available in literature [17]. Substitution, shuffling, number and date variance, null out/truncating, and hashing are most widely used data-masking techniques.

Substitution randomly replaces contents of a column of data with information that looks similar but is completely nonrelevant to real data, for instance, replacing surnames for a list of customers to be sanitized and replaced using values from a

| user.phone | user.id | user.name | user.email | weight | height | age |
|---|---|---|---|---|---|---|
| 06-54596481 | 1 | Alexis Mckinney | 1391464242296@gmail.com | 0 | 0 | 0 |
| 06-22112168 | 2 | Roman□ Williamson | 1391464242296@gmail.com | | 0 | 0 |
| 06-31491383 | 3 | Samantha Ortiz | 1391464242296@gmail.com | 0 | 0 | 18 |
| 06-74037961 | 4 | Brittany Phelps | 1391464242296@gmail.com | 54 | 174 | 19 |
| 06-83791334 | 5 | Brian Howard | 1391464242296@gmail.com | 70 | 174 | 22 |
| 06-12473983 | 6 | Perry Tucker | 1391464242296@gmail.com | 66 | 182 | 21 |
| 06-21110953 | 7 | Randall Ingram | 1391464242296@gmail.com | 0 | 0 | 0 |
| 06-95864805 | 8 | Ellis Andrews | 1391464242296@gmail.com | 70 | 178 | 20 |
| 06-66895955 | 9 | Barry Stephens | 1391464242296@gmail.com | 75 | 1 | 18 |
| 06-43741625 | 10 | Eva Mcguire | 1391464242296@gmail.com | 52 | 163 | 21 |
| 06-85877159 | 11 | Angel Garrett | 1391464242296@gmail.com | 0 | 0 | 18 |
| 06-17940993 | 12 | Lori Mont | ail.com | 72 | 188 | 19 |
| 06-50624684 | 13 | Jody Laws | ail.com | 65 | 185 | 19 |

Data Masking

| user.phone | user.id | user.name | user.email | weight | height | age |
|---|---|---|---|---|---|---|
| 06-*****481 | 202 | Kate | Kate@hotmail.com | 0 | 0 | 0-10 |
| 06-*****168 | 461 | Dave | Dave@gmail.com | 0 | 0 | 0-10 |
| 06-*****383 | 1234 | Adam | Adam@hotmail.com | .0 | 0 | 10-20 |
| 06-*****961 | 1184 | Evan | Evan@yahoo.com | 54 | 174 | 10-20 |
| 06-*****334 | 305 | Adam | Adam@gmail.com | 70 | 174 | 20-30 |
| 06-*****983 | 1152 | Dave | Dave@yahoo.com | 66 | 182 | 20-30 |
| 06-*****953 | 1149 | Evan | Evan@yahoo.com | 0 | 0 | 0-10 |
| 06-*****805 | 51 | Dianna | Dianna@infosys.com | 70 | 178 | 20-30 |
| 06-*****955 | 1019 | Frank | Frank@infosys.com | 75 | 1 | 10-20 |
| 06-*****625 | 726 | Evan | Evan@hotmail.com | 52 | 1.63 | 20-30 |
| 06-*****159 | 164 | Adam | Adam@gmail.com | 0 | 0 | 10-20 |
| 06-*****993 | 433 | Bob | Bob@infosys.com | 72 | 188 | 10-20 |
| 06-*****684 | 1145 | Eve | Eve@infosys.com | 65 | 185 | 10-20 |
| 06-*****618 | 409 | Frank | Frank@infosys.com | 65 | 178 | 10-20 |
| 06-*****784 | 222 | Evan | Evan@infosys.com | 80 | 185 | 10-20 |
| 06-*****604 | 1268 | Betty | Betty@gmail.com | 47 | 170 | 20-30 |
| 06-*****595 | 749 | Betty | Betty@infosys.com | 76 | 180 | 20-30 |
| 06-*****248 | 29 | Dave | Dave@hotmail.com | 85 | 185 | 20-30 |
| 06-*****664 | 394 | Dave | Dave@gmail.com | 75 | 175 | 20-30 |
| 06-*****484 | 834 | Betty | Betty@infosys.com | 90 | 189 | 20-30 |

**Fig. 11.4** Data masking on sample user data

random list of common surnames. Shuffling randomly moves the data in a column between rows until each data no longer holds any reasonable correlation with remaining rows. Numerical or date values using number variance technique are modified by a random percentage of its real value. Some values could be higher or some other could be lower, but no values are too far from original range. This technique is used to mask data fields like salary or birth dates. Null out/truncating simply deletes all data values for a given data set and replaces it with null values. Selective truncating is also used for masking values like credit card numbers, e.g., 4346 6454 0020 5379 is masked as 4346 xxxx xxxx 5379. Hashing substitutes an original data value with its hash value. Such values are highly difficult to decipher. Md5 hashing is most commonly used for masking password values.

Password hashing is the most common application of data masking. Password values are converted to md5 hash when collected from the user or device while registration or during a login attempt. While authenticating the user or device, the login function compares the available md5 value with the collected md5 hash password to permit/deny access to requested resource. The password values are never handled (transported, stored, or processed) in their actual form. This prevents possible security threat when a user or device's login information is revealed. The stakes are higher in case of banking and medical domains.

To understand how data masking would work in a typical IoT ecosystem, consider accident monitoring systems employed at various city junctions, which capture any mishaps happening at that location in terms of vehicle information, people involved (their id's or facial data), location, and time. These monitoring systems send the captured data to a central repository along with the system information. Suppose this data is being accessed by a third-party organization for assessing mishap index at a certain location over a period of time, to aide research for accident prevention or analyze deployment of emergency services in that location. For either case, only information about the mishap excluding user, monitoring system, or vehicle identity is required. These identities can be comfortably masked or even skipped while giving access to the third party for analysis. The data access system should thus be intelligent enough to anonymize the requested data in such a way that the involved identities must not be reengineered.

Choice of the masking technique to be applied to a given data set largely depends upon the intended usage or application. A dynamic data-masking engine shown in Fig. 11.5 decides the masking technique applicable to a given data access request. For usage purpose like testing, no specific piece of data should be skipped. User or device identity can be preserved using appropriate masking techniques. Post-masking the authentic look and feel of the data should be maintained. For example,

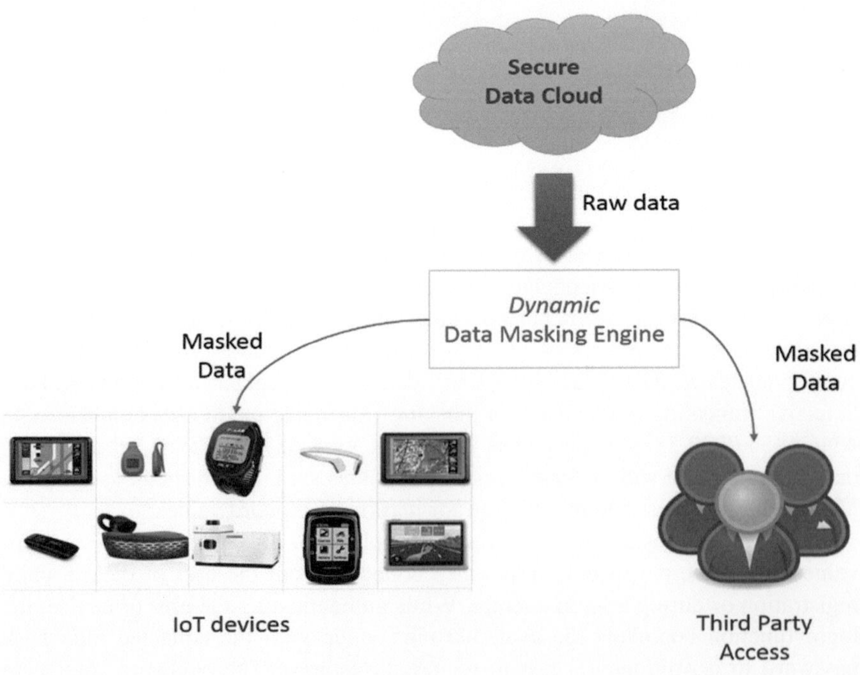


**Fig. 11.5** Dynamic masking for third-party access

while supplying information for testing the working of a chip-based credit card to a third party, sensitive information like credit card number, chip id, or display name could be substituted by some random values or numeric values be disguised by crossing out selective characters like 4562 xxxx xxxx 916x. The masked data comfortably disguises the user and chip identity without compromising the intended testing process. For any analysis or research purpose where substituted or null data values are not useful, techniques like data variance would be more appropriate where aggregate functions like average or mean do not differ if calculated with original values. Sensitive information like illness or workout stats, for which a common masking technique would not be applicable, user or device identity must be decoupled from it.

While applying masking to a data set, maintaining consistency in the data set as a whole is quite difficult to achieve as issues like synchronization, where-clause skips, sparse data, or mathematical operations inconsistency could occur. Hence, data masking though easy to implement but selecting the right technique is quite challenging. A right blend of IoT data with anonymization and other masking techniques is beneficial for securing sensitive sensor data without compromising on harnessing benefits of the data inference mechanisms like analytics or research.

### *11.4.3 Authorization Using OAuth in IoT*

Volumes of sensitive consumer data are stored, transported, and processed in IoT networks. With smart devices sensing, processing, and inferring data have led to minimal user intervention. However, it is quite essential for consumers to have a centralized control management for his/her sensitive data in Web space so that a device, application, or other user requesting access to a secure resource such as sensitive data have a seamless user experience, and no compromise is made to security and privacy of the protected resource. Hence, the use of OAuth 2.0 profiles such as OpenID connect and UMA [18] is recommended.

A new OAuth 2.0 authorization grant for the interaction between constrained clients and resource servers to obtain access tokens to access protected resources in IoT is proposed by Tschofenig [19]. It does so by leveraging prior work on OAuth 2.0, CoAP (Constrained Application Protocol), and DTLS (Datagram Transport Layer Security) protocols.

In case of the Internet, OAuth is an established security protocol for granting *delegated access* to third-party applications on behalf of the resource owner. Access tokens contain the level of granted access to the requester. Authorizing party or authorization server defines the access token including access permissions defined by the resource owner. In the IoT, OAuth is recommended to be implemented at device level. IoT devices and computing systems communicate with each other and send/receive sensitive sensor data. Context-based access control enables setting up access permissions based on contextual information in terms of environment,

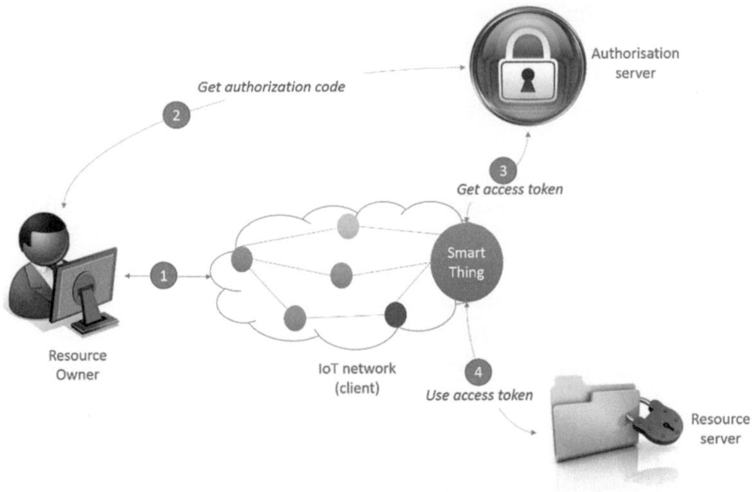


**Fig. 11.6** OAuth in IoT

network, user, and device. Context brings dynamism to a privacy and access control mechanism, whereas using OAuth access tokens baits granularity.

OAuth facilitates fine-grained access control for a third-party access request, where resource owner and authorizing authority are separate entities. Similarly, an IoT device holding a user's sensor data could contain access permissions defined by the user himself. An IoT device or third-party application attempting to access consumer data from another IoT device could obtain an access token from the device/application that owns the data. An access token will thus enable subsequent seamless communication between the paired devices. Figure 11.6 shows an indicative access control flow in an IoT ecosystem using OAuth.

To illustrate how OAuth could work for IoT networks, consider a Bluetooth heart rate monitor paired with a mobile device when it registers itself with a mobile app for workout activities. Heart rate monitor (HRM) authorizes the mobile app to access heart rate readings and corresponding timestamp as and when required. Once authenticated, the mobile app receives an access token from the application managing heart rate monitor device containing access permissions for accessing sensor readings. HRM device may choose to define a fine-grained access level for mobile app. When a workout starts, the mobile app initiates connection with heart rate monitor device using the received access token every time without having to go through authentication process all over again. The access token contains authentication details and also permitted access level for the mobile app. Hence a seamless but controlled pairing and data access is initiated between heart rate monitor and mobile device, providing access to only heart rate readings and timestamp.

A fine-grained access control enables secure access in a more controlled environment. Resource owner has a cohesive hold over data privacy while defining access permissions to more granular level. To understand fine-grained access control, consider a general example. While sending out an email to another user, the owner authorizes the user to read/forward/delete/copy the email sent. Microsoft Outlook offers an option to set up access permissions while sending an email. Owner can restrict forward or copy operations for the user receiving the email. This is the level of granularity available in email authorization. This feature lets an email user to define access/usage permissions in a more refined manner. Authorization server or authorizing party in OAuth offers similar functionality while defining access levels for requested resource on behalf of resource owner. In the OAuth context, for given example, email is the resource, and sending the email is the resource owner, whereas outlook is the authorizing party.

In addition to defining a standard for authorization across varied entities, OAuth saves on infrastructure cost for authentication and user and device management. Hence, there is less data to store. Access tokens are easier to manage than authentication information saving in terms of effort and cost. Device pairing could be done on the fly. Thus, users have more control over their data, device, and usage.

Consent-based access tokens decouple user-centric permissions from IoT devices. Consider a hotel room access card provided to a guest user upon check-in. The access card is activated at hotel reception with access to various devices or facilities in accordance to the guest plan. The access card can be used by any individual possessing it. The access permissions laden on the card can be controlled/modified using a centralized controller. If lost, another functionally identical card can be issued to the guest.

One of the major challenges while implementing OAuth for authorization services in IoT is securing transport layer where sensitive information could be compromised. Especially when devices or services are communicating with each other based on access permissions, data in transit could be attacked and thus must be protected. Devices should choose HTTPS over HTTP for communicating over Internet. Transport Layer Security mechanisms like TLS or VPN should be preferred for ensuring confidentiality of requests. Usage of trust certificates may be employed to mitigate possibilities of attack to authorizing servers and assured device pairing. For a better security mechanism, resource security and access management should be centralized. Activity or event logs need to be monitored regularly at both server and client sides to avoid any phishing vectors. Research by Lodderstedt [20] contains detailed account on possible threats and security considerations while using OAuth. A careful consideration of possible threats and appropriate measures could really help IoT enthusiasts to leverage the benefits of OAuth to the maximum.

### *11.4.4 Device-Based Certificates*

Communication patterns in IoT are immensely diverse as compared to standard patterns in a World Wide Web application. Embedded devices like camcorder, smart-grid devices, medical equipment, and industrial or home automation sensors may only off-load sensor data to cloud server, trigger other devices/applications, or request/receive data from other devices or server. With the presence of varied devices in IoT space, securing the connections between servers, machines, and devices is a challenging task. For instance, while devices communicate with each other or cloud services, authenticating the identity of devices mitigates the possibility of fraudulent activities. Device-based authentication shall be little useful in securing such device communications and help prevent rogue devices, employed by unauthorized users from accessing sensitive data. They provide better transport security and hence leverage benefits afforded by digital applications or embedded devices, while consistently safeguarding integrity and trust.

For end-to-end security mechanism in communication between two IoT nodes, certificate-based authentication is recommended to be implemented as well as managed at device level unlike Web. With more variety of sensor devices joining the IoT clan like home automation system, health tracking, and weather monitoring systems, it is quite difficult to establish a standardized communication protocol. Thus, communication privacy needs to be instigated on smarts devices while in production.

For mobile devices like smartphones, tablets, printers, and Wi-Fi hotspots, public key infrastructure (PKI)-based solutions have been most commonly used to aide secure information exchange. PKI is relied to offer security to a broad range of digital applications on World Wide Web. Specifically suited for distributed hardware devices to provide identity authentication, PKI platforms are based on a trusted certification authority (CA). CA issues, renews, revokes, and manages digital certificates used for valid identification. PKI-based digital certificates are embedded onto devices during assembly which communicates with a service provider to authenticate access to a service. Device-based certificate provider, DigiCert [21], provides Internet security products and services to over 80,000 customers in more than 180 countries, whereas Symantec PKI-based digital certificates [22] provide security to over 200 million devices worldwide.

A standardized hardware security model for authentication and transport security would bait an IoT ecosystem appropriately. These modules act as trust anchors to protect cryptographic infrastructure by securely managing, processing, and storing cryptographic keys inside a hardened, tamper-resistant embedded device. For one-to-one communication between devices, an embedded infrastructure would take care of crypto life cycle right from generation, distribution, rotation, storage, termination, and archival—in highly secure appliance. Crypto infrastructure could attach to network in a virtual/cloud environment.

Consider health monitor devices that record and assess temperature, heart rate, fatigue level, and step count. These individual devices regularly send recorded and processed sensor data to cloud for storage and available to health professionals for analysis and monitoring purpose. Third-party applications or health professionals can access data from cloud using another device or computing system. A device-based certificate mechanism is required to aide secure data transfer from device-device and device-cloud or vice versa. Fatigue analyzing devices and step counters, for example, access data from other devices like heart rate monitor for calculating sensor values. Embedded crypto infrastructure on these devices establishes trust relationship with paired devices for secure data exchange.

For the purpose of device data off-loading to cloud or another device, secure transport channel may sound completely reliable. However, for sensitive IoT data where data owner identity is equally significant to define usage or management of data, a mechanism for legitimating user identity to ensure incoming data is from reliable or intended source needs to be in place [21], for example, a medical hardware equipped with sensors that records and sends patient's vital data to hospital. The hospital needs to have a reliable account of patient's history, so that the physician can make decisions based on the data. For serving the purpose, sensor device digitally signs the data using the key assigned to it. While device sends the digitally signed message to cloud, the cloud checks the authenticity of the data by verifying the digital signature.

Similarly, when a device accesses data from the cloud using secure transport, only authorized devices be permitted, but it doesn't guarantee whether the user or application that tries to access the acquired data in turn is legitimate or not. Intruders or burglars can thus gain access to sensitive data in such case, which is quite dangerous. Therefore, an end-to-end security mechanism right from sensing to client access must be in place to provide a solution for security issues specific to IoT communication patterns. Organizations are constantly eyeing for authentication techniques to handle how devices communicate and access sensitive information and hence find digital certificates as the perfect answer.

## 11.5 Conclusion

IoT networks are not just about applications but also about disparate smart devices and assorted computing systems brought together in common shared space to make life easier. Given the growth of smart devices and the pace of innovation, the potential damage that could be triggered by the lack of proper security will continue to increase. However, the security and privacy needs in an IoT network are completely diverse and more challenging in nature. Hence, the general expectation is an entirely new, innovative security solution that is proven successful and amendable in the light of challenges and the constraints of connected devices, in other words, a uniquely tailored solution to IoT. Traditional security mechanisms require key features like dynamism, flexibility, and granularity to become adaptive to heterogeneous IoT networks. Unfortunately, there is no single solution that can adequately and comprehensively counter from every potential threat. Inclusion of contextual information while handling data in an IoT network makes the application more dynamic and scalable. Selective masking and permissions through access tokens improve flexibility and granularity. It also enhances user intervention in setting privacy and security for their own data. By applying these multilayered approaches in the IoT world, organizations can breeze through the technical challenges of deploying and managing a secure IoT ecosystem.

## 11.6 Future Direction

As the IoT is a relatively new field, security consequences are rising steeply. Unsecured smart devices curtail the power and growth of the Internet of Things. The varied constraints of networked devices require customized security solutions. This chapter throws some light on research directions in the IoT security and privacy field but still open issues like communication standards and protocols for heterogeneous environment exist. Trustworthiness among devices and users and policy compliance are still missing in implementation. With the traditional security solutions, there is a need for built-in security in the devices themselves. Device manufacturers need to consider the threats associated with data security in connected devices in the design phase. To protect identity, certificates could be embedded onto devices during assembly itself. A mindful design and a planned engineering of IoT devices would lay foundation for comprehensively secure IoT systems. In the future, security is of paramount concern when Internet of Things blends the virtual and physical worlds together at the same point.

## References

1. Evans D (2011) The internet of things: how the next evolution of the internet is changing everything, CISCO white paper-1, Apr 2011, https://www.cisco.com/web/about/ac79/docs/innov/IoT_IBSG_0411FINAL.pdf
2. F. T. Commission (2013) Internet of things—privacy and security in a connected world., workshop held on 19 Nov 2013
3. Yu S et al (2010) Achieving secure, scalable, and fine-grained data access control in cloud computing. IEEE INFOCOM'10 proceedings, 14–19 Mar 2010, pp 1–9
4. Blom R et al (1978) Encryption methods in data networks. Ericsson Technics 34:71
5. Freier A et al (1996) Secure socket layer 3.0. IETF Internet Draft, Nov 1996, pp 481–486
6. Iqbal A (2013) Security threats in integrated circuits. MIT SDM'11, 22 Oct 2013, http://sdm-blog.mit.edu/2013_10_01_archive.html. Accessed 20 May 2015
7. Hamilton BA (2015) Tech trends 2016. http://www.boozallen.com/insights/ 2015/ 12/ tech-trends-2016. Accessed July 2015
8. Jun B (2014) Make way for the internet of things. RSA conference '14, San Francisco, 24–28 Feb 2014. http://www.rsaconference.com/writable/presentations/file_upload/tech-r02-internet-of-things-v2.pdf
9. Suo H et al (2012) Security in the internet of things: a review. In: International conference on computer science and electronics engineering (ICCSEE '12), vol. 3, pp 648–651 IEEE, 23 Mar 2012
10. CISCO Security Systems, Securing the Internet of Things: a proposed network, http://www.cisco.com/web/about/security/intelligence/iot_framework.html. Accessed 15 June 2015

11. FTC Staff report (2015) Internet of Things. 27 Jan 2015. https://www.ftc.gov/system/files/documents/reports/federal-trade-commission-staff-report-november-2013-workshop-entitled-internet-things-privacy/150127iotrpt.pdf
12. Gang G et al (2011) Internet of things security analysis. IEEE International Conference on Internet Technology and Applications (iTAP '11) pp.1–4, 16–18 Aug 2011
13. Jha A, Sunil MC (2014) Security considerations for internet of things. Whitepaper, L&T Technology Services, 2014. http://www.lnttechservices.com/media/30090/whitepaper_security-considerations-for-internet-of-things.pdf
14. Riahi A et al (2013) A systemic approach for IoT security. IEEE International Conference on Distributed Computing in Sensor Systems (DCOSS '13). Boston pp. 351–355, 20 May 2013
15. Heer T et al (2011) Security challenges in the IP-based internet of things. Wirel Pers Commun 61:527–542
16. Wind River Systems (2015) Security in the internet of things. Whitepaper, 2015, http://www.windriver.com/whitepapers/security-in-the-internet-of-things/wr_security-in-the-internet-of-things.pdf. Accessed 29 July 2015
17. Roebuck K (2012) Data masking: high-impact strategies – what you need to know: definitions, adoptions, impact, benefits, maturity, vendors. Emereo Publishing, Aspley
18. Schwartz M (2014) OAuth2 for IoT security: why openID connect and UMA are the key, open internet consortium, 5 Nov 2014, http://www.slideshare.net/gluu/oic-security-wg-slides-on-uma-connect
19. Tschofenig H (2014) The OAuth 2.0 internet of things client credentials grant. ARM Limited, 4 July 2014. https://tools.ietf.org/pdf/draft-tschofenig-ace-oauth-iot-00.pdf
20. Lodderstedt T (2012) OAuth 2.0 threat model and security considerations, OAuth working Group, 6 Oct 2012, https://tools.ietf.org/pdf/rfc6819.pdf
21. Sabin J (2014) Authentication is the answer to data security in the internet of things, Digicert, 29 July 2014, https://www.digicert.com/news/2014-07-29-internet-of-things.htm. Accessed 25 July 2015
22. Symantec Corporation (2012), Symantec Device Certificate Service, http://www.symantec.com/content /en /us /enterprise /fact_sheets /b-device_certificate_service_DS_21195853.en-us.pdf?bcsi_scan_686bee1cf3c8ee0f=0 & bcsi_scan_filename=b-device_certificate_service_DS_21195853.en-us.pdf. Accessed 13 July 2015

# Chapter 12
# Access Control and Authentication in the Internet of Things Environment

**Aditya Kaushal Ranjan and Gaurav Somani**

## 12.1 Introduction

The scientific and business communities have realized the importance of IoT (Internet of Things) and its emergence in enhancing our day-to-day lifestyle. According to Gartner's forecast, there will be 20 billion devices connected to the IoT by 2020 [1]. Vast numbers of diverse devices from different vendors have already been connected towards achieving this target. The capabilities of these devices range from tiny measuring sensors to RFID mechanisms to traditional processing devices such as PCs and notebooks. The IoT application areas also vary from homes to hospitals, supply chain systems to industry automation, farming to electric grids, etc. It is important to address the concern of heterogeneity, scalability, energy efficiency (due to power and cost constraints of devices), integration and mining of enormous generated data (widely termed as Big Data), device configuration management, and most importantly the security (both at the logical level and physical level) and privacy.

Security of data and devices is one of the most significant concerns in the IoT. For example, security breaches and unwanted alterations in smart healthcare systems and faulty/irregular readings of health parameters of the patient could lead to unwanted or even fatal treatment. The whole credibility and deployability of the IoT solely depend on security aspects only. Authentication and access control are the first steps towards any security measures. With whom and up to what extent, one can access/communicate the devices in IoT scenario, are important aspects of security, especially when diverse devices with different capability have to perform collaborative tasks. The aim of this chapter is to introduce the reader with access

A.K. Ranjan (✉) • G. Somani
Department of Computer Science and Engineering, Central University of Rajasthan, Ajmer, India
e-mail: aditya.k.ranjan@ieee.org; gaurav@curaj.ac.in



Z. Mahmood (ed.), *Connectivity Frameworks for Smart Devices*,
Computer Communications and Networks, DOI 10.1007/978-3-319-33124-9_12

control granularities to abstract the various aspects, which are applicable to distributed environments. It is indeed important to differentiate the classical mobile computing literature from the modern IoT scenario. We will detail its present state of the art and future research direction in this chapter.

This chapter discusses the different architecture of IoT in Sect. 12.2, followed by Sect. 12.3 which describes the role of access control in connectivity of devices in both inter- and intra-domain. It is important to know how IoT paradigm is different from traditional ubiquitous computing. Therefore, Sect. 12.4 is devoted to it. Then we explore different issues and the current state of the art in Sect. 12.5. Section 12.6 outlines the various IoT aspects from distributed computing perspective. Access control and authentication in IoT have enormous scope for future research directions that are given in Sect. 12.7. We describe the guidelines for effective solutions in Sect. 12.8. The conclusions are presented in Sect. 12.9.

## 12.2 IoT Architecture from Security Perspective

For the sake of completeness, we would look at an abstract generic architecture for IoT. It would provide the reader a comprehensive as well as an abstract understanding between various components. In early days of IoT, numerous architectures have been proposed by the researchers and industry practitioners according to their specific needs. However, different federal agencies have also taken interest in this venture and presented numerous architecture such as IoT-A [2, 3, 6], SENSEI [5], and ETSI M2M [2, 4]. Additionally, a few allied architectures are also available, e.g., JCA-IoT [6], OGC [7], and IETF architectures. In this chapter, we attempt to provide an overview of some of these architectures for understanding the conceptual and actual elements. Readers are advised to refer to [2] for more details.

### *12.2.1 "IoT-A" Reference Architecture*

IoT-A [2, 3, 6], the European Lighthouse Integrated Project, has addressed the Internet-of-Things Architecture for 3 years (2010–2013) and created an architectural reference model together with the definition of an initial set of essential building blocks. Collectively, these blocks are envisioned as foundations for developing the emerging IoT products.

For better understanding, this architecture can be divided into two parts: the first being a reference model and the second being the reference architecture, as briefly discussed below:

- The reference model consists of IoT domain model, functional model, and communication model. For the IoT domain model, three types of devices are necessary: sensors, actuator, and tags. UML is used to describe the domain

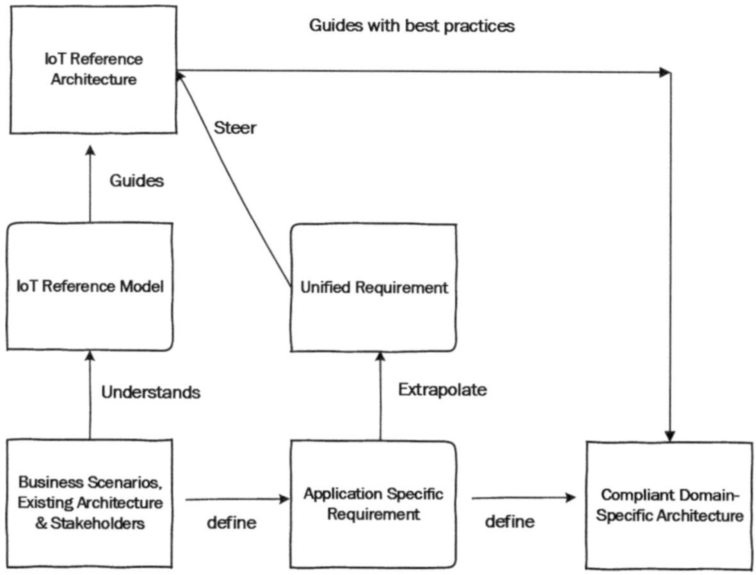


**Fig. 12.1** IoT-reference model and IoT-reference architecture dependency and model influences

model. Services are classified into three types: resource-level services, virtual entity services, and integrated services. In functional model mainly functional groups are divided, which consist of all functionalities of the respective entities. Communication model includes identification of endpoint interactions, traffic patterns, etc.

- Reference architecture is the beginning of established concrete architecture and actual systems. For addressing the concerns of concrete architecture, it could be divided into three parts: functional view, information view, and deployment/operational view. Figure 12.1 shows the influence factors and dependency of the IoT-A. IoT-reference model guides IoT-reference architecture. All business scenarios, stakeholder's interests, and previous architecture have been addressed in IoT-reference model only. These factors also govern application-specific requirement; that is also useful to derive domain-specific architectures and unified requirement that is finally useful to guide IoT-reference architecture.

### 12.2.2 ETSI M2M Architecture

The European Telecommunications Standards Institute (ETSI) established a Technical Committee (TC) on machine-to-machine (M2M) topics for producing a set of standards for communication among machines in 2009 [4]. In Fig. 12.2, it can be seen that it is divided into two domains: gateway and device domain and network domain, as follows:

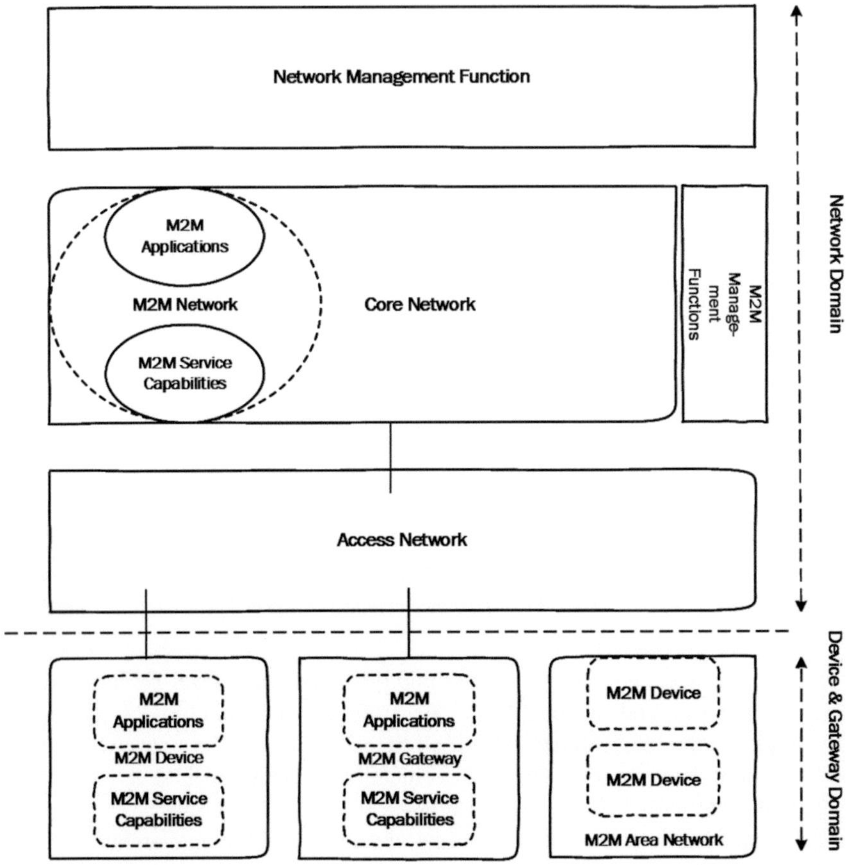


**Fig. 12.2** ETSI M2M high-level architecture

- Generally, gateway and device domain is connected through Bluetooth, IPv6 low-energy LAN, etc., and network domain connectivity is done through a higher-level network that is enabled to provide internet connectivity like GSM, 3G, 4G, 5G, etc. So this high-level architecture consists of both functional and topological view. It is more connection oriented in approach. However, we can also clearly see its topological aspects. Gateway is the main "connecting" entity between network and device domains. The topological view is associated with the physical elements like M2M devices and gateways.
- The network domain consists of access network, Core network, M2M service capabilities, M2M application, network management functions, and M2M management functions. A separate classification of service capabilities and resource management also exists with respect to this architecture [2].

### 12.2.3 SENSEI

The approach of SENSEI was to develop architectural and technological building block to enable integration of real world to the future Internet. The architecture includes real-world service interface plus wireless sensor and actuator network on the Internet at a global level. It is based on the separation of sensing actuating from real-world devices. The assumption for addressing mechanism is IP based [2, 5]. In Fig. 12.3, we note that it is divided into many domains connected through several interfaces, e.g., service interface, network support interface, and PnP interface. It is much more function oriented in its approach.

### 12.2.4 Open Geospatial Consortium Architecture

The Open Geospatial Consortium (OGC 2013) is an international industry consortium of a few hundred companies, government agencies, and universities that develop publicly available standards [7]. These standards provide geographical information support to the Web, wireless, and location-based services.

OGC developed many standards in the due course of time, which includes sensor Web enablement model (OGC SWE) that develops standards for sensor system models like Sense ML, sensor information model, and sensor services that follow

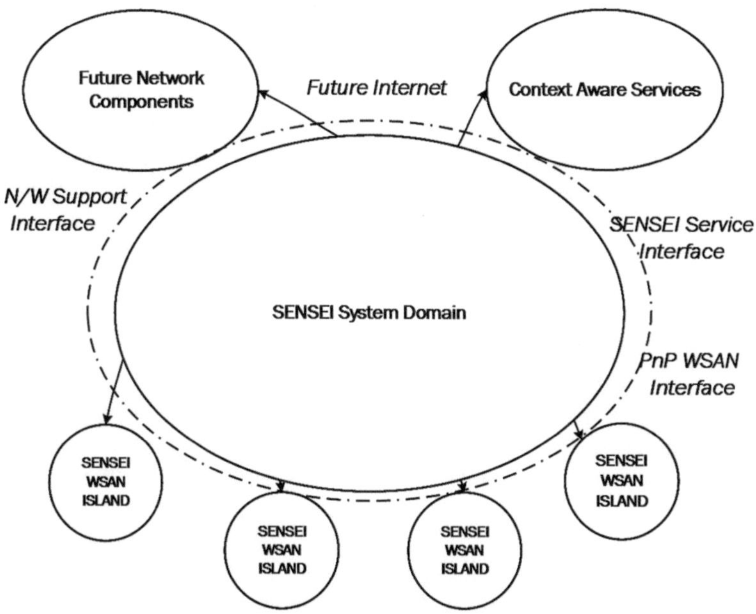


**Fig. 12.3** SENSEI architecture

service-oriented architecture. OGC SWE is more information centric than communication centric, similar to ETSI M2M [2].

### *12.2.5 Comparison Between Different IoT Architectures*

IoT-A describes the essential building blocks and identifies design requirements. It also provides guidelines to build architecture for a specific domain and is generic in nature. However, its emphasis is much less on topological part of the architecture. It is first of its kind for integrating all issues of IoT together. However, its generic nature is also a drawback to some extent, when there is a need to focus on a specific problem of certain IoT domain.

ETSI M2M is too specific in nature. It deals with a topological approach of IoT. It has provided a higher-level architecture, which addresses most connectivity needs of M2M paradigms. It lacks generality and cannot address building blocks and design requirements like IoT-A.

SENSEI and OGC are subsidiary architectures that concentrate on sensor issues that are helpful to realize IoT. It helps to understand primary architecture like ETSI M2M, IoT-A, etc. but lacks generality and broadness aspects of IoT architecture.

## 12.3 Access Control in Connectivity of Devices

To understand the significance of access control in connectivity of the device in the IoT scenario, let us take an example of a smart city. The building elements/domains behind "smart" city are smart home, smart sewerages, smart vehicle networks, smart water supply, smart hospital, smart traffic management, smart grids, electricity supply, etc. For better understanding, the connectivity of devices can be seen in two domains: intra-domain connectivity and inter-domain connectivity.

### *12.3.1 Intra-domain Connectivity*

In this section, we discuss connectivity issues in intra-domain communications while considering the buildings of the smart city. Basically, intra-domain connectivity can be done in several ways. For centralized system architecture, individual nodes could establish mutual trust or with the help of a gateway. Authentication and access control are the foremost requirements of trust establishment. Mutual authentication and application-level access control can be easily configured in this scenario. Several states of the art techniques are there for mutual authentication in IoT scenario [53]. For access control at the application level, we have given the present situation as shown in Table 12.1. However, for distributed architecture, the scenario

**Table 12.1** Present state of the art in layerwise approach

| | |
|---|---|
| Attribute and role-based access control, capability-based access control, authentication based on OAuth, admittance control algorithm, Kerberos and RADIUS-based access control, access Control in Contiki OS, user identity-based mechanism, aggregated proof-based hierarchical authentication mechanism, lightweight authentication based on IoT-A, zero-knowledge proof-based solutions, group authentication based on identity-based encryption | Application layer |
| Device identity-based mechanism, DTLS-based mechanism, OAuth based, delegated authentication, aggregated proof-based hierarchical authentication mechanism, conditional privacy preserving with access linkability with roaming service, authentication based on LISP, EAP-TLS-based authentication based, ECC-based authentication solutions, ECC-based authentication for M2M systems | Transportation layer |
| EAC framework for authentication, all authentication scheme of RFIDs, two-phase authentication for WSNs | Perception layer |

becomes slightly different as every device is capable of handling and processing the data itself through the vision of edge intelligence and collaboration. In that case, P2P-based distributed architecture [53] is helpful in that it brings all P2P-based mechanisms of authentication and access control into the picture. The delegation-based decision-making authority for decentralized-based architecture is also a possibility; as in this case, centralized access control mechanism will also be applied. However, in distributed architecture, heterogeneity will become a major issue. Scalability of such mechanism becomes an issue, as access control and authentication mechanism should be capable of handling millions of devices efficiently.

Figure 12.4 shows the abstract view of N to N communication scenario among building blocks/domains of a typical smart city. Bidirectional long arrows show the inter-domain communication between the different constituent domains, though short arrow depicts the intra-domain connectivity. If we evaluate this figure from distributed IoT point of view, then we find that intra-domain connectivity governs with collaborative paradigms and inter-domain connectivity governs with edge intelligence principle generally. That is why the communication takes place between inter-domain controllers, and intra-domain controller/gateway are achieved through P2P-based or delegation-based architecture as stated above. However, this figure can also be seen from the perspective of centralized architecture, where all connectivity is done through gateway/controller only.

## 12.3.2 *Inter-domain Connectivity*

Logically, connectivity issues of inter-domain remain the same as intra-domain issues; however, physically, they will be more diversified in connections. All present mechanisms of access control that is applicable to intra-domain at perception layer require major changes in inter-domain to fit on different kinds of

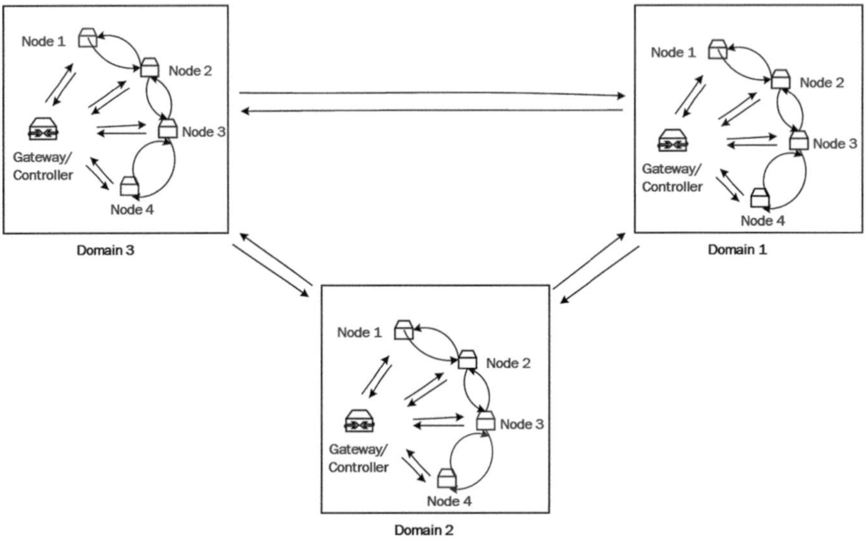


**Fig. 12.4** Abstract view of N to N communication scenario in distributed IoT

networks. In distributed IoT scenario, interaction could be dynamic, i.e., entities might not know/trust each other in advance, that is also one of the key challenges for authentication and access control mechanism in inter-domain communications. We frequently find dynamic N to N scenarios (refer to Fig. 12.4), where data providers are active entities and regularly require feedback from receiving entities [53]. Due to edge intelligence and collaboration principle, any node starts communicating to service provider's nodes directly, which requires that access control and authentication mechanisms must be presented to work at both local and global networks (in intra- and inter-domain).

## 12.4 IoT Security vs Traditional Ubiquitous Security

Ubiquitous computing is also termed as "everywhere, anywhere" computing, referring to embedding the capability of computing to everyday objects [2]. This vision of computing is realized by the sensors to RFID tags to handheld devices to wearable devices. The M2M systems, WSNs, and RFID tag networks are popular paradigms to realize this. However, M2M systems are meant for specific tasks while IoT devices are more generic and diverse in nature. Let us take one instance of body area network (BAN), which observes and computes several health parameters in a ubiquitous way. BANs usually send health readings to nearby hospital servers which process the data to suggest various outcomes to the medical

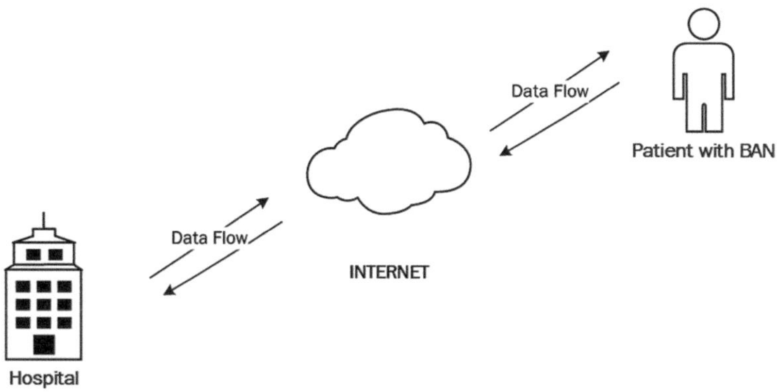


Fig. 12.5 Connectivity scenario of the healthcare IoT

practitioners. This also become part of quick decision-making based on history and machine learning techniques. Consequently, the medical prescription may be suggested by medical practitioners. Taking readings through BAN is a point-specific approach, while communicating with data processing server (hospitals in this case) involves the role of IoT (refer to Fig. 12.5).

Connecting the BAN with hospital and processing the data according to context-based requirements are possible due to Web services. Therefore, security concern applies to multiple layers in the case of IoT. It not only includes the security concern at local level but also the security concern of the Internet, different devices configuration issues, the privacy of generated and computed data, and so on. This makes the concerns more diverse in nature comparable to traditional ubiquitous computing.

In another example, we can take a typical IoT scenario where through a gateway, every device domain and external network domain is connected. Similar security concerns are applicable here also (Fig. 12.6).

Let us now discuss security of IoT in different layers. In all contemporary contributions, security issues can be divided into three layers of IoT, viz., perception/physical, transportation, and application layer [11]. We discuss these issues in the following subsections.

### *12.4.1 Security Issues at Physical/Perception Layer*

Basically, security issues of RFID tags and WSNs come into the picture, such as RFID tag's uniform coding [8], conflict collision, cryptographic algorithms, trust management [9], key management [10], heterogeneous integration and secure routing protocols in WSN, etc. [11]. Privacy protection can be solved by hardware-based schemes [12], password-based schemes, other trade-off-based solutions, etc. For trust management, security protocol, digital signature, etc. are

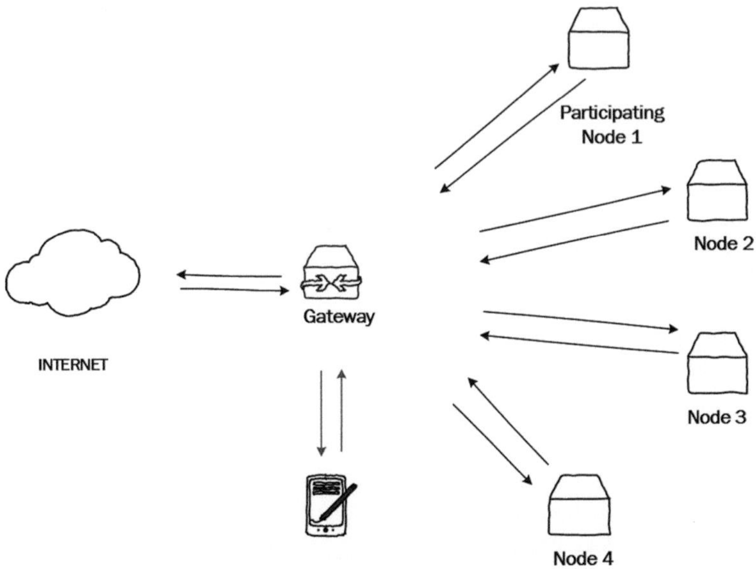


**Fig. 12.6** Typical connectivity of the home IoT scenario

beneficial. Symmetric key cryptography is mostly used in RFIDs due to their confidentiality and low computation cost. Different access control and access information format data processing methods are also integrated through heterogeneous technologies which are the core part of IoT.

### 12.4.2 Security Issues at Transportation Layer

At the transportation layer, phishing attacks, DDoS (distributed Denial of Services) attacks, secure routing issues, data security, information disclosure through creating fake login page or through injecting malicious script on target machine (known as phishing and scripting attack), and network paralysis could happen in various IoT scenarios. For mitigation of all these security issues, attack detection and prevention technologies are used. Access control and network encryption are also helpful for these scenarios [11].

### 12.4.3 Security Issues at Application Layer

At this layer, DDoS attacks, access control problem, service interruption, illegal intervention, etc. are the main issues that can be solved through middleware, attack detection, and prevention technologies. The information development platform can also prove helpful [11]. In the case of security issues of ubiquitous computing, we take M2M paradigms as an example. We present here the layerwise security issues and their solutions [13].

#### 12.4.3.1 Security Issues at Physical Layer

These attacks may be classified into active and passive attacks. Passive attacks involve traffic analysis and eavesdropping of wireless communications, while active attacks are more disruptive and may involve jamming and scrambling [14]. Increasing the power levels and employing techniques like spread spectrum, which have direct sequence spread spectrum (DSSS) or frequency hopping spread spectrum (FHSS), are the techniques useful to defend jamming, eavesdropping, and traffic analysis attacks [15].

#### 12.4.3.2 Security Issues at Medium Access Control Layer

Modification of MAC layer management, identity theft of appliances, data message modification, and Denial of Services attack could happen in this layer. Classic countermeasures of these attacks involve cryptographic mechanisms for encryption and authentication of participating entities. Cryptographic mechanisms are based on the public key and a symmetric key mechanism like ECC, X-509 mechanisms.

#### 12.4.3.3 Security Issues at Network and Adaption Layer

Interoperability between two communication domains is a major issue. Designing of compressed security headers is an important issue. Some issues are key management and management of security association.

#### 12.4.3.4 Security Issues at Transport Layer

Energy-efficient transport layer mechanisms include congestion control and reliability with minimal overhead and retransmissions. Several mechanisms currently exist like reliable message delivery, congestion control, and energy efficiency. The existing mechanisms are Distributed TCP Caching (DTCP) [16], Sensor Transmission Control Protocol (STCP) [17], Adjustable Parallel TCP [18], and Pump Slowly Fetch Quickly (PSFQ) [19].

#### 12.4.3.5 Security Issues at Application Layer

The main technology currently emerging is Constrained Application Protocol (CoAP) [20], which is an alternative to HTTP and is common in traditional computing systems. For security concern, CoAP uses DTLS for secure communications. For sensing application, ECC-based public key cryptography is used by CoAP.

### 12.4.4 Summary

After going through the security issues of IoT and M2M systems (as ubiquitous computing systems) separately, we can conclude that some security issues and its solutions overlap in both the environments. However, some issues are specific to IoT scenarios only like scripting and phishing attacks, etc. (described previously in Sect. 12.4.2). Therefore, IoT security issues are somewhat different from traditional computing environments. It involves some issues of traditional Internet as well ubiquitous computing; therefore, it is an important challenge to address these security issues in constrained device scenario.

## 12.5 Issues of Access Control and Authentication in IoT

The diversity of the devices and networks leads to the aggregation of several services and data from different sources and contexts. Each service and data providers have their own access control policies and authentication methods. Uniform privacy policy languages to express the different types of context, different types of data owner, and different types of request subjects needs to represent high-level aggregating requests and needs to change to the policies [21]. While designing and planning access policies, device resource (computing and storage) needs should be taken into account [22]. It is difficult to design access policies for resource-constrained devices where storage and processing are the main constraints. Location and enforcement points are the main factors, which needs to be considered while designing the efficient access policies. However, few advances have taken place in the area of managing access policies. Traditional methods like ACLs (access control lists), RBAC (role-based access control lists), etc. are there, but still, there is a need to implement some specific approaches which are feasible and consistent to IoT.

In order to see the present state of the art in access control, we classify various contributions in the following categories.

### 12.5.1 Modification/Improvisation of Existing Access Control Methods

Many efforts have been taking place to apply traditional methods of access control to IoT scenarios. Sun et al. [22] have evaluated ABAC (attribute-based access control) and RBAC (role-based access control) and found that RBAC cannot satisfy large-scale dynamic users but ABAC can satisfy dynamic problem; however, working mechanism is difficult. In order to cope with this problem, authors [22] have proposed ARBAC (attribute- and role-based access control) that has an advantage of both schemes. They presented the architecture and have shown the correspondence between attribute expressions and role with definitions of three relationships. They have also done a conflict detection and policy optimization. The advantages of proposed work on managing permissions, viz., modifying, adding, and deleting, are also mentioned. Real-time implementation and empirical data are missing to support the claims.

Another work that comes under this classification is by Mahalle et al. [23]. They have proposed the capability-based access control methods. They have suggested separate data structures with device id and access rights. Therefore, if any subject possesses the capability match with capability stored in the device, then access is granted.

One classical example of access control in IoT is presented in [24]. They used RBAC as a base access control techniques. They used thing's role and application in a particular network as a basis for access control, where extended RBAC has been used and named as context-based access control. Here access has been granted, based on a set of contextual information collected from environments of the system and user.

Fremantle [26] explored the use of OAuth for IoT systems that use MQTT 1.1 protocol. After implementations, they have concluded that both IoT and non-IoT clients can use OAuth tokens. It is also concluded that in IoT client secret security is much harder unlikely all Web application are deployed in a single phase.

Another work presented in [27] has used modified DTLS authentication to control access at the device level (physical/perception layer) where all resources hosted on the resource server are available to any client that has a right to connect.

The abovementioned works are a few recent reports and works on access control methods that use modifications or extensions of existing systems/mechanisms. They succeeded to show that existing mechanisms are also compatible with an IoT scenario with some modifications.

### *12.5.2 New Approaches to Access Control Mechanisms in IoT*

Liu [28] has defined a new admittance control algorithm, where new connection is adapted and a service call is launched in the current community when a user switches their current community. However, this algorithm follows the RBAC approach.

Pereira et al. [29] have combined the concept of Kerberos and RADIUS and implemented the mechanism on CoAP. They have successfully achieved their goals of access control in constrained devices. One more work on access control [30] that implements the access control mechanism in "Contiki OS" ensures that apps only use specified APIs and do not have arbitrary memory access. They proposed a mechanism from which apps can work only on specified memory location. Therefore, they cannot access the details of OS. They have used a third data structure called "permissions" for storing information, regarding access control. They have also introduced new APIs, which has many "get" functions especially for nonuser interactive functions which do not use inter-process communications.

Thuan [31] has proposed a user-centric identity management framework that consists of users, devices, service provider, and identity providers. They have also discussed udevID (universal device identity). Banerjee et al. [32] have proposed channel access control through novel zero-exposure slot allocation in which packet transmission timing is used to detect a collision, also for collision resolution and for scheduling.

### *12.5.3 Present State of the Art and Issues in Authentication*

Identity management is an important requirement for heterogeneity, without which successful realization of IoT is not possible. With this scenario, authentication is the most important aspect of identity management. There is a need to realize authentication in several layers. For privacy protection, password-based schemes are popular through the implementation of hash locks, random hash lock, hash chain, etc. for RFIDs and WSNs at physical layer [13]. Users, devices, and network authentication at application and transportation layers all come under access control. We can see the relevant solutions in Table 12.2.

In the case of authentication, we can see two types of schemes: certificate based and non-certificate based. Certificate-based solutions try to implement existing Internet standards like DTLS, DEX, minimal IKEv2, etc. [33, 34]. Let us see the present state of the art in authentication for IoT scenarios.

Mahalle et al. [23] proposed an authentication scheme based on the Diffie-Hellman algorithm for the secret key generation. The mechanism requires one or more KDC (key distribution center) to generate domain parameters. After this, they proposed a protocol for identity establishment for one-way and two-way authentication.

Liu et al. [24] have proposed authentication mechanism by using simple and secure key establishment method based on ECC. They have used federated identity management through home registration authority. They also proposed a framework for entity authentication, action authentication, and claim authentication and have done a formal analysis of these through CSP approach. They have shown that those mechanisms satisfied many requirements of IoT.

Hummen [33] proposed a delegation-based architecture for the expensive handshake of DTLS for constrained devices. They have presented empirical data for the entire process. The delegation server they presented establishes a connection on

**Table 12.2** Summary of the present state of the art

| Works | Base techniques | Real-time implementation | Security analysis |
|---|---|---|---|
| Sun et al. [22] | ARBAC+RBAC | No | No |
| Mahalle et al. [23] | Capability-based access control | Yes | No |
| Liu et al. [24] and Zhang et al. [25] | RBAC based, context based | No, No | No, No |
| Fremantle et al. [26] | OAuth | Yes | Yes |
| Sitenkov et al. [27] | DTLS based | Yes | Yes |
| Liu et al. [28] | EAC based | No | Yes |
| Pereira et al. [29] | SoA (service-oriented architecture) based | No | Yes |
| Mituca et al. [30] | MDSE (model-driven software engg.) | No | No |
| Thuan et al. [31] | Token based | No | No |
| Banerjee et al. [32] | Zero-exposure slot allocation | Yes | Yes |
| Hummen et al. [33] | DTLS | Yes | No |
| Gerdes et al. [34] | CoAP + DTLS | No | No |
| Ning et al. [35] | Aggregated proof based | No | Yes |
| Hernandez-Ramos et al. [36] | SEAPOL + EAP + RADIUS | Yes | No |
| Lai et al. [37] | Bilinear map + hybrid linear combination encryption | Yes | Yes |
| Jan et al. [38] | Challenge response based | Yes | No |
| Raheem et al. [39] | LISP based | No | Yes |
| Pawlowski et al. [40] | EAP-TEPANOM based | Yes | No |
| Druml et al. [41] | ECC based | Yes | No |
| Schukat et al. [42] | Zero-knowledge proofs | Yes | No |
| Flood et al. [43] | Zero-knowledge proofs | Yes | No |
| Porambage et al. [44] | Implicit certificate based | Yes | No |
| Yao et al. [45] | Nyberg's fast one-way accumulator | No | Yes |
| Kothmayr et al. [46] | DTLS | Yes | No |
| Lee et al. [47] | XOR based | Yes | No |
| Mahalle et al. [48] | TGCA | Yes | Yes |
| Adiga et al. [49] | Identity-based encryption | Yes | No |

behalf of constrained devices. The authors presented empirical data to show DTLS overheads on constrained devices.

Similar work has also been proposed by Gerdes et al. [34] by suggesting the protocols for delegating the client authentication and authorization in constrained devices that are based on symmetric key cryptography. These protocols rely on DTLS for data transfer. They have systematically pointed out the clear cut objectives and defined authorization- and authentication-related tasks.

Ning et al. [35] proposed aggregated proof-based hierarchical authentication scheme based on U2IoT architecture. The main features of the work include the establishment of aggregated proofs for multiple targets to achieve backward and forward anonymous data transmission. However, this mechanism lacks generality and works only for layered networks, although exhaustive proofs have been given for the protocol for a unit and ubiquitous IoT.

The work of Hernandez-Ramos [36] was part of IETF Authentication and Authorization for Constrained Environment (ACE). In their studies, they presented a lightweight version of Extensible Authentication Protocol over LAN (EAPOL) by integrating a standard mechanism for bootstrapping processes like EAP and RADIUS.

Lai et al. [37] used group signature schemes for an anonymous user linking function by presenting a mechanism of conditional preserving authentication with access linkability. It hides the real identity of the user and enables the authorized entity to link all access users' information without knowing the real identity of the user. Jan et al. [38] have proposed a mutual authentication mechanism without any device participation in communication. It facilitates less computation and communication overhead. Raheem et al. [39] have proposed a new authentication and key exchange scheme that is based on a locator/ID separation protocol routing architecture. They verified their scheme through AVISPA tool. They have claimed that there are no security flaws in their scheme.

Pawlowski [40] intermixed IEEE 802.15.4 authentication framework and TEPANOM (Trust extension protocol for authentication of newly deployed objects and sensor through the manufacturer). They showed that there is 42 % reduction in a message exchange and 32 % in transferred data. Druml et al. [41] presented ECC-based authentication scheme that shifted the computational intense part to authentication terminal from constraint device.

Schukat et al. [42] presented an authentication protocol for static M2M networks through zero-knowledge proofs. They have also evaluated several previously proposed zero-knowledge proofs. They claimed that their mechanism is suitable for resource-constrained devices. The work of Flood et al. [43] is also similar to Schukat et al.'s work. The work is an extension of previous works only.

Work reported by Porambage et al. [44] is based on traditional certificate-based methods that allow end user and sensor nodes to authenticate through implicit certificates. To prove the compatibility of their work, they have also shown the empirical data for memory utilization. The work of Yao et al. [45] is the modification of Nyberg's fast one-way accumulator as compatible to multicast with simpler computation. They have also evaluated the seven factors of the performance aspects of the proposed work. The work of Kothmayr et al. [46] is first to implement the DTLS in IoT scenario. Therefore, all strengths of DTLS in traditional computing are also valid here.

Lee et al. [48] proposed a lightweight authentication mechanism for RFID tags based on XOR manipulation. The work of Mahalle et al. [48] is meant for authentication of the devices in group communication through TCGA (Threshold Cryptography-based Group Authentication). They have shown the time analysis (by calculating asymptotic time complexity) and formal security analysis of the proposed scheme. Work reported by Adiga et al. [49] has implemented identity-based cryptography in secure M2M communications for an IoT scenario. They have shown the solution of many issues related to M2M scenario.

Some other lightweight ECC-based schemes have also been proposed, e.g., [50–52], mainly for RFIDs.

### *12.5.4 Issues in the Present State of the Art*

Let us look at the issues inherent in the present state of the art to help us find the research problems and future directions for further development in this field. A summary of the following studies is provided in Table 12.2.

The work of Liu et al. [28], Mahalle [23], and Druml [41] revolves around the ECC-based key exchange. However it is a well-proven and widely accepted mechanism, but it lacks specification for IoT. The work of Pereira et al. [29] is based on service-oriented architecture and uses the concept of Kerberos and RADIUS for access control and authentication. Again they use this popular mechanism and tried to make it compatible in IoT scenario somehow. Sun et al. [22] present a novel contribution in their approach by mixing the concept of ABAC and RBAC and developed as ARBHAC (attribute- and role-based hybrid access control). Its real-time implementation and empirical data are not there to support the claims.

Mituca [30] has presented a novel approach to implementing access control in "Contiki OS," but the real-time implementation is needed. Contributions of Hummen et al. [33] and Gerdes et al. [34] are solely dependent on DTLS mechanism. Conceptually, both works are quite similar in their approach. Both works have proposed delegation servers to perform computation intense tasks. Work reported by Thuan [31] concentrates on user-centric identity management. The way of approach in the paper is innovative, but again real-time implementation is not there to prove it. The work of Fremantle et al. [26] is based on OAuth. They developed a prototype to use in OAuth for access control. They implemented it and drew some fruitful conclusions. The work of Ning [35] is specifically concentrated on U2IoT. They presented authentication scheme for aggregated networks. That is why it lacks generality. The work of Pawlowski et al. [40] is meant for authentication in IoT by mixing the concept of TEPANOM and EAPs. Hummen et al. [33] have conducted a certificate-based authentication feasibility study in IoT scenario. This work is a preliminary of their one of the quoted work. Hernandez-Ramos et al. [36] have proposed a lightweight authentication and authorization protocol based on ARM architecture.

Work reported by Lai [37] is the conditional privacy-preserving authentication with access linkability. They talked about the access control while in roaming. The paper has provided detailed mathematical proofs and security analysis but lacks real-time empirical data.

Jan et al. [38] have proposed a lightweight authentication scheme with the application of AES (Advanced Encryption Standard) with a challenge-response mechanism. The proposed work also presented experimental data to firm its claim regarding feasibility in IoT scenario. Raheem [39] also proposed an authentication scheme using LISP, which just started emerging. They have also done a security analysis to firm its claims, but real-time implementations are not there. Schukat et al. [42] and its subset work of Flood [43] proposed authentication with zero-knowledge proofs. They have shown key exchange using graph methods.

The work of Porambage et al. [44] seems to be complete regarding theoretical and experimental aspects. They have specifically evaluated their protocol in terms of memory utilization, time, and energy consumption. The only drawback is that it depends on age-old authentication mechanism of certificates.

Work reported by Yao [45] seems promising at first sight. The scheme is novel, but its performance comparison with existing work is missing. The strength of this work is the main drawback of the work of Kothmayr et al. as all the drawback of certificate-based mechanism lies here.

The work of Lee et al. [47] is focused on RFID; therefore, it must experiment for other IoT devices and scenarios. The work of Mahalle [48] is novel, but it would be interesting to see a real-time application of it. Thorough security analysis of the work of Adiga et al. [49] is missing.

We can conclude that many schemes that are proposed in recent times lack real-time implementations. However, a few schemes have very strong fundamental claims like Schukat [42], Raheem [39], Lai et al. [37], Hernandez-Ramos et al. [36], Pawlowski [40], Ning et al. [35], Thuan [31], Mituca et al. [30], and Sun et al. [22], but real-time application of these is still missing. Some other research and developments are very specific to certain networks and for certain architectures that limit their applicability and feasibility. Although they have shown successfully that their work is fully robust to different attacks, there is a need to analyze their claims and verify further their results.

## 12.6 Access Control in the Perspective of Distributed Computing

As we have already discussed above, many access control/authentication works are suitable for certain networks or particular architectures only. For distributed and heterogeneous environments like IoT, there is a need for access control mechanism that caters interoperability issues efficiently. Scalability is also an important issue in distributed environment. So, to design and implement effective access control mechanism, we must consider also the scalability and heterogeneity issues very carefully and efficiently.

## 12.7 Research Direction in Access Control and Authentication for IoT

There is a vast scope for further research in authentication and access control in the IoT. Below, we summarize points regarding various research directions in IoT on access control and authentication:

- There is a lack of well-established access control architecture like AAA (authentication, authorization, and accounting) in IoT scenarios for M2M systems.
- Most of the existing work on access control is based on the traditional mechanism like ACLs, RBACs, etc., but there is a need to develop some access control paradigms specifically for resource-constrained environments.
- As we have pointed out in the previous section, there are very few access control management systems in constrained OSs like Contiki, contradicts with the high-end OSs like Android, etc. Hence, an initiative to develop access control management for constrained environment is needed much like traditional computing environment.
- Interoperability issues of access control mechanism of heterogeneous networks/devices in IoT scenarios are needed to be addressed.
- In existing work of authentication in IoT, a scenario can be classified into two types: certificate based and non-certificate based. Mostly certificate-based solution revolves around modified DTLS [46], etc. for IoT. There is a need to explore other certificate-based authentication mechanism for the IoT scenarios.
- In recent times, many interesting non-certificate-based authentication mechanism has been proposed. But still there are other authentication mechanisms for traditional computing environment that needs to be tested/implemented in IoT like anonymous authentication.
- There is a lack of a proper framework for user authentication in IoT environment. Usability and reliability aspects of user authentication are needed to be addressed.
- It has been observed during the state of the art surveys that a cross-validity of the present work is not there. So thorough security analysis and performance analysis are needed, so one can cross-validate the claims and make further improvements.
- Several security issues in IoT and relating paradigms remain unanswered. So, it will be better to propose some novel mechanisms to defend these.

## 12.8 Guidelines for Effective Solutions

It is observed in the present state of the art (as mentioned above) that there could be many access control and authentication solutions at different layers (as shown in Table 12.1). In the table, we have included best solutions for each layer from the present state of the art. It will help us to know what is already available and what needs to be done. All security solutions of RFIDs and WSN lie on the perception layer [7]. Therefore, we have included these solutions in perception layer only. Present solutions are mainly of generic nature; that is why most of the solutions lie in the application and network layers; however, if we see the work of WSN and RFIDs separately, then we can find that most works are at perception layer. All access control solutions must address scalability and complexity. Likewise the contribution of Sun et al. [22], RBAC, is not meant for dynamic users (scalability) and ABAC is complex in operations, so authors proposed ARBAC. The following are the directions and guidelines for designing effective solutions:

- Apart from complexity and scalability, heterogeneity and energy issues are also important. However, computational complexity and energy consumption are somewhat related, but these issues can be evaluated separately.
- Many researchers, e.g., [29, 30, 46] choose to propose access control and authentication solutions by making them compatible with widely accepted and implemented solutions of traditional computing systems in IoT scenario. We have seen many of these in the present state of the art.
- The foremost concern of authentication is scalability; therefore, the mechanisms must satisfy authentication operations of as many nodes as possible.
- However, standalone authentication solutions are suggested to be discouraged because of constrained resource issues. In many cases, devices cannot afford to engage all resources for authentication only. Therefore, it is better to propose complete access management frameworks [24].
- Authentication solutions should be simple and lightweight from the computation point of view, which will address the energy issues and computational resource issues effectively.
- The solution of access control and authentication must be dealt with for intra- and inter-domain connectivity and its interoperability and granularity. It is the most ignored part of the present state of the art.

## 12.9 Conclusion

In this chapter, we have comprehensively discussed scenarios of access control and authentication concerning the present state of the art and research community's progress. We started with the detailed differentiation of security issues in IoT and traditional ubiquitous computing. We have also evaluated present architectures to get familiar with actual and conceptual building block of IoT. In the present state of the art, we have pointed out certain significant contributions, their merits, and drawbacks and conducted a comparative study. Our goal has been to point certain important future directions for access control and authentication.

In Sect. 12.8, we have mentioned contemporary studies conducted at each layer, to frame the guidelines for future work. The chapter also explains the access control from the view of distributed computing to show how one should think about access control mechanisms for distributed computing environments.

## References


1. Gartner (2015), Gartner Says a thirty-fold increase in internet-connected physical devices by 2020 will significantly alter how the supply chain operates. http://www.gartner.com/newsroom/id/2688717. Accessed 12 June 2015
2. Holler J, Tsiatsis V, Mulligan C, et al (2014) From machine to machine to internet of things. Academic press, Elsevier, Oxford, UK
3. IoT (2015) IoT-ARM white paper. www.iot-a.eu. Accessed 12 June 2015
4. ETSI (2015) ETSI technical specification v 2.1.1. http://www.etsi.org. Accessed 17 June 2015
5. SENSEI (2015) SENSEI white papers. http://www.sensei-project.eu. Accessed 12 June 2015
6. ITU (2015) ITU Joint Coordination Activity on Internet of Things (JCA-IoT) white papers. www.itu.int. Accessed 12 June 2015
7. Open Geospatial Consortium (20115) Open geospatial consortium architecture. www.opengeospatial.org/pub/www/saa/saa_architecture.html. Accessed 17 June 2015
8. RFID (2015) RFIDs uniform coding. http://www.epc-rfid.info/tbd-1. Accessed 15 June 2015
9. Matt B, Joan F, John I, Angelos DK (2015) Trust management. http://www.cs.yale.edu/~jf/BFIK-SIP.pdf. Accessed 15 June 2015
10. Thales, (2015), Key management. https://www.thales-esecurity.com/solutions/by-technology-focus/key-management. Accessed 12 June 2015
11. Jing Q, Athanasios V et al (2014) Security of the internet of things: perspective and challenges. Wirel Netw 20(8):2481–2501, Springer US
12. Thales (2015) Hardware based scheme. https://www.thales-esecurity.com/products-and-services/products-and-services/hardware-security-modules. Accessed 12 June 2015
13. Granjal J, Monteiro E, De Silva J (2013) Security issues and wireless M2M systems, Wireless Networks and Security. Springer, Heidelberg, pp 133–164
14. Trung N (2015) A survey of WiMAX security threats project report. http://www.cse.wustl.edu/~jain/cse571-09/ftp/wimax2/. Accessed 17 June 2015
15. Stephen N (2015) Traffic analysis. http://www.sans.edu/research/security-laboratory/article/traffic-analysis. Accessed 12 June 2015
16. Dunkels A, Alonso J, Voigt T and Ritter H (2004) Distributed TCP caching for wireless sensor networks. Proceedings of 2004 modeling and optimization in mobile, Ad Hoc and wireless Networks, Cambridge, UK
17. Iyer YG, Gandham S, Venkatesan S (2005) STCP: a generic transport layer protocol for wireless sensor networks. Proceedings of 14th International Conference ICCCN 2005, pp 449–454
18. Yusung K, Kilnam C, Lisong XU (2008) Adjusting the aggregate throughput of parallel TCP flows without central coordination. IEICE Trans Commun 5:1615–1618, E91-B
19. Wan CY, Campbell AT, Krishnamurthy L (2005) Pump-slowly, fetch-quickly (PSFQ): a reliable transport protocol for sensor networks. IEEE J Sel Areas Commun 23(4):862–872
20. Shelby Z, Hartke K, Bormann C (2014) The Constrained Application Protocol (CoAP), request for comments: 7252. Internet Engineering Task Force (IETF)
21. Stankovic JA (2014) Research directions for the internet of things. IEEE J Internet Things 1 (1):3–9
22. Sun K, Yin L (2014) Attribute-role-based hybrid access control in the internet of things. In: Proceedings of workshop on APWeb 2014. Changsha, China, Springer LNCS 8710, pp 333–343

23. Mahalle PN, Anggorojati B et al (2014) Identity establishment and capability Based access control scheme for internet of things. In: Proceedings of 2009 12th international symposium on Wireless Personal Multimedia Communications (WPMC), Sendai, Japan, pp 187–191
24. Liu J, Xiao Y, Philip CL (2012) Authentication and access control in the internet of things. In: Proceedings of 2012 32nd International conference on distributed computing systems workshops, Macau, China, pp 588–592
25. Zhang G, Tian J (2010) An extended role based access control model for the internet of things. In: Proceedings of 2010 International Conference on Information, Networking and Automation (ICINA), Kunming, China, vol 1, pp 319–323
26. Fremantle P, Aziz B et al. (2014) Federated identity and access management for the internet of things. In: Proceedings of 2014 I.E. international workshop on secure internet of things, Wroclaw, Poland, pp 10–17
27. Sitenkov D (2014) Access control in the internet of things. Master's thesis; SICS
28. Liu L, Yin L et al (2014) EAC: a framework of authentication property for the IoTs. In: Proceedings of 2014 international conference on cyber-enabled distributed computing and knowledge discovery, Shanghai, China, pp 102–105
29. Pereira PP, Eliasson J, Delsing J (2014) An authentication and access control framework for CoAP-based internet of things. Proc 40th 2014 IECON, Dallas, US, pp 5293–5299
30. Mituca A, Moin HA, Prehofer C (2014) Access control for apps running on constrained devices in the internet of things. In: Proceedings of 2014 international workshop on secure internet of things, pp 1–9
31. Thuan DV, Butkus P, Thanh DV (2014) A user centric identity management for internet of things. In: Proceedings of 2014 international conference on IT convergence and security, pp 1–4
32. Banerjee D, Dong B et al (2014) Privacy-preserving channel access for internet of things. IEEE Internet Things J 1(5):430–445
33. Hummen R, Shafagh H et al. (2014) Delegation based authentication and authorization for the IP-based internet of things. In: Proceedings of 2014 I.E. international conference on Sensing, Communication and Networking (SECON), pp 284–292
34. Gerdes S, Bergmann O, Bormann C (2014) Delegated authentication authorization for constrained environments. In: Proceedings of IEEE 22nd international conference on network protocols, pp 654–659
35. Ning H, Liu H, Yang TL (2013) Aggregated-proof based hierarchical authentication scheme for the internet of things. IEEE Trans Parallel Distrib Syst 26(3):657–667
36. Hernandez-Ramos LJ, Pawlowski PM (2015) Toward a lightweight authentication and authorization framework for smart objects. IEEE J Sel Areas Commun 33(4):690–702
37. Lai C, Li H et al (2014) CPAL: a conditional privacy-preserving authentication with access linkability for roaming service. IEEE Internet Things J 1(1):46–57
38. Jan AM, Nanda P et al. (2014) A robust authentication scheme for observing resources in the internet of things environment. In: IEEE 13th International conference on trust, security and privacy in computing and communication, pp 205–211
39. Raheem A, Lasebae A, Loo J (2014) A secure authentication protocol for IP-based wireless sensor communications using the Location/ID Split Protocol (LISP). In: Proceedings of IEEE 13th international conference on trust, security and privacy in computing and communication, pp 840–845
40. Pawlowski PM, Jara JA and Ogorzalek JM et al. (2015) EAP for IoT:more efficient transport of authentication data- TEPANOM case study. In: Proceedings of 2015 29th international conference on advanced information networking and applications workshop, pp 694–699
41. Druml N, Menghin M, et al (2014) A flexible and lightweight ECC-based authentication solution for resource constrained systems. In: Proceeding of 2014 17th Euromicro conference on digital system design, pp 372–378
42. Schukat M, Flood P (2014) Zero-knowledge proofs in M2M communication. In: Proceedings of ISSC 2014/CHCT 2014, pp 269–273

43. Flood P, Schukat M (2014) Peer to peer authentication for small embedded systems. In: Proceedings of 10th international conference on digital technology, pp 68–72
44. Porambage P, Schmitt C et al (2014) Two phase authentication protocol for wireless sensor networks in distributed IoT applications. In: Proc IEEE WCNC 2014, pp 2728–2733
45. Yao X, Han X et al (2013) A lightweight multicast authentication mechanism for small scale IoT applications. IEEE Sensors J 13(10):3693–3701
46. Kothmayr T, Schmitt C et al (2012) A DTLS based end-to-end security architecture for the internet of things with two-way authentication. In: Proceedings of 2012 37th local computer network workshop, pp 956–963
47. Lee JY, Lin W, Huang Y (2014) A lightweight authentication protocol for internet of things. In: Proceedings of 2014 international symposium on next generation electronics, pp 1–2
48. Mahalle NP, Prasad RN, Prased R (2014) Threshold cryptography based group authentication scheme for internet of things. In: Proceedings of 2014 4th international conference on aerospace & electronic systems, pp 1–5
49. Adiga BS, Balamuralidhar P et al. (2012) An identity based encryption using Elliptic curve cryptography for secure M2M communication. In: Proceedings of 2012 SecurIT, pp 68–74
50. Liao Y, Hsiao C (2013) A secure ECC-based RFID authentication scheme using hybrid protocols. Adv Intell Syst Appl 2(21):1–13
51. Liao Y, Hsiao C (2014) A secure ECC-based RFID authentication scheme integrated with ID-verifier transfer protocol. Ad Hoc Netw 18:133–146
52. Chou J (2014) An efficient mutual authentication RFID scheme based on elliptic curve cryptography. J Supercomput 70(1):75–94
53. Roman R, Zhou J, Lopez J (2013) On the features and challenges of security and privacy in distributed internet of things. Comput Netw 57:2266–2279

# Chapter 13
# Internet of Things for Developing Smart Sustainable Cities (SSC): A Security Perspective

**S. Sivagurunathan, A. Sebastian, and K. Prathapchandran**

## 13.1 Introduction

Change, innovation, and growth are synonymous with the twenty-first century. Growth in economy, information technology, global business trends, resource utilization, and ecologically sensitive approaches are demanding urgent actions. In this context, Internet of Things (IoT) holds the key to meet these demands. In a report published in 2013, McKinsey Global Institute has identified 12 technologies that, by 2025, will have massive economically disruptive impact, driving profound changes in many dimensions: in citizen's lives, in business, and across global economy. Specifically, four technologies fall within Cyber-Physical Systems (CPS): (i) automation of knowledge work, (ii) Internet of Things, (iii) advanced robotics, and (iv) autonomous and near-autonomous vehicles. Among them, the IoT with an estimated value of 36 trillion of dollars is considered the CPS paradigm with the highest economy impact [1].

The term Internet of Things was first coined by Kevin Ashton in 1999 in the context of supply chain management. However, in the past decade, this definition has been more inclusive, covering a wide range of applications like healthcare, production and supply chain, transport, etc. [2]. The IoT is a new paradigm that combines aspects and technologies coming from different approaches. Ubiquitous computing, pervasive computing, Internet Protocol, sensing technologies, communication technologies, and embedded devices are merged together in order to form a system where the real and digital worlds meet and are continuously in symbiotic interaction. Smart, sensing, and intelligent objects are at the center of this IoT vision. By putting intelligence into everyday objects, they are turned into smart

S. Sivagurunathan (✉) • A. Sebastian • K. Prathapchandran
Department of Computer Science and Applications, Gandhigram Rural Institute – Deemed University, Gandhigram, Tamil Nadu, India
e-mail: svgrnth@gmail.com



Z. Mahmood (ed.), *Connectivity Frameworks for Smart Devices*,
Computer Communications and Networks, DOI 10.1007/978-3-319-33124-9_13

objects, able not only to collect information from the environment and control the physical world but also to be interconnected to each other through Internet to exchange data and information. The expected huge number of interconnected devices and the significant amount of available data open new opportunities to create services that will bring tangible benefits to the society, environment, economy, and individual citizens [1].

Urbanization is a fast-growing trend in many countries. Cities provide avenues for socioeconomic growth, education, employment, and social networking. This way, migration to urban cities is equated with opportunity and prosperity for millions of people around the world. According to the global health observatory, urban population accounted for more than half of total global population as of 2009 and will be more than 60 % by 2030 [3]. The UN World Economic and Social Survey 2013 suggested Africa, Asia, and other developing regions will be housing an estimate of 80 % of the world's urban population in the coming years. This way, the city is becoming the economic and social life core of a nation [1]. IoT will essentially turn a traditional city into a smart, sustainable city. The traditional and more emerging sectors such as business, transport logistics, healthcare, buildings, energy, living, and governance will also benefit from it.

The remainder of this chapter is organized as follows. In Sect. 13.2, we elaborate the need and justification for smart and sustainable cities and sum up related developments in smart sustainable city projects around the world. In Sect. 13.3, we discuss in detail how information becomes the foundation for smart sustainable city governance followed by the architectural view taking information and service-based approach to city governance. In this process, we also discuss automated decision-making and governance through cluster-based methods, citing examples from essential city services of a smart city. In Sect. 13.4, limitations of the IoT and the main challenges of security, privacy, and the possible security attacks are discussed. We also spell out the needed security requirements and possible solutions to develop a secure SSC in the IoT scenario. Conclusions and future research plans for SSC are discussed in Sect. 13.5.

## 13.2 Why Smart Sustainable Cities?

At its fifth meeting in June 2014, ITU-T's Focus Group on Smart Sustainable Cities (FG-SSC) agreed on the following definition of a smart sustainable city [4]: "A Smart Sustainable City (SSC) is an innovative city that uses Information and Communication Technologies (ICTs) and other means to improve the quality of life, efficiency of urban operation and services, and competitiveness, while ensuring that it meets the needs of present and future generations with respect to economic, social and environmental aspects." It is evident that, without loss of generality, a metropolitan area can be classified as smart when safety, enhanced public services, healthcare monitoring, green sustainability, intense social interaction, and efficient transportation systems become available to any citizen wherever he is located. All this requires designing, developing, deploying, and maintaining public and private infrastructures, based on advanced and integrated materials, sensors, electronics, computer systems, and database [4].

There are two modes in which a SSC is developed. The first and the easiest mode is to create smart cities from scratch or otherwise called planned new cities. New Songdo City in Korea is still today the most famous smart city project so far, covering all aspects from infrastructure to architecture, transportation, utilities, density, open space, and parks, in short everything that defines the substance of an urban area. There has also been the Ubiquitous Network Project of Tokyo University Professor Ken Sakamura, which started in the year 2007 with a field test in Tokyo's Ginza shopping district where more than 1,200 chips, 270 infrared spotlights, and 16 Wi-Fi stations were placed on lampposts, flower beds, stores, and underground subway tunnels. There are several initiatives taken to develop new smart cities, such as Plan IT Valley (Portugal), Skolkovo Innovation Center (Russia), Cyberport Hong Kong (China), Songdo International Business District (South Korea), Cyberjaya (Malaysia), Masdar City (Abu Dhabi, UAE), King Abdullah Economic City (KAEC) in Saudi Arabia, Gujarat International Finance Tec-City (GIFT) in India, and the Infocomm Development Authority (iDA) of Singapore. These cities are designed and built from scratch, showcasing leading edge "smart" technology and certifications of green physical planning. They are highly ambitious projects, tremendous investments for acquiring land, building infrastructure, and large-scale settlements. It is impressive that in China alone, as many as 154 proposals have been introduced to build smart city and population growth and migration will give rise to 81 new cities by the 2025.

The second and hard way to develop a SSC is to regenerate the long-lived urban areas. Many other cities are getting modernized, such as Amsterdam CITYNET in the Netherlands, Borlange City in Sweden, San Francisco Tech Connect in California, USA, Yangzhou in China's Jiangsu province, and Santander in Spain. Using the IoT technology that offers wireless communication and real-time data such as temperature, pressure, vibrations, and energy measurement between the devices which surround us, endless applications are being developed aiming at positioning cities as attractive global investment nodes for advanced manufacturing and service industries [5].

## 13.3 Information-Based Smart Sustainable City Governance

The most investigated use cases by EU projects are grouped into several macro categories, i.e., government and public administration, intelligent transportation systems, public safety, social, healthcare, educational, building and urban planning, environmental, and energy and water and waste management are some of them [4]. A SSC is governed by many entities such as government, agency

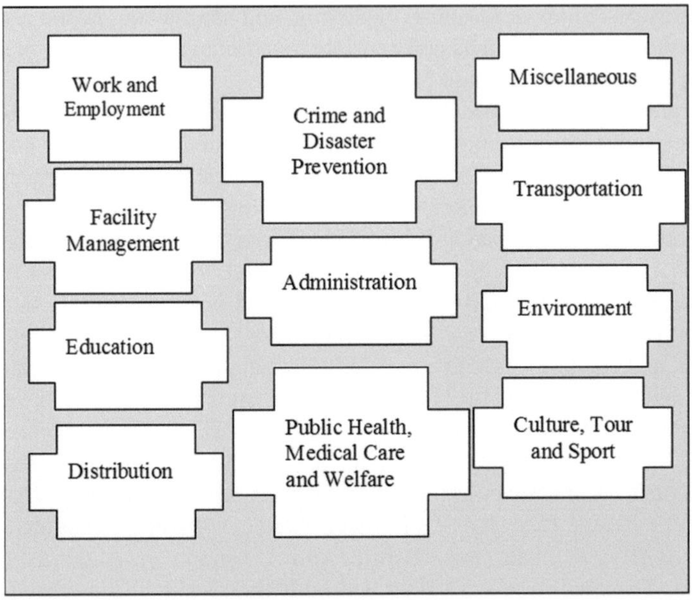


**Fig. 13.1** Model of smart city and related service categories

administration, business houses, and citizens. All of them are stakeholders in developing SSC. They jointly plan and execute operations and services to its citizens by effective use of available city infrastructure and human resource. However, as in Fig. 13.1, the responsibility and leadership lie with the city administration for innovation, smartness, and sustainability of a city. In this article, we attempt to suggest information-based automated smart sustainable city governance using IoT.

### *13.3.1 Information as Foundation of SSC Governance*

Business, revenues, suitable ambience for social activities, infrastructure, basic amenities, etc. are all parameters of a SSC. Growth and development of a city involve not only huge finance, landscape, good plan, and cooperation from people but also credible, accountable, and people-oriented governance. To develop a smart sustainable city, many research articles have suggested models for city transport logistics, healthcare, green environment, wastage management, smart grid for usage of power, smart meter for water, etc. In short, proposed smart city models are business oriented and technology laden. In our opinion, the success or failure of a SSC will depend upon the city administration or city governance. And this governance should be centered more on information and related knowledge and less by human methods and limitations. In such environment, data is the raw material that is processed into information. Individual data by itself is not very useful, but volumes of it, which is generated through the Internet of Things, can identify trends and patterns. This in combination with other information, then, comes together to form knowledge. This knowledge when combined with human experience brings forth wisdom [6].

Human beings evolve because they communicate, creating knowledge out of data and wisdom based on experience. Sensing objects with IoT technologies would enable knowledge derived from the data streams along with human experience bring the best in cities [6]. In SSC, along with human capital, information too becomes a potential capital. Using IoT, the city governance needs to possess correct information about the geography, infrastructure, climate, job opportunity, business environment, culture and ethics, and above all natural and human resource/capital that are under its territory. SSC governance involves administrative decisions which affect the growth, development, and sustainability of the city. Sustainability calls for concern for our environment and planet earth. So information of the past, present, and certain future is necessary for taking correct decisions at correct time. So this paper aims at suggesting information-based SSC governance using IoT. The good news is that we are living at a time where our understanding of urban areas is advancing. Our knowledge of the drivers of urban change is improving, and new data sets and analytical methodologies are emerging [7].

### *13.3.2 Information-Based IoT Architecture for SSC Governance*

Figure 13.2 illustrates the information-based IoT architecture for SSC governance. It is characterized by different interacting technologies and protocols and has different purposes and functions. Chiefly, it has three phases: the collection phase, the transmission phase, and the process, management, and utilization phase.

#### 13.3.2.1 Collection Phase

It refers to procedures for sensing the physical environment (e.g., temperature, humidity, brightness) or about objects (e.g., identity, state, and energy level). Data acquisition is encompassed by using different sensing technologies attached to sensors, cameras, and GPS terminals, while data collection is generally accomplished by short-range communications (e.g., Bluetooth, ZigBee, Dash7, Wireless M-Bus) collecting real-time physical data and reconstructing a general information system [1].

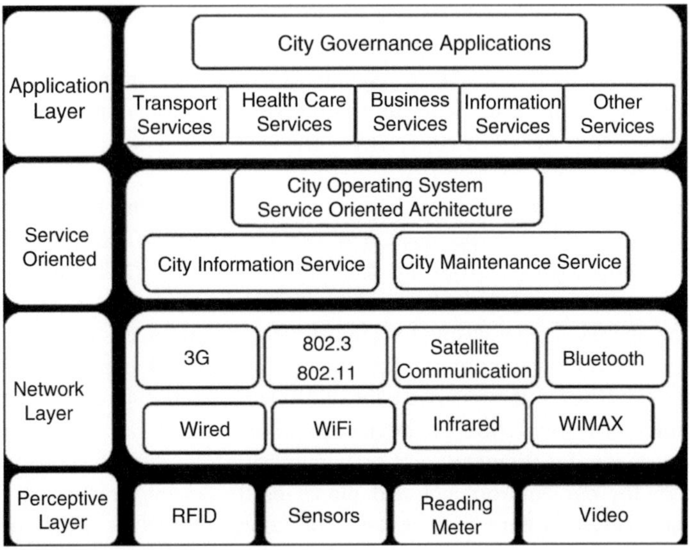


**Fig. 13.2** IoT architecture

#### 13.3.2.2 Transmission Phase

Once the data is gathered through sensing technologies, it needs to be transmitted across the network so that applications can consume it. Heterogeneous communication technologies form the backbone to access the network (e.g., Ethernet IEEE 802.3, coaxial cables, optical fiber, Wireless LAN, Wi-Fi 802.11a/b/g/n, WiMAX IEEE 802.16, broadband technological) [1].

#### 13.3.2.3 Process, Management, and Utilization Phase

In this phase, information flows are processed and then forwarded to applications. The service platform and enabler cover a fundamental role for managing the above operations. It is crucial for hiding the heterogeneity of hardware, software, data formats, technologies, and communication protocols characterizing IoT (e.g., SOA, P2P, and cloud computing) [1].

### *13.3.3 Cluster-Based IoT Architecture for SSC Governance*

Today, more people than ever are migrating to cities for better opportunities. To accommodate such demands, the city landscape has to be remodel or the city boundaries need to be redrawn. In either case, SSC governance has to process huge data which are gathered through IoT. No city or technology is in a position to

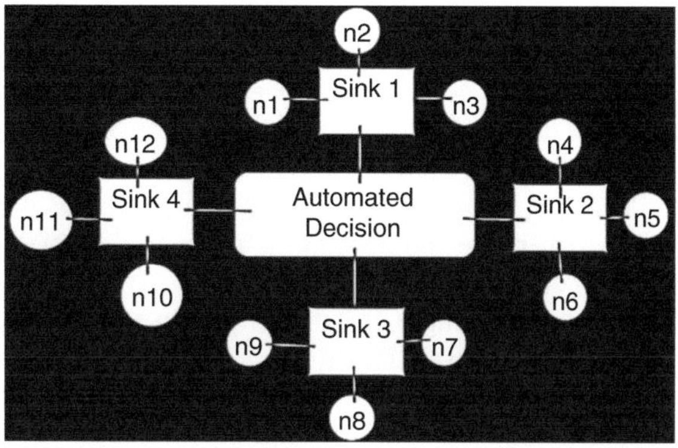


**Fig. 13.3** Nodes, sinks, and administrative processes in a cluster

handle such voluminous data and network. The existing centralized access and control mechanism is inefficient to handle such scenario. To meet this demand, it is necessary that information gathering by IoT is cluster based. The entire city can be clustered based on geographical accessibility or Internet service accessibility or any other manageable criteria. Figure 13.3 shows an example of such a cluster entity. Each cluster has many sinks and each sink in turn has many sensor nodes. The sensor nodes placed at various locations of the city perform the role of gathering data, perceptive component. The sink nodes gather all these data and do filtering methods for data redundancy and other checks and forward the data to administration process for automated decision generation. Administration process is a complex system which handles large amount of data. The administration will have many sink nodes and they constantly feed data. Once again, filtering the data for redundancy and duplication is handled here, and then by using powerful tools for analysis, decisions are generated. Various rules and test conditions are considered for making such decisions.

In SSC governance, based on past history, current data and future orientation emergency, normal service, maintenance service, etc. are considered. Along with this, the priority scale and quickness of action and time scale too are attached. The automated administrative decision process generates a list of actions to be taken. This way the cluster-based approach can help the SSC governance to grow towards smart sustainable city. Since the automated decisions are based on data from the past, present, and suggestive future, it holds value and truth about the nature and behavioral patterns of city dwellers. These decisions are information-based quick decisions which come handy in emergency and disaster-like situations.

### *13.3.4 Test Case for Information-Based Automated SSC Governance*

The information-based automated SSC governance can well be applied to any city environment. There are many services the city administration has to perform.

Among them, we propose two services, viz, City Information Service (CIS) and City Essential Maintenance Service (CEMS) which are critical to smart city governance. In normal city governance, these services are done based on time schedule of the city life or event driven or based on complaint from the citizens. But in our test case, these services can be easily automated based on information's collected by cluster-based IoT mechanism. This way of SSC governance will ensure that proper information is given to the citizens and quality of life is kept up at all times.

To cite an example, the street lights in a city are centrally controlled. They are switched on at a fixed time in the evening and switched off at a particular time in the morning irrespective of changes in season. Often we notice that these street lights burn at midday due to human negligence. But as we know, summer has longer days and rainy or winter has longer nights. However, as of now they keep burning through the night in all places. If some street lamps are not burning, the administration will not know unless someone complains. The city administration has to spend huge money to provide this basic service of providing electricity. Information-based automated SSC governance comes handy in bringing solution to this problem. If all street lamps have RFID tags and light sensors, they can be monitored in a clustered way. If there is malfunction in any street lamp, the automated system will raise alarm. The street lamps are made intelligent to switch on and off when light is needed or the intensity of light can be varied based on the need. This way the city can save electricity and maintain street lighting system at ease. By carefully adopting such technology, it gives way for sustainability and piper use of resources. In this way, the information gathered by IoT has potential for such deployment which will help the SSC governance, which is not possible in a human-driven city maintenance system.

#### 13.3.4.1 City Information Service (CIS)

Every day thousands of people enter the cities for various purposes. They come to a city for job, to get their official work done in offices, to get healthcare, to commute to other parts of the state and country, to buy and sell goods, or to conduct financial transactions. SSC governance must cater for the information needs of these people. The information should be at their reach.

City Information Service refers to the whereabouts of hospitals, banks, government offices, shopping malls, places of worship, public entertainment places, transport terminals, etc. which are situated in the town. The services will involve the directional map of the city, the distance from his/her current location, the nature of the building, available contact number if any, the time of office hours, if holidays, etc. The temperature, pollution level, precaution from various diseases, etc. are city services that can be given to citizens. Such information system can be of great help to all who enter the city and are in need of information.

Anybody who enters a city will be able to access these information by way of touch screen systems placed at prominent places. Every touch point can be accessed through Global Positioning Remote System (GPRS) and the user can get his/her required details. Along with this updates of the things happening in the city could be displayed. At this level of City Information System (CIS), a collaborated effort from various departments for infrastructure details and current event-driven updates can be collected from sensors placed across the city for various purposes. CIS can be provided by the city administration at commonplaces as well as in the form of applications to mobile, table, and PDA users who can download and avail these services either for free or at minimal cost. This way, CIS can make not only smart city but also the citizens' life smart. They can have fast and easy access to city landscape and all that is taking place in the city.

#### 13.3.4.2 City Essential Maintenance Service (CEMS)

SSC governance needs to provide Essential Maintenance Services to its citizens without fail. These services include basic necessities of life such as water, power, shelter, medicine, food provisions, garbage disposal, etc. without which the city will be in chaos. SSC governance needs to be alert at all times and be prepared to respond to these needs.

To cite an example, everyone in the city wants the city to be clean at all times. But garbage keeps getting accumulated regularly. The garbage disposal team normally collects garbage before city awakes. But due to business activities, garbage is full within few hours of business and it remains there creating big inconvenience to citizens and business. This problem could well be addressed by information-based SSC governance using IoT. If every garbage collection point is monitored through a camera, the automated system can generate alarm once the garbage has reached its maximum limit and the garbage disposal team can clear them during the day.

To cite another example, safe drinking water is a scarce resource in many cities. But the city administration has to provide them around the clock. Often we find, due to faulty taps and pipes, lots of precious water flow into drain. If sensors are attached to these taps to monitor the flow and report malfunction, immediate steps can be taken by the SSC governance. This will help in preserving the natural resource as well better utilization of resources.

Food provisions such as milk, vegetables, fruits, and other commodities too come under Essential Maintenance Service. Truckloads of these commodities reach the city market every day. At the end of the day, we find lots of these commodities unsold and thrown away as waste. Through information gathering, citizen's consuming behavior can be monitored through the year and through sensors the number of people those come to market can be counted; we can generate the actual need of the city. Then, we can monitor the amount of commodities that are brought to the city. This way we can deliver essential commodities through the year and store if more is produced in the farm. This will pave way for price control as well as avoid wastage and pollution of the city.

These are a few cited examples to clarify the point that cluster-based IoT technology with its sensors, cameras, and other things with intelligence can help the SSC governance in a big way. So gathering of information through objects and transmitting them across heterogeneous network to cluster and central sinks of the SSC governance and processing them through advanced techniques can generate the desired result for SSC governance. And the beauty is all these functions can be automated and these objects will deliver with promptness, dedication, accuracy, and least wear and tear.

## 13.4 Privacy and Security Issues in Automated SSC Governance

Developing automated SSC governance through the use of IoT, to improve quality of life as well as contribute towards better life for individuals through various facilities (such as governance, environment, society, economy, mobility, and living), is indeed a possibility. However, many challenges such as security, privacy, quality of services, scalability, location awareness, participatory sensing, data analysis, and more are still needed to be addressed before the vision of IoT becomes a reality [2]. SSC governance involves uninterrupted services to citizens, public and private officials, enterprises, and agencies over a communication network quickly and accurately.

The success of governance depends on its successful delivery of services but importantly delivery of these services with confidentiality and security is a big challenge. Keeping these advanced automated decisions that affect thousands of people away from intruders and antisocial elements is a huge task. Security and privacy alarms are great concerns because of the increase in vulnerabilities day by day; hence, they will threaten the developments of SSC governance. Basically, security-related issues arise not only due to the devices but also when two devices connect and communicate with each other, since IoT is mostly composed of RFID and wireless sensor nodes and in addition to networks and Internet provision to connect those devices. Therefore, security-related issues in the IoT are high compared to traditional network and as IoT plays a lead role for developing SSC with governance as the primary component. In IoT, there are a number of heterogeneous devices with limited resource capabilities that will connect and communicate; hence, such increased system complexity opens new doors and opportunities for security threats and vulnerabilities. Figure 13.4 represents the overall framework for security of SSC with a special focus on governance through IoT.

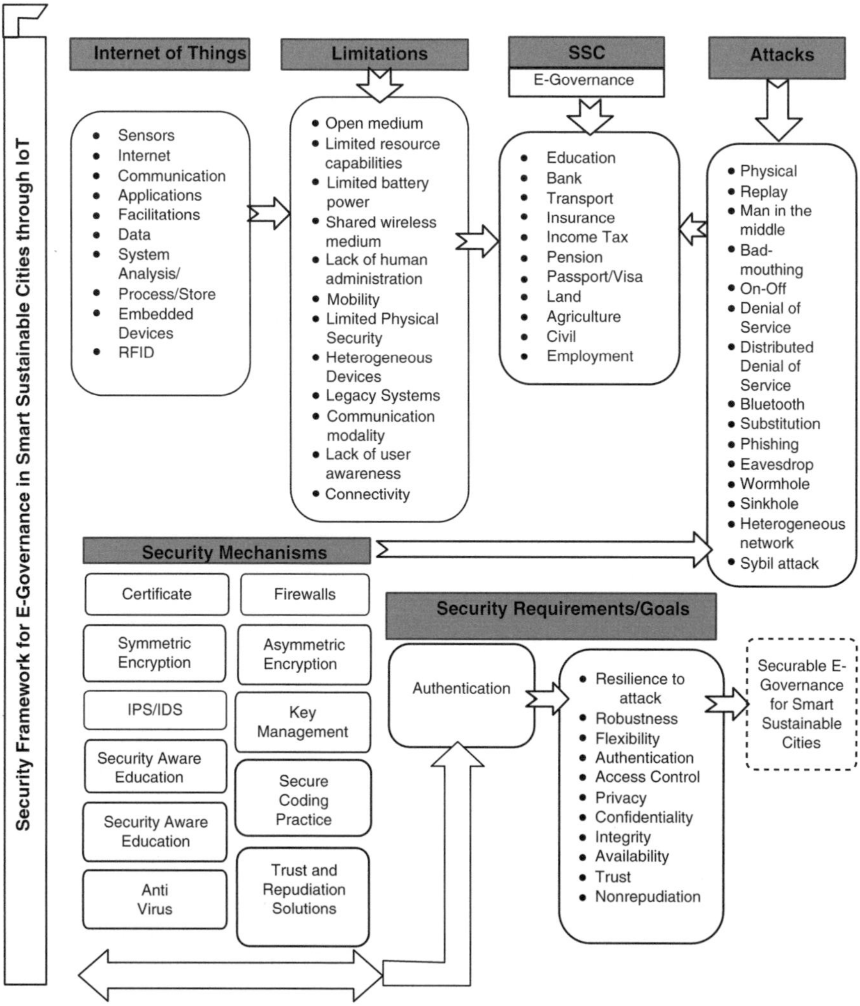


**Fig. 13.4** Security framework for e-governance in smart cities through IoT

### *13.4.1 Limitations of IoT and Implications for SSC Governance*

The automated SSC governance is carried out through various components involved in IoT such as devices, protocols, RFID, sensors, biometric-related smart camera, 2D and 3D bar codes, communication networks, controlling devices, and cloud computing technologies [8]. Typically, these components have limitations that lead to various challenges in developing SSC. The following section describes the limitations of IoT and how these limitations have potential to slow down the deployment of SSC and related security and privacy perceptive; therefore, it creates impact on public safety, environment, administration, intelligent transport, education, healthcare, and more.

#### 13.4.1.1 Open Medium

Typically, the IoT has both wired and wireless architecture that can be accessible to any object or devices because most of the IoT devices are located in public places and therefore less administration and human intervention. Possibility of getting physical damage is very high due to lack of awareness in using devices and devices are not in a situation to assess identity of correct users. Unidentified users can have access to data and systems that are supposed to be accessed by only authorized users [9].

Therefore, IoT devices should possess well-defined access control and privacy [10] management to maintain trust between government services and people. For instance, in transport service the sensors will observe the traffic and will send the information to the traffic control station. In that case, an attacker can physically damage sensor or take control over the sensor due to its wireless nature and try to send invalid traffic information to the control station.

#### 13.4.1.2 Limited Resource Capabilities

Compared with conventional network, IoT has limited resource capabilities in terms of memory, bandwidth, computation, and processing because the devices involved in IoT are mostly compact and tiny in size; perhaps those are mobile devices [11]. For instance, we can access and utilize the SSC information services via smartphones and tablets. Typically, these devices may not have any threats against them unless they are in the hands of attackers. But they will create harm when it is connected with other devices to execute or access services via Bluetooth and other means of wireless technology; therefore, there is a probability for intentional or accidental data leaks and data loss in SSC governance services.

#### 13.4.1.3 Limited Battery Power

Battery power determines the lifetime of IoT devices since the lifetime ranges from a few hours to many years. Basically, wireless devices have limited battery power. Excess utilization of devices will drain their battery completely and therefore result in unwanted data loss or data leakage [12]. For instance, intermediate devices play a vital role for data forwarding where devices are not in the same communication range; hence, each device depends on other device for forwarding especially where instant SSC service is required.

#### 13.4.1.4 Shared Wireless Medium

Every device as part of IoT works on either fixed architecture or shared wireless medium. If the communication medium is wired, we can regulate the data flow, but in wireless medium, too many devices will place a strain on the spectrum of wireless communication resulting in bandwidth consumption [9]. IoT devices are disseminated across various places and those who are trying to communicate a single server over wireless medium will create too much of data traffic that can make the server down. For instance, accessing SSC services over a shared wireless medium will enable bandwidth consumption and trouble the governance financially. Additionally wireless medium possesses a new challenge in terms of privacy violations. Healthcare services handling sensitive patient information without proper identity lead to trouble.

#### 13.4.1.5 Lack of Human Interaction

The devices in IoT are scalable and their deployment nature means one time or incremental or random human intervention is not possible. Initial deployment may require human intervention but later on IoT can work on its own due to its self-organization capabilities. Failure of self-organization will result in improper delivery of SSC services [13]. This will create negative opinion about governance and its services. For instance, notification and evacuation play an important role in physical safety and security of SSC governance. As urbanization becomes further mainstream, buildings are equipped with sensor capability to detect accidental causes like smoke, heat, gas, and flame. In most occasions administrators of the building are not paying too much attention over the sensors because of laziness or they are not in a situation to monitor so human security as well as device security is in question.

#### 13.4.1.6 Mobility

Devices involved in IoT have the ability to move within the range of the cluster [14]. Device movement may occur purposely or may depend on the deployment of its environment. Along with this, mobile devices are in a situation to get stolen or lost than other devices. For instance, due to mobility of devices, continuous assessment is required but it is not always possible and it will make additional burden in providing SSC services. Each mobile device has security policy agreements with their communicating neighbors. There is a problem to ensure the correct identity with other devices because their security policy may differ; therefore, it will create a problem in security as well as in privacy of SSC services. Additionally many mobile devices especially personally owned are untrustworthy; therefore, trying to acquire government services without any security mechanisms leads to security violations.

#### 13.4.1.7 Limited Physical Security

Conventional networks have high-security mechanisms because they can be easily controlled by any device or administrator. However, in IoT, security is always in question because of its open and shared medium and lack of central control [11]. Placing devices in the way of attackers may cause damage to devices accidentally or intentionally. Accessing SSC services without proper authentication via physical devices will harm the services potentially.

#### 13.4.1.8 Heterogeneous Devices

IoT environment comprises different heterogeneous devices [15, 16]. Therefore, security mechanism for one device may not be suitable for another one so it can lead to lack of interoperability, handover, and quality of services. This heterogeneity creates problem between citizen's requirements and SSC services in terms of accessibility, processing, and storing information resulting in undesirable data loss.

#### 13.4.1.9 Legacy Systems

Devices involved in IoT are often legacy systems [17] that are difficult to replace because of their widespread use. Therefore vendors no longer are concerned about updates. Most of the government departments depend on the private vendors in updating technologies. Different departments have different applications to provide SSC services to citizens and business people. Governance would need accumulative interactions among departments and with software and hardware vendors at various levels. Departments are not in situations to maintain and upgrade in case of version change and change in government policies and business rules. Lack of changes leads to negative opinion on government and also leads to data loss when upgraded devices communicate with one another.

#### 13.4.1.10 Communication Modality

Communication among the devices may be single hop or multi-hop. Whatever be the case, if the communication becomes wireless, possibilities of vulnerabilities are high. Before forwarding any information, each device is in situation to assess the identity of devices with which it is in communication because information is transferred via multiple intermediate nodes. In providing SSC services, a particular node belonging to one cluster may exchange information with the node belonging to some other cluster. This may lead to information leak and security vulnerabilities [17].

#### 13.4.1.11 Connectivity

Connectivity among the devices may be continuous, occasional, or periodic [17]. If it is occasional or periodic, the probability of security threats will be low. If it is continuous, the security threat will be high because devices always involve in processing and communication. This may result in unavailability of SSC services.

#### 13.4.1.12 Lack of User Awareness

People nowadays do not have proper knowledge about utilization of IoT devices. This can result in physical damage as well as data leakage [17].

### *13.4.2 Possible Security Attacks on SSC Governance*

In IoT, due to the limitations that we have discussed earlier, it is vulnerable to various kinds of attacks. Attack is nothing but an action that compromises the security of information owned by an organization [18]. In developing SSC governance using IoT, there are three types of possible attacks: physical, application, and network attacks. All attacks can take underlying limitations over the IoT devices and affect the successful development of SSC governance. However network and application attacks affect SSC governance more than physical attacks. It is due to the fact that network and application attacks are less detectable than physical and do not physically picture the attackers, certainly inexpensive, and further it can be launched from any geographically remote locations. Though they are identifiable, the prosecution is more problematic due to complex system structures involved in IoT. In the following section, we discuss some of the attacks that mainly affect the IoT environment SSC governance.

#### 13.4.2.1 Physical Attack

By means of natural disasters such as typhoons, floods, and earthquakes, serious emergencies such as fires and explosions, lack of awareness in using devices, and lack of concern for a long period of time cause physical attack and therefore financial losses and make damage to the electric assets [8, 19].

#### 13.4.2.2 Replay Attacks

An attacker can use previously captured information in order to replay a connection, authentication, or other session by the way to threaten message freshness without the remote device noticing. This attack generally executes when compromised system does not expose credentials [20].

#### 13.4.2.3 Man-in-the-Middle Attack

A malicious node simply occupies a place between a sender device and a receiver device and acts as a part of network and forwards false information to the destination as well as source [21].

#### 13.4.2.4 Bad-Mouthing

This type of attack will execute where trust management plays a significant role in assessing the trustworthiness of the devices. This attack originates from recommendations; sometimes there is a possibility for receiving dishonest recommendations, hence framing good parties or boosting trust value of malicious devices [22].

#### 13.4.2.5 On-Off Attack

In this category of attack, a malicious device behaves well or badly alternatively depending on the change in the condition of the environmental [22].

#### 13.4.2.6 Denial of Service Attack

A user of any device needs to send a request message to ask for access to a sensor device. In that situation, an attacker injects fake request messages with an invalid identity; the sensor node cannot authenticate the validity of the certificate as well as the access right of this user so that it tries to stop devices and services working properly [20].

#### 13.4.2.7 Distributed Denial of Service Attack

When Denial of Service attack executed by multiple devices, then it is called distributed Denial of Service attack. Here also attackers prevent system and services from working properly with the help of many devices with few resources [23].

#### 13.4.2.8 Bluetooth Attack

It is classified into two categories: first is blue jacking where an attacker sends unsolicited messages to Bluetooth-enabled devices by the way to get attention from its nearby devices and create annoyance for users of the devices. The second is blue snaring which is executed by accessing unauthorized data from Bluetooth-enabled devices [23].

#### 13.4.2.9 Substitution Attack

This attack will execute when a device leaves from one network with an Internet Protocol address and joins another. In this case, a malicious device can try to join other network with duplicate Internet address of ordinary node who really has to join and behave like an ordinary device in a network [23].

#### 13.4.2.10 Phishing

This attack is more dangerous where sensitive information is handled, for instance, banking, healthcare services, etc. Here the ultimate aim of an attacker is to capture individual's personal information where an attacker appears as legitimate user in the network and gains knowledge about the sensitive information regarding an individual [23].

#### 13.4.2.11 Client-Side Attack

This attack will mainly affect the client devices due to all-time Internet connection, a Web browser, and a sizable hard drive and CPU horsepower of client devices. An attacker can affect the devices via malware, worms, virus, adware, and spyware, and the aim is to degrade performance or collapse client devices [23].

#### 13.4.2.12 Eavesdropping

An attacker can easily have access to publically exchanged data due to availability of IoT devices in public. An attacker can easily know the energy consumption of presenting devices and here the aim is to drain the energy [24].

#### 13.4.2.13 Wormhole Attack

This attack is accomplished by one or more IoT devices in the network. They disrupt the routing by short circuiting the normal flow of routing packets by creating their own private network and forward through it [25].

#### 13.4.2.14 Sinkhole Attack

The attacking node offers extremely attractive links for the mobile devices in the network. Hence, a lot of traffic bypasses this device resulting in congestion in the IoT environment [26].

#### 13.4.2.15 Heterogeneous Network Attack

An attacker can take the advantage of heterogeneity among the devices and launch cyber-attacks to capture the sensitive information and devices [27].

#### 13.4.2.16 Sybil Attack

An attacker can manipulate false identities or misuse pseudo identities to compromise the efficiency of the IoT and even spread spam [28].

### *13.4.3 Security Requirements for Effective SSC Governance*

The first step in understanding SSC governance through IoT is identifying the security requirements at all levels of SSC governance structure like software, hardware, data, telecommunication, and networking. Hence, in the following section, we discuss the security requirement for securable SSC governance through IoT. It helps us to understand how the SSC governance should develop and operationalize its security features.

#### 13.4.3.1 Resilience to Attack

It represents that the SSC governance architecture or services should have an ability to recover from security compromises or attacks [29].

#### 13.4.3.2 Robustness

In case of an attack or incidents like natural disasters or emergency situations, SSC services should have the ability to maintain its performance and continuity in work progress [29].

#### 13.4.3.3 Flexibility

SSC governance services should have the ability to adapt to new circumstance, meaning ability to adapt to the situations [29].

#### 13.4.3.4 Authentication

Authentication ensures the identity of a device/user/data [18] prior to their communication with others for transmitting and receiving SSC services.

#### 13.4.3.5 Access Control

It limits the privileges of a device or applications or data so that they can be accessed only by the authorized SSC services [29].

#### 13.4.3.6 Privacy

It enables the protection of user's personal information from tampering or altering when they interact with SSC services or interact with themselves or when they are in movement [30].

#### 13.4.3.7 Confidentiality

SSC services may have sensitive information; hence, such information is never disclosed to unauthorized parties [18].

#### 13.4.3.8 Integrity

SSC services may exchange critical information between them or with third parties; therefore, it guarantees that a message being transferred is never corrupted [18].

#### 13.4.3.9 Availability

SSC services should have an ability to provide services at anytime and anywhere continuously despite any attack or incidents [18] like natural disaster or emergency.

#### 13.4.3.10 Non-repudiation

It ensures that SSC services cannot deny having sent the information to other services or denying from reception of information from other service [18].

#### 13.4.3.11 Trust

It ensures the trustworthiness of devices in SSC environment; therefore, each device ensures the trustworthiness of other device before communication begins to provide services [30, 31].

### *13.4.4 Impact of Authentication in SSC Governance*

SSC governance architecture involves various heterogeneous devices, and each device is in a situation to communicate with one another, to provide effective SSC governance services and attain the security requirements that we discussed above. Among the many security requirements, authentication is considered as the most significant requirement because it enables a device to ensure the identity to the receiver. Once authentication is achieved, the rest of the security requirements could easily be achieved. To ensure authentication, each device in IoT must trust other devices. Hence trust is a gateway for IoT devices to authenticate with each other. In order to execute the SSC governance services successfully, each device should cooperate with one another. When each device has trust on every other device in the network architecture, the IoT acts as a decentralized distributed network. Achieving cooperation among the devices in a decentralized distributed is a complicated task. The reason is that each device in the SSC network must trust every other device without any prior recommendations and interactions. But this blindness in communication will make it more vulnerable and affect the entire SSC network's performance. Hence, cooperating devices must trust each other in order to achieve the desired security level. Moreover, compared with traditional wired network, collecting trust evidences to evaluate a trustworthiness of a particular device in IoT is a crucial problem due to its complex and dynamic nature.

### 13.4.5 *Suggested Security Mechanisms for Effective Implementation of SSC Governance Using IoT*

The following section discusses the security mechanisms for IoT, and these mechanisms will play a vital role in the deployment of SSC governance because IoT will serve as a platform for the development of SSC governance. As IoT consists of heterogeneous devices, security mechanism for one device may not be suitable for another device. For instance, security mechanism for a server may not be suitable for sensor and RFID nodes. Servers are equipped with high-processing capabilities; hence, it supports complex security algorithms so we are in a situation to balance and maximize the security with less resource utilization, but RFID nodes have limited resources that we cannot apply complex security algorithms. Next, some devices may be wired with efficient resources; others may be wireless with less resources; for instance, mobile phone may act as a service provider to access SSC services through IoT. In such situations, mobile phone is equipped with wireless capabilities, whereas SSC service structure is full-fledged resources with wired architecture. Therefore, security mechanisms and policies for wired might not be applicable to wireless.

In addition, most of the IoT devices lack traditional operating system like windows, Linux, Mac, etc.; instead they are equipped with programs that are embedded in integrated chips. In a heterogeneous environment, there exist communication problems between systems that use operating systems and programs that are embedded in chips.

With these considerations in mind, we present some of the security mechanisms for IoT, and these mechanisms will provide significant contribution towards the development of SSC in security perspective. Each mechanism may differ depending on the context where it is used; by the way it will overcome all levels of security issues that will arise in the SSC governance development like application level, user level, data level, sensing level, system level, communication and networking level, and cyber level. Figure 13.5 shows the various security levels that we are concerned while developing SSC governance using IoT.

Primary security comes from ensuring authentication among the communicating devices. The authors [32–35] proposed security mechanisms to achieve authentication by various security mechanisms like public key infrastructure (PKI), trust- and repudiation-based mechanism, custom encapsulation mechanism, and emerging attribute signature, respectively. The authors of [36] proposed an elliptic curve cryptography-based authentication mechanism to establish a session key between communicating devices. In [37], the authors proposed a securing distributed storage for social Internet of Things using regeneration code and Blom key agreement. In addition, the authors [38–41] proposed security mechanism to ensure the privacy issues by context-aware k-anonymity privacy policies, adaptive clustering, discretionary and limited access, and privacy protection-enhanced domain naming system. The author of [42] proposed a public key and symmetric key algorithm to reduce the complexity of key distribution framework and reduce the power

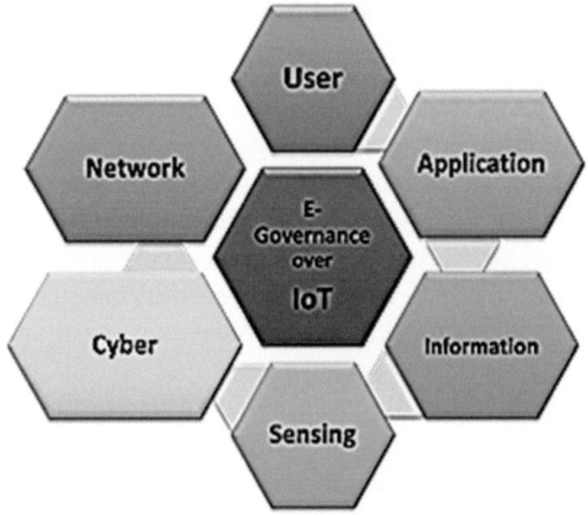


**Fig. 13.5** Various security concerns in e-governance development over IoT

consumption. To ensure confidentiality, the authors, in [43], proposed a symmetric key-based cryptography model where both the sender and receiver use a shared secret key by way of information security. To ensure integrity in the IoT, the authors in [44] proposed a symmetric key cryptography which is based on the digital signature to safeguard information while on transmission. The research reported in [45] proposed a model to address the security issues of heterogeneous integration in IoT environment. The work reported in [46] proposed a secure solution for IoT based on Trusted Cryptography Modules (TCM) to enable secure boot and secure storage by the way it ensures the system-level security.

For application-level security, research in [47] proposed a fully decentralized anonymous authentication protocol to ensure privacy preservation. In networking-level security, secure routing is important to achieve effective communication.

Another way of ensuring security in SSC governance is trust-based security mechanisms rather than cryptographic mechanisms. Normally it is quite suitable for resource-constrained devices since IoT devices share such nature. The ultimate aim of trust management is to take decision on devices before communicating with them. To ensure user-level security, the authors in [48] proposed a trust model based on service classification. The research appearing in [49] proposed a trust management model based on fuzzy repudiation to assess the IoT devices. To ensure information-level security, the author [50] proposed a trust model based on outlier detection algorithms. To ensure sensing-level security, the authors of [51] proposed a trust model which is based on multi-alteration technique. The proposal in [52] suggested a flow control technique to ensure data privacy in IoT environment.

From the above security mechanisms, we conclude that traditional security mechanisms like shared secret, public key infrastructure (PKI), digital signatures, digital certificate, intrusion detection systems/intrusion prevention systems (IDS/IPS), hash functions, system logs, etc. are suitable for fixed architecture-oriented services in SSC governance development, for instance, servers, desktops, and other well-equipped devices in processing as well as storing which will be involved in SSC governance services. Trust- and repudiation-based security mechanisms are quite useful for limited resource-constrained devices like wireless sensor nodes, RFID tags, etc., because these mechanisms do not require high-processing capabilities and high storage facility.

## 13.5 Conclusions

Today, good infrastructure, better living conditions, smart communication systems, and sustainable use of natural resources are indicators of growth and development. The city administrators across the world are clinging towards Internet of Things technology to meet these challenges. The IoT technology and related applications have the potential to meet these challenges. With modern techniques to manufacture sensors, RFID tags, and actuators with less cost and better processing ability, we have gone a step ahead in realizing the dream of developing smart sustainable cities. And this little step brings great hope that IoT can enhance human life and living conditions of people not only in cities but anywhere in the world. The next big step in this line is that IoT has brought about the revolution of converging all technologies into a single umbrella. Anything, Anytime, Anywhere, and Anyhow is the slogan of Internet of Things. Although this convergence makes the IoT technology a complex phenomenon, it brings with it innumerable possibilities by way of applications and deployments at every aspect of human society. By this convergence, information technology will have a dominant role on human living. It will affect everything we do in a new way.

The complexity cited above also calls for better ways to access devices, share informations, process computations, and store the voluminous data that IoT will generate. In IoT scenario, securing device, networks, and privacy are research challenges. Heterogeneous management, interoperability, scalability, and authentication are other research challenges in deploying IoT. In this chapter, we have attempted to suggest information- and knowledge-based automated SSC governance to coordinate the various services of the city. We also have analyzed the limitations of IoT, challenges in privacy and security and possible attacks, the possible security requirements, and solutions for effective automated SSC governance. Constructing new methods, standards, protocols, and security schemes both for date and network are research challenges in IoT and especially the deployment of information-based automated SSC governance.

## References

1. Borgia E (2016) The internet of things vision: key features, applications and open issue. Comput Commun 54:1–31
2. Gubbi J, Buyya R, Marusic S, Palaniswamia M (2013) Internet of things (IoT): a vision, architectural elements, and future directions. Futur Gener Comput Syst 29(7):1645–1660

3. Lee J, Lee H (2014) Developing and validating a citizen-centric typology for smart city services. Gov Inf Q Elsevier 31:93
4. Piro G (2014) Information centric services in smart cities. J Syst Softw 88:169–188
5. Sundmaeker H, Guillemin P, Friess P, Woelffléision S (2010) Vision and challenges for realising the internet of things. Eur Union. doi:10.2759/26127
6. Kyriazis D (2013) Smart, autonomous and reliable internet of things. Sci Dir 21:442–448
7. Kourtit K (2014) The new urban world: challenges and policy. Appl Geogr 49:1–3
8. Jing Q, Vasilakos AV, Wan J, Lu J, Qiu D (2014) Security of the internet of things: perspectives and challenges. Wirel Netw 20:2481–2501
9. Whitmore A, Agarwal A, Xu LD (2015) The internet of things—a survey of topics and trends. Inf Syst Front 17:261–274
10. Sicari S, Cappiello C, De Pellegrini F, Miorandi D, Coen-Porisini A (2015) A security-and quality-aware system architecture for internet of things. Inf Syst Front. doi:10.1007/s10796-014-9538-x
11. Bandyopadhyay D, Sen J (2011) Internet of things: applications and challenges in technology and standardization. Wirel Pers Commun 58:49–69
12. Yick J, Mukherjee B, Ghosal D (2008) Wireless sensor network survey. Comput Netw 52:2292–2330
13. Wanga F, Huang B, Yang LT (2012) SONR: a reliable reputation system of self-organized network. J Netw Comput Appl 35:914–926
14. Mantri DS, Prasad NR, Prasad R (2016) Mobility and heterogeneity aware cluster-based data aggregation for wireless sensor network. Wirel Pers Commun 86:975–993
15. De Poorter E, Moerman I, Demeester P (2011) Enabling direct connectivity between heterogeneous objects in the internet of things through a network-service-oriented architecture. EURASIP J Wirel Commun Netw, 61:1–14
16. Noll J, Mohammad MR, Chowdhury (2011) 5G: service continuity in heterogeneous environments. Wirel Pers Commun 57:413–429
17. Li S, Xu LD, Zhao S (2011) The internet of things: a survey. Inf Syst Front 17:243–259
18. Stallings W (2012) Network security essentials. Pearson, USA
19. Liu CH, Chung YF, Chen TS, Wang SD (2012) The enhancement of security in healthcare information systems. J Med Syst 36:1673–1688
20. Yu H, He J, Zhang T, Xiao P, Zhang Y (2013) Enabling end-to-end secure communication between wireless sensor networks and the Internet. World Wide Web 16:515–540
21. Ning H (2013) A security framework for the internet of things based on public key infrastructure. Adv Mater Res 671–674
22. Feng R, Che S, Wang X, Yu N (2013) Trust management scheme based on D-S evidence theory for wireless sensor networks. Int J Distrib Sensor Netw. doi:10.1155/2013/948641
23. Miorandi D, Sicari S, De Pellegrini F, Chalamtac I (2013) Internet of things: vision, applications and research challenges. Ad Hoc Networks 10:1497–1516
24. Bekara C (2014) Security issues and challenges for the IoT-based smart grid. Procedia Comput Sci 34:532–537
25. Xu Y, Chen G, Ford J, Makedon F (2008) Critical infrastructure protection. IFIP- Int Fed Inf Process 253:267–279
26. Shafieia H, Khonsaria A, Derakhshia H, Mousavia P (2014) Detection and mitigation of sinkhole attacks in wireless sensor networks. J Comput Syst Sci 80(3):644–653
27. Zhao Y (2013) Research on data security technology in internet of things. In: 2013 2nd International Conference on Mechatronics and Control Engineering, ICMCE 2013, Dalian, China, 2013, 1752–1755
28. Liang X, Lu R, Shen X (2010) Sybil attacks and their defenses in the internet of things. Internet Things J 1(5):372–383
29. Heer T, Garcia-Morchon O, Hummen R, Keoh SL, Kumar SS, Wehrle K (2011) Security challenges in the IP-based internet of things. Wirel Pers Commun 61:527–542
30. Sicari S, Rizzardi A, Grieco LA, Coen-Porisini A (2015) Security, privacy and trust in internet of things: the road ahead. Comput Netw 76:146–164

31. Velloso PB, Laufer RP, de O Cunha D et al (2010) Trust management in mobile Ad Hoc networks using a scalable maturity-based model. IEEE Trans Netw Serv Manag 7:3
32. Tianshui WU, Gang Z (2014) A novel risk assessment model for privacy security in internet of things. Wuhan Univ J Nat Sci 19(5):398–404
33. Roman R (2011) Key management systems for sensor networks in the context of the internet of things. Comput Electr Eng 37(2):147–159
34. Kothmayr T, Schmitt C et al (2013) Dtls based security and two-way authentication for the internet of things. Ad Hoc Netw 11(8):2710–2723
35. Zhao, Ling Y (2013) Research on data security technology in internet of things. Appl Mech Mater 1752:433–435
36. Ye N, Zhu Y et al (2014) An efficient authentication and access control scheme for perception layer of internet of things. Appl Math Inf Sci 8(4):1617–1624
37. Wu J, Dong M, Ota K et al (2014) Securing distributed storage for social internet of things using regenerating code and blom key agreement. Peer-to-Peer Netw Appl. doi:10.1007/s12083-014-0286-y
38. Huang X, Fu R et al (2012) User interactive internet of things privacy preserved access control. In: 7th international conference for Internet Technology and Secured Transactions, ICITST 2012, London, pp 597–602
39. Cao J, Carminati B, Ferrari E, Tan KL (2011) CASTLE: continuously anonymizing data streams. IEEE Trans Dependable Secure Comput 8(3):337–352
40. Yang J, Fang B (2011) Security model and key technologies for the internet of things. J China Univ Posts Telecommun 8(2):109–112
41. Wang Y, Wen Q (2011) A privacy enhanced dns scheme for the internet of things, In: IET international conference on Communication Technology and Application, ICCTA 2011, Beijing, pp 699–702
42. Karlof C, Wagner D (2003) Secure routing in wireless sensor networks: attacks and countermeasures. Proc First IEEE Int Work Sensor Netw Protoc Appl 1(2):293–315
43. Delfs H, Knebl H (2007) Symmetric key encryption. In: Introduction to cryptography, Berlin: Springer, pp 11–13
44. Vucinic M, Tourancheau B, Rousseau F, Duda A, Damon L, Guizzetti R (2015) OSCAR: object security architecture for the internet of things. Retrieved on 25.05.2015, available on http://arxiv.org/abs/1404.7799
45. Zhang GG, Bi Y, Li C (2013) Massive internet data security processing model research. Small Microcomput Syst 34(9):2090–2094
46. Qiu-Xin W, Han L (2013) Secure solution of trusted internet of things base on TCM. J China Univ Posts Telecommun, 47–52
47. Alcaide A, Palomar E, Castillo JM, Ribagorda A (2013) Anonymous authentication for privacy preserving IoT target driven applications. Comput Secur 37:111–123
48. Liu M, Zhang A (2010) A solution to privacy preserving two party sign test on vertically partitioned data using data disguising techniques. In: Proceedings of the international conference on networking and information technology, pp 526–534. doi. 10.1109/ICNIT.2010.5508458
49. Chen D, Chang G, Sun D, Li J, Jia J, Wang X (2011) TRM-IoT: a trust management model based on fuzzy repudiation for internet of things. Comput Sci Inf Syst 8(4):1207–1228
50. Javed N, Wolf T (2012) Automated sensor verification using outlier detection in the internet of things. In: Proceedings of the 32nd international conference on distributed computing systems workshop, pp 261–266
51. Sicari S, Coen-Porisini A, Riggio R (2013) DARE: evaluating data accuracy using node repudiation computer networks. 57(15):3098–3111
52. Evans D, Eyers DM (2012) Efficient data tagging for managing privacy in the internet of things. In: Proceedings of the IEEE international conference on green computing and communications, pp 244–248

# Chapter 14
# Connectivity of Smart Devices: Addressing the Security Challenges of the Internet of Things

**Stephen Kwamena Aikins**

## 14.1 Introduction

The Internet of Things (IoT) entails interconnection of smart devices in a network based on the possibility of seamless integration of physical objects such as sensors or home appliances which can be loosely defined as a network of interface that explores a piece of functionality [1]. IoT is a network of billions of addressable, smart, mobile, and possibly, minuscule devices [2]. It promises a revolution in computing and communications technology and also offers revolution in the way we live, potentially providing intelligent support in all aspects of our lives [3]. While there is no global consensus on the meaning of the term, it is clear that the main idea behind the IoT concept is the ability to connect loosely defined smart objects and enable them to interact with other objects, the environment, or more complex and legacy computing devices [4].

New developments in radio-frequency identification (RFID) and wireless sensor networks (WSNs) mean that more things can be interconnected, tracked, and even made intelligent, with the hope of benefiting society. Despite its huge potential, there are numerous concerns about the security and privacy of IoT. A crucial data management challenge for the IoT is that of maintaining appropriate security in a wireless environment. The wireless environment of IoT allows the network to go where wires cannot go. Users are no longer limited to certain workplaces, but this mobility and flexibility have properties inherently different from those of conventional networks, with major implications for security vulnerabilities [2]. Given the security and privacy concerns of IoT, a high degree of reliability is needed in order for the concept to gain wider acceptance. The purpose of this chapter is to discuss

S.K. Aikins (✉)
School of Public Affairs, University of South Florida, Tampa, FL, USA
e-mail: saikins@usf.edu



Z. Mahmood (ed.), *Connectivity Frameworks for Smart Devices*,
Computer Communications and Networks, DOI 10.1007/978-3-319-33124-9_14

some of the security concerns of IoT, as well as some existing and in-progress security protocols and technologies for addressing those concerns.

The rest of the chapter is organized as the following sections: domain areas of IoT and security implications, the benefits of secured IoT to society, IoT security challenges and related research, security automation and interoperability requirements of IoT, and security protocols and solutions to IoT challenges.

## 14.2 Domain Areas of IoT and Security Implications

The IoT entails connectivity of things such as smart devices, the notion of which encompasses a wider range of devices that use TCP/IP and protocols on top of that to communicate with PCs and other devices. These include mobile phones, car navigators, handheld cameras, and other embedded devices. Many of these use Web service technology as a means to communicate or synchronize themselves with other devices on the Internet [1]. Currently, the application of IoT in real life is mostly made up of a loose collection of disparate, purpose-built networks. For example, today's cars have multiple networks to control engine function, safety features, communication systems, etc. Healthcare services are relying on increased home sensing to support remote medicine and wellness [5]. Commercial and residential buildings also have various control systems for heating, venting, and air conditioning (HVAC), telephone service, security, and lighting. The emergence of applications of sensor networks has room for adoption by law enforcement, military, border patrol, custom, etc. Vibration sensors distributed along national borders form an effective virtual fence [6]. Utility meters rely on machine-to-machine communications, eliminating the need for a human meter reader and allow fully automated billing. Weather forecasting infrastructure collaborates with in-ground sensors and irrigation-control software, thereby enabling the irrigation system to engage based on intelligent decision involving the level of moisture in the soil and the likelihood of precipitation [6]. Additionally, many factory shop floors are typically filled with sensors, robots, and other smart embedded devices connected to a network, with the potential benefit of getting these production line embedded devices to engage in real-time communication based on predefined specifications.

Effective communication of the smart objects involved in the functions described above depends on proper security. For example, messages from smart utility meters must be authenticated so that the utility provider can verify that the sensor reading was generated by the right smart meter to avoid sending wrong invoices, and the smart meter must be able to verify that a command is actually from the right provider. Additionally, it is desirable to encrypt the sensor data in transit to ensure message confidentiality [7]. Security is a major concern in large-scale deployment of networks such as those of the interconnected smart devices on the IoT. There can be many ways the system could be attacked—disabling the network availability, pushing erroneous data into the network, accessing personal

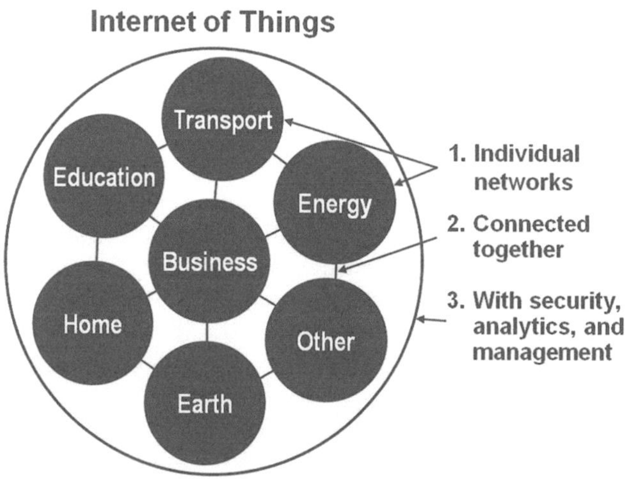


**Fig. 14.1** IoT can be viewed as a network of networks. Source: Evans [12]. Cisco Internet Business Solution Group, April 2011

information, etc. Two key physical components of IoT—RFID and WSN—are vulnerable to such attacks. Security is critical to any network [8, 9], and the first line of defense against data corruption is cryptography. RFID seems to be the most vulnerable as it allows person tracking as well as the objects and no high-level intelligence can be enabled on these devices [10]. These complex problems however have solutions that can be provided using cryptographic methods and require more research before they are widely accepted. Against outsider attackers, encryption ensures data confidentiality, whereas message authentication codes ensure data integrity and authenticity [11]. Encryption, however, does not protect against insider malicious attacks. Consequently, non-cryptographic means are needed to combat such attacks, particularly in WSNs. Figure 14.1 shows how IoT can be viewed as a network of networks of devices in various domains such as transportation, education, energy, home, and business, with security and other implications. As IoT evolves, these networks and many others will have to be connected with added security, analytics, and management capabilities [12].

## 14.3 The Benefits of Secured IoT to Society

Recently, WSNs and traditional Internet Protocol (IP) networks are integrated using Internet Protocol version 6 (IPv6) and IPv6 over Low-Power Wireless Personal Area Network (6LoWPAN). The introduction of IPv6 and Web services as fundamental building blocks for IoT applications brings a number of potential basic advantages, including (i) a homogenous protocol ecosystem that allows simple integration with Internet hosts, (ii) a simplified development of very different appliances, and (iii) a unified interface for applications, removing the need for application-level proxies [13]. Such features greatly simplify the development of envisioned scenarios ranging from building automation to production environments to personal area networks, in which very different things such as a temperature sensor, a luminaire, or an RFID tag might interact with each other, with a human carrying a smartphone, or with backend services [13].

The significance of the connectivity of smart devices in the IoT lies in the huge amount of data that can be gathered and processed for the benefit of mankind. This benefit stems from the principle of sharing information and building on discoveries as humans process data to gain information, knowledge, and wisdom [12]. For this to work effectively, the security of the data in the networks of connected smart devices is crucial in order to maintain confidentiality, reliability, and integrity. Data consists of text, images, or sound that may or may not be pertinent for a particular purpose. It is the raw material that is processed into information. Individual data by itself is not very useful but volumes of it can identify trends and patterns that provide information to form knowledge [12]. Therefore, knowledge can be viewed as information of which a person is aware, while wisdom is born out of knowledge and experience. The key issue is that the more data that is created, the more knowledge and wisdom humans can obtain, and IoT dramatically increases the amount of data available for us to process [12].

Stankovic [14] suggests the steady increasing of sensing, and the sophistication of the associated processing will make a significant qualitative change in how humans work and live, as we will truly have systems of systems that synergistically interact to form totally new and unpredictable services. Given this potential, the question is, what will be the platform or platforms that support the IoT vision? One possibility is a global sensing and actuation utility connected to the Internet. Sensing and actuation in the form of IoT platform will become a utility, and IoT will not be seen as individual systems, but as a critical, integrated infrastructure upon which many applications and services can run [14]. This critical infrastructure will be meaningful in helping to realize the dream of IoT only if the appropriate security parameters of the interconnected devices are developed, installed, and well managed in order to enable humans to further advance by turning data into wisdom. Figure 14.2 depicts the benefits of humans turning data into wisdom.

To realize the vision of IoT, there is a need for substantial progress in research achievements in several fields. Firstly, today there is no single way of identifying an object in the Internet of Things: there are several standards, such as 2-D bar codes, GS1, uID, IPv6 addresses, and RFID, but they are not all compatible [15]. Moreover, reference architectures which can lead the way to any kind of real-life system implementation must be identified and standardized. Additionally, there is the need for security mechanisms that ensure reasonable safety and privacy properties. Communication protocols, from physical layer to interfaces with services and applications, need substantial advances, which can be made possible through research, in order to leverage the upcoming of any IoT vision [15]. The following section reviews the literature on IoT security challenges and the research on connectivity of smart devices.

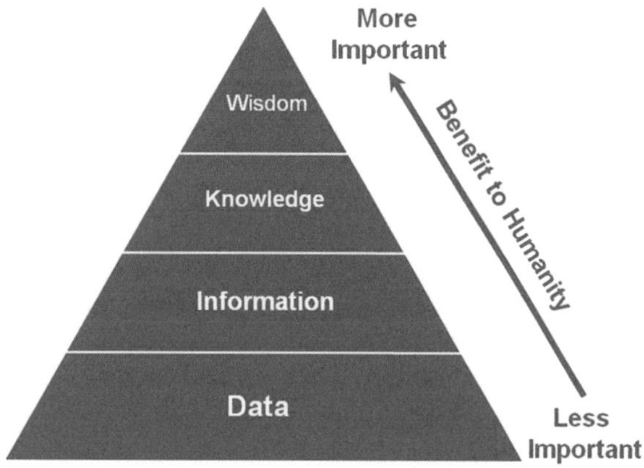


**Fig. 14.2** Humans turn data into wisdom. Source: Evans [12]. Cisco Internet Business Solution Group, April 2011

## 14.4 Research on IoT Security Challenges

As argued by several scholars [8, 9, 14, 16], a fundamental and pervasive problem concerning IoT that needs resolution is dealing with security attacks. Security attacks are problematic for the IoT because of the minimal capacity of the devices being used; the physical accessibility to sensors, actuators, and objects; and the openness of the systems, including the fact that most devices will communicate wirelessly. This security problem is complicated by the transient and permanent random failures and vulnerabilities that can be exploited by attackers [14]. This implies the need for IoT applications to be able to operate satisfactorily during, and recover effectively from, security attacks including strong attack detection capabilities if they are to meet realistic system requirements that derive from long-lived and unattended operations [17]. Given the types of low-capacity devices involved in the IoT, there is the need for a system that can detect and diagnose security attacks and deploy countermeasures in a lightweight manner [13]. Additionally, the real-time nature of many IoTs requires that the detection, countermeasures, and recoveries from attacks must run in real time as part of runtime self-healing architecture. However, most of today's mainframe security solutions require heavy-weight computations and large memory requirements, implying a major research challenge for IoT [14].

Several research projects are underway to address many of the abovementioned challenges. In the area of health, the AIRE project of the University of Murcia in Spain designs and develops an IoT platform to support remote monitoring and detect and predict anomalies in patients with breathing problems. The same institution is working on an IoT-based personal device for diabetes therapy management in ambient-assisted living [18]. From a technical point of view, the architecture of IoT is based on data communication tools, primarily RFID-tagged items. A key industry proposal for IT infrastructure for the IoT is based on an Electronic Product Code (EPC). The "things" are physical objects carrying RFID tags with a unique EPC. The infrastructure can offer and query EPC Information Services (EPCIS) both locally and remotely to subscribers [19]. Although the information is not fully saved on an RFID tag, a supply of the information by distributed servers on the Internet is made available through linking and cross-linking with the help of an Object Naming Service (ONS) [20]. Thus, EPC connects the physical and virtual worlds with the help of ONS and physical markup language (PML). This connectivity is possible only when the integration at various levels of EPC network takes place. Any EPC deployment will need to address device integration, data integration, application integration, and process-level integration with EPC network infrastructure [21] with enormous security challenges. Figure 14.3 shows integration between organization's EPC systems. Information sharing, data security, inter-organization messaging, and communication for collaborative automation are key requirements for integration between EPC systems [21].

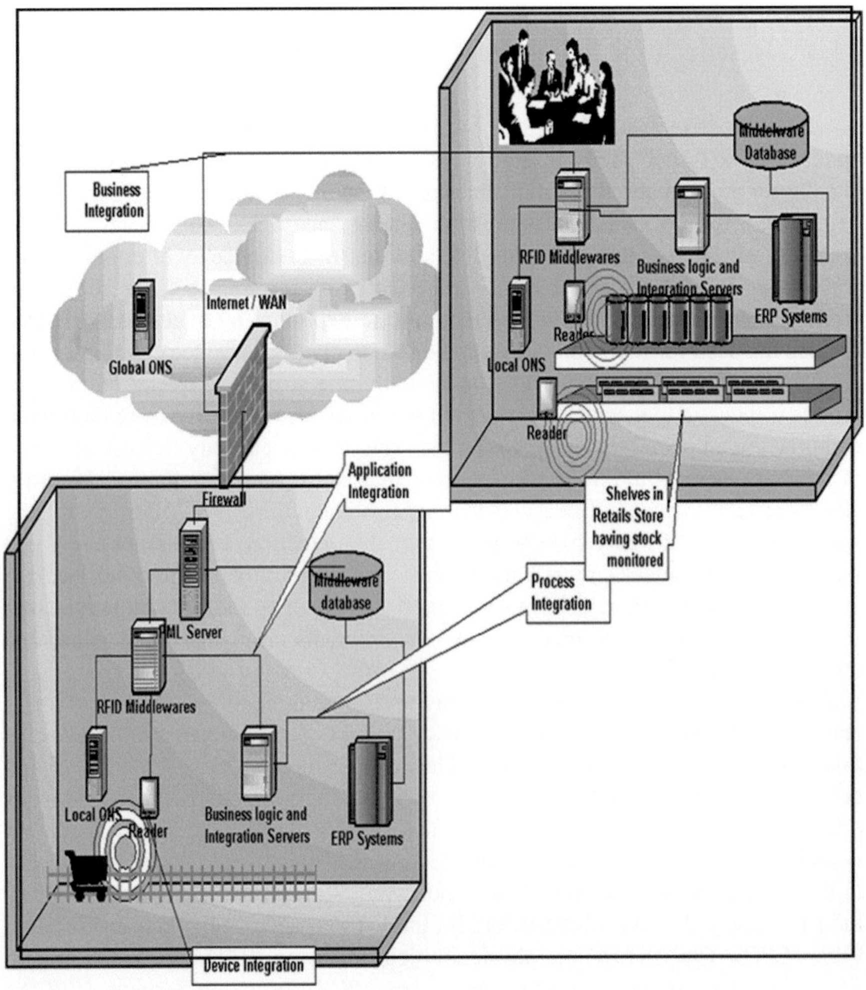


**Fig. 14.3** Inter-enterprise EPC network (Adopted from [21])

In recent years, the introduction of RFID tags has raised privacy concerns because anyone might access and track tags. Considering the fact that IoT involves both passive devices as well as active and sensing devices, the IoT might deeply intrude into people's privacy. Therefore, IoT protocols should be designed to avoid these privacy threats in its operation [4].

In transportation, for example, the aviation industry faces the threat of inappropriate parts. Safety and security of the service can be achieved by protecting them from counterfeiting through RFID tags with authentication of digital signatures on the real product and wireless monitoring of parts with intelligent sensing devices. Similar problems abound in retail logistics and supply chain management. Researchers at the Hasso Plattner Institute are working on RFID as a basis for anti-counterfeiting by providing enhancements to existing business processes through the usage of EPCs for identification [22].

In the case of ONS, the entity that assigns the EPC to the concerned item is the entity having centralized change control over the information about the EPC. Consequently, the architecture can also serve as backbone for ubiquitous computing, enabling smart environments to recognize and identify objects and receive information from the Internet to facilitate their adaptive functionality [19, 20]. As stated by [19], ONS is based on Domain Name Service (DNS). In order to use DNS to find information about an item, the item's EPC must be converted into a format that the DNS can understand. Given the fact that EPC is encoded into syntactically correct domain name and used within the existing DNS infrastructure, the ONS can be considered a subset of DNS. Therefore, the ONS will also inherit all of the well-documented DNS weaknesses, including limited redundancy in practical implementation and the creation of single point of failure [19]. This technical architecture of IoT has an impact on the security and privacy of stakeholders. The attribution of tags to objects may not be known to users, and there may not be an acoustic or visual signal to draw the attention of the object's user. Consequently, individuals can be followed without them knowing about it and would leave their data or traces in cyberspace [10].

The abovementioned concern calls for security and privacy requirements in the areas of interoperability and automation to strengthen the connectivity of smart devices as part of overall IoT. The advanced research on information security and privacy project (ARES), funded by the Spanish Ministry of Science, aims at bringing security to the information society while preserving individual rights. It focuses on ubiquitous computing with emphasis on WSNs and RFID, protection of critical information infrastructures, and secure electronic commerce and digital content distribution, while tackling different tactical challenges in the areas of cryptography, smart cards, personal identification and biometrics, access control and authentication, network security, and trust generation [23]. French researchers, including GSI France, France Telecom Group, and RFID European Lab, are working on a large-scale EPC global network in which only one ONS root will exist in Europe and will be managed on a shared basis, security in vehicular networks, systems to track patients, medical personnel, drugs and equipment, and a smart planet using mobile enterprise systems. Researchers in the USA are working on efficient cryptographic techniques to speed up integrity verification and detection of integrity corruptions in vehicular networks and business policies, as well as government policies that shape the IoT [6].

For communication of devices to be secured in the various IoT application domains, protocol compatibility will be essential. Machine-to-machine interfaces and protocols of electronic communication set the rules of engagement for two or more nodes on a network. IP has become the standard for all data communication. Consequently, it provides the easy way for data transmission over the Internet [7]. Examples of protocols that can be used in lower-power radio for communication are Link Layer, ISA 100A, Wireless HART, ZigBee, and IPv6 [7]. The advantage of IPv6 is that it helps to address the challenges of interoperability of different existing systems. For this reason, the system of objects connected via the Internet can develop the same way that the current Internet developed [7]. In order to enhance effectiveness, security automation and interoperability requirements are essential for protocol compatibility of smart objects connected via the Internet.

### 14.4.1 Security Automation and Interoperability Requirements

IoT involves and leverages on current knowledge in automatic identification and communication of connected devices. For pervasive computing to be realized, the embedded devices within IoT should be able to communicate and interoperate with each other in order to cooperate. For communication between connected smart devices, there is a need to develop a convergence between different communication means. Several communication mechanisms (as shown in Table 14.1) are deployed in current applications, and any novel technologies will need to guarantee interoperability between different protocols [15].

There is a need to also consider that the lifetime of network technologies might be much shorter than the one of the physical objects connected to it, where that same technology is applied [15]. In the "common" Internet, the interoperability between low-layer technology and services is assured by the use of the IP. This implies a set of requirements that can be expressed in terms of the quantity and resources connected, density of the connections, and complexity to manage both elements. These requirements include interoperability and automation. The interoperability issue in the security of connected smart devices can be separated in three main domains. These domains are semantic communication, grammar of communication, and operation connection [1]. For connected smart devices to understand each other, there is the need to be able to know the meaning of the exchanged data. Two mechanisms have been created to address this translation protocol and standardized semantics. For example, security ontologies and translation mechanisms have been developed in order for different firewall and antivirus software to exchange data [24, 25].

**Table 14.1** Protocols of popular physical communication interfaces exploited by communication

| Physical communication interface type | Communication type | Protocols | OSI layer |
|---|---|---|---|
| 802.15.X series (ZigBee, Bluetooth, RFID, etc.) | Wireless | NWK/APS/API defined by each standardization body (all non-IP) | Network/ transport/ upper |
| Wi-Fi | Wireless | IP/TCP-UDP | Network/ transport/ upper |
| UWB | Wireless | Baseband/LinkManager/L2CAP (non-IP) | Network/ transport/ upper |
| Sensor network busses (e.g., CAN, Profibus, etc.) | Fixed | Up to data link | Data link |
| Serial | Fixed | Up to data link | Data link |
| USB | Fixed, wireless | Up to data link | Data link |
| DeviceNet | Fixed | DeviceNet network and transport | Network/ transport/ upper |
| ControlNet | Fixed | ControlNet network and transport | Network/ transport/ upper |
| Ethernet/IP | Fixed | IP/TCP-UDP | Network/ transport/ upper |
| Power line (KNX, LonWorks) | Fixed | Network/transport layers according network layer/transport to KNX and LonWorks specifications | Network/ transport |

Source: Anzelmo et al. [15]. Discussion Paper Commissioned by the Commission for Internet and Society, Berlin

Connected smart devices do not necessarily use shared grammar to understand the semantics of the data exchanges. Therefore, several grammars have been developed and used for security-related issues and could benefit IoT by providing a standard access control policy language replacing many application-specific languages, for example, eXtensible Access Control Markup Language.

XACML is an XML-based OASIS [26] Web service-oriented standard for communicating access control policies between services. Security Assertion Markup Language (SAML) is a standard in OASIS standardized specification for expressing, requesting, and delivery assertions regarding credentials of entities such as users, computers, printers, etc. Developed by Microsoft Corporation, SecPAL is a policy and token authoring language that combines access control policies and security tokens under the same grammar which in turn conforms to a formal model [27].

Automation of security task is essential in order to effectively manage the ever-growing connected smart objects, as well as their increased level of associations and potential usage. Given that not all smart objects on a network can be manually made aware of all new threats as they evolve, automation facilitates detection of threats to connected devices on a network and the actions taken to address such threats. With interoperability, connected devices are capable of understanding each other's security-related information. Therefore, automation can promote a more advanced interoperability regarding the exposure of management-type interfaces which allow exchanging data and permit devices to know how to communicate with each other.

A security requirement regarding interoperability can be illustrated with the installation of Building Automation Control (BAC) system in the life cycle of a connected device on IoT. A BAC system consists of a network of interconnected nodes that perform various functions including HVAC, lighting, safety, etc. Most BAC systems use legacy building control standards such as BACNet [28, 29] with independent networks for each subsystem such as HVAC. However, this compartmentalization of functionality entails complications with additional configuration and maintenance costs for the different networks within the same building. Consequently, more recent building control networks employ IP-based standards allowing seamless control over the various nodes with a single management system.

Although the shift to IP-based standards in the network allows for easier integration, it also results in new requirements regarding the implementation of IP security protocols on constrained devices and the network. This calls for security architecture with the elements to manage security relationships between devices, as well as security model of the various nodes to ensure effective management of the security parameters, processes, and applications. It also implies the need for authentication and authorization of devices as well as the transfer of security parameters allowing for trusted operation. Additionally, there is the need for network security to prevent attackers from endangering or modifying the expected operation of connected devices on the network. Effective deployment of network security requires understanding the various threats to network communication and IoT systems vulnerabilities.

Furthermore, application security is essential to guarantee that only trusted instances of applications running on the IoT can communicate with each other. Table 14.2 provides a synthesis of common threats per network communication layer to give the reader an idea of the vulnerabilities IoT systems face [15]. The next section discusses some of the security protocols being implemented to address some of the challenges of the IoT network.

### 14.4.2 Security Protocols and Technologies for Addressing IoT Challenges

As stated above, the IoT is a resource-constrained network. This is because it relies on low-bandwidth channels for communication between small nodes, regarding

**Table 14.2** Threats to network communication layer depicting IoT systems vulnerabilities

| Layer | Threat | Requirements | Targets [1] | Approaches |
|---|---|---|---|---|
| Transport | Ping/ICMP flood | Attacker being part of the network, ICMP | All connected devices | |
| | Synflood | TCP, attacker being part of the network | All connected devices | |
| Network | Neighbor discovery attack | Neighbor discovery protocol | Networks using unauthenticated ND protocol | Authentication support for ND protocols |
| | Wormhole | Mesh networking | Multi-hop wireless | Specific hardware, time |
| | | | Networks | Constraints on packet delivery |
| | Black hole | Attacker being part of the network | Multi-hop wireless<br>Networks | Don't use plain distance-vector-based protocols |
| Link | Spoofing | – | All networks, especially wireless | Packet authentication |
| | Eavesdropping | – | Wireless networks | Encryption |
| | DoS—collision | – | Wireless networks | Use UWB, increase data rate |
| | DoS—exhaustion | – | Embedded wireless<br>Networks | Link-layer intrusion detection |
| | Replay protection att | Replay protection | Multi-hop wireless<br>Networks | RANBAR, Tesla |

Source: Anzelmo et al. [15]. Discussion Paper Commissioned by the Commission for Internet and Society, Berlin

CPU memory and energy budget. The limited energy budget available to IoT nodes requires careful protocol design and usage to reduce both the energy consumption during normal operation and also during DoS (Denial of Service) attacks. In general, the energy consumption of IoT devices differs from other devices classes. This implies the need for tailor-made IoT implementation of particular protocol in order to have informed judgment on the energy consumption of any particular protocol. The limited memory and processing constraints of connected devices on IoT elevate attacks which may be difficult to notice before the service becomes unavailable because of battery or memory exhaustion.

As a DoS countermeasure, protocols such as the Internet Key Exchange (IKEv2)/IPsec (Internet Protocol Security) and the Host Identity Protocol (HIP) which reside at or above the network layer of the OSI model, implement return routability check, and help to delay the establishment of state at the responding host until the addresses of the initiating host are verified, although the effectiveness of these defenses strongly depends on the routing topology of the network [13]. Although return routability checks are particularly effective if hosts cannot receive packets addressed to other hosts and if addresses present meaningful information as is the case in today's Internet, they are less effective in broadcast media or when attackers can influence the routing and addressing of hosts [13].

IPsec defines an Authentication Header (AH) and an Encapsulating Security Payload (ESP). The AH can be used to provide data integrity and authentication, while ESP provides data confidentiality, integrity, and authentication. Additionally, either each one of them or both can be used to secure IPv6 packets in transit [7]. ESP is used to encrypt the payload of an IP packet but in contrast to AH, it does not secure the IP header. If ESP is applied, the IP header is followed by the ESP IP extension header which contains the encrypted payload. ESP includes an SPI (Security Parameter Index) which identifies the SA (Security Associations) used, a sequence number to prevent replay attacks, the encrypted payload, padding which may be required by some block ciphers, a reference to the next header and optional authentication data [7]. Encryption in ESP includes Payload Data, Padding, Pad Length, and Next Header. Selected authentication includes all header fields in ESP. It is important to note that the protocols AH and ESP support two different modes—the transport mode and tunnel mode. In the transport mode, the IP header and payload are directly secured, while in the tunnel mode, a new IP header is placed in front of the original packet and security functions are applied to the encapsulated (tunneled) IP packet.

The characteristics of IoT directly impact the threats to and the design of security protocols for the IoT domain [13]. For example, the use of small packets such as IEEE 802.15.4 to support 127 byte-sized packets at the physical layer of data communication may result in fragmentation of larger packets of security protocols and may open new attack vectors like DoS attacks. Packet fragmentation downgrades the overall system performance due to fragment losses and the need for retransmission. Inadequate CPU memory resources limit the use of resource demanding public key cryptography that is used in most Internet security standards. As noted by [13], this is especially true if the basic cryptoblocks need to be used frequently or if the underlying application demands a low delay.

Message authentication and encryption in WSNs are generally performed using well-known cryptographic mechanisms such as block ciphers as part of standard-based protocols such as IEEE 802.15.4. However, these mechanisms are difficult to implement on resource-constrained sensor nodes as cryptographic mechanisms can be expensive in terms of code size and processing speed. Additionally, it is necessary to distribute and maintain key, and it is difficult to implement efficient key distribution protocols for resource-constrained sensor nodes [7]. Several research work such as EEC [30] and NanEEC [31] aims at reducing complexity of cryptographic mechanisms or to simplify key distribution. Examples of these include the proposal for pairwise key distribution [32] and the DHB-KEY [33]. Although a standardized way of implementing security services remains an issue, the above-mentioned improvements make cryptographic mechanisms in the context of WSNs more viable.

Efforts have been made to create a HIP variant termed Diet HIP [34] that takes into account the low-power networks at the authentication and key exchange level of data communication. Additionally, Transport Layer Security (TLS) provides security for TCP and requires a reliable transport, while its datagram-oriented variant (DTLS) secures and uses datagram-oriented protocols. End-to-end security can be provided by the widely used TLS standard. By operating between the transport layer and the application layer, it guarantees security between applications, includes a key exchange mechanism, and provides authentication between Internet hosts in addition to confidentiality and integrity. As a counterpart, TLS can only be used over TCP, which is rarely used in wireless sensor networks. DTLS is an adaptation of TLS for UDP (User Datagram Protocol), but it is not widely used and would require to be implemented in conjunction with TLS in order to provide full IP support, but this involves additional complexity overhead [7]. The Extensible Authentication Protocol (EAP) is a framework for supporting multiple authentication methods and runs directly over the data link layer, meaning it does not require the deployment if IP, and it supports duplicate detection and retransmission without allowing for packet fragmentation [13].

A network-layer transport for EAP that enables network access authentication between clients and the network infrastructure is the Protocol for Carrying Authentication for Network Access (PANA), an EAP lower layer that runs between the EAP peer and the EAP authenticator [13]. The IPsec protocol suite, mandated by IPv6, provides end-to-end security for any IP communication. Like TLS, it includes a key exchange mechanism and provides authentication in addition to confidentiality and integrity. By operating at the network layer, it can be used with any transport protocols, including potential future one. Additionally, it ensures the confidentiality and integrity of the transport-layer headers (as well as integrity of IP headers), which cannot be done with a higher-level solution like TLS [7]. For these reasons, researchers [35–37] and 6LoWPAN standardization groups [38] consider IPsec a potential security solution for IP-based WSN. 6LoWPAN aims at integrating existing IP-based infrastructure and sensor networks by specifying how IPv6 packets are to be transmitted over and IEEE 802.15.4 network. The maximum physical layer packet size of 802.154 packets is $127byte$ and the maximum frame header size is $25byte$. This implies an IPv6 packet has therefore to fit $102byte$. Given that packet headers of a pack would already consume $48byte$ of the available $102byte$, it is obvious that header compression mechanisms are an essential component of the 6LoWPAN standard [7].

In other efforts to address WSN security challenges of connected smart devices in the IoT, a variety of key agreement and privacy protection protocols tailored to IoT scenarios have been introduced. For example, random key pre-distribution [39] or Security Protocols for Sensor Networks [SPINS] [40] have been proposed for key establishment in WSNs. Furthermore, the ZigBee standard leverages the security model of IEEE 802.15.4 MAC sublayer which specifies four security services—access control, data encryption, frame integrity, and sequential freshness. The frame integrity is to protect data from being modified without cryptographic key, and the sequential freshness is to reject data frames that have been relayed [41]. The ZigBee standard defines a security architecture based on an online trust center that is in charge of handling the security relationships within a ZigBee network. Personal privacy in ubiquitous computing has also been studied extensively, e.g., [42]. However, these solutions often implement a collapsed cross-layer optimized communication stack. For example, such solutions are implemented without task-specific network layers and layered packet headers, due to resource constraints and specialization to meet specific requirements. As a result of the nature of their design, they cannot directly be adapted to the requirements of the Internet [13].

With the evolvement of IoT, it is expected that connected smart devices such as wearable sensors and user devices will be mobile in that they are attached to different networks during the lifetime of a security association [13]. Built-in mobility signaling can greatly reduce the overhead of the cryptographic protocols due to the potential avoidance of unnecessary and costly reestablishments of the session. HIP offers a simple and effective mobility management by allowing hosts to signal changes to their associations [43]. As argued by [13], slight adjustment might be necessary to reduce cryptographic costs. This can be done by making the public key signatures in the mobility messages optional. IKEv2 supports host mobility with mobility and multi-homing protocol [MOBIKE] extension [44, 45]. Although MOBIKE refrains from applying burdensome cryptographic extensions for mobility, it mandates the use of IPsec tunnel mode which requires transmission of an additional IP header in each packet. This additional overhead could be alleviated by using header compression methods or the Bound End-to-End Tunnel (BEET) mode [46].

To enable RFID and EPCglobal standard solutions in practice, technical, social, and educational constraints—particularly in the area of security—must be overcome. BRIDGE (Building Radio-frequency IDentification solutions for the Global Environment) addresses these problems by extending the EPC network architecture [47]. For security purposes, it is crucial that an RFID tag attached to an object can be disabled at a later date to provide customers the discretion on the future use of the tag. To disable RFID tags, they may be put in a protective mesh of foil known as "Faraday cage" which is impenetrable by radio signals of certain frequencies or they may be "killed" by removing and destroying them [48]. Although putting tags in a special cage is relatively safe, the disadvantage of this approach is that it requires that every tag from every single product is put in that cage if a customer so desires.

There is also a good chance that certain tags will be overlooked and left with the client, thereby making it possible for the client to be traced. Regarding the "killing" of tags, it leaves room to the possibility of reactivation or that some identifying information could be left on the tag [48]. A way of addressing this weakness could be the dissolution of the connection between the tag and the identifiable object, by deleting the information on the ONS to protect the privacy of the owner of the tagged object. While the tag can still be read in such instance, further information regarding the owner of the tagged object is not retrievable [19]. In H2T and T2T interactions, privacy-aware identifiers might be used to prevent unauthorized user tracking. Similarly, authentication can be used to prove membership of a group without revealing unnecessary individual information. TLS and DTLS provide the option of only authenticating the responding host, so that the initiating host can stay anonymous.

Given the need for effectively functioning security protocols, as well as the limited memory, energy budget, and processing constraints of IoT network, sensors will need to be self-sustaining if IoT is to reach its full potential. With billions of devices connected, it is impossible to change batteries of all those devices deployed across the planet. Consequently, there is the need for a way for sensors to generate electricity from environmental elements such as vibrations, light, and airflow [49]. In a significant breakthrough, scientists announced, at the 241st National Meeting and Exposition of the American Chemical Society in March 2011, a commercially viable nanogenerator, a flexible chip that uses body movements such as the pinch of the finger to generate electricity [12]. Considering the fact that many of the components of IoT will be battery powered, energy consumption will often be at a premium. Therefore, methods need to be devised to achieve the required functionality and security of connected devises while minimizing energy use.

## 14.5 Conclusion

As a radical evolution of the Internet into a network of connected smart devices, IoT offers enormous opportunity to increase the generation of information from the environment through sensing and to interact with the physical world through processes such as actuation, in order to facilitate information exchange about goods and people to improve the livelihood of mankind. Despite its huge potential, there are numerous concerns about the security and privacy of IoT. This chapter discussed the security concerns and challenges of IoT as well as the protocols for addressing some of those challenges. The recent adaptation of enabling wireless technologies, such as RFID tags and embedded sensor and actuator nodes, is enabling IoT as the next revolutionary technology in fully integrating the Internet. RFID technology enables the design of microchips for wireless data communication and helps in automatic identification of objects they are attached to, acting as an electronic barcode. However, RFID seems to be the most vulnerable as it allows person tracking and no high-level intelligence can be enabled on these devices.

Technological advances have also made available efficient, low-cost, low-power devices for use in remote sensing applications and improved the viability of utilizing network of intelligent sensors, enabling the collection, processing, analysis, and dissemination of valuable information, gathered in a variety of environments. Security attacks are problematic for the IoT because of the minimal capacity of the devices being used; the physical accessibility to sensors, actuators, and objects; and the openness of the systems, including the fact that most objects will communicate wirelessly. In recognition of this problem, several protocols and technologies are being implemented to address some of the IoT security challenges.

For IoT technologies, applications, and solutions to be widely adopted by relevant stakeholders, there needs to be security guarantees in terms of system-level confidentiality, authenticity, and privacy. These include definition of an authentication mechanism as well as an object identification process with related identity management system to help promote the benefits of securely connected smart objects.

## References


1. de Leusse P, Periorellis P, Dimitrakos T, Nali SK (2009) Self- managed security cell, a security model for the Internet of things and services. Paper presented at First International Conference on Advances in Future Internet
2. Hamad F, Smalov L, James A (2009) Energy-aware security in m-commerce and Internet of things. IETE Tech Rev 26(5):357–362
3. ITU (2005) The Internet of things. ITU Internet Report, Executive Summary. http://www.itu.int/osg/spu/publications/internetofthings/InternetofThings_summary.pdf. Accessed 16 Mar 2015
4. Medaglia CM, Serbanati A (2010) An overview of privacy and security issues in the Internet of things. In: Guisto D et al (eds) The internet of things: 20th Tyrrhenian Workshop on Digital Communication. Springer Science+Business Media, New York, NY, pp 389–395
5. Dickerson R, Gorlin E, Stankovic J (2011) Empath: a continuous remote emotional health monitoring system for depressive illness. Wireless health. http://www.cs.virginia.edu/~stankovic/psfiles/robempath.pdf. Accessed 16 June 2015
6. Dlodlo N, Foko T, Mvelase P, Mathaba S (2012) The state of affairs in Internet of things research. Electron J Inf Syst Eval 15(3):244–258
7. Raza S, Chung T, Duquennoy S, Yazar D, Voigt T, Roedig U (2011) Securing Internet of things with lightweight IPsec. SIC Tech Rep T2010:08
8. Navajo M, Ballesteros I, D'Elia S, Sassen A, Goyet M, Santaella J et al (2010) Draft report of the task force on interdisciplinary research activities applicable to the future Internet. European Union Task Force Report. Rejected 29 July 2015. http://www.future-internet.eu/fileadmin/documents/reports/FI-content/Report_on_the_Future_Internet_Content_v4.1.pdf
9. Tang D (2009) Event detection in sensor networks. School of Engineering and Applied Sciences, The George Washington University. Rejected 18 July 2015. http://media.proquest.com/media/pq/classic/doc/1729680731/fmt/ai/rep/NPDF?_s=IhmVfasgHkWNpdWJayKhnXDAmkE%3D
10. Juels A (2006) Security and privacy: a research survey. IEEE J Sel Areas Commun 24:381–394
11. Neill DB (2011) Fast Bayesian scan statistics for multivariate event detection and visualization. Stat Med 30:455–469
12. Evans D (2011) The Internet of things. How the next evolution of the Internet is changing everything. Cisco Internet Business Solutions Group (IBSG), San Jose, CA
13. Heer T, Garcia-Morchon O, Hummen R, Keoh SL, Kumar SS, Wehrle K (2011) Security challenges in the IP-based Internet of things. Int J Wirel Pers Commun 61(3):527–542
14. Stankovic JA (2014) Research directions for the Internet of Things. http://dx.doi.org/10.1109/JIOT.2014.2312291. Accessed 25 June 2015
15. Anzelmo E, Bassi A, Capiro D, Dodson S, Cranenburg R, Ratto M (2011) Discussion paper on the Internet of Things Commissioned by the Institute for Internet and Society, Berlin. http://www.theinternetofthings.eu/sites/default/files/Rob%20van%20Kranenburg/Internet%20of%20Things%20Institute%20for%20Internet%20&%20Society%20Discussion%20Paper.pdf. Accessed 14 June 2015

16. Xu W, Trappe W, Zhang Y, Wood T (2005) The feasibility of launching and detecting jamming attacks in wireless networks. Proc of MobiHoc 46–57
17. Wood A, Stankovic J, Virone G, Selavo L, He T, Cao Q, Doan T, Wu Y, Fang L, Stoleru R (2008) Context-aware wireless sensor networks for assisted living and residential monitoring. IEEE Netw. 22(4):26–33
18. Jara A, Zamora MA, Skarmeta FG (2011) An ambient assisted living platform to integrate biometric sensors to detect respiratory failures for patients with serious breathing problems. http://ants.inf.um.es/projects/aire/files/IWAAL_2011.pdf. Accessed 2 July 2015
19. Weber RH (2010) Internet of things – new security and privacy challenges. Comput Law Secur Rev 26:23–30
20. Fabian B (2008) Secure name services for the Internet of things. Dissertation. http://edoc.hu-berlin.de/dissertationen/fabian-benjamin-2008-08-07/PDF/fabian.pdf. Accessed 25 Apr 2015
21. Sule S, Shah S (2004) Integration in RFID. A Patni White Paper
22. Hasso Plattner Institute (2012) Integration of RFID Technology in enterprise platforms. https://hpi.de/fileadmin/user_upload/fachgebiete/plattner/projects/GoRFID/RFID_Poster.pdf. Accessed 2 May 2015
23. ARES (2012) Advanced research on information security and privacy. Funded by Spain Ministry of Science. https://www.nics.uma.es/projects/ares. Accessed 2 July 2015
24. Benali F, Ubeda S, Legrand V (2008) Collaborative approach to automatic classification of heterogeneous information security. In: Emerging security information systems and technologies. 2nd IEEE International Conference, Cap Esterel, France, pp 294–299
25. Kagal L, Finin T, Joshi A (2003) A policy based approach to security for the semantic web. Paper presented at the 2nd International Semantic Web Conference (ISWC2003)
26. OASIS (2013) Extensible access control mark up language (XACML) v2. http://docs.oasis-open.org/xacml/3.0/xacml-3.0-core-spec-os-en.pdf. Accessed 16 June 2015
27. Becker MY, Fournet C, Gordone AD (2006) SecPAL: design and semantics of a decentralized authorization language. Technical Report MSR-TR-2006-120, Microsoft Research
28. Newman H (2013) BACnet today and the smart GRID. http://www.bacnet.org/Bibliography/BACnet-Today-13/Newman-2013.pdf. Accessed 14 June 2015
29. DALI (2011) Dali by design. http://www.dalibydesign.us/dali.html. Accessed 26 May 2015
30. Liu A, Ning P (2008) TinyECC: a configurable library for elliptic curve cryptography in wireless sensor networks. http://discovery.csc.ncsu.edu/pubs/ipsn08-TinyECC-IEEE.pdf. Accessed 2 July 2015
31. Szczechowiak L, Oliviera L, Scott M, Collier M, Dahab R (2008) Nanoecc: testing the limits of elliptic curve cryptography in sensor networks. http://www.ic.unicamp.br/~leob/publica tions/ewsn/NanoECC.pdf. Accessed 2 July 2015
32. Liu A, Ning P (2003) Establishing pairwise keys in distributed sensor networks. In 10th ACM conference on Computer and Communication Security (CCS), New York
33. Chung A, Roeding U (2008) DHB-KEY: an efficient key distribution scheme for wireless sensor networks. In: Mobile Ad Hoc and sensor systems. 5th IEEE international conference, Atlanta
34. Moskowitz R (2011) HIP diet exchange (DEX), draft-moskowitz-hip-rg-dex-01. https://tools.ietf.org/html/draft-moskowitz-hip-dex-01. Accessed 2 July 2015
35. Granjal J, Silva R, Monteiro E, Silva JS, Boavida F (2008) Why is IPsec a viable option for wireless sensor networks. https://eden.dei.uc.pt/~edmundo/Conf%20Internacionais/CI113%202008%20MASS%20Granjal.pdf. Accessed 2 July 2015
36. Riaz R, Kim K, Ahmed HF (2009) Security analysis survey and framework design for ip connected lowpans. In: International Symposium on Autonomous Distributed Systems (ISADS), IEEE
37. Roman R, Lopez J (2009) Integrating wireless sensor networks and the Internet: a security analysis. Internet Res 19(2):246–259
38. Deloche G, Kushalnagar N, Hui J, Culler D (2007). Transmission of IPv6 Packets over IEEE 802.15.4 Networks. RFC 4944, September 2007

39. Chan H, Perrig A, Song D (2003) Random key predistribution schemes for sensor networks. In: Proceedings of the 2003 I.E. Symposium on Security and Privacy
40. Perrig A, Szewczyk R, Wen V, Culler D, Tygar JD (2002) Spins: security protocols for sensor networks. http://users.ece.cmu.edu/~adrian/projects/mc2001/mc2001.pdf. Accessed 15 July 2015
41. Ahamed SS (2009) The role of ZigBee technology in future data communication system. J Theor Appl Inf Technol 129–235
42. Langheinrich M (2005) Personal privacy in ubiquitous computing. PhD Thesis, ETH Zurich. http://www.vs.inf.ethz.ch/publ/papers/langheinrich-phd-2005.pdf. Accessed 26 May 2015
43. Nikander P, Henderson T, Vogt T, Arkko J (2008) End-host mobility and multihoming with the host identity protocol. RFC 5206. http://www.rfc-base.org/rfc-5206.html. Accessed 21 Apr 2015
44. Eronen P (2006) IKEv2 mobility and multihoming protocol (MOBIKE). RFC4555. https://www.ietf.org/rfc/rfc4555.txt. Accessed 16 Apr 2015
45. Kivinen T, Tschofenig H (2006) Design of the IKEv2 mobility and multihoming (MOBIKE) protocol. RFC 4621. http://www.rfc-base.org/rfc-4621.html. Accessed 16 Apr 2015
46. Nikander P, Melen J (2009) A bound end-to-end tunnel (BEET) mode for ESP, draft-nikandar-esp-beet-mode-09. https://tools.ietf.org/html/draft-nikander-esp-beet-mode-09. Accessed 5 July 2015
47. BRIDGE (2011) Building radio frequency identification solutions for the global environment. RFID applied research and development project funded by the European Commission. http://www.bridge-project.eu/data/File/Brochure%20Overview.pdf. Accessed 26 May 2015
48. Eschet G (2005) Protecting privacy in the web of radio frequency identification. Jurimetrics 45:301–332
49. Shwe YW, Liang CL (2009) Smart dust sensor networks with piezoelectric energy harvesting. http://www.icita.org/papers/34-sg-Liang-217.pdf. Accessed 16 May 2015

# Index





Z. Mahmood (ed.), *Connectivity Frameworks for Smart Devices*,
Computer Communications and Networks, DOI 10.1007/978-3-319-33124-9

MIX
Papier aus verantwortungsvollen Quellen
Paper from responsible sources
FSC® C105338
FSC
www.fsc.org

If you have any concerns about our products,
you can contact us on
**ProductSafety@springernature.com**

In case Publisher is established outside the EU,
the EU authorized representative is:
**Springer Nature Customer Service Center GmbH**
**Europaplatz 3, 69115 Heidelberg, Germany**

Printed by Libri Plureos GmbH
in Hamburg, Germany